THE
WORLD ALMANAC®
OF PRESIDENTIAL
QUOTATIONS

THE WORLD ALMANAC®
OF PRESIDENTIAL
QUOTATIONS

Quotations from
America's Presidents

Edited by
Elizabeth Frost-Knappman

PHAROS BOOKS '93
A SCRIPPS HOWARD COMPANY
NEW YORK

The World Almanac of Presidential Quotations

Copyright © 1988 by New England Publishing Associates

Originally published as The Bully Pulpit: Quotations From America's Presidents

New and revised material copyright © 1993 by Pharos Books

First Pharos edition published in 1993.

Library of Congress Cataloging-in-Publication Data

The World almanac of presidential quotations / Elizabeth
 Frost, editor.
      p.   cm.
  Includes index.
  ISBN 0-88687-734-2
  1. Presidents—United States—Quotations. 2. United
States—Politics and government—Quotations, maxims,
etc. 3. Quotations, American. I. Frost, Elizabeth.
E176.1.W926 1993
973'.099—dc20   92-39243
                                      CIP

Printed in the United States of America

Cover design: Sara Stemen

Pharos Books
A Scripps Howard Company
200 Park Avenue
New York, NY 10166

10 9 8 7 6 5 4 3 2 1

Pharos Books are available at special discounts on bulk purchases for sales promotions, premiums, fundraising or educational use. For details, contact the Special Sales Department, Pharos Books, 200 Park Avenue, New York, NY 10166

For Ed

Contents

Acknowledgments

The author acknowledges with gratitude the courtesy and contributions of the following people.

The author wishes to thank, in particular, Gloria Eustis and the staff of the Chester (Connecticut) Public Library who, with patience and persistence, located many of the references used in this book.

The author would like to express her gratitude to John Gable, Executive Director of the Theodore Roosevelt Association, for providing the origin of the title of this book.

The author greatly appreciates the work of Maura McDermott for helping to compile the Bibliography and Alice Misiewicz for carefully copyediting the manuscript.

A sincere expression of thanks goes to the staff of Facts On File for their advice and guidance, particularly to John Thornton, Norman Mitgang, Doug Schulkind, Joe Reilly, Marjorie Bank, Olivia McKean and the production staff.

Finally, the author appreciates, more than she can say, the lively interest and many contributions of her husband, Ed, to whom this book is dedicated.

INTRODUCTION

"The White House is a bully pulpit," said Theodore Roosevelt to George Putnam. Indeed, from George Washington to Ronald Reagan, America's thirty-nine presidents have used their office to speak out on every conceivable subject. Their statements have been wise and foolish, profound and shallow, momentous and trivial, solemn and irreverent, eloquent and tongue-tied, generous and malicious, witty and ponderous. Many of them still resonate, such as Thomas Jefferson's famous tribute to truth: "It is error alone which needs the support of government. Truth can stand by itself." Some have become the clichés of election campaigns, for instance, Richard Nixon's plea: "It is time for the great silent majority of Americans to stand up and be counted." Still others were quickly forgotten but deserve resurrection, as with James Buchanan's remark about Congress: "Abstract propositions should never be discussed by a legislative body."

The World Almanac of Presidential Quotations is a collection of approximately 3,000 of the most significant and interesting quotations by America's presidents. While the book contains most of the more well-known statements, a majority are less familiar. Yet these are often the more revealing ones, best expressing the personalities and opinions of the men themselves. Woodrow Wilson's sense of irony, for instance, is clearly reflected in this wry observation on the failing campaign of his opponent, Governor Charles Evans Hughes: "Never murder a man who is committing suicide." This book is neither hagiographic nor muckraking in purpose. Rather, quotations have been included on the basis of their historic significance, intrinsic human interest, and colorful or eloquent language.

When I began this volume, I visualized it as a compilation of the most memorable statements made by presidents during their White House years. But, as my research progressed, it became clear that many of their best observations fell outside this period. Either the fire of a campaign, the privacy of a long-kept diary, or the reflection and perspective associated with retirement gave rise to eloquent commentary that could not be left out of this book. Therefore, while I have tried to focus on the presidential years, I have also included apt quotations from earlier, or later, dates.

Some readers may wonder to what extent the words of presidents were, in fact, their own. Actually, most were. The early presidents prided themselves on writing their own speeches (although Alexander Hamilton may have helped George Washington with his farewell address). Not until Warren G. Harding, himself a newspaper editor, hired Judson Welliver as his "literary clerk," did an American president have a formal speech writer. And only after World War II did elected officials have the money and large staffs necessary to accommodate full-time speech writers.

But ghosted or not, the words of American presidents record the political and social history of the country itself. Their words trace great themes in American history, reflect the changing beliefs of the American people, and articulate the best and the worst in the American spirit. Some, such as those about Congress or the presidency itself, reveal how American government and politics really work. (Who can resist Thomas Jefferson's skewering of Congress: "That 150 lawyers should do business together ought not to be expected"?) And a great many skillfully articulate the core principles of American democracy.

The words of the chief executives also vividly reflect their personalities. No president was as combative as Theodore Roosevelt, who, in 1911, proudly proclaimed: "I took the canal zone and let Congress debate, and while the debate goes on the canal does also." Few were as humorous as Abraham Lincoln, who, in reply to a friend who asked how it felt to be president wrote: "You have heard about the man tarred and feathered and ridden out of town on a rail? A man in the crowd asked him how he liked it, and his reply was that if it wasn't for the honor of the thing, he would much rather walk."

Finally, many Americans forget what keen observers of other politicians our chief executives are. Consider, for example, Gerald Ford's perceptive description of the White House staff under Richard Nixon, which, he wrote: "viewed Congress in much the same way that the chairman of the board of a huge corporation regards his regional sales managers."

Although other books have been published that quote from presidential speeches or writings, these have either been of the "wit and wisdom" variety or have been devoted to one individual. None but Caroline Thomas Harnsberger's 1964 collection has attempted to bring together the most significant quotes from all the presidents. *The World Almanac of Presidential Quotations* differs by including comments by the presidents about each other, and selections from presidents of the last two decades, covering as they do such critical events as Watergate and the Vietnam war.

The World Almanac of Presidential Quotations is organized alphabetically by topic. Under each heading, quotes are arranged chronologically. This format has the advantage of allowing the reader to easily trace the views of the presidents on long-standing issues without having to flip back and forth in the book. All entries contain the original date and source whenever possible, and the back of the book contains a list of presidents and their dates of birth, death, and term of office so that each quote can be placed according to whether the president was on the campaign trail, in retirement, or living at 1600 Pennsylvania Avenue.

Most of the quotations come from press reports, state papers, speeches, diaries, or autobiographies; others are from secondary sources. As a result of this range of sources, peculiarities of punctuation and spelling have generally been modernized throughout in the interest of readability and consistency. However, in some quotations, particularly the older ones, such peculiarities have been let stand where they appeared to cause no confusion.

As my family and editors can attest, this book might never have been completed without the pressure of the publisher's kindly but firm deadline. But for this, the book might easily have extended far beyond the two years it took me to research and compile. Doubtless I have omitted a noble or familiar quote which, but for the need to finally complete this book, might otherwise have been included. For this, I can only apologize to the disappointed reader.

Elizabeth Frost-Knappman

THE
WORLD ALMANAC®
OF PRESIDENTIAL
QUOTATIONS

A

Accomplishment

Far better it is to dare mighty things, to win glorious triumphs, even though checkered by failure, than to take rank with those poor spirits who neither enjoy much nor suffer much, because they live in the gray twilight that knows not victory nor defeat.

Theodore Roosevelt
Speech
April 10, 1899

You know, the greatest epitaph in the country is here in Arizona. It's in Tombstone, Arizona, and this epitaph says, "Here lies Jack WIlliams. He done his damnest." I think that is the greatest epitaph a man could have. Whenever a man does the best he can, then that is all he can do.

Harry S. Truman
Informal campaign remarks, Winslow, Arizona
June 15,·1948

Accomplishment will prove to be a journey, not a destination.

Dwight D. Eisenhower
Speech, NATO Council
December 16, 1957

Action

Get action. Do things; be sane, don't fritter away your time; create, act, take a place wherever you are and be somebody; get action.

Theodore Roosevelt
1900

Actions speak louder than words.

Theodore Roosevelt
Cited in William Henry Harbaugh, *Power and Responsibility: The Life and Times of Theodore Roosevelt*

Life does not consist in thinking, it consists in acting.

Woodrow Wilson
Speech, New York, New York
September 28, 1912

Perhaps one of the most important accomplishments of my administration has been minding my own business.

Calvin Coolidge
Comment, news conference
March 1, 1929

There are many ways it [the Depression] can be helped, but it can never be helped by merely talking about it. We must act, and we must act quickly.

Franklin D. Roosevelt
First inaugural address
March 4, 1933

The country needs and, unless I mistake its temper, the country demands bold, persistent experimentation. It is common sense to take a method and try it; if it fails, admit it frankly and try another. But above all, try something. The millions who are in want will not stand by silently forever while the things to satisfy their needs are within reach.

Franklin D. Roosevelt
Speech, Oglethorpe University, Atlanta, Georgia
January 8, 1936

John Adams

He is vain, irritable, and a bad calculator of the force and probable effect of the motives which govern men. This is all the ill which can possibly be said of him. He is as disinterested as the Being who made him.

Thomas Jefferson
Letter, James Madison
1787

John Adams and Thomas Jefferson were political enemies, but they became fast friends. And when they passed away on the same day, the last words of one of them was, "The country is safe. Jefferson still lives." And the last words of the other was, "John Adams will see that things go forward."

Harry S. Truman
Informal remarks, Quincy, Massachusetts
October 28, 1948

John Quincy Adams

I am a man of reserved, cold, austere, and forbidding manners; my political adversaries say, a gloomy misanthropist, and my personal enemies, an unsocial savage.

John Quincy Adams
Diary
June 4, 1819

His disposition is as perverse and mulish as that of his father.

James Buchanan
Letter, Hugh Hamilton
March 22, 1822

He loved his country, desired to serve it, and was properly conscious of the honor of doing so.

Martin Van Buren
Cited in Richard Kenin and Justin Wintle, *The Dictionary of Biographical Quotations*

Advice

The President gets the best advice he can find, uses the best judgment at his command, and leaves the event in the hands of Providence.

Calvin Coolidge
The Autobiography of Calvin Coolidge
1929

The President cannot function without advisers or without advice, written or oral. But just as soon as he is required to show what kind of advice he has had, who said what to him, or what kind of records he has, the advice he receives will be worthless.

Harry S. Truman
Memoirs
1956

I have had enough experience in all my years, and have read enough of the past, to know that advice to grandchildren is usually wasted. If the second and third generations *could* profit by the experience of the first generation, we would not be having some of the troubles we have today.

Harry S. Truman
Statement
1960

My doctor ordered me to shut up, which will make every American happy.

Bill Clinton
Informal Comment
April 1992

Advisers

[They should have a] passion for anonymity.

Franklin D. Roosevelt
Cited in *Newsweek*
March 9, 1987

There's only one man who has seen more of the world and talked with more people and knows more than he [John Foster Dulles] does—and that's me.

Dwight D. Eisenhower
Comment, Emmet Hughes
1952

I would like to discuss it [the congressional power to declare war] with [Secretary of State John] Foster Dulles, but having talked to him, I am sure that we are in absolute agreement as to what we mean about it.

Dwight D. Eisenhower
Press conference
Spring 1954

It's much easier to make speeches than it is to finally make the judgments, because unfortunately your advisers are frequently divided. If you take the wrong course, and on occasion I have, the President bears the burden, responsibility, quite rightly. The advisers may move on to new advice.

John F. Kennedy
CBS interview
December 17, 1962

Congressmen are always advising Presidents to get rid of presidential advisers. That's one of the most constant threads that run through American history, and Presidents ordinarily do not pay attention.

John F. Kennedy
Press conference
May 8, 1963

When I became President, I did not want to have a powerful chief of staff. Wilson had his Colonel House, Eisenhower his Sherman Adams, Nixon his Haldeman, and I was aware of the trouble those top assistants had caused my predecessors.

Gerald Ford
A Time to Heal
1979

Age

I have lived in this old and frail tenement a great many years; it is very much dilapidated; and, from all that I can learn, my landlord doesn't intend to repair it.

John Adams
To Daniel Webster, cited in Peter Harvey, *Reminiscences and Anecdotes of Daniel Webster*

Of all the faculties of the human mind that of memory is the first which suffers decay with age.

Thomas Jefferson
Letter, B. H. Latrobe
1812

Having outlived so many of my contemporaries, I ought not to forget that I may be thought to have outlived myself.

James Madison
Cited in Paul Wilstach, *Patriots off Their Pedestals*
1831

My eyes are threatening to fail me. My hands tremble like an aspen leaf. My memory daily deserts me. My imagination is fallen into the sear and yellow leaf and my judgment sinking into dotage.

John Quincy Adams
1839

As you get older, you get tired of doing the same things over and over again, so you think Christmas has changed. It hasn't. It's you who has changed.

Harry S. Truman
Statement
December 1955

You know, by the time you reach my age, you've made plenty of mistakes, and if you've lived your life properly, so you learn. You put things in perspective. You pull your energies together. You change. You go forward.

Ronald Reagan
Speech, Iran-contra arms affair
March 4, 1987

Aggression

No man has a natural right to commit aggression on the equal rights of another; and this is all from which the laws ought to restrain him.

Thomas Jefferson
Letter, F. W. Gilmer
1816

You cannot win a battle in any arena merely by defending yourself.

Richard Nixon
Six Crises
1962

The central lesson of our time is that the appetite of aggression is never satisfied. To withdraw from one battlefield means only to prepare for the next.

Lyndon B. Johnson
Address, Johns Hopkins University, Baltimore, Maryland
April 7, 1965

Appeasement does not work. As was the case in the 1930's, we see in Saddam Hussein an aggressive dictator threatening his neighbors.

George Bush
Television address
August 8, 1990

Agriculture

The small landholders are the most precious sort of a state.

Thomas Jefferson
Letter, James Madison
1785

I think our governments will remain virtuous for many centuries; as long as they remain chiefly agricultural; and this will be as long as there shall be vacant lands in any part of America. When they get piled upon one another in large cities, as in Europe, they will become corrupt as in Europe, and go to eating one another as they do there.

Thomas Jefferson
Letter, Reverend James Madison
December 20, 1787

I know of no pursuit in which more real and important services can be rendered to any country than by improving its agriculture, its breed of useful animals, and other branches of a husbandman's cares.

George Washington
Letter, John Sinclair
July 20, 1794

The first and most precious of all the arts.

Thomas Jefferson
Letter, Robert R. Livingston
1800

No occupation is so delightful to me as the culture of the earth.

Thomas Jefferson
Letter, C. W. Peale
1811

[Farming] affords nothing sufficiently interesting to trouble my friends by communicating with them on the subject.

Zachary Taylor
Letter, J. C. Breckenridge
April 12, 1817

I am more of a farmer than a soldier. I take little or no interest in military affairs.

Ulysses S. Grant
Comment, Otto Von Bismarck, Potsdam, Germany
1879

The farmer's son, not satisfied with his father's simple and laborious life, joins the eager chase for easily acquired wealth.

Grover Cleveland
Fourth annual message, Congress
December 3, 1888

The moment the government engages in buying and selling, by that act it is fixing prices.

Calvin Coolidge
Speech, American Farm Bureau Federation, Chicago, Illinois
December 7, 1925

Farming looks mighty easy when your plow is a pencil, and you're a thousand miles from a corn field.

Dwight D. Eisenhower
Speech, Peoria, Illinois
September 25, 1956

Allies

Our allies are the millions who hunger and thirst after righteousness.

Harry S. Truman
Inaugural address
January 20, 1940

We cannot live alone, and we've got to find some way for our allies to earn a living, because we do not want to carry them on our backs.

Dwight D. Eisenhower
Legislative leaders meeting
March 29, 1954

We failed to halt Hirohito, Mussolini, and Hitler by not acting in unity and in time. That marked the beginning of many years of stark tragedy and desperate peril. May it not be that our nations have learned something from that lesson?

Dwight D. Eisenhower
Telegram, Winston Churchill, urging unity in Vietnam
April 4, 1954

Ambition

Ambition is the subtlest Beast of the Intellectual and Moral Field. It is wonderfully adroit in concealing itself from its owner.

John Adams
Letter, John Quincy Adams
January 3, 1794

I want the voice of honest praise,
    To follow me behind,
And to be thought, in future days,
    The friend of humankind;
That after-ages, as they rise,
    Exulting may proclaim,
In choral union to the skies,
    Their blessings on my name.

John Quincy Adams
"The Wants of Man"
c. 1787

I had rather be shut up in a very modest cottage, with my books, my family and a few old friends, dining on simple bacon, and letting the world roll on as it liked, than to occupy the most splendid post which any human power can give.

Thomas Jefferson
Letter, A. Donald
1789

Every man who takes office in Washington either grows or swells, and when I give a man an office, I watch him carefully to see whether he is swelling or growing.

Woodrow Wilson
Speech, Washington D.C.
May 15, 1916

America

America is a great, unwieldy body. Its progress must be slow. It is like a large fleet sailing under convoy. The fleetist sailers [*sic*] must wait for the dullest and slowest.

John Adams
Letter, Abigail Adams
June 17, 1775

Its soul, its climate, its equality, liberty, laws, people, and manners. My God! how little do my countrymen know what precious blessings they are in possession of, and which no other people on earth enjoy!

Thomas Jefferson
Letter, James Monroe
June 17, 1785

The preservation of the sacred fire of liberty and the destiny of the republican model of government are justly considered, perhaps as *deeply*, as *finally*, staked on the experiment intrusted to the hands of the American people.

George Washington
First inaugural address
April 30, 1789

The name of American, which belongs to you in your national capacity, must always exalt the just pride of patriotism more than any appellation derived from local discriminations. With slight shades of difference, you have the same religion, manners, habits and political principles. You have in common cause fought and triumphed together. The independence and liberty you possess are the work of joint councils and joint efforts, of common dangers, sufferings, and successes.

George Washington
Farewell address
September 17, 1796

Wherever the standard of freedom and independence has been or shall be unfurled, there will be America's heart, her benedictions and her prayers. But she does not go abroad in search of monsters to destroy. She is the champion and vindicator only of her own.

John Quincy Adams
Address
July 4, 1821

As a nation of free men, we must live through all time, or die by suicide.

Abraham Lincoln
Speech, Springfield, Illinois, on U.S. freedom from external threat
January 27, 1838

The stars upon your banner have become nearly threefold their original number; your densely populated possessions skirt the shores of the two great oceans.

Franklin Pierce
Inaugural address
March 4, 1853

A nation may be said to consist of its territory, its people, and its laws. The territory is the only part which is of certain durability. Laws change, people die; the land remains.

Abraham Lincoln
Message, Congress
December 1, 1862

Tallyrand once said to the first Napoleon that "the United States is a giant without bones." Since that time our gristle has been rapidly hardening.

James A. Garfield
Speech
July 2, 1873

Have you not learned that not stocks or bonds or stately homes, or products of mill or field are our country? It is the splendid thought that is in our minds.

Benjamin Harrison
Cited in Clifton Fadiman, *The American Treasury*

The Yankee intermingles with the Illinoisian, the Hoosier with the Sucker, and the people of the South with them all; and it is this commingling which gives that unity which marks the American nation.

Benjamin Harrison
Speech, San Diego, California
April 23, 1891

The American people are slow to wrath, but when their wrath is once kindled it burns like a consuming flame.

Theodore Roosevelt
First annual message, Congress
December 3, 1901

From the beginning our people have markedly combined practical capacity for affairs with power of devotion to an ideal. The lack of either quality would have rendered the possession of the other of small value.

Theodore Roosevelt
Speech, Philadelphia, Pennsylvania
November 22, 1902

Americanism is a question of principle, of purpose, of Idealism, or Character; it is not a matter of birthplace or creed or line of descent.

Theodore Roosevelt
Speech, Washington, D.C.
1909

America is not a mere body of traders; it is a body of free men. Our greatness is built upon our freedom—is moral, not material. We have a great ardor for gain; but we have a deep passion for the rights of man.

Woodrow Wilson
Speech, New York, New York
January 29, 1911

The things that will destroy America are prosperity-at-any-price, peace-at-any-price, safety-first instead of duty-first, the love of soft living and the get-rich-quick theory of life.

Theodore Roosevelt
Letter, S. S. Menken
January 10, 1917

Some people call me an idealist. Well, that is the way I know I am an American. America is the only idealist nation in the world.

Woodrow Wilson
Speech, Sioux Falls, South Dakota
September 8, 1919

This country would not be a land of opportunity, America would not be America, if the people were shackled with government monopolies.

Calvin Coolidge
Speech
August 14, 1924

This generation of Americans has a rendezvous with destiny.

Franklin D. Roosevelt
Acceptance speech, renomination for presidency, Philadelphia, Pennsylvania
June 27, 1936

The overwhelming majority of Americans are possessed of two great qualities—a sense of humor and a sense of proportion.

Franklin D. Roosevelt
Speech, Savannah, Georgia
November 18, 1945

America was not built on fear. America was built on courage, on imagination and an unbeatable determination to do the job at hand.

Harry S. Truman
Special message, Congress
January 8, 1947

You know that being an American is more than a matter of where your parents came from. It is a belief that all men are created free and equal and that everyone deserves an even break. It is respect for the dignity of men and women without regard to race, creed, or color. That is our creed.

Harry S. Truman
Informal remarks, Indiana and Ohio
October 26, 1948

Whatever America hopes to bring to pass in this world must first come to pass in the heart of America.

Dwight D. Eisenhower
Inaugural address
January 20, 1953

The American, by nature, is optimistic. He is experimental, an inventor and a builder who builds best when called upon to build greatly.

John F. Kennedy
Speech, Washington, D.C.
January 1, 1960

We are a nation of lovers and not a nation of haters. We are a land of good homes, decent wages and decent medical care for the aged. Yes, we want a land of hope and happiness, but never a land of harshness and hate.

Lyndon B. Johnson
Remarks, State Democratic Committee, Harrisburg, Pennsylvania
September 10, 1964

Our own freedom and growth have never been the final goal of the American dream. We were never meant to be an oasis of liberty and abundance in a worldwide desert of disappointed dreams. Our Nation was created to help strike away the chains of ignorance and misery and tyranny wherever they keep man less than God wants him to be.

Lyndon B. Johnson
State of the union address
January 4, 1965

This is what America is all about. It is the uncrossed desert and the unclimbed ridge. It is the star that is not reached and the harvest that is sleeping in the unplowed ground.

Lyndon B. Johnson
Inaugural address
January 20, 1965

The promise of America is a simple promise: Every person shall share in the blessings of this land. And they shall share on the basis of their merits as a person. They shall not be judged by their color or by their beliefs, or by their religion, or by where they were born, or the neighborhood in which they live.

Lyndon B. Johnson
News conference, the White House
March 13, 1965

We have no sense of arrogance—we honestly, almost naively, like people and want to get along with them. We lack often a sense of subtlety but that will come after a few hundred more years of civilization.

Richard Nixon
Diary
February 1972

I don't believe that the people I've met in almost every state in the union are ready to consign this, the last island of freedom, to the dustbin of history.

Ronald Reagan
Campaign speech, Republican presidential nomination
1976

Three weeks after Pearl Harbor, Winston Churchill came to North America and he said, "We have not journeyed all this way across the centuries, across the oceans, across the mountains, across the prairies because we are made of sugar candy." We Americans have courage. Americans have always been on the cutting edge of change. We've always looked forward with anticipation and confidence.

Jimmy Carter
Acceptance speech, Democratic National Convention, New York, New York
August 14, 1980

Our American values are not luxuries but necessities—not the salt in our bread but the bread itself. Our common vision of a free and just society is our greatest source of cohesion at home and strength abroad—greater than the bounty of our material blessings.

Jimmy Carter
Farewell address
January 14, 1981

I've always believed that this land was set aside in an uncommon way, that a divine plan placed this great continent between the oceans to be found by a people from every corner of the earth who had a special love of faith, freedom and peace.

Ronald Reagan
Speech, Washington, D.C.
November 11, 1982

Back over the years, citizens like ourselves have gathered within these walls when our nation was threatened; sometimes when its very existence was at stake. Always, with courage and common sense they met the crises of their time and lived to see a stronger, better and more prosperous country . . . . Yes we still have problems—plenty of them. But it is just plain wrong—unjust to our country and unjust to our people—to let those problems stand in the way of the most important truth of all: America is on the mend.

Ronald Reagan
State of the union address
January 25, 1983

America is too great for small dreams.

Ronald Reagan
Speech, Congress
January 1, 1984

He [Michael Dukakis] sees America as another pleasant country on the U.N. roll call, somewhere between Albania and Zimbabwe. And I see America as the leader, a unique nation with a special role in the world.

George Bush
Acceptance speech, Republican Convention
August 18, 1988

America is never wholly herself unless she is engaged in high moral principle. We as a people have such a purpose today. It is to make kinder the face of the nation and gentler the face of the world.

George Bush
Inaugural Address
January 20, 1989

Appeasement

Establish the eternal truth that acquiescence under insult is not the way to escape war.

Thomas Jefferson
Cited in Bruce Bohle, *The Home Book of American Quotations*

We must especially be aware of that small group of selfish men who would clip the wings of the American eagle in order to feather their own nests.

Franklin D. Roosevelt
Four Freedoms Speech
January 6, 1941

We . . . would rather die on our feet than live on our knees.

Franklin D. Roosevelt
Third inaugural address
January 20, 1941

The path we have chosen for the present is full of hazards, as all paths are. But it is the one most consistent with our character and courage as a nation and our commitments around the world. The cost of freedom is always high, but Americans have always paid it. And one path we shall never choose, and that is the path of surrender, or submission.

John F. Kennedy
Speech to the nation announcing blockade of Cuba during missile crisis
October 22, 1962

Appointments and Patronage

If due participation of office is a matter of right, how are vacancies to be obtained? Those by death are few; by resignation, none.

Thomas Jefferson
Letter, Elias Simpson et al.
July 12, 1801

Whenever a man has cast a longing eye on offices, a rottenness begins in his conduct.

Thomas Jefferson
Letter, Tench Coxe
1820

On the appointment to office, I have been forc'd either to distribute the offices among the friends of the candidates, to guard myself against the imputation of favoritism, or to take my own course, and appoint those whom I knew & confided in, without regard to them. Had I pursued the former, the office in my hands, for two or three years of the latter term, would have sunk to nothing. I therefore adopted the latter, and have steadily pursued it, believing that I had given sufficient proof of respect for, and confidence in each of the members of the administration, by appointing & continuing him in his place.

James Monroe
Letter, Thomas Jefferson
March 22, 1824

At the removal of my many friends from office you may readily conceive my concern. My attachment to them was not of a transient nature, for, being founded on long and thorough knowledge of their worth, and the most friendly, in many instances confidential intercourse, it could never be removed. In their future welfare I shall always take a deep interest.

James Monroe
Letter, Judge Southard
April 17, 1829

If you have a job in your department that can't be done by a Democrat, then abolish the job.

Andrew Jackson
Comment, Secretary of War
Cited in Vic Fredericks, *The Wit and Wisdom of the Presidents*

Permit me to premise, that in appointing persons to office it is not incumbent on the President to assign the reasons which govern his conduct. . . . It is by his acts that he is in the respect to be judged by his constituents.

Andrew Jackson
Letter, R. Y. Hayne
February 8, 1831

I believe that no one appointment has been made in this country that I had the honor to recommend. . . . I regret it not. It has no power to grant what I have any desire to receive.

Millard Fillmore
Letter, Thurlow Weed
April 1839

The right to remove from office, while subjected to no just restraint, is inevitably destined to produce a spirit of crouching servility with the official corps, which, in order to uphold the hand that feeds them, would lead to direct and active interference in the elections, both State and Federal.

John Tyler
Inaugural address
April 9, 1841

I begin, more than I have ever done before, to distrust the disinterestedness and honesty of all mankind. Some selfish or local petty feeling seems to influence even members of Congress in their recommendations for office, much more than principle. When I act upon the information which they give me, and make a mistake, they leave me to bear the responsibility, and never have the manliness to assume it themselves.

James K. Polk
The Diary of James K. Polk
December 10, 1846

The passion for office among members of Congress is very great, if not absolutely disreputable, and greatly embarrasses the operations of the government. They create offices by their own votes and then seek to fill them themselves. I shall certainly refuse to appoint them, though it be at the almost certain hazard of incurring their displeasure . . . . [T]heir appointment would be most corrupting in its tendency.

James K. Polk
The Diary of James K. Polk
June 22, 1846

The people of the United States have no idea of the extent to which the President's time, which ought to be devoted to more important matters, is occupied by the voracious and often unprincipled persons who seek office. If a kind Providence permits me . . . . I will, after I retire from the Presidential office, write the secret and hitherto unknown history of the workings of the government in this respect. It requires great patience and self-command to repress the loathing I feel towards a hungry crowd of unworthy office-hunters who often crowd my office.

James K. Polk
The Diary of James K. Polk
April 6, 1848

In the midst of the annoyances of the herd of lazy, worthless people who come to Washington for office instead of going to work . . . I am sometimes amused at their applications . . . . One of these office seekers placed his papers of recommendation. . . . No particular office was specified . . . but he answered that he thought he would be a good hand at making Treaties . . . and would like to be a minister abroad. This is about as reasonable as many other applications which are made to me.

James K. Polk
The Diary of James K. Polk
April 10, 1848

There is no class of our population by whom I am annoyed so much, or for whom I entertain a more sovereign contempt, than for the professed office-seekers who have beseiged me ever since I have been in the Presidential office.

James K. Polk
The Diary of James K. Polk
October 19, 1848

The appointment is made by the Constitution to consist of three acts—the nomination, the approach by the Senate, and the commissioning. The first and last devolve on the President.

Martin Van Buren
The Autobiography of Martin Van Buren
1854

The distribution of patronage of the Government is by far the most disagreeable duty of the President. Applicants are so numerous, and their applications are pressed with such eagerness by their friends both in and out of Congress, that the selection of one for any desirable office gives offence to many.

James Buchanan
Message, House of Representatives
June 22, 1860

A fellow once came to me to ask for an appointment as a minister abroad. Finding he could not get that, he came down to some more modest position. Finally, he asked to be made a tide-waiter. When he saw he could not get that, he asked me for an old pair of trousers. It is sometimes well to be humble.

Abraham Lincoln
Washington, D.C.
1865

The spirit of that clause of the constitution which shields them [members of Congress] from arrest "during their attendance on the session of their respective houses, and in going to and from the same," should also shield them from being arrested from their legislative work, morning, noon, and night, by office-seekers.

James Garfield
"A Century of Congress," *Atlantic*
1887

Nothing brings out the lower traits of human nature like office seeking. Men of good character and impulses are betrayed by it into all sorts of meanness. Disappointment makes them unjust to the last degree.

Rutherford B. Hayes
August 9, 1878

Let no man be put out merely because he is Mr. [Chester] Arthur's friend, and no man put in merely because he is our friend.

Rutherford B. Hayes
Letter, General Edwin A. Merrit
February 4, 1879

The President has neither time, nor authority, neither means nor men, to gather the information required to make appointments and removals.

Rutherford B. Hayes
Diary
July 11, 1880

It will cost me some struggle to keep from despising the office seeker.

James Garfield
Journal
March 16, 1881

My day is frittered away by personal seeking of people, when it ought to be given to the great problem[s] which concern the whole country. Four years of this kind of intellectual dissipation may cripple me for the remainder of my life. What might not a vigorous thinker do, if he could be allowed to use the opportunities of a presidential term in vital, useful activity! Some Civil Service reform will come by necessity after the wearisome years of wasted Presidents have paved the way for it.

James A. Garfield
Journal
June 13, 1881

The applicants for office are generally respectable and worthy men . . . . but at the end of one hundred days of this work the President should not be judged too harshly if he shows a little wear, a little loss of effusiveness, and even a hunted expression in his eyes.

Benjamin Harrison
This Country of Ours
1897

This dreadful, damnable office-seeking hangs over me and surrounds me—and makes me feel like resigning.

Grover Cleveland
Cited in Arthur Bernon Tourtellot, *The Presidents on the Presidency*

They open their mouths for a horse, but are perfectly willing to settle for a fly.

James A. Garfield
Cited in Vic Fredericks, *The Wit and Wisdom of the Presidents*, describing office seekers as alligators

I venture to hope that we shall never again be remitted to the system which distributes public positions purely as rewards for partisan service. Doubts may well be entertained whether our government could survive the strain of a continuance of this system, which, upon every change of administration, inspires an immense army of claimants for office to lay siege to the patronage of government, engrossing the time of public officers with their importunities, spreading abroad the contagion of their disappointments, and filling the air with the tumult of their discontent.

Grover Cleveland
First annual message, Congress
December 8, 1885

All appointments *hurt*. Five friends are made cold or hostile for every appointment; no *new* friends are made. All patronage is perilous to men of real ability or merit. It aids only those who lack other claims to public support.

Rutherford B. Hayes
Letter, William McKinley
December 27, 1892

I hate to use the patronage as a club unless I have to.

William Howard Taft
Cited in Arthur Bernon Tourtellot, *The Presidents on the Presidency*

Every man who takes office in Washington either grows or swells, and when I give a man an office, I watch him carefully to see whether he is swelling or growing. The mischief of it is that when they swell, they do not swell enough to burst.

Woodrow Wilson
Washington, D.C.
May 15, 1916

In the days before the present civil service law, a sense of obligation to the President for the places held, made practically all the civil employees his political henchmen. In those halcyon times, even the humblest charwoman or the most poorly paid janitor felt a throb of deep personal interest in the political health of the President.

William Howard Taft
The President and His Powers
1916

Machine politics and the spoils system are as much an enemy of a proper and efficient government system of civil service as the boll weevil is of the cotton crop.

William Howard Taft
The President and His Powers
1916

I have to appoint human beings to office.

Calvin Coolidge
Comment, reporters, regarding scandals in his administration
1925

You have to stand every day three or four hours of visitors. Nine-tenths of them want something they ought not to have. If you keep dead-still they will run down in three or four minutes. If you even cough or smile they will start up all over again.

Calvin Coolidge
To Herbert Hoover
1928

It is a handicap to any man to succeed a member of his own party as President. He has little patronage with which to reward his personal supporters.

Herbert Hoover
Memoirs
1951-1952

No one should be appointed to political office if he is a seeker after it.

Dwight D. Eisenhower
Diary
January 1, 1953

[The Republicans] did not look upon the results of the [1952] election as the threshold of opportunity; rather it was the end of a long and searing drought, and they were at last reveling again in luxurious patronage.

Dwight D. Eisenhower
To Emmett Hughes
December 10, 1953

The last thing I would ever ask any man that I appoint to a high office is what are going to be his decisions in specific cases.

Dwight D. Eisenhower
March 30, 1955

Patronage is almost a wicked word. By itself it could well-nigh defeat democracy.

Dwight D. Eisenhower
Diary
January 5, 1956

Army

The good sense of people will always be found to be the best army.

Thomas Jefferson
Letter, Edward Carrington
January 16, 1787

A standing army is one of the greatest mischiefs that can possibly happen.

James Madison
Debates, Virginia convention
1787

I think with the Romans of old, that the general of today should be a common soldier tomorrow, if necessary.

Thomas Jefferson
Letter, James Madison
1797

None but an armed nation can dispense with a standing army.

Thomas Jefferson
Letter
February 25, 1803

Always remember[ing] that an armed and trained militia is the firmest bulwark of republics—that without standing armies their liberty can never be in danger, nor with large ones safe.

James Madison
First inaugural address
March 4, 1809

Good officers will make good soldiers.

Andrew Jackson
Journal
January 18, 1815

The axe, pick, saw & trowel, has become more the implement of the American soldier than the cannon, musket or sword.

Zachary Taylor
Letter, Thomas Jesup
June 18, 1820

A military education will be but of little service . . . unless practice be blended with theory.

Zachary Taylor
Letter, Thomas Jesup
September 18, 1820

From Caesar to Cromwell, and from Cromwell to Napoleon . . . . history presents the same solemn warning—beware of elevating to the highest civil trust the commander of your victorious armies.

James Buchanan
Speech, Greensburg, Pennsylvania
October 7, 1852

My dear McClelland: If you don't want to use the Army I should like to borrow it for a while.

Abraham Lincoln
Unsent Letter, George Brinton McClelland, protest-
    ing his "waiting campaign" of 1862

[There is] but one debt contracted in the last four years which the people of the United States cannot pay. That is the debt of gratitude to the rank and file of our Army and Navy.

Ulysses S. Grant
Letter, J. J. Talmadge
May 25, 1865

And we must not forget that it is often easier to assemble armies than it is to assemble army revenues.

Benjamin Harrison
Speech, Marquette Club Banquette, Chicago, Illinois
March 20, 1888

The people want us to hold everything but the soldiers, forgetting that without them we could not hold anything.

William McKinley
Annexation of the Philippines
1898

I am not one of those who believe that a great standing army is the means of maintaining peace, because if you build up a great profession those who form parts of it want to exercise their profession.

Woodrow Wilson
Speech in Pittsburgh, Pennsylvania
January 29, 1916

No nation ever had an army large enough to guarantee it against attack in time of peace, or insure it victory in time of war.

Calvin Coolidge
Speech
1925

The necessary and wise subordination of the military to civil power will be best sustained when lifelong professional soldiers abstain from seeking high political office.

Dwight D. Eisenhower
Letter to a friend, quoted in Harry Truman, *Years of Trials and Hope*

In the council of government we must guard against the acquisition of unwanted influence, whether sought or unsought, by the military-industrial complex . . . . We must never let the weight of this combination endanger our liberties or democratic processes. We should take nothing for granted. Only an alert and knowledgeable citizenry can compel the proper meshing of the huge industrial and military machinery of defense with our peaceful methods and goals so that security and liberty may prosper together.

Dwight D. Eisenhower
Farewell Address
January 17, 1961

The Chinese philosopher, Sun Tzu, 2,500 years ago said winning a hundred victories in a hundred battles is not the acme of skill; to subdue the enemy without fighting is the acme of skill. A truly successful army is one that, because of its strength and ability and dedication, will not be called upon to fight because no one will dare to provoke it.

Ronald Reagan
Speech, U. S. Military Academy, West Point, New York
May 27, 1981

Chester A. Arthur

He seems more afraid of his enemies . . . than guided either by his judgement, personal feelings, or friendly influences.

Ulysses S. Grant
Comment, Adam Badeau, Adam Badeau's *Grant in Peace*
1867

The sop thrown to [Senator Roscoe] Conkling in the nomination of [Chester Arthur] only serves to emphasize the completeness of his defeat. He was so crushed that it was from sheer sympathy that this bone was thrown to him.

Rutherford B. Hayes
Diary, describing the nomination of Chester A. Arthur as Republican candidate for vice president and James A. Garfield for president
June 11, 1880

Arthur for President! [Senator Roscoe] Conkling the power behind the throne!

Rutherford B. Hayes
Diary
c. 1881

Nothing like it ever before in the Executive Mansion—liquor, snobbery, and worse.

Rutherford B. Hayes
Comment on Chester Arthur's White House
c. 1882

A non-entity with side whiskers.

Attributed to Woodrow Wilson
Cited in Richard Kenin and Justin Wintle, *The Dictionary of Biographical Quotations*

Assassination

I have been informed that part of the business to be transacted on the present occasion is the assassination of the individual who now has the honor of addressing you. . . . Therefore, if any man has come here tonight for the purpose indicated, I do not say to him, let him speak, but, let him shoot.

Andrew Johnson
Campaign speech for governor of Tennessee in Know-Nothing stronghold
1855

If I am shot at, I want no man to be in the way of the bullet.

Andrew Johnson
Rejecting bodyguards after assassination threat when governor of Tennessee
1850s

Hannah, if they do kill me, I shall never die another death.

Abraham Lincoln
Response, Hannah Armstrong's comment, "They'll kill ye, Abe." Springfield, Illinois
1860

But, if this country cannot be saved without giving up that principle [equality] . . . I would rather be assassinated on this spot than surrender it.

Abraham Lincoln
Speech, Independence Hall
February 22, 1861

If it [the Ship of State] should suffer attack now, there will be no pilot ever needed for another voyage.

Abraham Lincoln
Speech, New Jersey Assembly, Trenton, New Jersey
1861

When the hour comes for dealing with slavery, I trust I will be willing to do my duty though it cost my life.

Abraham Lincoln
Comment, Reverend Moncure Daniel Conway
Summer 1862

Why put up the bars when the fence is done all around? If they kill me, the next man will be just as bad for them; and in a country like this, where habits are simple, and must be, assassination is always possible, and will come if they are determined upon it.

Abraham Lincoln
Comment, Harriet Beecher Stowe
Winter 1862-1863

If it is [God's] will that I must die at the hand of an assassin, I must be resigned. I must do my duty as I see it, and leave the rest with God.

Abraham Lincoln
Statement, Washington, D.C.
1864

I have been almost overwhelmed by the announcement of the sad event [Lincoln's assassination] which has so recently occurred. I feel incompetent to perform duties so important and responsible as those which have been so unexpectedly thrown upon me.

Andrew Johnson
First statement as president
April 15, 1865

God reigns and the Government at Washington still lives.

James A. Garfield
Reassuring a crowd on Wall Street after Lincoln's
   assassination
April 15, 1865

I have been told that if I repeated here today what I said on former occasions, perhaps I would be assassinated. But these two eyes have never yet beheld the man that this heart feared.

Andrew Johnson
Speech, campaign for Senate, Tennessee
Fall 1874

I am receiving what I suppose to be the usual number of threatening letters on that subject. Assassination can be no more guarded against than death by lightening; and it is best not to worry about either.

James A. Garfield
Cited in John M. Taylor, Garfield of Ohio: The Available Man

My God! what is this?

James A. Garfield
Overheard by James Blaine at the time of Garfield's
   assassination
July 21, 1881

He must have been crazy. None but an insane person could have done such a thing. What could he have wanted to shoot me for?

James A. Garfield (on his deathbed, after the
   assassination attempt by Charles Guiteau)
Washington, D.C.
July 1881

All personal considerations and political views must be merged in the national sorrow. I am an American among millions grieving for their wounded chief.

Chester A. Arthur
Comment, reporter who alluded to newspaper
   editorials linking him with James A. Garfield's
   assassin, Charles Guiteau
July 1881

Men may die, but the fabrics of free institutions remain unshaken.

Chester A. Arthur
Inauguration address
September 22, 1881

I should think the people would be tired of having me dished up to them in this way.

James Garfield
Comment, press after he was shot
1881

If we bar out the irresponsible crank, so far as I can see the President is in no peril, except that he may be killed by the superabundant kindness of the people.

Benjamin Harrison
Speech, Waterbury, Vermont
August 26, 1891

I have no enemies. Why should I fear?

William McKinley
Comment, friends, a few days before his assassina-
   tion, Canton, Ohio
August 1901

My wife—be careful, Cortelyou, how you tell her—oh, be careful.

William McKinley, to George Courtelyou, after being
   shot by Leon Czolgosz
Temple of Music, Buffalo, New York
September 6, 1901

I do not believe there is any danger of any assault upon my life . . . and if there were it would be simple nonsense to try to prevent it, for as Lincoln said, though it would be safer for a President to live in a cage, it would interfere with his business.

Theodore Roosevelt
Letter, Henry Cabot Lodge
August 6, 1906

Friends, I shall ask you to be as quiet as possible. I don't know whether you fully understand that I have been shot; but it takes more than that to kill a Bull Moose.

Theodore Roosevelt
Five minutes after being shot, Milwaukee, Wisconsin
October 14, 1912

I am delighted to learn that the dastardly attack was unsuccessful. The resort to violence is out of place in our twentieth-century civilization.

William Howard Taft
Comment, New York Times reporter, on the
   attempted assassination of Theodore Roosevelt
October 1912

A President has to expect those things. The only thing you have to worry about is bad luck. I never have bad luck.

Harry S. Truman
Comment, after an attempt on his life at Blair House, reported in *Time*
November 13, 1950

All I have I would have given gladly not to be here today.

Lyndon B. Johnson
First address, Congress, after John F. Kennedy's burial
November 27, 1963

An assassin's bullet has thrust upon me the awesome burden of the Presidency. I am here to say that I need the help of all Americans, in all America.

Lyndon B. Johnson
First address, Congress, after John F. Kennedy's burial
November 27, 1963

What in the name of conscience will it take to pass a truly effective gun-control law? Now in this new hour of tragedy, let us spell out our grief in constructive action.

Lyndon B. Johnson
Speech, following the assassination of Senator Robert F. Kennedy
June 6, 1968

The American people want a dialogue between them and their President. . . . And if we can't have that opportunity of talking with one another, seeing one another, shaking hands with one another, something has gone wrong in our society.

Gerald Ford after two assassination attempts
September 22, 1975

I never felt the "there but for the grace of God go I" reaction to Kennedy's death that many people seemed to imagine I would. After eight years as Vice President I had become fatalistic about the danger of assassination.

Richard Nixon
The Memoirs of Richard Nixon
1978

We were sure that ours was a nation of the ballot, not the bullet, until the murders of John Kennedy, Robert Kennedy, and Martin Luther King, Jr.

Jimmy Carter
Speech, the White House
July 15, 1979

Atomic Warfare

Sixteen hours ago an American airplane dropped one bomb on Hiroshima. . . . It is a harnessing of the basic power of the universe. The force from which the sun draws its powers has been loosened against those who brought the war to the Far East.

Harry S. Truman
Speech announcing first atomic bomb explosion
August 6, 1945

If a [decision to drop the atomic bomb] had to be made for the welfare of the United States and the democracies of the world, I wouldn't hesitate to make it again.

Harry S. Truman
Statement
April 10, 1949

It is part of my responsibility as Commander-in-Chief of the armed forces to see to it that our country is able to defend itself against any possible aggressor. Accordingly, I have directed the Atomic Energy Commission to continue its work on all forms of atomic weapons, including the so-called hydrogen or super-bomb.

Harry S. Truman
Announcement, hydrogen bomb program
January 31, 1950

The worst to be feared and the best to be expected can be simply stated. The worst is atomic war. The best would be this: a life of perpetual fear and tension; a burden of arms draining the wealth and labor of all peoples. Every gun that is made, every warship launched, every rocket fired, signifies, in the final sense, a theft from those who hunger and are not fed, those who are cold and are not clothed.

Dwight D. Eisenhower
The Chance for Peace Speech, Washington, D.C.
April 16, 1953

This is not a way of life at all, in any true sense. Under the cloud of threatening war, it is humanity hanging from a cross of iron.

Dwight D. Eisenhower
The Chance for Peace Speech, Washington, D.C.
April 16, 1953

We've just got to let the American people know how terrible this thing [Hydrogen bomb] is.

Dwight D. Eisenhower
Bernard Shanley Diary
July 9, 1953

This titanic force must be reduced to the fruitful service of mankind.

Dwight D. Eisenhower
News conference
October 8, 1953

The dread secret, and the fearful engines of atomic might, are not ours alone.

Dwight D. Eisenhower
Speech, United Nations (Atoms for Peace Program)
December 8, 1953

It is not enough to take this weapon [the atomic bomb] out of the hands of soldiers. It must be put into the hands of those who will know how to strip its military casing and adapt it to the arts of peace.

Dwight D. Eisenhower
Speech, United Nations (Atoms for Peace Program)
December 8, 1953

But for me to say that the defense capabilities of the United States are such that they could inflict terrible losses upon an aggressor—for me to say that the retaliation capabilities of the United States are such that such an aggressor's land would be laid waste—all this, while fact, is not the true expression of the purpose and the hope of the United States. To pause there would be to confirm the hopeless finality of a belief that two atomic collosi are doomed malevolently to eye each other indefinitely across a trembling world.

Dwight D. Eisenhower
Speech, United Nations (Atoms for Peace Program)
December 8, 1953

The things we really need are the things the other fellow looks at and respects [the bomb].

Dwight D. Eisenhower
Speech, Republican congressional leaders
December 1953

War is a contest, and you finally get to a point where you are talking merely about race suicide, and nothing else.

Dwight D. Eisenhower
Republican leaders meeting
February 14, 1954

In any combat where these things [small atomic weapons] can be used on strictly military targets and for strictly military purposes, I see no reason why they shouldn't be used just exactly as you would use a bullet or anything else.

Dwight D. Eisenhower
News conference
March 16, 1954

You boys must be crazy. We can't use those awful things against those Asians for the second time in less than ten years. My God.

Dwight D. Eisenhower
Comment, Bobby Cutler, on National Security Council paper exploring the use of atomic bombs in Vietnam
April 30, 1954

How many times do we have to destroy Russia?

Dwight D. Eisenhower
Comment, advisers, concerning DOD budget request for fiscal 1960
November 1958

Destruction is not a good police force.

Dwight D. Eisenhower
News conference
March 11, 1959

The atomic bomb was no "great decision." ...It was merely another powerful weapon in the arsenal of righteousness.

Harry S. Truman
Seminar, Columbia University, New York, New York
April 28, 1959

The world is very different now. For man holds in his mortal hands the power to abolish all forms of human poverty and all forms of human life.

John F. Kennedy
First inaugural address
January 20, 1961

Men no longer debate whether armaments are a symptom or cause of tension. The mere existence of modern weapons—ten million times more destructive than anything the world has ever known, and only minutes away from any target on earth—is a source of horror, of discord, of distrust. . . . The risks inherent in disarmament pale in comparison to the risks inherent in an unlimited arms race.

John F. Kennedy
Speech, United Nations General Assembly, New York, New York
September 25, 1961

It was clear to me by 1969 that there could never be absolute parity between the U.S. and the U.S.S.R. . . . Consequently, at the beginning of my administration I began to talk in terms of *sufficiency* rather than *superiority* to describe my goals for our nuclear arsenal.

Richard Nixon
The Memoirs of Richard Nixon
1978

It is precisely because we have fundamental differences with the Soviet Union that we are determined to bring this dangerous dimension of our military competition under control.

Jimmy Carter
Speech, Georgia Institute of Technology, Atlanta, Georgia
February 20, 1979

Yet this kind of twilight peace [since Hiroshima] carries the everpresent threat of a catastrophic nuclear war, a war that in horror and destruction massive death would dwarf all the combined wars of man's long and bloody history.

Jimmy Carter
Address, Congress
June 18, 1979

It has now been 35 years since the first atomic bomb fell on Hiroshima. The great majority of the world's people cannot remember a time when the nuclear shadow did not hang over the earth. Our minds have adjusted to it, as after a time our eyes adjust to the dark.

Jimmy Carter
Farewell address
January 14, 1981

In an all-out nuclear war, more destructive power than in all of World War II would be unleashed every second for the long afternoon it would take for all the missiles and bombs to fall. A World War II every second—more people killed in the first few hours than [in] all the wars of history put together. The survivors, if any, would live in despair amid the poisoned ruins of a civilization that had committed suicide.

Jimmy Carter
Farewell address
January 14, 1981

Up until now we have increasingly based our strategy of deterrence upon the threat of retaliation. But what if free people could live secure in the knowledge that their security did not rest upon the threat of instant United States retaliation to deter a Soviet attack; that we could intercept and destroy strategic ballistic missiles before they reached our own soil or that of our allies?

Ronald Reagan
Speech, proposing Strategic Defense Initiative research, Washington, D.C.
March 3, 1983

If the Soviet Union will join with us in our effort to achieve major arms reduction we will have succeeded in stabilizing the nuclear balance. Nevertheless it will still be necessary to rely on the specter of retaliation—on mutual threat, and that is a sad commentary on the human condition.

Ronald Reagan
Speech, Washington, D.C.
March 23, 1983

The treaty [SALT] was really nothing but the legitimizing of an arms race.

Ronald Reagan
Press conference, Washington, D.C.
June 11, 1986

B

Banks

I sincerely believe that banking establishments are more dangerous than standing armies, and that the principle of spending money to be paid by posterity, under the name of funding, is but swindling futurity on a large scale.

Thomas Jefferson
Letter, John Taylor
May 28, 1816

I do not think the Congress has a right to create a corporation out of the ten miles square.

Andrew Jackson
Suspected unsigned letter, Nicholas Biddle
1829

Many of our rich men have not been content with equal protection and equal benefits, but have besought us to make them richer by act of Congress.

Andrew Jackson
Veto, Bank Bill
July 10, 1832

If our power over means is so absolute that the Supreme Court will not call into question an act of Congress . . . it becomes to us to proceed in our legislation with the utmost caution.

Andrew Jackson
Veto, Bank Bill
July 10, 1832

A permanent electioneering engine.

Andrew Jackson
Paper read to cabinet
September 18, 1833

Public money is but a species of public property. It can not be raised by taxation or customs, nor brought into the Treasury in any other way except by law; but whenever or however obtained, its custody always has been and always must be, unless the Constitution be changed, intrusted to the executive department.

Andrew Jackson
Protest, Senate
April 15, 1834

But where is the difference in principle whether the public property be in the form of arms, munitions of war, and supplies or in gold and silver or bank notes? None can be perceived; none is believed to exist. Congress cannot, therefore, take out of the hands of the executive department the custody of the public property or money without an assumption of executive power and a subversion of the first principles of the Constitution.

Andrew Jackson
Protest, Senate
April 15, 1834

You can rest assured that, as long as I am President, the gentlemen in Wall Street are not to control the operations of the International Bank.

Harry S. Truman
Letter
1947

James Buchanan

I voted for Buchanan because I didn't know him and voted against [John C.] Fremont because I did know him.

Ulysses S. Grant
November 1856

Our present granny executive.

Ulysses S. Grant
Letter, friend

Budget

The accounts of the United States ought to be, and may be made, as simple as those of a common farmer, and capable of being understood by common farmers.

Thomas Jefferson
Letter, James Madison
1796

I hold it the duty of the Executive to insist upon frugality in the expenditures, and a sparing economy is itself a great national resource.

Andrew Johnson
First annual message, Congress
December 4, 1865

The bane of an overflowing treasury.

Chester A. Arthur
Speech
1882

The course of unbalanced budgets is the road to ruin.

Herbert Hoover
Speech, Senate, on a balanced budget
May 31, 1932

For three long years I have been going up and down this country preaching that government. . . costs too much. I shall not stop that preaching.

Franklin D. Roosevelt
Acceptance speech, Democratic National Convention
July 2, 1932

We can afford all that we need; but we cannot afford all we want.

Franklin D. Roosevelt
Veto, Soldier's Bonus Bill
May 22, 1935

Look, I'd like to know what's on the other side of the moon. But I won't pay to find out this year!

Dwight Eisenhower
Comment, Cabinet
November 1, 1957

We cannot substitute last year's achievements for next year's goals; nor can we meet next year's challenge with last year's budget.

Lyndon B. Johnson
Budget Message, Congress
January 25, 1965

It's discouraging how hard it is for a President to slice away large chunks from a $305 billion budget.

Gerald Ford
A Time to Heal
1979

The . . . purchase of unnecessary military equipment is undoubtedly the most wasteful element in American government.

Jimmy Carter
Keeping Faith
1982

It's time we reduced the Federal budget and left the family budget alone.

Ronald Reagan
State of the union address
February 2, 1986

Bureaucracy

I think we have more machinery of government than is necessary, too many parasites living on the labor of the industrious.

Thomas Jefferson
Letter, Charles Yancey
1816

Restraint, restraint . . . this Federal Government is nothing but a system of restraints from beginning to end.

James Buchanan
c. 1844

Presidents may go to the seashore or to the mountains, Cabinet Officers may go about the country explaining how fortunate the country is in having such an administration, but the machinery at Washington continues to operate under the army of faithful non-commissioned officers, and the great mass of governmental business is uninterrupted.

William Howard Taft
The President and His Powers
1916

Our federal machinery is the result of a hundred years of patchwork and has lagged lamentably behind the skill in organization of our people.

Herbert Hoover
October 1919

If we do not halt this steady process of building commissions and regulatory bodies and special legislation like huge inverted pyramids over every one of the simple constitutional provisions, we shall soon be spending many billions of dollars more.

Franklin D. Roosevelt
Radio address
March 2, 1930

One of the enduring truths of the nation's capital is that bureaucrats *survive*.

Gerald Ford
A Time to Heal
1982

The federal government too often treats government programs as if they are of Washington, by Washington and for Washington. Once established, federal programs seem to become immortal.

George Bush
State of the union address
January 29, 1991

George Bush

Mr. Bush, for 12 years you've had it your way; you've had your chance and it didn't work. It's time to change.

Bill Clinton
Presidential Debate
October 11, 1992

Business and Capitalism

These capitalists generally act harmoniously and in concert, to fleece the people.

Abraham Lincoln
Speech, Illinois Legislature
January 1837

The prudent capitalist will never adventure his capital . . . if there exists a state of uncertainty as to whether the Government will repeal to-morrow what it has enacted to-day.

John Tyler
Second annual message, Congress
December 6, 1842

Capital and capitalists . . . are proverbially timid.

James Buchanan
Comment, Franklin Pierce
1854

That irresistible tide of commercial expansion.

Grover Cleveland
First annual message, Congress
c. 1885

Must we always look for the political opinions of our business men precisely where they suppose their immediate pecuniary advantage is found?

Grover Cleveland
Speech, Commercial Exchange, Philadelphia, Pennsylvania
September 16, 1887

They [trusts] are dangerous conspiracies against the public good.

William McKinley
Letter of acceptance of presidential nomination
September 1900

I have sometimes heard men say politics must have nothing to do with business, and I have often wished that business had nothing to do with politics.

Woodrow Wilson
Speech, New York, New York
1904

There can be no delusion more fatal to the nation than the delusion that the standard of profits, of business prosperity, is sufficient in judging any business or political question.

Theodore Roosevelt
Annual message, Congress
December 1905

There can be no effective control of corporations while their political activity remains.

Theodore Roosevelt
The New Nationalism
1910

The truth is, we are all caught in a great economic system which is heartless.

Woodrow Wilson
The New Freedom
1912-1913 speeches

There was a time when corporations played a minor part in our business affairs, but now they play the chief part, and most men are the servants of corporations.

Woodrow Wilson
The New Freedom
1912-1913 speeches

We must insist that when anyone engaged in big business honestly endeavors to do right, he himself shall be given a square deal.

Theodore Roosevelt
Speech
1913

The business of America is business.

Calvin Coolidge
Speech, Society of American Newspaper Editors, Washington, D.C.
January 1925

Commercial business requires a concentration of responsibility. Self-government requires decentralization and many checks and balances to safeguard liberty. Our Government to succeed in business would need to become in effect a despotism. There at once begins the destruction of self-government.

Herbert Hoover
Speech on rugged individualism, New York, New York
October 22, 1928

Our country has become the land of opportunity to those born without inheritance, not merely because of the wealth of its resources and industry but because of this freedom of initiative and enterprise.

Herbert Hoover
Speech, New York, New York
October 22, 1928

There runs through the ranks of the great captains of industry as high a type of conscience as can be found even on the floor of the United States Senate.

Warren G. Harding
While in the U.S. Senate
c. 1917

Free speech does not live many hours after free industry and free commerce die.

Herbert Hoover
Speech, New York, New York
October 22, 1928

The royalists of the economic order have conceded that political freedom was the business of government, but they have maintained that economic slavery was nobody's business.

Franklin D. Roosevelt
Acceptance speech, Democratic National Convention
June 27, 1936

Concentration of wealth and power has been built upon other people's money, other people's business, other people's labor. Under this concentration, independent business . . . has been a menace to . . . American society.

Franklin D. Roosevelt
Acceptance speech, Democratic National Convention
June 27, 1936

Private enterprise is ceasing to be free enterprise.

Franklin D. Roosevelt
Message, Congress, proposing monopoly investigation
1938

No political party can be a friend of the American people which is not a friend of American business.

Lyndon B. Johnson
Speech, Houston Chamber of Commerce, Houston, Texas
August 12, 1963

Free enterprise is a rough and competitive game. It is a hell of a lot better than a government monopoly.

Ronald Reagan
Speech, 77th Congress of American Industry, National Association of Manufacturers, New York, New York
December 8, 1972

We do not need an Energy Department to solve our basic energy problems: as long as we let the forces of the marketplace work without undue interference, the ingenuity will do that for us.

Ronald Reagan
Speech, White House
September 24, 1981

Millions of individuals making their own decisions in the marketplace will always allocate resources better than any centralized government planning process.

Ronald Reagan
Speech, Annual Joint Meeting of the Board of Governors of the World Bank and International Monetary Fund, Washington, D.C.
September 27, 1983

Excellence does not begin in Washington.

Ronald Reagan
State of the union address
January 25, 1984

Somewhere along the way these folks in Washington have forgotten that the economy is business. Business creates new products and new services. Business creates jobs. Business creates prosperity for our communities and our nation as a whole.

Ronald Reagan
Speech, business and congressional leaders, Washington, D.C.
September 23, 1985

Entrepreneurs share a faith in a bright future. They have a clear vision of where they are going and what they are doing, and they have a pressing need to succeed. If I didn't know better, I would be tempted to say that "entrepreneur" is another word for America.

Ronald Reagan
"Reflections of a Self-Made American," *Success* magazine
1986

A decade ago, Americans earned higher wages than anyone else in the world. Now we're thirteenth and falling. In Europe and Japan our competitors' economies grew three and four times faster than ours because their leaders decided to invest in their people and Washington did not.

Bill Clinton
Putting People First
1992

We can never again allow the corrupt do-nothing values of the 1980s to mislead us. Today, the average CEO at a major American corporation is paid 100 times more than the average worker. Our government rewards that excess with a tax break for executive pay, no matter how high it is, no matter what performance it reflects. And then the government hands out tax deductions to corporations that shut down their plants here and ship our jobs overseas. That has to change.

Bill Clinton
Putting People First
1992

C

Cabinet

There are, however, other relations between the President and a head of Department beyond these defined legal relations, which necessarily attend them, though not expressed. Chief among these is mutual confidence. This relation is so delicate that it is sometimes hard to say when or how it ceases. A single flagrant act may end it at once, and then there is no difficulty. But confidence may be just as effectively destroyed by a series of causes too subtle for demonstration. As it is a plant of slow growth, so, too, it may be slow in decay.

Andrew Johnson
To Senate
December 12, 1867

1. A new Cabinet—no holdovers from the Grant administration; 2. no presidential candidates; 3. no appointment to "take care" of anybody.

Rutherford B. Hayes
Diary
February 18, 1877

No trades, no shackles, and as well fitted for defeat or victory as ever.

James A. Garfield
Diary, on his Cabinet appointments
August 9, 1880

Kitchen cabinet.

Harry S. Truman
Referring to mythical group consisting of a Secretary for Inflation, a Secretary of Reaction, a Secretary of Semantics, etc.
Cited in Bruce Bohle, *The Home Book of American Quotations*

Campaigns

I am sensible that by being removed from the turbulent and disgusting scene of perpetual electioneering I am spared many a detail of vexation which I should otherwise be obliged to suffer.

John Quincy Adams
Letter, Thomas Boylston Adams
December 20, 1800

I need not say to you that I have no desire to run. . . . I am not willing to be treacherously killed by this pretended kindness. . . . Do not suppose for a moment that I think they desire my nomination.

Millard Fillmore
Letter, Francis Granger, objecting to possible nomination for governor of New York, instead of vice president
April 7, 1844

So I am in for it and there is no escape.

Millard Fillmore
Letter, Thurlow Weed, after Fillmore's nomination for governor of New York
September 16, 1844

I must have shook hands with several thousand persons. . . . Some gentlemen asked me if my arm was not sore. . . . I told them that I had found that there was a great art in shaking hands. . . .[I]f a man surrendered his arm to be shaken . . . he could not fail to suffer severely from it, but that if he would shake and not be shaken, grip and not be gripped, taking care always to squeeze the hand of his adversary as hard as he squeezed him, that he suffered no inconvenience from it.

James K. Polk
The Diary of James K. Polk
January 1, 1849

It [campaigning] has been done, so far as I remember, by but two presidential candidates heretofore, and both of them were public speakers and both were beaten. I am no speaker and I don't want to be beaten!

Ulysses S. Grant
Comment, Senator Roscoe Conkling, presidential election
1872

I spoke almost every day till the election, but it now appears that we are defeated by the combined power of rebellion, Catholicism and whiskey, a trinity very hard to conquer.

James A. Garfield
Comment, James G. Blaine, on attempts to unite Republicans for the presidential elections of 1880

I said to one of the first delegations that visited me that this was a contest of great principles; that it would be fought out upon the high plains of truth, and not in the swamps of slander and defamation. Those who will encamp their army in the swamp will abandon the victory to the army that is on the heights.

Benjamin Harrison
Speech, Indianapolis, Indiana
October 25, 1888

If elected, I shall see to it that every man has a square deal, no less and no more.

Theodore Roosevelt
Speech
November 1904

The New Nationalism puts the national needs before sectional or personal advantage. . . . The man who wrongly holds that every human right is secondary to his profit must now give way to the advocate of human welfare who rightly maintains that every man holds his property subject to the general right of the community to regulate its use to whatever degree the public welfare may require.

Theodore Roosevelt
Speech, Osawatomie, Kansas
August 31 1910

My hat's in the ring. The fight is on and I'm stripped to the buff.

Theodore Roosevelt
Announcement of his presidential candidacy
1912

I feel as fit as a bull moose.

Theodore Roosevelt
Reply, reporter, on eve of the Progressive Party Convention
August 7, 1912

A presidential campaign may easily degenerate into a mere personal contest, and so lose its real dignity. There is no indispensable man.

Woodrow Wilson
Speech accepting Democratic nomination for the presidency
August 7, 1912

Harry, it's awful.
What's awful?
This stumping the country and howling for myself.

Warren G. Harding
Comment, Harry M. Daugherty, U.S. Senate campaign
c. 1914

It is better not to press a candidacy too much, but to let it develop on its own merits without artificial stimulation. If the people want a man they will nominate him, if they do not want him he had best let the nomination go to another.

Calvin Coolidge
The Autobiography of Calvin Coolidge
1929

Never murder a man who is committing suicide.

Woodrow Wilson
On the failing campaign of his opponent, Governor Charles Evans Hughes
Cited in John Dos Passos, Mr. Wilson's War

Two cars in every garage.

Herbert Hoover
Campaign speech
1929-1930

I pledge to you, I pledge myself, to a new deal for the American people.

Franklin D. Roosevelt
Acceptance speech, Democratic National
  Convention
July 2, 1932

I consider it a public duty to answer falsifications with facts. I will not pretend that I find this an unpleasant duty. I am an old campaigner, and I love a good fight.

Franklin D. Roosevelt
Speech, Philadelphia, Pennsylvania
October 23, 1940

I'm going to fight hard. I'm going to give them hell.

Harry S. Truman
Comment, Senator Alben Barkeley, *Memoirs: Years
  of Trial and Hope*

We can take heart from a comment made by that great American heavyweight champion Joe Lewis. In one fight, some time ago, he had a hard time catching up with his opponent. But Joe finally did catch up with him, and he knocked him out. After the fight, this is what Joe said: "Well, he could run away, but he couldn't hide."

Harry S. Truman
Address, Convention Hall, Philadelphia,
  Pennsylvania
October 6, 1948

It isn't important who is ahead at one time or another in either an election or a horse-race. It's the horse that comes in first at the finish that counts.

Harry S. Truman
Statement
October 17, 1948

I am going to campaign up and down America until we drive the crooks and the Communists and those that defend them out of Washington.

Richard Nixon
Checkers Speech, Hollywood, California
1952

We stand today on the edge of a new frontier—the frontier of the 1960's—a frontier of unknown opportunities and perils—frontier of unfulfilled hopes and threats.

John F. Kennedy
Acceptance speech, Democratic National Conven-
  tion, Los Angeles, California
July 15, 1960

I personally have lived through ten Presidential campaigns, but I must say the eleventh makes me feel like I lived through twenty-five.

John F. Kennedy
Speech, New York, New York
September 14, 1960

I am deeply touched—not as deeply touched as you have been by coming to this dinner, but nevertheless, it is a sentimental occasion.

John F. Kennedy
Speech, $100-a-plate fund-raising dinner, presiden-
  tial campaign, Salt Lake City, Utah
September 23, 1960

Franklin Roosevelt started his campaign here in Ohio. I don't know what has happened to politics, but whenever I read about the 1932 campaign, Franklin Roosevelt stayed in Albany all winter, spring, summer, didn't go to the convention until he was nominated. He then took a boating trip up the coast of Maine with his son, started his campaign late in September, made some speeches, and was elected by a tremendous majority.

John F. Kennedy
Speech, Dayton, Ohio
October 17, 1960

It is time for the great silent majority of Americans to stand up and be counted.

Richard Nixon
Election Speech
October 1970

Having lost a close one eight years ago and having won a close one this year, I can say this—winning's a lot more fun.

Richard Nixon
Speech, after winning presidential election, New York, New York
1972

I am here to confess that in my first campaign for President—of my senior class in South High School in Grand Rapids, Michigan—I headed the Progressive Party ticket, and lost. Maybe that is why I became a Republican.

Gerald Ford
Address, Congress
August 12, 1974

In 1948 Harry Truman had campaigned to cries of "Give 'em hell." Eisenhower's parting admonition in 1956 was, "Give 'em heaven."

Richard Nixon
The Memoirs of Richard Nixon
1978

We were faced by an [Kennedy] organization that had equal dedication and unlimited money that was led by the most ruthless group of political operators ever mobilized for a presidential campaign.

Richard Nixon
The Memoirs of Richard Nixon, on the 1960 campaign
1978

A campaign is a disagreement, and disagreements divide. But an election is a decision, and decisions clear the way for harmony and peace. I mean to be president of all the people, and I want to work for the hopes and interests not only of my supporters but of the governor's [Dukakis] and of those who didn't vote at all.

George Bush
Campaign victory speech
November 8, 1988

Canada

We cannot bear that Great Britain should have a canady [sic] on our west [Texas] as she has on our North.

Andrew Jackson
Jackson Correspondence
c. 1844

Geography has made us neighbors. History has made us friends. Economics has made us partners; and necessity has made us allies.

John F. Kennedy
Speech, Canadian Parliament
May 17, 1961

Jimmy Carter

Teddy Roosevelt . . . once said "Speak softly and carry a big stick." Jimmy Carter wants to speak loudly and carry a fly swatter.

Gerald Ford
Campaign speech, presidential election
October 16, 1976

Look, we tried this once before, combining the Democratic governor of a small southern state with a very liberal vice president and a Democratic Congress. America doesn't need Carter II.

George Bush
Acceptance speech, Republican Convention
August 20, 1992

Change

The earth belongs to the living, not the dead.

Thomas Jefferson
Letter, John Wayles Eppes
June 24, 1813

If you want to make enemies, try to change something.

Woodrow Wilson
Speech, Detroit, Michigan
July 10, 1916

We do not need to burn down the house to kill the rats.

Herbert Hoover
The Challenge to Liberty
1934

Since the beginning of our American history we have been engaged in change—in a perpetual peaceful revolution—a revolution which goes on steadily, quietly adjusting itself to changing conditions—without the concentration camp or the quick-lime in the ditch.

Franklin D. Roosevelt
Four Freedoms Speech
January 6, 1941

Whatever America hopes to bring to pass in this world must first come to pass in the heart of America.

Dwight D. Eisenhower
Inaugural address
January 20, 1953

Neither a wise man nor a brave man lies down on the tracks of history to wait for the train of the future to run over him.

Dwight D. Eisenhower
Time
October 6, 1952

We must change to master change.

Lyndon B. Johnson
State of the union address
January 12, 1966

The people's right to change what does not work is one of the greatest principles of our system of government.

Richard Nixon
"Manpower Report of the President"
March 1972

The very key to our success has been our ability, foremost among nations, to preserve our lasting values by making change work for us rather than against us.

Ronald Reagan
Speech, Washington, D.C.
January 25, 1983

Character

He is happiest of whom the world says least, good or bad.

Thomas Jefferson
Letter, John Adams
August 27, 1786

The little spice of ambition which I had in my younger days has long since evaporated, and I set still less store by a posthumous than a present name.

Thomas Jefferson
Letter, James Madison
April 1795

I laid it down as a law to myself, to take no notice of the thousand calumnies issued against me, but to trust my own conduct, and the good sense and candor of my fellow citizens.

Thomas Jefferson
Letter, Wilson C. Nicholas
1809

Did you ever see a portrait of a great man without perceiving strong traits of pain and anxiety?

John Adams
Letter, Thomas Jefferson
May 6, 1816

A man is known by the company he keeps, and also by the company from which he is kept out.

Grover Cleveland
Cited in Vic Fredericks, *The Wit and Wisdom of the Presidents*

That's all a man can hope for during his lifetime—to set an example—and when he is dead, to be an inspiration for history.

William McKinley
Comment, George B. Cortelyou, Cortelyou Diary
December 29, 1899

Character is the only secure foundation of the state.

Calvin Coolidge
Address, New York, New York
February 12, 1924

A man cannot have character unless he lives within a fundamental system of morals that creates character.

Harry S. Truman
Statement, press conference
1950

China

If it is commercialism to want possession of a strategic point giving the American people an opportunity to maintain a foothold in the markets of that great Eastern country, for God's sake let's have commercialism.

Theodore Roosevelt
New York Times
July 31, 1898

An unconquerable China will play its proper role in maintaining peace not only in Eastern Asia but in the whole world.

Franklin D. Roosevelt
Speech
April 28, 1942

The Chinese, as you know, are fundamentally anti-foreign, and we must be exceedingly careful to see that this anti-foreign sentiment is not turned in our direction.

Harry S. Truman
Letter, Arthur H. Vandenberg
March 1950

But those damned little offshore islands [Quemoy and Matsu]. Sometimes I wish they'd sink.

Dwight D. Eisenhower
To Republican leaders
February 16, 1956

If there is anything I want to do before I die, it is to go to China. If I don't, I want my children to.

Richard Nixon
Time
October 1972

I am really probably older than they [Chinese leaders] are—I have only ten months to live [politically]—or at most four years and ten months, and I must get results now. That is why now is the hour for me, even more than for them, despite the fact that they are older in conventional terms.

Richard Nixon
Diary, after trip to China
1972

[Secretary of Defense] Harold Brown reported a meeting with Huang Chen from the People's Republic of China, and the high criticism by him of our military posture. He was particularly critical about our having changed strategic planning from a "2 1/2" capability to a "1 1/2" capability in recent years. When Harold pointed out that the other war plan had been designed for use against the People's Republic of China, his criticisms were attenuated.

Jimmy Carter
Diary
November 14, 1977

One reason we found the Chinese appeared to be so agreeable to deal with was their total lack of conceit or arrogance.

Richard Nixon
The Memoirs of Richard Nixon
1978

China had few lawyers, and he [Deng Xiaoping] was in a quandary about whether the country would be better off with more of them.

Jimmy Carter
Keeping Faith
1982

Deng [Xiaoping] informed me that there was no equating China and the Soviet Union on the immigration question, and added, "If you want me to release ten million Chinese to come to the United States, I'd be glad to do so."

Jimmy Carter
Keeping Faith
1982

Citizenship

When we assumed the soldier, we did not lay aside the citizen.

George Washington
Speech, Provincial Congress of New York
June 6, 1775

So long as he [the American citizen] can discern every star in its place upon that ensign, without wealth to purchase for him preferment or title to purchase for him place, it will be his privilege, and must be his acknowledged right, to stand unabased even in the presence of princes, with a proud consciousness that he is himself one of a nation of sovereigns.

Franklin Pierce
Inaugural address
March 4, 1853

No citizen of our country should permit himself to forget that he is a part of its Government and entitled to be heard in the determination of its policy and its measures, and that therefore the highest considerations of personal honor and patriotism require him to maintain by whatever power or influence he may possess the integrity of the laws of the Republic.

Franklin Pierce
Special message, Congress
January 24, 1856

There is here a great melting pot in which we must compound a precious metal. That metal is the metal of nationality.

Woodrow Wilson
Speech, Washington, D.C.
April 19, 1915

It is the duty of a citizen not only to observe the law but to let it be known that he is opposed to its violation.

Calvin Coolidge
Message, Congress
December 6, 1923

Self-reliance includes failure to fulfill the recognized responsibilities of citizenship. It is the worst form of laziness and leads, inevitably, to centralization of power.

Dwight D. Eisenhower
New York Times
September 11, 1959

Civil Disorder

Mobs do not discriminate, and the punishments inflicted by them have no repressive or salutary influence.

Benjamin Harrison
Acceptance speech, second Republican nomination
September 3, 1892

I can't imagine any set of circumstances that would ever induce me to send federal troops into . . . any area to enforce the orders of a federal court, because I believe that [the] common sense of America will never require it.

Dwight D. Eisenhower
Comment, Merriman Smith, press conference, before sending troops into Little Rock, Arkansas, September 24, 1957
July 16, 1957

Mob rule cannot be allowed to override the decisions of our courts.

Dwight D. Eisenhower
Address on the situation in Little Rock, Arkansas
September 24, 1957

I deplore the need or the use of troops anywhere to get American citizens to obey the orders of constituted courts; but I want to point this one thing out: there is no person in this room whose basic rights are not involved in any successful defiance to the carrying out of court orders.

Dwight D. Eisenhower
News conference, Arkansas's defiance of Supreme Court desegregation order during crises in Little Rock
May 14, 1958

Evil acts of the past are never rectified by evil acts of the present.

Lyndon B. Johnson
Statement, riots in New York City
July 21, 1964

There is no American right to loot stores, or to burn buildings, or to fire rifles from the rooftops. That is crime—and crime must be dealt with forcefully and swiftly, and certainly—under law.

Lyndon B. Johnson
Radio and television speech
July 27, 1967

Civilization

To correct evils, great and small, which spring from want of sympathy and from positive enmity among strangers, as nations or as individuals, is one of the highest functions of civilizations.

Abraham Lincoln
Speech, Milwaukee, Wisconsin
September 30, 1859

We may divide the whole struggle of the human race into two chapters: first, the fight to get leisure; and then the second fight of civilization—what shall we do with our leisure when we get it.

James A. Garfield
Speech, presidential campaign
1880

No people is wholly civilized where the distinction is drawn between stealing an office and stealing a purse.

Theodore Roosevelt
Speech, Chicago, Illinois
June 22, 1912

Civilization and profits go hand in hand.

Calvin Coolidge
Speech, New York, New York
November 27, 1920

·

Civil Rights

A measure which makes at once 4,000,000 people voters who were heretofore declared by the highest tribunal in the land not citizens of the United States, not eligible to become so, . . . is indeed a measure of grander importance than any other act of the kind from the foundation of our free Government to the present day.

Ulysses S. Grant
Message, Congress, 15th Amendment
March 30, 1870

Social equality is not a subject to be legislated upon.

Ulysses S. Grant
Second inaugural address
March 4, 1873

What questions are we to grapple with? What unfinished work remains to be done? It seems to me that the work that is unfinished is to make that constitutional grant of citizenship, the franchise to the colored men of the South, a practical and living reality.

Benjamin Harrison
Speech, Marquette Club Banquette, Chicago, Illinois
March 20, 1888

It was my good fortune at Santiago to serve beside colored troops. A man who is good enough to shed his blood for the country is good enough to be given a square deal afterward. More than that no man is entitled to, and less than that no man shall have.

Theodore Roosevelt
Speech, Springfield
July 4, 1903

Let the black man vote when he is fit to vote, prohibit the white man voting when he is unfit to vote.

Warren G. Harding
Speech, Birmingham, Alabama
August 1921

We can no longer afford the luxury of a leisurely attack upon prejudice and discrimination. There is much that state and local governments can do in providing positive safeguards for civil rights. But we cannot any longer await the growth of a will to action in the slowest state or the most backward community. Our national government must show the way.

Harry S. Truman
Address, National Association for the Advancement of Colored People
June 29, 1947

I do not see how any American can justify—legally, or logically, or morally—a discrimination in the expenditure of those [federal] funds as among our citizens. If there is any benefit to be derived from them, I think it means all share, regardless of such inconsequential factors as race and religion.

Dwight D. Eisenhower
Comment, Alice Dunningham, Associated Negro Press
April 1953

I will use the full power of the United States including whatever force will be necessary to prevent any obstruction of the law and to carry out the orders of the Federal Court.

Dwight D. Eisenhower
Statement, day before sending federal troops into
    Little Rock, Arkansas, to inforce the integration
    of Central High School
September 23, 1957

It's a matter of decency.

Dwight D. Eisenhower
Comment, Republican leaders
February 12, 1959

I want every American to stand up for his rights, even if he has to sit down for them.

John F. Kennedy
Campaign speech on black civil rights
    demonstrations
August 3, 1960

No one has been barred on account of his race from fighting or dying for America—there are no "white" or "colored" signs on the foxholes or graveyards of battle.

John F. Kennedy
Message, Congress, civil rights bill
June 19, 1963

We have talked long enough in this country about equal rights. We have talked for one hundred years or more. It is time now to write it in the books of law.

Lyndon B. Johnson
Speech, Congress
November 27, 1963

We must open the doors of opportunity. But we also must equip our people to walk through those doors.

Lyndon B. Johnson
Speech, National Urban League Conference,
    Washington, D.C.
December 10, 1964

Freedom is not enough. You do not wipe away the scars of centuries by saying: Now you are free to go where you want, and do as you desire, and choose the leaders you please. You do not take a person who for years has been hobbled by chains and liberate him, bring him to the starting line of a race and then say, "you are free to compete with all the others," and still justly believe that you have been completely fair. Thus it is not enough just to open the gates of opportunity. All citizens must have the ability to walk through those gates. This is the next and most profound stage of the battle for civil rights. We seek not just legal equity but human stability, not just equality as a right and a theory but equality as a fact and equality as a result.

Lyndon B. Johnson
Commencement Address, Howard University,
    Washington, D.C.
June 4, 1965

I do not want to be the President who built empires or sought grandeur or extended dominion. I want to be the President who helped the poor find their own way and who protected the right of every citizen to vote in every election. I want to be the President who helped end hatred among his fellow men.

Lyndon B. Johnson
Speech in support of legislation giving blacks the vote
    in the South
1965

We've got to stop using the classrooms and the kids as the cutting edges for social and economic problems that will have to be solved elsewhere. Our goal should be education, not litigation.

Richard Nixon
Comments, Cabinet Committee on Education
February 1970

I feel that busing for the purpose of achieving racial balance in our schools is wrong, and that the great majority of Americans are right in wanting to bring it to an end.

Richard Nixon
Readers Digest
June 1972

As a child, I rode a bus to school each day with the other white students, while the black children walked, and never gave a thought to the lack of equality inherent in the separateness.

Jimmy Carter
Keeping Faith
1982

Surely a tired woman on her way to work at six in the morning on a subway deserves the right to get there safely. And surely, it's true that everyone who changes his or her life because of crime—from those afraid to go out at night to those afraid to walk in the parks they pay for—surely these people have been denied a basic civil right.

George Bush
State of the union message
January 28, 1992

Civil War

If those forts [in Charleston] should be taken by South Carolina in consequence of our neglect to put them in defensible condition, it were better for you and me both to be thrown into the Potomac with millstones tied about our necks.

James Buchanan
Comment, Secretary of War John B. Floyd
1860

Our Union rests upon public opinion, and can never be cemented by the blood of its citizens shed in civil war.

James Buchanan
Message, Congress
December 3, 1860

No terms except unconditional and immediate surrender can be accepted. I propose to move immediately upon your works.

Ulysses S. Grant
Dispatch, General Simon Buckner at Fort Donelson
February 16, 1862

The horrible sights I have witnessed on this field, I can never describe. No blaze of glory that flashed around the magnificent triumphs of war can ever atone for the unwritten and unutterable horrors of the scene of carnage.

James Garfield
Letter, wife
1862

Three years of civil war have desolated the fairest portion of our land, loaded the country with an enormous debt that the sweat of millions yet unborn must be taxed to pay; arrayed brother against brother, father against son in mortal combat; deluged our country with fraternal blood, whitened our battle-fields with the bones of the slain, and darkened the sky with the pall of mourning.

Millard Fillmore
Speech, Buffalo, New York
February 1864

[I will not] hire a house at the capital and direct the war from an armchair in Washington.

Ulysses S. Grant
New York Tribune
March 10, 1864

I purpose to fight it out on this line if it takes all Summer.

Ulysses S. Grant
Dispatch, H. M. Halleck, near Spotsylvania, Virginia
May 11, 1864

Fondly do we hope—fervently do we pray—that this mighty scourge of war may speedily pass away. Yet, if God wills that it continue until all the wealth piled by the bondman's two hundred and fifty years of unrequited toil shall be sunk, and until every drop of blood drawn with the lash be paid by another drawn with the sword, as was said three thousand years ago, so still it must be said, "The judgments of the Lord are true and righteous altogether."

Abraham Lincoln
Second inaugural address
March 4, 1865

And thus there will be some black men who can remember that with silent tongue, and clenched teeth, and steely eye, and well-poised bayonet, they have helped mankind on to this great consumation, while I fear there will be some white ones unable to forget that with malignant heart and deceitful speech they strove to hinder it.

Abraham Lincoln
Letter, James Conkling

When news of the [Lee's] surrender first reached our lines our men commenced firing salute of a hundred guns in honor of the victory. I at once sent word, however, to have it stopped. The Confederates were now our prisoners, and we did not want to exult over their downfall.

Ulysses S. Grant
Personal Memoirs of U. S. Grant
1886

Some of us fancied that the Southern people were given to vaporing—that each one of them was equal to five Northern soldiers. But the South learned that Paul Revere still rode the highways of Massachusetts, and that the man of Concord still plowed the fields. And we, on our part, learned that the spirit of the cavalier which was found in the Southern army was combined with the reserve and steadfastness of Cromwell's Ironsides.

Benjamin Harrison
Speech, Soldiers and Sailors Monument, Rochester, New York
May 30, 1892

Colonialism

"Why, do you not *know*," replied he [Stratford Canning, British foreign minister], "that we have a claim [to the mouth of the Columbia River]?"

"I do not *know*," said I, "what you claim nor what you do not claim. You claim India; you claim Africa; you claim—"

"Perhaps," said he, "a piece of the moon."

"No," said I; "I have not heard that you claim exclusively any part of the moon; but there is not a spot on *this* habitable globe that I could affirm you do not claim."

John Quincy Adams
Diary
January 27, 1821

A policy of acquisition of new and distant territory or the incorporation of remote interests with our own.

Grover Cleveland
Cited in Eugene E. Brussell, *Dictionary of Quotable Definitions*

Benevolent assimilation.

William McKinley
Cited in Eugene E. Brussell, *Dictionary of Quotable Definitions*

We need Hawaii just as much and a good deal more than we did California. It is Manifest Destiny.

William McKinley
Comment, Charles S. Olcott
1898

Did we need their [the Filipinos'] consent to perform a great act for humanity? We had it in every aspiration of their minds, in every hope of their hearts.

William McKinley
Speech, Congress
February 27, 1899

If old Dewey had just sailed away when he smashed the Spanish fleet, what a lot of trouble he would have saved us.

William McKinley
Cited in Foster Rhea Dulles, *America's Rise to World Power: 1898-1954*

Jingo nonsense.

William McKinley
When taking office
Cited in Foster Rhea Dulles, *America's Rise to World Power: 1898-1954*

We stand supreme in a Continent, in a hemisphere. East and West we look across two great oceans toward the larger world life in which, whether we will or not, we must take an ever-increasing share.

Theodore Roosevelt
Inaugural address as vice president
March 4, 1901

Our place must be great among the nations. We may either fail greatly or succeed greatly; but we cannot avoid the endeavor from which either great failure or great success must come. Even if we would, we cannot play a small part. If we should try, all that would follow would be that we should play a large part ignobly or shamefully.

Theodore Roosevelt
Message, Congress
1902

I thought first we would take only Manila; then Luzon; then other islands, perhaps . . .

William McKinley
Comment, visiting clergymen, *Christian Advocate*
January 22, 1903

I wish that all Americans would realize that American politics is world politics.

Theodore Roosevelt
Comment, Andre Tardieu
1908

The standing of the United States as the most powerful of the anti-colonial powers is an asset of incalculable value to the free world.

Dwight D. Eisenhower
Unpublished section of *Memoirs*

Communism

Communism is a hateful thing, and a menace to peace and organized government. But the communism of combined wealth and capital, the outgrowth of overweening cupidity and selfishness, which insidiously undermines the justice and integrity of free institutions is not less dangerous than the communism of oppressed poverty and toil which, ex-

asperated by injustice and discontent, attacks with wild disorder the citadel of rule.

Grover Cleveland
Fourth annual message, Congress
December 3, 1888

The menace of communism lies primarily in those areas of American life where the promise of democracy remains unfulfilled.

Harry S. Truman
Address, Chicago Swedish Pioneer Centennial Association, Chicago, Illinois
June 4, 1948

But the great danger of communism does not lie in its false promises. It lies in the fact it is an instrument of an armed imperialism which seeks to extend its influence by force.

Harry S. Truman
Address, Alexandria, Virginia
February 22, 1950

You say, why do I think it [my country] is in danger? And I say look at the record. Seven years of the Truman-Acheson Administration, and what's happened? Six hundred million people lost to the Communists.

Richard Nixon
Checkers Speech, Hollywood, California
September 23, 1952

Unless we can put things in the hands of people who are starving to death we can never lick Communism.

Dwight D. Eisenhower
Comment, Cabinet
January 12, 1953

This is not just a casual argument against slightly different philosophies. This is a war of light against darkness, freedom against slavery, Godliness against atheism.

Dwight D. Eisenhower
Speech, Columbia University, New York, New York
January 1953

We face a hostile ideology—global in scope, atheistic in character, ruthless in purpose, and insidious in method.

Dwight D. Eisenhower
Farewell address
January 17, 1961

Neutrality where the Communists are concerned means three things: we get out; they stay in; they take over.

Richard Nixon
Speech, Sales Executive Club of New York
January 26, 1965

I have never seen a Communist government come to power as a result of a free election. I have never seen Communist aggression bow before its little neighbor's weakness. Communist power respects only its neighbor's strength.

Lyndon B. Johnson
Speech, Democratic Dinner, Des Moines, Iowa
June 30, 1966

As I looked at America's position in the world and examined our relations with other nations, I could see that the central factor in 1968 on the eve of my presidency was the same as it had been in 1947. . . . America now, as then, was the main defender of the free world against the encroachment and aggression of the Communist world.

Richard Nixon
The Memoirs of Richard Nixon
1978

Communist leaders believe in Lenin's precept: Probe with bayonets. If you encounter mush, proceed; if you encounter steel, withdraw.

Richard Nixon
The Memoirs of Richard Nixon
1978

[One] of the simple, but overwhelming facts of our time is this: of all the millions of refugees we have seen in the modern world, there flight is always away from, not toward, the communist world.

Ronald Reagan
Speech, British Parliament
June 8, 1982

For more than 40 years, America and its allies held communism in check and insured that democracy would continue to exist. And today, with communism crumbling, our aim must be to insure democ-

racy's advance, to take the lead in forging peace and freedom's best hope, a great and growing commonwealth of free nations.

George Bush
State of the union address
January 31, 1990

Congress

I have accepted a seat in the House of Representatives, and thereby have consented to my own ruin, to your ruin, and the ruin of our children. I give you this warning, that you may prepare your mind for your fate.

John Adams
Comment, Abigail Adams
May 1770

The business of the Congress is tedious beyond expression. . . . Every man in it is a great man, an orator, a critic, a statesman; and therefore every man upon every question must show his oratory, his criticism, and his political abilities.

John Adams
Letter, Abigail Adams, on the Continental Congress
October 9, 1774

But is not man, in the shape of a senator or a representative, as fond of power as a president? . . . Are not ambition and favoritism, and all other vicious passions and sinister interests, as strong and active in a senator or a representative as in a president? Cannot, indeed, the members of the legislature conceal their private views and improper motives more easily than a president?

John Adams
Review of propositions to amend the Constitution
1808

My election as President of the United States was not half as gratifying to my innermost soul [as his election to the Twenty-Second Congress]. No election or appointment ever gave me so much pleasure.

John Quincy Adams
Diary
November 6, 1830

If our power over means is so absolute that the Supreme Court will not call into question an act of Congress . . . it becomes to us to proceed in our legislation with the utmost caution.

Andrew Jackson
Veto, Bank Bill
July 10, 1832

If he [the president] speaks to Congress, it must be in the language of truth.

Andrew Jackson
Letter, Martin Van Buren
October 27, 1834

When I was a member of either House of Congress I acted under the conviction that to *doubt* as to the constitutionality of a law was sufficient to induce me to give my vote against it; but I have not been able to bring myself to believe that a *doubtful opinion* of the Chief Magistrate ought to outweigh the solemnly pronounced opinion of the representatives of the people and of the States.

John Tyler
Message, Congress
June 25, 1842

There is more selfishness and less principle among members of Congress . . . than I had any conception of, before I became President of the U.S.

James K. Polk
The Diary of James K. Polk
December 16, 1846

Abstract propositions should never be discussed by a legislative body.

James Buchanan
Comment
c. 1844

That one hundred and fifty lawyers should do business together ought not to be expected.

Thomas Jefferson
Autobiography
1853

In a body where there are more than one hundred talking lawyers, you can make no calculation upon the termination of any debate and frequently, the more trifling the subject, the more animated and protracted the discussion.

Franklin Pierce
Cited in Bill Adler, *Presidential Wit from Washington to Johnson*

Congress does from a third to a half of what I think is the minimum that it ought to do, and I am profoundly grateful that I get as much.

Theodore Roosevelt
Comment, Leonard Wood
December 1904

I have a very strong feeling that it is a President's duty to get on with Congress if he possibly can, and that it is a reflection upon him if he and Congress come to a complete break.

Theodore Roosevelt
Letter, Theodore Roosevelt, Jr.
January 31, 1909

There is a well-known aphorism that men are different, but all husbands are alike. The same idea may be paraphrased with respect to Congressmen. Congressmen are different, but when in opposition to an administration they are very much alike in their attitude and in their speeches.

William Howard Taft
The President and His Powers
1916

No one has as good opportunity to know Senators and Congressmen as the President, because in asking the Presidential favor, the Senator or Congressman frequently bares his motives and discloses his inmost traits of character in the confidence and secrecy of the Executive Office. It is more or less an unconscious confessional.

William Howard Taft
The President and the Presidency
1916

If you see ten troubles coming down the road, you can be sure that nine will run into the ditch before they reach you and you have to battle with only one of them.

Calvin Coolidge
Herbert Hoover, *Memoirs*
1920-1933

The President has tended to become the champion of the people because he is held solely responsible for his acts, while in the Congress where responsibility is divided it has developed that there is much greater danger of arbitrary action.

Calvin Coolidge
The Autobiography of Calvin Coolidge
1929

The Congress has sometimes been a sore trial to Presidents.

Calvin Coolidge
The Autobiography of Calvin Coolidge
1929

Nobody will deny that the majority of the Congress have been reduced to a rubber stamp for the Executive. They don't deny it themselves.

Herbert Hoover
Addresses upon the American Road
1933-1960

On the Congress of the United States falls the primary responsibility for the adoption of methods, but on the President falls the responsibility of recommending objectives. This is in accordance with the Constitution.

Franklin D. Roosevelt
Letter, Senator Alben Barkley
July 15, 1937

If you tell Congress everything about the world situation, they get hysterical. If you tell them nothing, they go fishing.

Harry S. Truman
Statement
July 17, 1950

But presidents cannot always kick evil-minded persons out of the front door. Such persons are often selected by the electors to represent them.

Herbert Hoover
Memoirs
1951-1952

The selfishness of the members of Congress is incredible. . . . They are just about driving me nuts.

Dwight D. Eisenhower
Comment, James C. Hagerty
July 27, 1954

When it comes down to the relations of any President with a Congress controlled by the opposite party, I just say this: it is no bed of roses.

Dwight D. Eisenhower
Press conference
July 15, 1959

It is much easier in many ways for me—and for other Presidents, I think, who felt the same way—when Congress is not in town.

John F. Kennedy
Press conference
June 28, 1962

Washington is not the problem; their Congress is the problem.

Gerald Ford
Acceptance speech, Republican National
   Convention
August 19, 1976

The behind-the-scenes power structure in Washington is often called the "iron triangle": a three-sided set of relationships composed of congressional lobbyists, congressional committee and subcommittee members and their staffs.

Richard Nixon
The Memoirs of Richard Nixon
1978

The White House staff [under Richard Nixon] viewed Congress in much the same way that the chairman of the board of a huge corporation regards his regional sales managers.

Gerald Ford
A Time to Heal
1979

Conscience

Labor to keep alive in your breast that little spark of celestial fire called conscience.

George Washington
Early Copybook
1746

The moral sense, or conscience, is as much a part of man as his leg or arm. It is given to all human beings in a stronger or weaker degree, as force of members is given them in a greater or less degree.

Thomas Jefferson
Letter, Peter Carr
1787

Conscience is the most sacred of all property. . . . To guard a man's house as his castle, to pay public and enforce private debts with the most exact faith, can give no title to invade a man's conscience which is more sacred than his castle.

James Madison
National Gazette
March 29, 1792

We are bound, you and I, and every one, to make common cause, even with error itself, to maintain the common right of freedom of conscience.

Thomas Jefferson
Letter, Doctor Benjamin Rush
1813

Stand with anybody that stands right, stand with him while he is right and part with him when he goes wrong.

Abraham Lincoln
Speech, Peoria, Illinois
October 16, 1854

Conservatism

What is conservatism? Is it not adherence to the old and tried, against the new and untried?

Abraham Lincoln
Speech, Cooper Institute, New York, New York
February 27, 1860

Conservatism is the policy of "make no change and consult your grandmother when in doubt."

Woodrow Wilson
1918

He [Senator Barry Goldwater] wants to repeal the present and veto the future.

Lyndon B. Johnson
Speech, Cleveland, Ohio
October 8, 1964

If being a liberal means federalizing everything, then I'm no liberal. If being a conservative means turning back the clock, denying problems that exist, then I'm no conservative.

Richard Nixon
The Memoirs of Richard Nixon
1978

Constitution

The thought that we might be driven to the sad Necessity of breaking our Connection with G[reat] B[ritain] exclusive of the Carnage & Destruction which it was easy to see must attend the separation, always gave me a great deal of grief. And even now, I would chearfully retire from public life forever, renounce all Chance for Profits or Honours from the public, nay I would chearfully contribute my little Property to obtain Peace and Liberty. But all these must go and my life too before I can surrender the Right of my Country to a Free Constitution.

John Adams
Letter, Abigail Adams
October 7, 1775

The body politic is . . . a social compact, by which the whole people covenants with each citizen, and each citizen with the whole people, that all shall be governed by certain laws for the common good.

John Adams
Constitution of Massachusetts (the only state constitution in the United States that has survived to this day)
c. 1776

The basis of our political systems is the right of the people to make and to alter their constitutions of government. But the constitution, which at any time exists, until changed by an explicit and authentic act of the whole people, is sacredly obligatory upon all.

George Washington
Farewell address
September 17, 1776

Should the states reject this excellent constitution, the probability is that an opportunity will never again offer to make another in peace—the next will be drawn in blood.

George Washington
Upon signing the Constitution
September 17, 1787

A Miracle has been wrought.

George Washington
Summer 1787

There are very good articles in it, and very bad. I do not know which preponderate.

Thomas Jefferson
Letter, W. S. Smith
November 1787

The Constitution . . . is unquestionably the wisest ever yet presented to men.

Thomas Jefferson
Letter, David Humphreys
March 1789

The earth belongs always to the living generation: they may manage it, then and what proceeds from it, as they please, during their usufruct. They are masters, too, of their own persons, and consequently may govern them as they please. But persons and property make the sum of the objects of government. The constitution and the laws of their predecessors are extinguished then, in their natural course, with those whose will gave them being. This could preserve that being, till it ceased to be itself, and no longer. Every constitution, then, expires at the end of thirty-four years. If it be enforced longer, it is an act of force, not of right.

Thomas Jefferson
Letter, James Madison
September 6, 1789

Every word [of the Constitution] decides a question between power and liberty.

James Madison
National Gazette
January 19, 1792

In Europe, charters of liberty have been granted by power. America has set the example, and France has followed it, of charters of power granted by liberty.

James Madison
National Gazette
January 19, 1792

If, in the opinion of the people, the distribution or modification of the constitutional powers be in any particular wrong, let it be corrected by an amendment in the way which the Constitution designates. But let there be no change by usurpation.

George Washington
Farewell address
September 17, 1796

In questions of power let no more be heard of confidence in man, but bind him down from mischief by the chains of the constitution.

Thomas Jefferson
Kentucky Resolutions
November 1798

Our Constitution professedly rests upon the good sense and attachment of the people. This basis, weak as it may appear, has not yet been found to fail.

John Quincy Adams
Letter, William Vans Murray
January 27, 1801

By the tables of mortality, of the adults living at one moment of time, a majority will be dead in about nineteen years. At the end of that period, then, a new majority is come into place; or, in other words, a new generation. Each generation is as independent of the one preceding, as that was of all which had gone before. It has, like them, a right to chose for itself the form of government it believes most promotive of its own happiness; consequently, a solemn opportunity of doing this every nineteen or twenty years should be provided by the Constitution.

Thomas Jefferson
Letter, W. H. Torrance
1815

Some men look at constitutions with sanctimonious reverence, and deem them like the Ark of the Covenant, too sacred to be touched. They ascribe to the men of the preceding age a wisdom more than human, and suppose what they did to be beyond amendment. I knew that age well; I belonged to it, and labored with it. It deserved well of its country. It was very like the present, but without the experience of the present, and forty years of experience in government is worth a century of book-learning.

Thomas Jefferson
Letter, Samuel Kercheval
July 12, 1816

We find that brevity is a characteristic of the instrument [Constitution].

James Monroe
Views on the Subject of Internal Improvements, Veto
   of the Cumberland Road Bill
1822

When an honest observance of constitutional compacts cannot be obtained from communities like ours, it need not be anticipated elsewhere, and the cause in which there has been so much martyrdom, and from which so much was expected by the friends of liberty, may be abandoned, and the degrading truth that man is unfit for self-government admitted. And this will be the case if expediency be made a rule of construction in interpreting the Constitution.

Andrew Jackson
Veto message on the Lexington Turnpike Road Bill
May 27, 1830

You know, I never despair. I have confidence in the virtue and good sense of the people. God is just, and while we act faithfully to the Constitution, he will smile upon and prosper our exertions.

Andrew Jackson
Letter, Martin Van Buren
November 1, 1831

Perpetuity is stamped upon the constitution by the blood of our Fathers.

Andrew Jackson
Letter, J. R. Poinsett
December 2, 1832

The Constitution of the United States, then, forms a *government*, not a league . . . .It is a government in which all the people are represented, which operates directly on the people individually, not upon the States.

Andrew Jackson
Proclamation to the People of South Carolina
December 10, 1832

[Constitutions are] restraints imposed, not by arbitrary authority, but by people upon themselves and their own representatives.

James Buchanan
c. 1844

The storm of frenzy and faction must inevitably dash itself in vain against the unshaken rock of the Constitution.

Franklin Pierce
Third annual message, Congress
December 31, 1855

There is nothing stable but Heaven and the Constitution.

James Buchanan
Baltimore Sun
May 13, 1856

Honest conviction is my courage; the Constitution is my guide.

Andrew Johnson
Speech, Washington, D.C.
February 22, 1866

An heroic though perhaps lawless act.

Martin Van Buren
Inquiry into the origin and course of political parties,
   in reference to the ratification process
1867

Unlike many other people less happy, we give our devotion to a Government, to its Constitution, to its flag, and not to men.

Benjamin Harrison
Speech, Monterey, California
April 30, 1891

The Constitution was made for the people and not the people for the Constitution.

Theodore Roosevelt
Comment, Representative James E. Watson
1902

The Constitution was not made to fit us like a straitjacket. In its elasticity lies its chief greatness.

Woodrow Wilson
Speech, New York, New York
November 19, 1904

The Constitution of the United States is not a mere lawyers' document; it is a vehicle of life, and its spirit is always the spirit of the age.

Woodrow Wilson
1908

The more I study it [the Constitution] the more I have come to admire it, realizing that no other document devised by the hand of man ever brought so much progress and happiness to humanity.

Calvin Coolidge
The Autobiography of Calvin Coolidge
1929

The United States Constitution has proved itself the most marvelously elastic compilation of rules of government ever written.

Franklin D. Roosevelt
Radio speech
March 2, 1930

Our Constitution is so simple and practical that it is possible always to meet extraordinary needs by changes in emphasis and arrangement without loss of essential form.

Franklin D. Roosevelt
Inaugural speech
March 4, 1933

I hope your committee will not permit doubts as to constitutionality, however reasonable, to block the suggested legislation.

Franklin D. Roosevelt
Letter, Ways and Means Committee, House of Representatives (on the Guffey-Snyder Coal Bill)
July 1935

No treaty or international agreement can contravene the Constitution.

Dwight D. Eisenhower
Letter, Senator William Knowland, on the Bricker Amendment
January-February 1954

The Constitution of the United States applies to every American, of every race, of every religion in this beloved country. If it doesn't apply to every race, to every region, to every religion, it applies to no one.

Lyndon B. Johnson
Speech, Gainsville, Georgia
May 8, 1964

The Constitution is the bedrock of all our freedoms; guard and cherish it; keep honor and order in your own house; and the republic will endure.

Gerald Ford
State of the union address
January 12, 1977

If our Constitution means anything it means that we, the Federal Government, are entrusted with preserving life, liberty and the pursuit of happiness.

Ronald Reagan
Press conference, Washington, D.C., in answer to question about Supreme Court's decision not to interfere with women's right to abortion
June 11, 1986

Our Constitution is to be celebrated not for being old, but for being young.

Ronald Reagan
State of the union address
January 27, 1987

Why is the Constitution of the United States so exceptional? . . . Just three words: We the people. In . . . other constitutions, the Government tells the people of those countries what they are allowed to do. In our Constitution, we the people tell the Government what it can do.

Ronald Reagan
State of the union address
January 27, 1987

Corruption

When a government becomes totally corrupted, the system of God Almighty in the government of the world, and the rules of all good government upon earth, will be reversed, and virtue, integrity, and ability will become the objects of malice, hatred, and revenge of the men in power, and folly, vice, and villainy will be cherished and supported.

John Adams
Diary
c. 1770-1771

Few men have virtue to withstand the highest bidder.

George Washington
Letter, Robert Howe
August 17, 1779

The time to guard against corruption and tyranny is before they shall have gotten hold of us. It is better to keep the wolf out of the fold than to trust to drawing his teeth and talons after he shall have entered.

Thomas Jefferson
"Notes on Virginia"
1782

The only remedy [for corruption] is to throw the rich and the proud into one group, in a separate assembly, and there tie their hands; if you give them scope with the people at large or their representatives, they will destroy *all equality and liberty, with the consent and acclamations of the people themselves.*

John Adams
A Defence of the Constitutions of the Government of the United States of America
1787-1788

I would take no one step to advance or promote pretensions to the Presidency. If that office was to be the prize of cabal and intrigue, of purchasing newspapers, bribing by appointments, or bargaining for foreign missions, I had no ticket in that lottery.

John Quincy Adams
Diary
February 25, 1821

There are, perhaps, few men who can for any length of time enjoy office and power without being more or less under the influence of feelings unfavorable to the faithful discharge of their political duties. Their integrity may be proof against improper considerations immediately addressed to themselves but they are apt to acquire a habit of looking with indifference upon the public interests and of tolerating conduct from which an unpracticed man would revolt.

Andrew Jackson
First annual message, Congress
December 4, 1829

If such corruption exists in the green tree, what will be in the dry?

Andrew Jackson
Letter, Cryer
April 7, 1833

The prosperity of the country, independent of all agency of the Government, is so great that the people have nothing to disturb them but their own waywardness and corruption.

John Quincy Adams
Diary
October 9, 1834

Under government ownership corruption can flourish just as rankly as under private ownership.

Theodore Roosevelt
Letter, Lincoln Steffens
June 1908

Courage

One man with courage makes a majority.

Andrew Jackson
Veto, Bank Renewal Bill
July 10, 1832

I wish some of you would tell me the brand of whiskey that Grant drinks. I would like to send a barrel of it to my other generals.

Abraham Lincoln
Ascribed to him by the *New York Herald*
November 26, 1863

There is something better, if possible, that a man can give than his life. That is his living spirit to a service that is not easy, to resist counsels that are hard to resist, to stand against purposes that are difficult to stand against.

Woodrow Wilson
Speech, Suresnes Cemetary, France
May 30, 1919

America was not built on fear, America was built on courage, on imagination and an unbeatable determination to do the job at hand.

Harry S. Truman
Special message, Congress
January 8, 1947

Any dangerous spot is tenable if brave men will make it so.

John F. Kennedy
Radio and television address
July 26, 1961

The test before us as a people is not whether our commitments match our will and our courage; but whether we have the will and the courage to match our commitments.

Lyndon B. Johnson
Message, Congress
August 3, 1967

Crime

I do believe that some crimes are so heinous, so brutal, so outrageous...and for those real brutal crimes I do believe in the death penalty.

George Bush
Television debate with Michael Dukakis
October 13, 1988

Crisis

The only temper that honors a nation is that which rises in proportion to the pressure upon it.

John Quincy Adams
Ghent, Belgium
September 14, 1814

A complete remedy to a political disease is seldom found until something like a crisis occurs, and this is promoted by the abuse of those who have rendered the most important services, and whose characters will bear the test of enquiry.

James Monroe
Letter, James Madison
March 20, 1829

The man who can look upon a crisis without being willing to offer himself upon the altar of his country is not fit for public trust.

Millard Fillmore
Louisville Journal
March 16, 1854

The spiritual nature of men has a power of its own that is manifest in every great emergency from Runnymede to Marston Moor, from the Declaration of Independence to the abolition of slavery.

Calvin Coolidge
The Autobiography of Calvin Coolidge
1929

What determines success or failure in handling a crisis is the ability to keep coldly objective when emotions are running high.

Richard Nixon
Six Crises
1962

The ability to be cool, confident, and decisive in crisis is not an inherited characteristic but is the direct result of how well the individual has prepared himself for the battle.

Richard Nixon
Six Crises
1962

Going through the necessary soul-searching of deciding whether to fight a battle, or to run away from it, is far more difficult than the battle itself.

Richard Nixon
Six Crises
1962

The ox is in the ditch!

Lyndon B. Johnson
Comments, Staff, describing catastrophes

Criticism

Defamation is becoming a necessity of life; inasmuch as a dish of tea in the morning or evening cannot be digested without that stimulant.

Thomas Jefferson
Letter, John Norvell
June 11, 1807

I could never do anything but was ascribed to sinister motives.

John Adams
Letter, Benjamin Rush
August 28, 1811

I go into it [retirement] with a combination of parties and of public men against my character and reputation such as I believe never before was exhibited against any man since this Union existed.

John Quincy Adams
Diary
February 28, 1829

Until the wit of man shall be able to devise some plan of representation by which all who think themselves qualified may be at the same time admitted to a participation in the Administration of its affairs, we must not expect to be relieved from the spirit of complaining, nor even surprised to find it most vehement at a period of the greatest prosperity.

Martin Van Buren
Albany Argus
June 1835

If both factions, or neither, shall abuse you, you will probably be about right. Beware of being assailed by one, and praised by the other.

Abraham Lincoln
Letter, General John M. Schofield
c. October 1863

I have endured a great deal of ridicule without much malice, and have received a great deal of kindness not quite free from ridicule.

Abraham Lincoln
Letter, J. H. Hackett
November 2, 1863

As a general rule, I abstain from reading the reports of attacks upon myself, wishing not to be provoked by that to which I cannot properly offer an answer.

Abraham Lincoln
Last public address
April 11, 1865

Notwithstanding a mendacious press; notwithstanding a subsidized gang of hirelings who have not ceased to traduce me, I have discharged all my official duties and fulfilled my pledges. And I say here tonight that if my predecessor [Lincoln] had lived, the vials of wrath would have poured out upon him.

Andrew Johnson
Trial, Cleveland, Ohio
September 3, 1866

I enjoy being President, and I like to do the work and have my hand on the lever. But it is very worrying and puzzling, and I have to make up my mind to accept every kind of attack and misrepresentation.

Theodore Roosevelt
To Kermit Roosevelt
October 2, 1903

The truth is it is not the height of my ambition to be popular. I have even become quite philosophical with respect to the dislike the people may feel for me.

William Howard Taft
Letter, Mrs. Taft
July 20, 1912

It isn't fair. This premature criticism [that he was "getting pouty"] is a serious menace to popular government.

Warren G. Harding
New York Times
March 6, 1921

I shall always consider it the highest tribute to my administration that the opposition have based so little of their criticism on what I have really said and done.

Calvin Coolidge
The Autobiography of Calvin Coolidge
1929

Perhaps one of the reasons I have been a target for so little abuse is because I have tried to refrain from abusing other people.

Calvin Coolidge
The Autobiography of Calvin Coolidge
1929

Many years ago I concluded that a few hair shirts were part of the mental wardrobe of every man. The President differs only from other men in that he has a more extensive wardrobe.

Herbert Hoover
Speech, Gridiron Club, Washington, D.C.
December 14, 1929

Presidents have long since learned that one of the undisclosed articles in the Bill of Rights is that criticism and digging of political graves are reserved exclusively to members of the legislative arm.

Herbert Hoover
Speech, Gridiron Club, Washington, D.C.
December 14, 1929

These Republican leaders have not been content with attacks upon me, or on my wife, or on my sons—no, not content with that, they now include my little dog Fala. Unlike the members of my family, he resents this.

Franklin D. Roosevelt
Speech, Teamster's Union
September 23, 1944

A President may dismiss the abuse of scoundrels, but to be denounced by honest men honestly outraged is a test of greatness that none but the strongest men can survive.

Harry S. Truman
Address, Raleigh, North Carolina
October 19, 1948

About the meanest thing you can say about a man is that he means well.

Harry S. Truman
Speech, Pendleton, Oregon
May 10, 1950

I pinned a medal on General MacArthur the other day, and I told him I wished I had a medal like that, and he said that it was my duty to give medals, not to receive them. That is always the way. About all I receive are the bricks. It's a good thing I have got a pretty hard head, or it would have been broken a long time ago.

Harry S. Truman
Address, United Nations General Assembly, New York, New York
October 24, 1950

I refer you to the second term of President Washington . . . when I compare the weak, inconsequential things said about me, compared to what they said about the man who I think is the greatest human the English-speaking race has produced, then I can be quite philosophical about it.

Dwight D. Eisenhower
Speech
August 7, 1957

The men who create power make an indispensable contribution to the nation's greatness. But the men who question power make a contribution just as indispensable.

John F. Kennedy
Speech, Amhurst, Massachusetts
October 1963

As the attacks became more personal, I sometimes wondered where party loyalty left off and masochism began.

Richard Nixon
The Memoirs of Richard Nixon, on the 1954 election
1978

Remember the flap when I said, "We begin bombing in five minutes"? Remember when I fell asleep during my audience with the pope? Remember Bitburg? Boy, those were the good old days.

Ronald Reagan
Speech, Gridiron Club, Washington, D.C.
Newsweek
April 13, 1987

I am sick and tired every night of hearing one of these carping little liberal Democrats jumping all over my you-know-what.

George Bush
Campaign speech
January 1992

D

Death

It is well. I die hard, but I am not afraid to go.

George Washington
December 14, 1799

I have had a father and lost him. I have had a mother and lost her. I have had a wife and lost her. I have had children and lost them. I have had honorable and worthy Friends and lost them—and instead of suffering these Griefs again, I had rather go forward and meet my destiny.

John Adams
Letter, Thomas Jefferson

I hope and trust to meet you in Heaven, both white and black—both white and black.

Andrew Jackson
Comment, household, including slaves
June 8, 1845

This is the last of earth. I am content.

John Quincy Adams
Comment, doctors, on his deathbed
February 21, 1848

You have fought the good fight, but you cannot make a stand.

Zachary Taylor
Comment, doctors, on his deathbed
Letter, E. P. Prentice
July 5, 1850

Approaching death to me is a mere shadow of God's protecting wing.

Andrew Johnson
June 9, 1873

When I die, I desire no better winding sheet than the Stars and Stripes, and no softer pillow than the Constitution of my country.

Andrew Johnson
Cited by George F. Milton, ''The Tennessee Epilogue,'' in Eric L. McKitrick, *Andrew Johnson: A Profile*

It's mighty lonesome in here.

William McKinley
Comment, George Cortelyou, on his deathbed
September 1901

It's useless, gentlemen. I think we ought to have a prayer.

William McKinley
Comment, doctors, on his deathbed
September 13, 1901

Good-bye—good-bye, all. It's God's way. His will, not ours, be done. Nearer, my God to Thee, nearer to Thee.

William McKinley
Last words to his wife
September 13, 1901

Only those are fit to live who do not fear to die; and none are fit to die who have shrunk from the joy of life and the duty of life. Both life and death are parts of the same Great Adventure.

Theodore Roosevelt
Editorial, *Kansas City Star*, on the death of his son in World War I
Summer 1918

Mr. President, we have all been praying for you.

Which way, Senator?

Woodrow Wilson
Comment, Senator Albert Fall, after the President's
    stroke
December 1919

Everybody is headed for the same place, and they are headed on the same train, and under the same engineer.

Harry S. Truman
Remarks, members of the Associated Church press,
    Washington, D.C.
March 28, 1951

I want to go; God take me.

Dwight D. Eisenhower
Last words, John Eisenhower, Walter Reed Hospital
March 28, 1969

Debt and Deficit Spending

I go on the principle that a public debt is a public curse.

James Madison
Letter, Henry Lee
April 13, 1790

I sincerely believe that banking establishments are more dangerous than standing armies, and that the principle of spending money to be paid by posterity, under the name of funding, is but swindling futurity on a large scale.

Thomas Jefferson
Letter, John Taylor
May 28, 1816

It is incumbent on every generation to pay its own debts as it goes—a principle which, if acted on, would save one-half the wars of the world.

Thomas Jefferson
Letter, Destutt Tracy
1820

I am one of those who do not believe that a national debt is a national blessing, but rather a curse to a republic; inasmuch as it is calculated to raise around the administration a moneyed aristocracy dangerous to the liberties of the country.

Andrew Jackson
Letter, L. H. Coleman
April 26, 1824

If a national debt is considered a blessing, then we can get on by borrowing. But [if] as I believe it is a national curse, my vow shall be to pay the national debt.

Andrew Jackson
Letter
July 4, 1824

We now pride ourselves upon having given freedom to 4,000,000 of the colored race; it will then be our shame that 40,000,000 of people, by their own toleration of usurpation and profligacy, have suffered themselves to become enslaved, and merely exchanged slave owners for new taskmasters in the shape of bondholders and taxgatherers.

Andrew Johnson
Fourth annual message, Congress
December 9, 1868

The harpy of Public Extravagance devours the [treasury] surplus and impudently calls upon its staggering victims to bring still larger supplies within the reach of its insatiate appetite.

Grover Cleveland
Cleveland Democracy Speech, Buffalo, New York
May 12, 1891

It [extravagance] is the most fatal of all the deadly brood born of governmental perversion. It hides beneath its wings the betrayal of the people's trust, and holds powerless in its fascinating glance the people's will and conscience. It brazenly exhibits to-day a Billion dollar Congress.

Grover Cleveland
Cleveland Democracy Speech, Buffalo, New York
May 12, 1891

There are crimes far worse than murder for which men should be reviled and punished.

Herbert Hoover
On credit inflation, cited in Eugene Lyons, *Herbert Hoover: A Biography*

Borrowed money, even when owing to a nation by another nation, should be repaid. They hired the money, didn't they? Let them pay it.

Calvin Coolidge
Comment on the allies' war debt
1925

Public debt [is] a burden on all the people.

Calvin Coolidge
The Autobiography of Calvin Coolidge
1929

Nothing is easier than spending the public money. It does not appear to belong to anybody. The temptation is overwhelming to bestow it on somebody.

Calvin Coolidge
Cited in *Reader's Digest*
June 1960

If the nation is living within its income its credit is good. . . . But if, like the spendthrift, it throws discretion to the winds . . . extends its taxing up to the limit of the people's power to pay, and continues to pile up deficits, it is on the road to bankruptcy.

Franklin D. Roosevelt
Speech, Pittsburgh, Pennsylvania
October 19, 1932

As quickly as you start spending federal money in large amounts, it looks like free money.

Dwight D. Eisenhower
February 9, 1955

The communist objective is to make us spend ourselves into bankruptcy.

Dwight D. Eisenhower
Joint Chiefs of Staff meeting
March 8, 1959

We cannot mortgage the material assets of our grandchildren without risking the loss also of their political and spiritual heritage. We want democracy to survive for all generations to come, not to become the insolvent phantom of tomorrow.

Dwight D. Eisenhower
Farewell address
January 17, 1961

If we want to restore confidence in ourselves as working politicians, the first thing we all have to do is to learn to say No.

Gerald Ford
Address, Congress
August 12, 1974

Always we've had the best of intentions. But in the recent past we sometimes forgot the sound principles that guided us through most of our history. . . . We tried to be a policeman abroad and the indulgent parent at home.

Gerald Ford
State of the union address, referring to the federal budget
January 20, 1976

If you've been wondering why you don't seem as well off as you were a few years back, it's because Government makes a profit on inflation. It gets an automatic tax increase without having to vote on it. We intend to stop that.

Ronald Reagan
Speech, Washington, D.C.
July 27, 1981

Our interest payments on the [national] debt alone are now running more than $96 billion a year. That's more than the total combined profits last year of the 500 biggest companies in the country; or to put it another way, Washington spends more on interest than on all of its education, nutrition and medical programs combined.

Ronald Reagan
Speech, White House
September 24, 1981

Government always finds a need for whatever money it gets.

Ronald Reagan
Speech, Washington, D.C.
April 29, 1982

America must never again use inflation to profit at the people's expense.

Ronald Reagan
Speech, Congress
January 25, 1984

We do not face large deficits because American families are undertaxed; we face those deficits because the Federal Government overspends.

Ronald Reagan
State of the union address
February 2, 1986

Decisions

I never sit on a fence. I am either on one side or another.

Harry S. Truman
Remarks, Bellefontaine, Ohio
October 30, 1948

In politics . . . the time comes when you've got to pee or get off the pot.

Richard Nixon
Cited in Stewart Alsop, *Nixon and Rockefeller: A Double Portrait*

Some of the best decisions ever made by Presidents were made when they were not too popular.

Richard Nixon
Speech, Chicago, Illinois
March 15, 1974

Declaration of Independence

The die was now cast; I had passed the Rubicon. Sink or swim, live or die, survive or perish with my country, was my unalterable determination.

John Adams
Letter, Jonathan Sewell, after deciding to vote for the Declaration of Independence
1776

He [King George III] has erected a multitude of new offices, and set hither swarms of officers to harass our people and eat out their substance.

Thomas Jefferson
The Declaration of Independence count in the indictment of George III
April 14, 1776

The second day of July, 1776, will be the most memorable Epocha, in the history of America. I am apt to believe that it will be celebrated, by succeeding generations, as the great anniversary festival. It ought to be commemorated as the day of deliverance, by solemn acts of devotion to God Almighty. It ought to be solemnized with pomp and parade, with shews, games, sports, guns, bells, bonfires, and illuminations from one end of this continent to the other from this time forward forever more.

John Adams
Letter, Abigail Adams
July 3, 1776

Yesterday the greatest question was decided which was ever debated in America; and a greater perhaps never was, nor will be, decided upon men. A resolution was passed without one dissenting colony, that those United Colonies are, and of right ought to be, free and independent states.

John Adams
Letter, Abigail Adams
July 3, 1776

When in the course of human events, it becomes necessary for one people to dissolve the political bands which have connected them with another, and to assume among the powers of the earth the separate and equal station to which the Laws of Nature and of Nature's God entitle them, a decent respect to the opinions of mankind requires that they should declare the causes which impel them to the separation. . . .

Thomas Jefferson
Declaration of Independence
July 4, 1776

We hold these truths to be self-evident, that all men are created equal, that they are endowed by their Creator with certain unalienable Rights, that among these are Life, Liberty and the pursuit of Happiness. That to secure these rights, Governments are instituted among Men, deriving their just powers from the consent of the governed. That whenever any Form of Government becomes destructive of those ends, it is the Right of the People to alter or abolish it, and to institute a new Government, laying its foundation on such principles and organizing its power in such form, as to them shall seem most likely to effect their Safety and Happiness.

Thomas Jefferson
Declaration of Independence
July 4, 1776

If it be the pleasure of Heaven that my country shall require the poor offering of my life, the victim shall be ready, at the appointed hour of sacrifice, come when that hour may. But while I do live, let me have a country, and that a free country. . . . All I have, and all that I am, and all that I hope, in this life, I am now ready to stake upon it; and I leave off as I began, that live or die, survive or perish, I am for the declaration.

John Adams
Speech
1776

The declaration of independence confirmed in form what had existed before in substance. It announced to the world new States, possessing and exercising complete sovereignty, which they were resolved to maintain.

James Monroe
Views on the subject of Internal Improvements,
    reasons for Veto of the Cumberland Road Bill
1822

This holy bond of our Union.

Thomas Jefferson
Letter, James Monroe
1825

May it [the Declaration of Independence] be to the world what I believe it will be (to some parts sooner, to others later, but finally to all): the signal of arousing men to burst the chains under which monkish ignorance and superstition have persuaded them to bind themselves and assume the blessings and security of self-government.

Thomas Jefferson
Letter, Roger C. Weightman
June 24, 1826, ten days before his death

They [the authors of the Declaration of Independence] knew the proneness of prosperity to breed tyrants, and they meant when such should reappear in this fair land and commence their vocation, they should find left for them at least one hard nut to crack.

Abraham Lincoln
Speech, Springfield, Illinois
June 27, 1857

Free speech, free press, free religion, the right of free assembly, yes, the right of petition . . . well, they are still radical ideas.

Lyndon B. Johnson
Speech, International Platform Association, the
    White House
August 3, 1965

Defeat

No one knows and few conceive the agony of mind that I have suffered from the time that I was made by circumstances, and not by my own volition, a candidate for the Presidency till I was dismissed from that station by the failure of my reelection. They were feelings to be suppressed; and they were suppressed.

John Quincy Adams
Diary
1829

All is gone but honor!

Millard Fillmore
Letter, Henry Clay
November 11, 1844

My deliverance has been the greatest case of emancipation since the rebellion commenced.

Andrew Johnson
Speech, Baltimore, Maryland, after losing the Republican nomination to Grant
March 11, 1869

I feel that defeat will be a great relief—a setting free from bondage.

Rutherford B. Hayes
Diary, on the day of his nomination as Republican nominee for president
June 16, 1876

The men of both Lee's and Johnson's armies were, like their brethren of the North, as brave as men can be; but no man is so brave that he may not meet such defeats and disasters as to discourage him and dampen his ardor for any cause, no matter how just he deems it.

Ulysses S. Grant
Personal Memoirs of U. S. Grant
1886

I am greatly grieved at your defeat. If the intrepid leader fell outside the breastworks, the column, inspired by his courage, went on to victory.

Benjamin Harrison, president-elect
Letter to defeated Republican candidate for governor of New York, Warner Miller
November 9, 1888

In the time of darkest defeat, victory may be nearest.

William McKinley
Comment, Philander C. Knox, when the latter referred to the 1910 congressional elections as a "landslide"
1910

If I am defeated I hope that somebody, sometime, will recognize the agony of spirit that I have undergone.

William Howard Taft
Letter, Horace D. Taft

What I got was the irreducible minimum of the Republican Party.

William Howard Taft
Describing his defeat in the presidential election of 1912, *New York World*
November 6, 1912

Victory has a thousand fathers but defeat is an orphan.

John F. Kennedy
Attributed upon defeat of Bay of Pigs invasion
April 1961

I have never been a quitter. To leave office before my term is completed is abhorrent to every instinct in my body.

Richard Nixon
Resignation speech, Washington, D.C.
August 8, 1975

In 1961 I found that virtually everything I did seemed unexciting and unimportant by comparison with national office. When you win, you are driven by the challenges you have to meet; when you lose, you must drive yourself to do whatever is required.

Richard Nixon
The Memoirs of Richard Nixon
1978

Defense

There is nothing so likely to produce peace as to be well prepared to meet an enemy.

George Washington
Letter, Elbridge Gerry
January 29, 1780

Whatever enables us to go to war, secures our peace.

Thomas Jefferson
Letter, James Monroe
July 11, 1790

Experience has taught us that neither the pacific dispositions of the American people nor the pacific character of their political institutions can altogether exempt them from that strife which appears beyond the ordinary lot of nations to be incident to the actual period of the world, and the same faithful monitor demonstrates that a certain degree of preparation for war is not only indispensable to avert disasters in the onset, but affords also the best security for the continuance of peace.

James Madison
Speech, Senate and House
February 18, 1815

Preparation for war is a constant stimulus to suspicion and ill-will.

James Monroe
On signing the Rush-Bagot Pact with Britain
April 28, 1818

The right of self-defense never ceases. It is among the most sacred, and alike necessary to nations and to individuals.

James Monroe
Second annual message, Congress
November 16, 1818

If there be a people on earth whose more especial duty it is to be at all times prepared to defend the rights with which they are blessed, and to supress all others in sustaining the necessary burthens, and in submitting to sacrifices to make such preparations, it is undoubtedly the people of these States.

James Monroe
Sixth annual message, Congress
December 3, 1822

For mere vengeance I would do nothing. This nation is too great for revenge. But for the security of the future I would do everything.

James A. Garfield
Speech, New York, New York
April 15, 1865

To maintain peace in the future it is necessary to be prepared for war.

Ulysses S. Grant
Personal Memoirs of U. S. Grant
1885

The Spanish fleet is in Cuban waters and we haven't enough ammunition on the Atlantic seacoast to fire a salute.

William McKinley
May 1900

I had rather have everybody on my side than be armed to the teeth.

Woodrow Wilson
Speech, Columbus, Ohio
September 4, 1919

The core of our defense is the faith we have in the institutions we defend.

Franklin D. Roosevelt
Reader's Digest
January 1934

Do not let us be hair-splitters. Let us not ask ourselves whether the Americas should begin to defend themselves after the first attack, or the fifth attack, or the tenth attack, or the twentieth attack. The time for active defense is now.

Franklin D. Roosevelt
Fireside chat, after the sinking of the U.S.S. *Greer*,
    September 4, 1941, Washington, D.C.
September 11, 1941

Never before have we had so little time in which to do so much.

Franklin D. Roosevelt
Radio address
February 23, 1942

Weakness cannot cooperate with anything. Only strength can cooperate.

Dwight D. Eisenhower
State of the union address
February 2, 1953

There is no amount of military force that can possibly give you real security, because you wouldn't have that amount unless you felt that there was almost a similar amount that could threaten you somewhere in the world.

Dwight D. Eisenhower
Press conference
March 19, 1953

This is not a way of life at all, in any true sense. Under the cloud of threatening war, it is humanity hanging from a cross of iron.

Dwight D. Eisenhower
The Chance for Peace Speech, Washington, D.C.
April 16, 1953

Anybody who bases his defense on his ability to predict the day and the hour of attack is crazy. If you are going on the defensive, you have got to get a level of preparation you can sustain over the years.

Dwight D. Eisenhower
News conference
April 23, 1953

Every gun that is fired, every warship launched, every rocket fired signifies, in the final sense, a theft from those who hunger and are not fed, those who are cold and are not clothed. The world in arms is not spending money alone. It is spending the sweat of its laborers, the genius of its scientists, the hopes of its children.

Dwight D. Eisenhower
Speech, American Society of Newspaper Editors,
   Washington, D.C.
April 16, 1953

Dollars and guns are no substitutes for brains and will power.

Dwight D. Eisenhower
Radio panel
June 3, 1953

Safety cannot be assumed by arms alone. Their usefulness becomes concentrated more and more in their characteristics as deterrents than in instruments with which to obtain victory.

Dwight D. Eisenhower
Letter, publisher
1956

Above all, words alone are not enough. The United States is a peaceful nation. And where our strength and determination are clear, our words need merely to convey conviction, not belligerence. If we are strong, our strength will speak for itself. If we are weak, words will be of no help. I realize that this nation often tends to identify turning points in world affairs with the major addresses which precede them. But it was not the Monroe Doctrine that kept all Europe away from this hemisphere—it was the strength of the British fleet and the width of the Atlantic Ocean. It was not General Marshall's speech at Harvard which kept communism out of Western Europe—it was the strength and stability made possible by our military and economic assistance.

John F. Kennedy
Text of speech written but not delivered at Dallas,
   Texas, on the day of his death, *New York Times*
November 24, 1963

In short, we must be constantly prepared for the worst and constantly acting for the best—strong enough to win a war and wise enough to prevent one.

Lyndon B. Johnson
State of the union address
January 8, 1964

The American defense establishment should never be a sacred cow, but on the other hand, the American military should never be anybody's scapegoat.

Richard Nixon
Speech, U.S. Air Force Academy, Colorado Springs
June 1969

We will maintain strength so sufficient that it need not be proven in combat—a quiet strength based not merely on the size of an arsenal but on the nobility of ideas.

Jimmy Carter
Inaugural address
January 20, 1977

No nation that placed its faith in parchment paper, while at the same time it gave up its protective hardware, ever lasted long enough to write many pages in history.

Ronald Reagan
Speech, U.S. Military Academy, West Point,
   New York
May 27, 1981

The defense policy of the United States is based on a simple premise: the United States does not start fights. We will never be an aggressor. We maintain our strength in order to deter and defend against aggression—to preserve freedom and peace.

Ronald Reagan
Speech, Washington, D.C.
March 3, 1983

Too often, the demands of prosperity and security are viewed as competitors when, in fact, they are complementary, natural and necessary skills.

Ronald Reagan
Speech, Annual Joint Meeting of Governors of the
   World Bank and International Monetary Fund,
   Washington, D.C.
September 27, 1983

Nations do not mistrust each other because they are armed; they are armed because they mistrust each other.

Ronald Reagan
Speech, United Nations General Assembly, New York, New York
September 22, 1986

But we cannot lead a new world abroad if, at home, it's politics as usual on American defense and diplomacy. It's time to turn away from the temptation to protect unneeded weapons systems and obsolete bases.

George Bush
Address to Congress
March 6, 1991

Demagogues

One of our defects as a nation is the tendency to use what have been called "weasel words." When a weasel sucks an egg, the meat is sucked out of the egg; and if you use a "weasel word" after another there is nothing left of the other.

Theodore Roosevelt
Speech, St. Louis, Missouri
May 1916

To play the demagogue for purposes of self-interest is a cardinal sin against the people in a democracy, exactly as to play the courtier for such purposes is a cardinal sin against the people in other forms of government.

Theodore Roosevelt
Autobiography
1926

Half-truth, hypocrisy and hate are departments in the art of demagogues. The polite phrase for all this is intellectual dishonesty.

Herbert Hoover
Speech, Kansas City, Missouri

Usurpation . . . justifies itself by a precaution against usurpation.

James Madison
Virginia Assembly
January 23, 1799

Democracy

Kings we never had among us. Nobles we never had. Nothing hereditary ever existed in the country; nor will the country require or admit of any such thing. But governors and councils we have always had, as well as representatives.

John Adams
Autobiography
October 1775

If there is a form of government, then, whose principle and foundation is virtue, will not every sober man acknowledge it better calculated to promote the general happiness than any other form?

John Adams
"Thoughts on Government"
January 1776

You are afraid of the one, I, of the few. . . . You are apprehensive of monarchy, I, of aristocracy.

John Adams
Letter, Thomas Jefferson
December 6, 1787

I have no fear that the result of our experiment will be that men may be trusted to govern themselves without a master. Could the contrary of this be proved I should conclude either that there is no God or that He is a malevolent being.

Thomas Jefferson
Letter, David Hartley
1787

Democracy, simply democracy, never had a patron among men of letters.

John Adams
"A Defence of the Constitutions of Government of the United States of America"
1787-1788

In the first place, what is your definition of a republic? Mine is this: *A government whose sovereignty is vested in more than one person.*

John Adams
Letter, Roger Sherman
July 17, 1789

The essence of a free government consists in an effectual control of rivalries.

John Adams
Discourses on Davila
1789

The republican is the only form of government which is not eternally at open or secret war with the rights of mankind.

Thomas Jefferson
Letter, William Hunter
March 11, 1790

A government deriving its energy from the will of the society . . . is the government for which philosophy has been searching, and humanity been fighting, from the most remote ages. Such are republican governments which it is the glory of America to have invented, and her unrivalled happiness to possess.

James Madison
National Gazette
February 20, 1792

Free government is founded in jealousy, and not in confidence, which prescribes limited constitutions, to bind down those whom we are obliged to trust with power.

Thomas Jefferson
The Kentucky Resolutions
1798

Sometimes it is said that man can not be trusted with the government of himself. Can he, then, be trusted with the government of others? Or have we found angels in the form of kings to govern him? Let history answer this question.

Thomas Jefferson
First inaugural address
March 4, 1801

Democracy is Lovelace and the people is Clarissa.

John Adams
Letter, William Cunningham
March 1804

Nor was it uninteresting to the world, that an experiment should be fairly and fully made, whether freedom of discussion, un-aided by power, is not sufficient for the propagation and protection of truth—whether a government, conducting itself in the true spirit of its constitution, with zeal and purity, and doing no act which it would be unwilling the whole world should witness, can be written down by falsehood and defamation.

Thomas Jefferson
Second inaugural address
March 4, 1805

There never was a democracy yet that did not commit suicide. It is in vain to say that democracy is less vain, less proud, less selfish, less ambitious, or less avaricious than aristocracy or monarchy.

John Adams
Speaking of direct, not representative, democracy
After 1812

Democracy. Sovereignty in the many. That is, in the whole nation, the whole body, assemblage, congregation, or if you are an Episcopalian, you may call it, if you please *church*, of the whole people.

John Adams
Letter, John Taylor
April 15, 1814

We of the United States are constitutionally and conscientiously democrats.

Thomas Jefferson
Letter, Du Pont de Nemours
1816

In this great nation there is but one order, that of the people.

James Monroe
Second inaugural address
March 4, 1821

No other example can be found of a Government exerting its influence to lessen its own powers.

James Monroe
Views on the Subject of Internal Improvements,
reasons for veto of the Cumberland Road Bill
1822

Our system of government is new, and we find little cause for consolation in the example, and fate, of other republics, all of which have failed.

James Monroe
Letter, S. M. Edwards
April 6, 1829

But I contend that the strongest of all governments is that which is most free.

William Henry Harrison
Letter, Simon Bolívar
September 27, 1829

Democracy, pure democracy, has at least its foundation in a generous theory of human rights.

John Quincy Adams
Address, Constituents

Foreign powers do not seem to appreciate the true character of our government.

James K. Polk
Inaugural address
March 4, 1845

Democracy is a ladder, corresponding in politics to the one spiritual which Jacob saw in his vision; one up which all, in proportion to their merit, may ascend. While it extends to the humblest of all created beings, here on earth below, it reaches to God on high.

Andrew Johnson
Inaugural address, governor of Tennessee
1853

No man is good enough to govern another man without that other's consent.

Abraham Lincoln
Speech, Peoria, Illinois
October 16, 1854

We have to maintain inviolate the great doctrine of the inherent right of popular self-government.

Franklin Pierce
Second annual message, Congress
December 4, 1854

A majority held in restraint by constitutional checks and limitations, and always changing easily with deliberate changes of popular opinions and sentiments, is the only true sovereign of a free people. Whoever rejects it does, of necessity, fly to anarchy or to despotism.

Abraham Lincoln
First inaugural address
March 4, 1861

Men may die, but the fabrics of free institutions remain unshaken.

Chester A. Arthur
Inaugural address
September 22, 1881

The political revolution which accompanied the birth of our party was not accomplished while the principles of Democracy were kept laid away in a napkin.

Grover Cleveland
Speech, Democratic Club, New York, New York
April 13, 1891

Every people has a right to choose the sovereignty under which they shall live.

Woodrow Wilson
Speech, Washington, D.C.
May 27, 1916

A great democracy must be progressive or it will soon cease to be a great democracy.

Theodore Roosevelt
Cited by Franklin D. Roosevelt, dedication of the
   Theodore Roosevelt Memorial

Self-determination is not a mere phrase. It is an imperative principle of action, which statesmen will henceforth ignore at their peril.

Woodrow Wilson
Address, Congress
February 11, 1918

It was the bitter experience of all public men from George Washington down that democracies are at least contemporarily fickle and heartless.

Herbert Hoover
1919

The highest form of self-government is the voluntary cooperation within our people.

Herbert Hoover
Fourth annual message, Congress
December 6, 1932

Democracy is not a static thing. It is an everlasting march.

Franklin D. Roosevelt
Speech, Los Angeles, California
October 1, 1935

Democracy is a harsh employer.

Herbert Hoover
Comment, former secretary
C. 1936

My anchor is democracy—and more democracy.

Franklin D. Roosevelt
Speech, Roanoke Island, North Carolina
August 18, 1937

We must be the great arsenal of democracy.

Franklin D. Roosevelt
Fireside chat
December 29, 1940

There is nothing mysterious about the foundations of a healthy and strong democracy. . . . They are: equality of opportunity for youth and for others; jobs for those who can work; security for those who need it; the ending of special privilege for the few; the preservation of civil liberties for all; the enjoyment of the fruits of scientific progress in a wider and constantly rising standard of living.

Franklin D. Roosevelt
Four Freedoms Speech
January 6, 1941

The democratic aspiration is no mere recent phase of human history. It is human history.

Franklin D. Roosevelt
January 20, 1941

Yes, the decisions of our democracy may be slowly arrived at. But when that decision is made, it is proclaimed not with the voice of one man but with the voice of one hundred and thirty million.

Franklin D. Roosevelt
White House Correspondents Association Dinner
March 1941

No government is perfect. One of the chief virtues of a democracy, however, is that its defects are always visible and under democratic processes can be pointed out and corrected.

Harry S. Truman
Speech to Congress requesting aid for Greece and
   Turkey
March 12, 1947

Hitler learned that efficiency without justice is a vain thing. Democracy does not work that way. Democracy is a matter of faith—a faith in the soul of man—a faith in human rights. That is the kind of faith that moves mountains—that's the kind of faith that hurled the Iron Range at the Axis and shook the world at Hiroshima. Faith is much more than efficiency. Faith gives value to all things. Without faith, the people perish.

Harry S. Truman
Address, St. Paul, Minnesota
October 13, 1948

There isn't a word in the English language that has been so severely abused during the last ten years as the word democracy.

Harry S. Truman
Statement
March 20, 1949

Any system of government will work when everything is going well. It's the system that functions in the pinches that survives.

John F. Kennedy
State of the union address
January 14, 1963

Democracy is a constant tension between truth and half-truth and, in the arsenal of truth, there is no greater weapon than fact.

Lyndon B. Johnson
Remarks, accepting honorary membership, National Forensic League
May 12, 1964

Democracy rests on the voice of the people. Whatever blunts the clear expression of that voice is a threat to democratic government.

Lyndon B. Johnson
Message, Congress
May 25, 1967

The best way to enhance freedom in other lands is to demonstrate here that our democratic system is worthy of emulation.

Jimmy Carter
Inaugural address
January 20, 1977

We are a nation that has a government—not the other way around. And that makes us special among the nations of the earth.

Ronald Reagan
Inaugural address
January 20, 1981

Democratic Party

I am a Democrat now; I have been one all my life; I expect to live and die one . . . they shall never divert me from the polar star by which I have ever been guided from early life—the great principles of Democracy upon which this Government rests.

Andrew Johnson
Speech
1862

A gentleman told me recently he doubted if I would vote for the Angel Gabriel if found at the head of the Democratic party, to which I responded that the Angel Gabriel would never be found in such company.

Theodore Roosevelt
Address, Young Men's Republican Club, New York, New York
October 1884

Its [Democratic] history reminds me of the boulder in the stream of progress, impeding and resisting its onward flow and moving only by the force that it resists.

Benjamin Harrison
Speech, Detroit, Michigan
February 22, 1888

We cannot match ages with the Democratic party any more than that party can match achievements with us. It has lived longer, but to less purpose. "Moss-backed" cannot be predicted of a Republican. Our Democratic friends have a monopoly on that distinction, and it is one of the few distinguished monopolies they enjoy; and yet when I hear a Democrat boasting himself of the age of his party I feel like reminding him that there are other organized evils in the world, older than the Democratic party.

Benjamin Harrison
Speech, Chicago, Illinois
March 20, 1888

Those rattled-oated people who are doing so much wild talking.

William McKinley
Comment, Admiral George Dewey
1900

I am all kinds of a democrat, so far as I can discover—but the root of the whole business is this, that I believe in the patriotism and energy and initiative of the average man.

Woodrow Wilson
Speech, Philadelphia, Pennsylvania
June 29, 1916

Of course, almost every Democrat thinks the sovereign remedy for any of our ills is an appropriation of public money.

Calvin Coolidge
1932

Once upon a time, there were a number of citizens who thought that Andrew Jackson ought to have a suitable coffin. At great expense, they went to Syria and purchased a marble sarcophagus. A sarcophagus, as you know, is a tomb—a big marble coffin with a marble lid. These citizens then shipped this big marble box to Washington, which was quite a job as it weighed four or five tons. At last, they thought, a suitable resting place had been provided for Andrew Jackson. Well, the only trouble with the project was that Andrew Jackson wasn't dead. Moreover, he wasn't ready to die. And he did not intend to be hurried to his grave. Courteously but firmly he wrote to these well-meaning citizens, and said, "I must decline the intended honor." And they never did get Old Hickory into that thing. You can still see it, if you're interested, out in front of the Smithsonian Institution. It still sits there. Andy wouldn't even be buried in it. I think that this little story has a moral in it. It is this: Before you offer to bury a good Democrat, you better be sure he is dead.

Harry S. Truman
Address, Jefferson-Jackson Day Dinner
February 24, 1949

The vice president has claimed Al Smith for his work in his later years and I claimed him for his work in the 1928 campaign. Neither one of us indicated what Al Smith would do in 1960. It is possible he would have *voted* Republican, but I think he would have *prayed* Democratic this year.

John F. Kennedy
Speech, New York, New York
October 20, 1960

I suppose it might be said that a good Democrat needs a good head and a good heart all the time, and good legs and feet at election time, and certainly a good stomach in between times.

Lyndon B. Johnson
Speech, Democratic Congressional Dinner, Washington, D.C.
June 24, 1965

I [am] a free man first, and an American second, and a public servant third, and a Democrat fourth, in that order, and I guess as a Democrat, if I had to . . . place a label on myself, I would want to be a progressive who was prudent.

Lyndon B. Johnson
Television and radio interview
March 15, 1964

The Democratic Party . . . brought us the minimum wage. It brought us the maximum hours.

Lyndon B. Johnson
Speech, Pasedena, Texas
November 2, 1964

He [Lyndon B. Johnson] doesn't want McGovern [Senator George McGovern] under any circumstances but, of course, feels that he can't leave his party. As he puts it, he has been sucking at the tit of the Democratic Party for years and can't let go now, even though the milk may have turned a bit sour because of what the poor cow is eating.

Richard Nixon
Diary
October 1972

Unlike Republicans, Democrats are usually able to swallow their differences and unite behind their party's nominee.

Richard Nixon
The Memoirs of Richard Nixon
1978

The Democratic leadership would chart the most dangerous course for a nation since the Egyptians tried to make a short cut through the Red Sea.

Ronald Reagan
Speech, cited in the *New York Times*
1986

Despotism, Dictatorship, and Tyranny

The accumulation of all power, legislative, executive, and judiciary, in the same hands, whether of one, a few, or many, and whether hereditary, self-appointed, or elective, may justly be pronounced the very definition of tyranny.

James Madison
Federalist, XLVII
February 1, 1788

When a people shall have become incapable of governing themselves, and fit for a master, it is of little consequence from what quarter he comes.

George Washington
Letter, marquis de Lafayette
April 28, 1788

It is not denied that there may be cases in which a respect to the general principles of liberty, the essential rights of the people, or the overruling sentiments of humanity, might require a government, whether new or old, to be treated as an illegitimate despotism.

James Madison
Letter, Thomas Jefferson
May 13, 1798

Force [is] the vital principle and immediate parent of despotism.

Thomas Jefferson
First inaugural address
March 4, 1801

The fundamental article of my political creed is that despotism, or unlimited sovereignty, or absolute power, is the same in a majority of a popular assembly, an aristocratical council, an oligarchical junta, and a single emperor.

John Adams
Letter, Thomas Jefferson
November 13, 1815

We might as well require a man to wear still the coat which fitted him as a boy, as civilized society to remain ever under the regimen of their barbarous ancestors.

Thomas Jefferson
Letter, Samuel Kercheval
July 12, 1816

The plea of necessity, that eternal argument of all conspirators.

William Henry Harrison
Letter, Simon Bolívar
September 27, 1829

The chains of military despotism once fastened upon a nation, ages might pass away before they could be shaken off.

William Henry Harrison
Letter, Simon Bolívar
September 27, 1829

If by . . . strong government . . . one without responsibility is intended, which may put men to death, and immure them in dungeons, without trial, and one where the army is everything, and the people nothing, I must say, that . . . the wildest anarchy would be preferable.

William Henry Harrison
Letter, SImon Bolívar
September 27, 1829

When the white man governs himself, that is self-government; but when he governs himself and also governs another man, that is more than self-government—that is despotism.

Abraham Lincoln
Speech, Peoria, Illinois
October 16, 1854

Personal freedom, property, and life, if assailed by the passion, the prejudice, or the rapacity of the ruler, have no security whatever.

Andrew Johnson
Third annual message, Congress, on reconstruction
     and military rule
December 3, 1867

People will endure their tyrants for years, but they tear their deliverers to pieces if a millennium is not created immediately.

Woodrow Wilson
Cited in John Dos Passos, *Mr. Wilson's War*

I am not afraid of a knave. I am not afraid of a rascal. I am afraid of a strong man who is wrong, and whose wrong thinking can be impressed upon other persons by his own force of character and force of speech.

Woodrow Wilson
1912

The ultimate failures of dictatorship cost humanity far more than any temporary failures of democracy.

Franklin D. Roosevelt
1937

No man can tame a tiger by stroking it.

Franklin D. Roosevelt
Radio speech
December 29, 1940

At the present moment in world history nearly every nation must choose between alternative ways of life. The choice is too often not a free one.

Harry S. Truman
Message, Congress (The Truman Doctrine)
March 12, 1947

Whenever you have an efficient government you have a dictatorship.

Harry S. Truman
Seminar, Columbia University, New York, New York
April 28, 1959

In the past, those who foolishly sought power by riding the back of the tiger ended up inside.

John F. Kennedy
First inaugural address
January 20, 1961

Our motto is what it has always been—progress yes, tyranny no.

John F. Kennedy
Proposal, Alliance for Progress
March 13, 1961

Optimism comes less easily today, not because democracy is less vigorous but because democracy's enemies have refined their instruments of repression.

Ronald Reagan
Speech, British Parliament
June 6, 1982

It would be cultural condescension, or worse, to say that any people prefer dictatorship to democracy. Who would voluntarily choose not to have the right to vote; decide to purchase government propaganda handouts instead of independent newspapers; prefer government- to worker-controlled unions; opt for land to be owned by the state instead of those who till it; want government repression of religious liberty, a single political party instead of a free choice, a rigid cultural orthodoxy instead of democratic tolerance and diversity?

Ronald Reagan
Speech, British Parliament
June 8, 1982

All through history, it has been the dictatorships and the tyrannies that have surrendered first to the cult of militarism and the pursuit of war. Countries based on the consent of the governed, countries that recognize the unalienable rights of the individual, do not make war on each other.

Ronald Reagan
Speech, United Nations General Assembly, New York, New York
September 22, 1986

Diplomacy

Let what will be said or done, preserve your *sang-froid* immovably, and to every obstacle oppose patience, perseverance and soothing language.

Thomas Jefferson
To William Short
March 18, 1792

A little flattery will support a man through great fatigue.

James Monroe
Letter, F. D. Vanderkemp
January 24, 1818

Take things always by their smooth handle.

Thomas Jefferson
Letter, Thomas Jefferson Smith
February 21, 1825

There are a large number of well-meaning ambassadors . . . who belong to what I call the pink-tea type.

Theodore Roosevelt
Letter, R.H. Davis
January 3, 1905

Keep in harmony with the other interested parties.

Calvin Coolidge
Comment, Secretary of State Frank B. Kellogg, Swampscott, Massachusetts
1925

Our Golden Rule as far as international diplomacy is concerned is: "Do unto others as they do unto you."

"Plus ten percent," Kissinger quickly added.

Richard Nixon
State Dinner in honor of Golda Meir,
    Washington, D.C.
September 25, 1969

The conventional way to handle a meeting at the summit like this, while the whole world is watching, is to have meetings for several days, which we will have, to have discussions and discover differences, which we will do, and then put out a weasel-worded communique covering up the problems.

Richard Nixon
Comment, Chou En-lai
February 1972

Duty

My great wish is to go on in a strict but silent performance of my duty; to avoid attracting notice, and to keep my name out of the newspapers.

Thomas Jefferson
Letter, Francis Hopkinson
January 11, 1789

I discharged my duty to my country, but I committed the unpardonable sin against *Party*.

John Quincy Adams
Letter, Skelton Jones
April 17, 1809

It ought to be a maxim in politics, as well as in law, that an officer of your Government, high in the confidence of the people, shall be presumed to have done his duty, until the reverse of the proposition is proved.

James Buchanan
Speech, House of Representatives
1821

A great nation cannot abandon its responsibilities. Responsibilities abandoned today will return as more acute crises tomorrow.

Gerald Ford
Speech
December 9, 1975

E

Economics

A perfect system [of trade] is the system which would be my choice.

James Madison
Letter, James Monroe
August 7, 1785

Let the influx of money be ever so great, if there be no confidence, property will sink in value. . . . The circulation of confidence is better than the circulation of money.

James Monroe
Speech, Virginia Convention
June 20, 1788

Increased prosperity, which is sure to come, will outrun the malingerer and the vilifier.

William McKinley
Editorial for the *Repository*, written on election night
1890

I would rather have my political economy founded upon the everyday experience of the puddler or the potter than the learning of the professor.

William McKinley
Cited in Richard Kenin and Justin Wintle, *The Dictionary of Political Quotations*

[W]hen the question is raised whether our people shall have the necessaries of life at a cheaper rate, we are not ashamed to confess ourselves "in full sympathy with the demand for cheaper coats"; and we are not disturbed by the hint that this seems "necessarily to involve a cheaper man or woman under the coats."

Grover Cleveland
Speech, Thirman Birthday Banquet, Columbus, Ohio
November 13, 1890

Every dollar of fixed and stable value has, through the agency of confident credit, an astonishing capacity of multiplying itself in financial work. Every unstable and fluctuating dollar falls as a basis of credit and in its use begets gambling speculation and undermines the foundations of honest enterprise.

Grover Cleveland
Message, Congress
December 2, 1895

The truth is, we are all caught in a great economic system which is heartless.

Woodrow Wilson
The New Feedom
1912-1913 speeches

We are reaching and maintaining the position . . . where the property class and the employed class are not separate, but identical. There is a relationship of interdependence which makes their interests the same in the long run. . . . This is the ideal economic condition.

Calvin Coolidge
Have Faith in Massachusetts
1919

Economy is idealism in its most practical form.

Calvin Coolidge
Inaugural address
March 4, 1925

Our productive capacity is sufficient to maintain us all in a state of prosperity if we give sufficient attention to thrift and industry.

Calvin Coolidge
The Autobiography of Calvin Coolidge
1929

There is no dignity quite so impressive, and no independence quite so important, as living within your means. In our country a small income is usually less embarrassing than the possession of a large one.

Calvin Coolidge
The Autobiography of Calvin Coolidge
1929

If our institutions and our cities and states and nation only spent the money they had in hand, we wouldn't be in the mess we are today.

Calvin Coolidge
Comment, Stanley King
1930

Economic depression cannot be cured by legislative action or executive pronouncement. Economic wounds must be healed by the action of the cells of the economic body.

Herbert Hoover
Second annual message, Congress
December 2, 1930

The royalists of the economic order have conceded that political freedom was the business of government, but they have maintained that economic slavery was nobody's business.

Franklin D. Roosevelt
Acceptance speech, Democratic National
    Convention
June 27, 1936

We have always known that heedless self-interest was bad morals; we know now that it is bad economics.

Franklin D. Roosevelt
Second inaugural address
January 20, 1937

I see one-third of a nation ill-housed, ill-clad, ill-nourished.

Franklin D. Roosevelt
Second inaugural address
January 20, 1937

It's a recession when your neighbor loses his job; its a depression when you lose your own.

Harry S. Truman
Cited in *The Observer*
April 6, 1958

On the subject of depressions I may mention that once upon a time my political opponents honored me as possessing the fabulous intellectual and economic power by which I created a worldwide depression all by myself. At least I might claim from these tributes that I must know something about depressions.

Herbert Hoover
N. Y. Chamber of Commerce
1958

As President, my interest is in an economy which will be strong enough to absorb the potential of a rapidly expanding population, steady enough to avert the wide swings which bring grief to so many of our people, and noninflationary enough to persuade investors that this country holds a steady promise of growth and stability.

John F. Kennedy
Speech to the U. S. Chamber of Commerce
May 1962

The mere absence of war is not peace. The mere absence of recession is not growth.

John F. Kennedy
Speech
January 4, 1963

We are no longer prisoners in an economy of scarcity where one man's wealth causes another man's misery.

Lyndon B. Johnson
Speech, Presidential Breakfast, Shoreham Hotel,
    Washington, D.C.
February 4, 1965

Only two of my predecessors have come here in person to call upon Congress for a declaration of war, and I shall not do that. But I say to you that our inflation, our public enemy number one, will, unless whipped, destroy our country, our homes, our liberties, our property and finally our national pride as surely as will any well-armed wartime enemy. I concede there will be no sudden Pearl Harbor to shock us into unity and to sacrifice, but I think we have had enough early warnings. The time to intercept is right now.

Gerald Ford
Speech, Congress, Joint Session, "WIN" Campaign
October 8, 1974

I was the first president since Herbert Hoover to take office at a time of declining expectations about personal well-being.

Gerald Ford
A Time to Heal
1979

We are not talking here about some static, lifeless econometric model—we are talking about the greatest productive engine in human history, an economy that is historically revitalized not by government but by people free of government interference, needless regulation, crippling inflation, high taxes and unemployment.

Ronald Reagan
Five-Year Economic Program for the United States,
   Let's Get America Working Again, International
   Business Council, Chicago, Illinois
September 9, 1980

To paraphrase Winston Churchill, I did not take the oath I've just taken with the intention of presiding over the dissolution of the world's strongest economy.

Ronald Reagan
Inaugural address
January 20, 1981

Our aim is to increase our national wealth so all will have more, not just redistribute what we already have, which is just a sharing of scarcity. We can begin to reward hard work and risk-taking by forcing this Government to live within its means.

Ronald Reagan
Speech, Washington, D.C.
February 5, 1981

The key to a dynamic decade is economic growth. We might as well begin with common sense Federal budgeting; Government spending no more than it takes in.

Ronald Reagan
Speech, Congress
January 25, 1984

The most powerful force we can enlist against the Federal deficit is an ever-expanding American economy, unfettered and free.

Ronald Reagan
State of the union address
February 2, 1986

Most people are working harder for less money than they were making 10 years ago. It is because we are in the grip of a failed economic theory. And this decision you're about to make better be about what kind of economic theory you want.

Bill Clinton
Presidential Debate
October 15, 1992

Education and Knowledge

The preservation of the means of knowledge among the lowest ranks is of more importance to the public than all the property of all the rich men in the country.

John Adams
Dissertation on the Canon and the Feudal Law
August 1765

In a word, let every sluice of knowledge be opened and set a-flowing.

John Adams
Dissertation on the Canon and Feudal Law
August 1765

Liberty cannot be preserved without general knowledge among people.

John Adams
Dissertation on the Canon and the Feudal Law
August 1765

Illuminate, as far as practicable, the minds of the people at large, and more especially to give them knowledge of those facts, which history exhibiteth, that, possessed thereby of the experience of other ages and countries, they may be enabled to know ambition under all its shapes, and prompt to exert their natural powers to defeat its purposes.

Thomas Jefferson
Bill of 1779 (for the more general diffusion of knowledge)

It is universally admitted that a well-instructed people alone can be permanently a free people.

James Madison
Second annual message, Congress
December 5, 1810

We must train and classify the whole of our male citizens, and make military instruction a regular part of collegiate education. We can never be safe until this is done.

Thomas Jefferson
Letter, James Monroe
1813

Knowledge . . . can never be equally divided among mankind, any more than property, real or personal, any more than wives or women.

John Adams
Letter, John Taylor
April 15, 1814

And after all that can be done to disseminate knowledge, you can never equalize it.

John Adams
Letter, John Taylor
April 15, 1814

Education! Oh, education! the greatest grief of my heart, and the greatest affliction of my life!

John Adams
Letter, Thomas Jefferson
July 16, 1814

Caesar and Virgil, and a few books of Euclid, do not really contain the sum of all human knowledge.

Thomas Jefferson
Letter, Thomas Cooper
October 7, 1814

Knowledge is power . . . knowledge is safety . . . knowledge is happiness.

Thomas Jefferson
Letter, George Ticknor
November 25, 1817

It is only when the People become ignorant and corrupt, when they degenerate into a populace, that they are incapable of exercizing their sovereignty. . . . Let us, by all wise and constitutional measures, promote intelligence among the People, as the best means of preserving our liberties.

James Monroe
Inaugural address
March 4, 1817

Books constitute capital. A library book lasts as long as a house, for hundreds of years. It is not, then, an article of mere consumption but fairly of capital, and often in the case of professional men, setting out in life, it is their only capital.

Thomas Jefferson
Letter, James Madison
September 16, 1821

Learned institutions ought to be favorite objects with every free people. They throw that light over the public mind which is the best security against crafty and dangerous encroachments on the public liberty.

James Madison
Letter, W. T. Barry
August 4, 1822

A popular Government, without popular information, or the means of acquiring it, is but a Prologue to a Farce or a Tragedy; or, perhaps both. Knowledge will forever govern ignorance; and a people who mean to be their own Governors, must arm themselves with the power which knowledge gives.

James Madison
Letter, W. T. Barry
August 4, 1822

The diffusion of knowledge is the only guardian of true liberty.

James Madison
Letter, George Thompson
June 30, 1825

I had not the advantage of a classical education, and no man should, in my judgement, accept a degree he cannot read.

Millard Fillmore
Comment, declining a degree from Oxford
  University
1855

In the civilized countries of the world the question is how to distribute most generally and equally the property of the world. As a rule where education is most general the distribution of property is most general. When we see what wealth is doing and what wealth can do we begin to doubt the aphorism, "Knowledge is power." As knowledge spreads, wealth spreads. To diffuse knowledge is to diffuse wealth. To give all an equal chance to acquire knowledge is the best and surest way to give all an equal chance to acquire property.

Rutherford B. Hayes
Diary
May 15, 1878

Education was early in the thought of the framers of our Constitution as one of the best, if not the only guarantee of their perpetuation. . . . How shall one be a safe citizen when citizens are rulers who are not intelligent? How shall he understand those great questions which his suffrage must adjudge without thorough intellectual culture in his youth?

Benjamin Harrison
Speech, Knox College, Galesburg, Illinois
October 8, 1889

Where the children of rich and poor mingle together on the play ground and in the school-room, there is produced a unity of feeling and a popular love for public institutions that can be brought about in no other way.

Benjamin Harrison
Speech, Provo City, Utah
May 9, 1891

You do not know the world until you know the men who have possessed it and tried its ways before ever you were given your brief run upon it.

Woodrow Wilson
The Forum
December 1896

The use of university is to make young gentlemen as unlike their fathers as possible.

Woodrow Wilson
1914

A muttonhead, after an education at West Point—or Harvard—is a muttonhead still.

Theodore Roosevelt
Comment, Newton D. Baker
April 1917

My education began with a set of blocks which had on them the Roman numerals and the letters of the alphabet. It is not yet finished.

Calvin Coolidge
The Autobiography of Calvin Coolidge
1929

The gains of education are never really lost. Books may be burned and cities sacked, but truth, like the yearning for freedom, lives in the hearts of humble men.

Franklin D. Roosevelt
Acceptance speech, Democratic National
  Convention
June 27, 1936

You know that education is one thing that can't be taken away from you. Nobody can rob you of your education, because that is in your head; that is, if you have any head and are capable of holding it. Most of us are capable of holding an education, if we try to get it.

Harry S. Truman
Informal remarks, Oregon
June 11, 1948

I have a little hesitation about addressing this august body, shall I say, everybody with degrees emeritus and all the other $40 words that go with an education. The only degree that I ever earned was at George Washington University in Washington, D.C. My daughter went to school there for four years and earned me a degree.

Harry S. Truman
Speech, California
June 12, 1948

Don't join the book burners. Don't think you are going to conceal faults by concealing evidence that they ever existed. Don't be afraid to go in your library and read every book.

Dwight D. Eisenhower
Dartmouth College Commencement, Hanover, New Hampshire
June 14, 1953

What we need now in this nation, more than atomic power, or airpower, or financial, industrial, or even manpower, is brain power. The dinosaur was bigger and stronger than anyone else—but he was also dumber. And look what happened to him.

John F. Kennedy
Address, Washington, D.C.
April 16, 1959

It might be said now that I have the best of both worlds. A Harvard education and a Yale degree.

John F. Kennedy
Comment, on receiving an honorary degree from Yale University, *New York Times*
June 12, 1962

This is the richest, most powerful country which ever occupied this globe. The might of past empires is little compared to ours. But I do not want to be the President who built empires, or sought grandeur, or extended dominion. I want to be the president who educated young children to the wonders of their world.

Lyndon B. Johnson
Speech, Congress, Joint Session
March 15, 1965

The world is engaged in a race between education and chaos.

Lyndon B. Johnson
Radio and television speech
July 12, 1966

Once we considered education a public expense; we know now that it is a public investment.

Lyndon B. Johnson
Speech, Crossman Senior High School, Camp Springs, Maryland
April 27, 1967

What are our schools for if not indoctrination against Communism?

Richard Nixon
Quoted, *Avant-Garde*
January 1968

Efficiency

We must centralize ideas but decentralize execution.

Herbert Hoover
Senate Committee, Food Administration Bill
1917

The best form of efficiency is the spontaneous cooperation of a free people.

Woodrow Wilson
Cited in James M. Burns, *Roosevelt: The Soldier of Freedom 1940-1945*

Dwight D. Eisenhower

I like Ike—I like Ike so well I would send him back to the Army if I had a chance.

Harry S. Truman
Statement
October 12, 1952

He'll sit here, and he'll say, "Do this! Do that!" And nothing will happen. Poor Ike—it won't be a bit like the Army.

Harry S. Truman
Campaign speech
1952

The General doesn't know any more about politics than a pig knows about Sunday.

Harry S. Truman
Campaign speech
1952

I never had enough money to play golf.

Harry S. Truman
Quote Magazine
September 25, 1955

I like Ike, but not as President. He has gotten mixed up with those damn Republicans and doesn't know which way is up.

Harry S. Truman
Statement
October 1956

President Eisenhower's whole life is proof of the stark but simple truth—that no one hates war more than one who has seen a lot of it.

Richard Nixon
Radio and television address, Moscow
August 1959

Eisenhower also knew that to maintain his above-the-battle position he needed a running mate who was willing to engage in all-out combat, and who was good at it. In a sense, the hero needed a point man.

Richard Nixon
The Memoirs of Richard Nixon
1978

While he had an engaging, outgoing personality, he also had a very definite sense of dignity. He was not the kind of man who appreciated undue familiarity. I remember the chilling looks he gave to those who tugged at his sleeve or slapped him on the back. In this respect he could not have been more different from Lyndon Johnson, who seemed unable to carry on a conversation without nudging or poking or even shaking the other person.

Richard Nixon
The Memoirs of Richard Nixon
1978

Elections

Elections, my dear sir, to offices which are a great object of ambition, I look at with terror.

John Adams
Letter, Thomas Jefferson
December 6, 1787

Corruption in Elections has heretofore destroyed all Elective Governments. What Regulations or Precautions may be devised to prevent it in future, I am content with you to leave Posterity to consider. You and I shall go to the Kingdom of the just or at least shall be released from the Republik of the Unjust, with Hearts pure and hands clean of all Corruption in Elections; so much I firmly believe.

John Adams
Letter, Thomas Jefferson, Philadelphia, Pennsylvania
April 6, 1796

The ballot box is the surest arbiter of disputes among freemen.

James Buchanan
Fourth annual message, Congress
December 3, 1860

It is now for them [the people] to demonstrate to the world that those who can fairly carry an election can also suppress a rebellion; that ballots are the rightful and peaceful successors of bullets; and that when ballots have fairly and constitutionally decided, there can be no successful appeal back to bullets; that there can be no successful appeal, except to ballots themselves, at succeeding elections. Such will be a great lesson of peace: teaching men that what they cannot take by an election, neither can they take it by war; teaching all the folly of being the beginners of war.

Abraham Lincoln
Message, Congress, Special Session
July 4, 1861

I do not want to be re-elected.

Chester A. Arthur
Comment, Frank B. Conger
May 1883

How shall those who practise election fraud recover that respect for the sanctity of the ballot which is the first condition and obligation of good citizenship? The man who has come to regard the ballot-box as a juggler's hat has renounced his allegiance.

Benjamin Harrison
Inaugural address
March 4, 1889

When the American people make a major decision like the election of a President they do not offer themselves to the highest bidder. . . . Promises and good intentions are not enough.

Calvin Coolidge
Speech
1932

It isn't important who is ahead at one time or another in either an election or a horse-race. It's the horse that comes in first at the finish that counts.

Harry S. Truman
Statement
October 17, 1948

These polls that the Republican candidate is putting out are like pills designed to lull the voters into sleeping on Election Day. You ought to call them sleeping polls.

Harry S. Truman
Speech, Cleveland Municipal Auditorium,
    Cleveland, Ohio
October 26, 1948

A President needs political understanding to *run* the government, but he may be *elected* without it.

Harry S. Truman
Memoirs
1956

Enemies

An injured friend is the bitterest of foes.

Thomas Jefferson
French Treaties Opinion
April 28, 1793

I have labored with holy zeal to rid this devoted state [New York] of a Junta which sits like the nightmare upon her. . . . We have scotched the snake, not killed it.

Martin Van Buren
Letter, Gorham Worth
June 1, 1820

My course has been always to put my enemies at defiance, and pursue my own course.

Andrew Jackson
Letter, Frank Blair
February 20, 1839

I'm ready to forgive the whole crews of them [his enemies] collectively, but not as individuals.

Andrew Jackson
Comment, Parson, on his deathbed
1845

Well, we have met the enemy and we are theirs.

James Buchanan
Letter, Harriet Lane, after election loss
October 1858

A well-bred man will respect me; all others I will make do it.

Andrew Johnson
Speech, Senate
1858

I just won't get into a pissing contest with that skunk [Senator Joe McCarthy].

Dwight D. Eisenhower
Comment, Milton Eisenhower
1953

No conversation is sweeter than that of former political enemies.

Harry S. Truman
Statement, cited in *Quote* Magazine
April 1954

I'd much rather have that fellow inside my tent pissing out, than outside my tent pissing in.

Lyndon B. Johnson
Comment on J. Edgar Hoover, cited by John Kenneth
    Galbraith in the *Guardian Weekly*
December 18, 1971

Environment and Energy

[Conservation is] the chief material question that confronts us, second only—and second always—to the great fundamental question of morality.

Theodore Roosevelt
Speech, White House
May 13, 1908

As a people, we have the problem of making our forests outlast this generation, our iron outlast this century, and our coal the next; not merely as a matter of convenience or comfort, but as a matter of stern national necessity.

William Howard Taft
Cited in Paolo E. Coletta, *The Presidency of William Howard Taft*

When I talk about energy, I am talking about jobs. Our American economy runs on energy. No energy—no jobs.

Gerald Ford
Address to the nation on energy policy
May 27, 1975

We cannot continue to depend on the price and supply whims of others. The Congress cannot drift, dawdle and debate forever with America's future.

Gerald Ford
Address to the nation on energy policy
May 27, 1975

This difficult effort [to solve the energy crisis] will be the "moral equivalent of war," except we will be uniting our efforts to build and not to destroy.

Jimmy Carter
Address to the nation
April 18, 1977

Equality

The foundation on which all [our constitutions] are built is the natural equality of man, the denial of every preeminence but that annexed to legal office, and particularly the denial of a preeminence by birth.

Thomas Jefferson
Letter, George Washington
1784

It is the law of nature between master and servant that the servant shall spoil or plunder the master.

John Quincy Adams
Diary
December 17, 1810

Equal laws protecting equal rights are . . . the best guarantee of loyalty & love of country.

James Madison
Letter, Jacob De La Motta
August 1820

All eyes are opened or opening to the rights of man. The general spread of the lights of science has already opened to every view the palpable truth, that the mass of mankind has not been born with saddles on their backs, nor a favored few booted and spurred, ready to ride them legitimately, by the grace of God.

Thomas Jefferson
Letter, R. C. Weightman
June 24, 1826

Many of our rich men have not been content with equal protection and equal benefits, but have besought us to make them richer by act of Congress.

Andrew Jackson
Veto, Bank Bill
July 10, 1832

I believe and I say it is true Democratic feeling, that all the measures of Government are directed to the purpose of making the rich richer and the poor poorer.

William Henry Harrison
Speech
October 1, 1840

We admit of no government by divine right, believing that so far as power is concerned the Beneficient Creator has made no distinction amongst men.

William Henry Harrison
Inaugural address
March 4, 1841

Our progress in degeneracy appears to me to be pretty rapid. As a nation, we began by declaring *"all men are created equal."* We now practically read it "all men are created equal, *except negroes.*" When the Know-Nothings get control, it will read "all men are created equal, except negroes, *and foreigners and catholics.*" When it comes to this I should prefer emigrating to some country where they make no pretense of loving liberty—to Russia, for instance, where despotism can be taken pure, and without the base alloy of hypocrisy.

Abraham Lincoln
Letter, Joshua Speed
1855

I think the authors of that notable instrument [the Declaration of Independence] intended to include *all* men, but they did not intend to declare all men equal *in all respects*. They did not mean to say all were equal in color, size, intellect, moral developments, or social capacity. They defined with tolerable distinctness in what respects they did consider all men created equal—equal with "certain inalienable rights, among which are life, liberty, and the pursuit of happiness." This they said, and this they meant.

Abraham Lincoln
Speech, Springfield, Illinois
June 27, 1857

But, if this country cannot be saved without giving up that principle [equality] . . . I would rather be assassinated on this spot than surrender it.

Abraham Lincoln
Speech, Independence Hall
February 22, 1861

Four score and seven years ago our fathers brought forth on this continent, a new nation, conceived in Liberty, and dedicated to the proposition that all men are created equal.

Abraham Lincoln
Gettysburg Address
November 19, 1863

It is now true that this is God's country, if equal rights—a fair start and an equal chance in the race of life are everywhere secured to all.

Rutherford B. Hayes
Diary
July 25, 1880

The equal and exact justice of which we boast, as the underlying principle of our institutions, should not be confined to the relations of our citizens to each other. The government itself is under bond to the American people that, in the exercise of its functions and powers, it will deal with the body of our citizens in a manner scrupulously honest and fair, and absolutely just. It is agreed that American citizenship shall be the only credential necessary to justify the claim of equality before the law, and that no condition in life shall give rise to discrimination in the treatment of the people by their government.

Grover Cleveland
Fourth annual message, Congress
December 3, 1888

We stand committed to the proposition that freedom is not a half-and-half affair. If the average citizen is guaranteed equal opportunity in the polling place, he must have equal opportunity in the market place.

Franklin D. Roosevelt
Acceptance speech, Democratic National
    Convention
June 27, 1936

As a nation we are committed to the principle of freedom because we believe that men are created equal. Freedom is a relationship between equals.

Harry S. Truman
Speech, Madison, Wisconsin
January 27, 1952

Finally, it should be clear by now that a nation can be no stronger abroad than she is at home. Only an America which practices what it preaches about equal rights and social justice will be respected by those whose choice affects our future.

John F. Kennedy
Speech prepared for delivery, Dallas, Texas
November 22, 1963

For too long we've been told about "us" and "them." Each and every election we see a new slate of arguments and ads telling us that "they" are the problem, not "us." But there can be no "them" in America. There's only us.

Bill Clinton
Putting People First
1992

Error

Reason and free inquiry are the only effectual agents against error.

Thomas Jefferson
"Notes on Virginia"
1781-1782

Delay is preferable to error.

Thomas Jefferson
Letter, George Washington
May 16, 1792

It is better to bear the ills we have than to fly to others we know not of.

James Buchanan
Cited in Philip S. Klein, *President James Buchanan*
c. 1819

We are all liable to error, and those who are engaged in the management of public affairs are more subject to excitement and to be led astray by their particular interests and passions than the great body of our constituents, who, living at home in the pursuit of their ordinary avocations, are calm but deeply interested spectators of events and of the conduct of those who are parties to them.

James Monroe
Seventh annual message, Congress
December 2, 1823

I had much rather you should impute to me great error of judgment than the smallest deviation from sincerity.

John Quincy Adams
Letter, John Greenleaf Whittier
1837

A faithful and conscientious magistrate will concede very much to honest error, and something even to perverse malice, before he will endanger the public peace.

Andrew Johnson
Third annual message, Congress
December 3, 1867

My failures have been errors of judgment, not of intent.

Ulysses S. Grant
Eighth annual message, Congress
December 5, 1876

You may write down in your books now, the largest percentage of blunders which you think I will be likely to make, and you will be sure to find in the end that I have made many more than you have calculated, many more.

James A. Garfield
Speech, Washington, D.C.
March 3, 1881

I have made mistakes, but I am an honest man.

Richard Nixon
Press conference, San Francisco, California, on loan from Hughes Tool Company to his brother
October 1, 1962

Now what should happen when you make a mistake is this: You take your knocks, you learn your lessons and then you move on. That's the healthiest way to deal with a problem.

Ronald Reagan
Address to the nation, Iran-contra arms affair
March 4, 1987

It wasn't my finest hour. It wasn't even my finest hour and a half.

Bill Clinton
Comments on his poorly received speech to the Democratic Convention
1988

Europe

The great rule of conduct for us in regard to foreign nations is, in extending our commercial relations to have with them as little *political* connection as possible. . . .

Why, by interweaving our destiny with that of any part of Europe, entangle our peace and prosperity in the toils of European ambition, rivalship, interest, humor, or caprice? It is our true policy to steer clear of permanent alliances with any portion of the foreign world. . . . We may safely trust to temporary alliances for extraordinary emergencies. . . . There can be no greater error than to expect or calculate upon real favors from nation to nation. It is an illusion which experience must cure, which a just pride ought to discard.

George Washington
Farewell address
September 17, 1796

The less we do with the amities or enmities of Europe, the better.

Thomas Jefferson
Letter, Thomas Leiper
1815

They are nations of eternal war.

Thomas Jefferson
Letter, James Monroe
1823

Separated as we are from Europe by the great Atlantic ocean, we can have no concern in the wars of the European Governments no[r] in the causes which produce them.

James Monroe
Eighth annual message, Congress
December 7, 1824

If any South American State misbehaves toward any European country, let the European country spank it.

Theodore Roosevelt
Letter, Speck Von Sternberg
July 12, 1901

We can make war but we do not and cannot make peace in Europe.

Herbert Hoover
After Munich
1938-1939

Our founding fathers perhaps owed more of their initial ideas to Ancient Greece and Rome than to Europe of their time.

Herbert Hoover
The Memoirs of Herbert Hoover: Years of Adventure
    1874-1920
1951

Too many Americans do not realize to what extent our ideas and our way of life have grown apart from Europe in these three hundred years of separation. American Society with a capital S, and many of our Intellectuals with a capital I, have made a fetish of their spiritual home in Europe. They fail to realize that ours is a setting three centuries distant.

Herbert Hoover
The Memoirs of Herbert Hoover: Years of Adventure
    1874-1920
1951

I get weary of the European habit of taking our money, resenting any slight hint as to what *they* should do, and then assuming, in addition, full right to criticize us as bitterly as they may desire. In fact, it sometimes appears that their indulgence in this kind of criticism varies in direct ratio to the amount of help we give them.

Dwight D. Eisenhower
Comment, Alfred Gruenther
October 27, 1953

I came to Europe to reassert as clearly and persuasively as I could that the American commitment to the freedom of Europe is reliable—not merely because of goodwill, although that is strong; not merely because of a shared heritage, though that is deep and wide; and not at all because we seek to dominate, because we do not. I came to make it clear that this commitment rests upon the inescapable requirement of intelligent self-interest—it is a commitment whose wisdom is confirmed by its absence when two World Wars began and by its presence in eighteen years of well-defended peace.

John F. Kennedy
Speech, Naples, Italy
July 1963

Evil

Wherever there is an interest and power to do wrong, wrong will generally be done, and not less readily by a powerful & interested party than by a powerful and interested prince.

James Madison
Letter, Thomas Jefferson
October 20, 1788

It is more honorable to repair a wrong than to persist in it.

Thomas Jefferson
To the Cherokee Chiefs
January 10, 1806

In the turbid stream of political life, a conscientious man must endeavor to do justice to all, and to return good for evil, but he must always expect evil in return.

John Quincy Adams
Debate
1835-1836

No man is justified in doing evil on the ground of expedience.

Theodore Roosevelt
Speech, Chicago, Illinois
1899

Expansion

If there be one principle more deeply rooted than any other in the mind of every American, it is that we should have nothing to do with conquest.

Thomas Jefferson
Letter, William Short
1791

I know the acquisition of Louisiana has been disapproved by some, from a candid apprehension that the enlargement of our territory would endanger its union. But who can limit the extent to which the federative principle may operate effectively. The larger our association, the less will it be shaken by local passions; and in any view, is it not better that the opposite bank of the Mississippi should be settled by our own brethren and children, than by

strangers of another family? With which shall we be most likely to live in harmony and friendly intercourse?

Thomas Jefferson
Second inaugural address
March 4, 1805

It is evident, that the further acquisition of territory, to the West and South, involves difficulties, of an internal nature, which menace the Union itself. We ought therefore to be cautious in making the attempt.

James Monroe
Letter, Thomas Jefferson
May 1820

So seducing is the passion for extending our territory, that if compelled to take our own redress it is quite uncertain within what limit it will be confined.

James Monroe
Letter, Albert Gallatin
May 26, 1820

Have you not enough Indians to expel from the land of their fathers? Are you not large and unwieldly enough already?

John Quincy Adams
Speech, House of Representatives, arguing against
    annexation of Texas
May 18, 1836

What, sir! prevent the American people from crossing the Rocky Mountains? You might as well command Niagara not to flow. We must fulfill our destiny.

James Buchanan
c. 1837

In the face of this House and the face of Heaven, I avow . . . that the annexation of an independent foreign power [Texas] to this government would be ipso facto a dissolution of this Union. The question is whether a foreign nation, a nation damned to everlasting fame by the reinstitution of that detested system of slavery after it had once been abolished within its borders, should be admitted into union with a nation of freemen. For that name, thank God, is still ours!

John Quincy Adams
Speech, House of Representatives
1838

Our title to the country of the Oregon is "clear and unquestionable," and already are our people preparing to perfect that title by occupying it with their wives and children.

James K. Polk
Inaugural address
March 4, 1845

The policy of my administration will not be controlled by any timid forebodings of evil from expansion. Indeed it is not to be disguised that our attitude as a nation and our position on the globe render the acquisition of certain possessions not within our jurisdiction eminently important for our protection, if not in the future essential for the preservation of commerce and the peace of the world . . . if your past is limited, your future is boundless.

Franklin Pierce
Third annual message, Congress
December 31, 1855

It is beyond question the destiny of our race to spread themselves over the continent of North America. . . . The tide of emigrants will flow to the South.

James Buchanan
Letter, Hiram Swarr
December 31, 1858

They yearn for the protection of our free institutions and laws, our progress and civilization. Shall we refuse them?

Ulysses S. Grant
Speech, Senate, on Dominican Republic
May 31, 1870

Maintaining, as I do, the tenets of a line of precedents from Washington's day, which proscribe tangling alliances with foreign states, I do not favor a policy of acquisition of new and distant territory or the incorporation of remote interests with our own.

Grover Cleveland
Message, Congress
December 8, 1885

I speak not of forcible annexation, for that cannot be thought of. That by our code of morality would be criminal aggression.

William McKinley
First annual message, Congress, on alternatives in Cuba
December 6, 1897

We have good money, we have ample revenues, we have unquestioned national credit, but what we want is new markets, and as trade follows the flag it looks very much as if we were going to have new markets.

William McKinley
Speech for Republican congressional candidates, annexation of the Philippines
1898

Who will darken the counsels of the Republic in this hour requiring the united wisdom of all? Shall we deny ourselves what the rest of the world so freely and so justly accords to us?

William McKinley
Speech for Republican congressional candidates, annexation of the Philippines
1898

[It was not] a good time for the liberator to submit important questions concerning liberty and government to the liberated while they are engaged in shooting down their rescuers.

William McKinley
On asking the consent of the Filipinos to American annexation at the time of victory over Spain, Banquet of the Home Market, Mechanics Hall, Boston, Massachusetts
February 16, 1899

When great nations fear to expand, shrink from expansion, it is because their greatness is coming to an end. Are we still in the prime of our lusty youth, still at the beginning of our glorious manhood, to sit down among the outworn people, to take our place with the weak and the craven? A thousand times no.

Theodore Roosevelt
Speech in Akron, Ohio, justifying the U.S. war against Spain
September 1899

The use of power in the extension of American institutions presents an inconsistency whose evil and dangerous tendency ought to be apparent to all who love these institutions and understand their motives and purposes.

Grover Cleveland
Letter, condemning the war against Spain
October 8, 1899

[I have] about the same desire to annex it [the Dominican Republic] as a gorged boa constrictor might have to swallow a porcupine wrong-end-to.

Theodore Roosevelt
Comment on request of Dominican minister of foreign affairs that America establish a protectorate over the islands, Washington, D.C.
January 1904

When you try to conquer other people or extend yourself over vast areas you cannot win in the long run.

Harry S. Truman
1950

Experience

The ordinary affairs of a nation offer little difficulty to a person of any experience.

Thomas Jefferson
Letter, James Sullivan
1808

It was my fortune, or misfortune, to be called to the office of Chief Executive without any previous political training. From the age of seventeen I had never even witnessed the excitement attending a Presidential campaign but twice antecedent to my own candidacy, and but one of them was I eligible as a voter.

Ulysses S. Grant
Eighth annual message, Congress
December 5, 1876

You don't set a fox to watching the chickens just because he has a lot of experience in the hen house.

Harry S. Truman
Comment, Richard Nixon's candidacy for the Presidency
October 30, 1960

F

Family

Pecuniary concerns I never regarded, and indeed I now feel that I have regarded too little the just claims of my family.

James Monroe
Letter, General Andrew Jackson
July 3, 1825

Sometimes I think that I get far less leisure than any other mortal and have far less of the enjoyments of life. It is a fearful price to pay for a little publicity—to be obliged to throw away all the dear pleasures of home and family just at a time when enjoyment has the keenish relish.

James A. Garfield
As a congressman
February 1864

A man's rootage is more important than his leafage.

Woodrow Wilson
Speech, Baltimore, Maryland
April 29, 1912

They [his family] all taught me to be faithful over a few things. If they had any idea that such a training might some day make me a ruler over many things, it was not disclosed to me.

Calvin Coolidge
The Autobiography of Calvin Coolidge
1929

Children and dogs are as necessary to the welfare of this country as Wall Street and the railroads.

Harry S. Truman
Remarks, National Conference on Family Life
May 6, 1948

Fear

The only thing we have to fear is fear itself—nameless, unreasoning, unjustified terror.

Franklin D. Roosevelt
Inaugural address
March 4, 1933

There is no panic on our agenda.

Lyndon B. Johnson
Speech, Los Angeles, California
February 21, 1964

Millard Fillmore

I'll tell you at a time when we needed a strong man, what we got was a man that swayed with the slightest breeze. About all he ever accomplished as President, he sent Commodore Perry to open up Japan to the West, but that didn't help much as far as preventing the Civil War was concerned.

Harry S. Truman
Cited in Merle Miller, *Plain Speaking: An Oral Biography of Harry S. Truman*

Flattery

Let those flatter who fear: it is not an American art.

Thomas Jefferson
"The Rights of British America"
1774

85

A little flattery will support a man through great fatigue.

James Monroe
Letter, F. A. Vanderkemp
January 24, 1818

Force

Force cannot give right.

Thomas Jefferson
"The Rights of British America"
1774

Is uniformity obtainable? Millions of innocent men, women, and children, since the introduction of Christianity, have been burnt, tortured, fined, imprisoned; yet we have not advanced an inch toward uniformity. What has been the effect of coercion? To make one half the world fools, and the other half hypocrits. To support roguery and error all over the earth.

Thomas Jefferson
"Notes on Virginia"
1782

Germany has once more said that force, and force alone, shall decide whether peace and justice shall reign in the affairs of men, whether right as America conceives it, or dominion as she conceives it, shall determine the destinies of mankind. There is, therefore, but one response possible from us: force, force to the uttermost, force without stint or limit, the righteous and triumphant force which shall make right of the law of the world and cast every selfish dominion down in the dust.

Woodrow Wilson
Speech, Baltimore, Maryland
April 6, 1918

A long time ago down in Texas I learned that telling a man to go to hell and making him go there are two different propositions.

Lyndon B. Johnson
Campaign speech
1964

Foreign Affairs

It is the sincere wish of America to have nothing to do with the political intrigues, or squabbles of European nations.

George Washington
Letter, Earl of Buchan
April 22, 1793

My ardent desire is . . . to keep the United States free from political connections with every other country, to see them independent of all and under the influence of none.

George Washington
Letter, Patrick Henry
October 9, 1795

I have always given it as my decided opinion that no nation had a right to intermeddle in the internal concerns of another; . . . and that, if this country could, consistent with its engagements, maintain a strict neutrality and thereby preserve peace, it was bound to do so by motives of policy, interest, and every other consideration.

George Washington
Letter, James Monroe
August 25, 1796

Observe good faith and justice toward all nations. Cultivate peace and harmony with all. . . . The nation which indulges toward another an habitual hatred or an habitual fondness is in some degree a slave. It is a slave to its animosity or to its affection, either of which is sufficient to lead it astray from its duty and its interest.

George Washington
Farewell address
September 17, 1796

Against the insidious wiles of foreign influence . . . the jealousy of a free people ought to be *constantly* awake. . . . But that jealousy, to be useful, must be impartial, else it becomes the instrument of the very influence to be avoided, instead of a defense against it.

George Washington
Farewell address
September 17, 1796

The great rule of conduct for us in regard to foreign nations is, in extending our commercial relations to have with them as little *political* connection as possible.

George Washington
Farewell address
September 17, 1796

There can be no greater error than to expect, or calculate upon, real favors from nation to nation.

George Washington
Farewell address
September 17, 1796

Equal and exact justice to all men, of whatever state or persuasion, religious or political; peace, commerce and honest friendship with all nations—entangling alliances with none.... [T]hese principles . . . should be the creed of our political faith.

Thomas Jefferson
First inaugural address
March 4, 1801

Nations are sometimes called upon to perform to each other acts of humanity and kindness, of which we see so many illustratious examples between individuals in private life.

James Monroe
Views on the Subject of Internal Improvements, Veto
  of Cumberland Road Bill
1822

Our nation is too great, both in material strength and in moral power, to indulge in bluster or to be suspected of timorousness.

Benjamin Harrison
Acceptance speech, Republican nomination, In-
  dianapolis, Indiana
September 11, 1888

We Americans have no commission from God to police the world.

Benjamin Harrison
Campaign speech
1888

It is most appropriate that a people whose storehouses have been so lavishly filled with all the fruits of the earth by the gracious favor of God should manifest their gratitude by large gifts to his suffering children in other lands.

Benjamin Harrison
Speech, Senate and House, on the famine in Russia
January 5, 1892

I never take a step in foreign policy unless I am assured that I shall be able eventually to carry out my will by force.

Theodore Roosevelt
Comment
1905

In the field of world policy I would dedicate this nation to the policy of the good neighbor—the neighbor who resolutely respects himself and, because he does so, respects the rights of others—the neighbor who respects his obligations and respects the sanctity of his agreements in and with a world of neighbors.

Franklin D. Roosevelt
First inaugural address
March 4, 1933

The rest of the world—ah! There is the rub.

Franklin D. Roosevelt
Message, Congress
1936

The issue is really whether our civilization is to be dragged into the tragic vortex of unending militarism punctuated by periodic wars, or whether we shall be able to maintain the ideal of peace, individuality and civilization as the fabric of our lives.

Franklin D. Roosevelt
Hands Off the Western Hemisphere speech, Pan-
  American Day
April 14, 1939

We have the right to say that there shall not be an organization of world affairs which permits us no choice but to turn our countries into barracks unless we are to be vassals of some conquering empire.

Franklin D. Roosevelt
Hands Off the Western Hemisphere speech, Pan-
  American Day
April 14, 1939

We want no domination over any nation. We want no indemnities. We want no special privileges. But we do want the freedom of nations from the domination of others, call it by whatever name we will—liberation of peoples, self-government or just restored sovereignty.

Herbert Hoover
Republican National Convention, Chicago, Illinois
June 27, 1944

We must have a policy to guide our relations with every country in every part of the world. No country is so remote from us that it may not some day be involved in a matter which threatens the peace. Remember that the First World War began in Serbia; that the peace of Versailles was first broken in Manchuria; and the Second World War began in Poland. Who knows what may happen in the future? Our foreign policy must be universal.

Harry S. Truman
Address, Army Day, Chicago, Illinois
April 6, 1946

International relations have traditionally been compared to a chess game in which each nation tries to outwit and checkmate the other.

Harry S. Truman
Address, Mexico City
March 3, 1947

You have the broader considerations that might follow what you would call the "falling domino" principle. You have a row of dominos set up, you knock over the first one, and what will happen to the last one is the certainty that it will go over very quickly.

Dwight D. Eisenhower
News conference
April 7, 1954

I will not be a party to any treaty that makes anybody a slave; now that is all there is to it.

Dwight D. Eisenhower
Press conference
July 7, 1954

A major American goal is a world of open societies.

Dwight D. Eisenhower
Statement, U-2 incident
May 25, 1960

I believe in building bridges but we should build only our end of the bridge.

Richard Nixon
Lakeside speech, Bohemian Grove, California
July 1967

Regimes planted by bayonets do not take root.

Ronald Reagan
Speech, British Parliament
June 8, 1982

Our policy is simple: We are not going to betray our friends, reward the enemies of freedom, or permit fear and retreat to become American policies, especially in this hemisphere. None of the four wars in my lifetime came about because we were too strong. It is weakness—it is weakness that invites adventurous adversaries to make mistaken judgments.

Ronald Reagan
Speech, Republican National Convention, Dallas, Texas
August 23, 1984

France

I consider all Reasoning upon French Affairs of little moment. The Fates must determine hereafter as they have done heretofore. Reasoning has been lost. Passion, Prejudice, Interest, Necessity has governed and will govern; and a Century must roll away before any permanent and quiet System will be established. An Ameliorization of human affairs I hope and believe will be the result, but You and I must look down from Battlements of Heaven if We have the pleasure of Seeing it.

John Adams
Letter, Thomas Jefferson, Philadelphia, Pennsylvania
January 31, 1796

Of all nations of any consideration, France is the one which, hitherto, has offered the fewest points on which we could have any conflict of right, and the most points of a communion of interests. From these causes, we have ever looked to her as our *natural friend*. . . . Her growth, therefore, we viewed as our own, her misfortunes ours. There is on the globe one single spot, the possessor of which is our natural and habitual enemy. It is New Orleans, through which the produce of three-eighths of our territory must pass to market. . . . France, placing herself in that door, assumes to us an attitude of defiance. . . .[These] circumstances render it impossible that France and the United States can continue long friends, when they meet in so irritable a position.

Thomas Jefferson
Letter, Robert R. Livingston, U.S. minister to France
April 18, 1802

As for France and England, with all their preeminence in science, the one is a den of robbers, and the other of pirates. And if science produces no better fruits than tyranny, murder, rapine and destitution of national morality, I would rather wish our country to be ignorant, honest and estimable, as our neighboring savages are.

Thomas Jefferson
Letter, John Adams
January 21, 1812

The revolution of France undoubtedly took its origin from that of the United States. Her citizens fought and bled within our service. They caught the spirit of liberty here, and carried it home with them.

James Monroe
Letter, J. M. Cowperthwaite
1830

The wit who describes the government of France as despotism tempered by epigram was really formulating one of the approaches to constitutional government.

Woodrow Wilson
1908

Freedom

The love of power, which has been so often the cause of slavery—has, whenever freedom has existed, been the cause of freedom.

John Adams
"Dissertion on the Canon and the Feudal Law"
August 1765

If it be the pleasure of Heaven that my country shall require the poor offering of my life, the victim shall be ready, at the appointed hour of sacrifice, come when that hour may. But while I do live, let me have a country, and that a free country.

John Adams
Speech
1776

Posterity! You will never know how much it cost the present generation to preserve your freedom! I hope you will make good use of it! If you do not, I shall repent it in Heaven that I ever took half the pains to preserve it!

John Adams
Letter to Abigail Adams
April 26, 1777

We, the General Assembly of Virginia, do enact that no man shall be compelled to frequent or support any religious worship, place, or ministry whatsoever, nor shall be enforced, restrained, molested, or burthened in his body or goods, or shall otherwise suffer, on account of his religious opinions or belief; but that all men shall be free to profess, and by argument to maintain, their opinions in matters of religion, and that the same shall in no wise diminish, enlarge, or affect their civil capabilities.

Thomas Jefferson
Virginia Act for Religious Freedom
1786

The nation which reposes on the pillow of political confidence, will sooner or later end its political existence in a deadly lethargy.

James Madison
Virginia Assembly
January 23, 1799

No man is good enough to govern another man without that other's consent.

Abraham Lincoln
Speech, Peoria, Illinois
October 16, 1854

I am for the people of the whole nation doing just as they please in all matters which concern the whole nation; for that of each part doing just as they choose in all matters which concern no other part; and for each individual doing just as he chooses in all matters which concern nobody else.

Abraham Lincoln
Speech
October 1, 1858

Those who deny freedom to others deserve it not for themselves. And, under a just God, cannot long retain it.

Abraham Lincoln
Letter, H. L. Pierce
April 6, 1859

In giving freedom to the slave we assure freedom to the free,—honorable alike in what we give and what we preserve.

Abraham Lincoln
Message, Congress
December 1, 1862

In their cry for freedom, it may truly be said, the voice of the people is the voice of God.

Grover Cleveland
Speech, Washington Inauguration Centennial, New York, New York
April 30, 1889

Here in America, where the tablets of human freedom were first handed down, their sacred word has been flouted. Today the stern task is before the Republican party to restore the Ark of that Covenant to the temple in Washington.

Herbert Hoover
Speech, Republican Convention, Cleveland, Ohio
1932

We stand committed to the proposition that freedom is not a half-and-half affair. If the average citizen is guaranteed equal opportunity in the polling place, he must have equal opportunity in the market place.

Franklin D. Roosevelt
Acceptance speech, Democratic National Convention, Philadelphia, Pennsylvania
June 27, 1936

We believe that the only whole man is a free man.

Franklin D. Roosevelt
Speech
October 2, 1940

The winds that blow through the wide sky in these mountains, the winds that sweep from Canada to Mexico, from the Pacific to the Atlantic—have always blown on free men.

Franklin D. Roosevelt
Speech
October 2, 1940

Freedom means the supremacy of human rights everywhere. Our support goes to those who struggle to gain those rights or keep them.

Franklin D. Roosevelt
Four Freedoms Speech
January 6, 1941

In the future days, which we seek to make secure, we look forward to a world founded upon four essential human freedoms.

The first is freedom of speech and expression—everywhere in the world.

The second is freedom of every person to worship God in his own way—everywhere in the world.

The third is freedom from want . . . everywhere in the world.

The fourth is freedom from fear . . . anywhere in the world.

Franklin D. Roosevelt
Four Freedoms Speech
January 6, 1941

In the long run our security and the world's hopes for peace lie not in measures of defense or in the control of weapons, but in the growth and expansion of freedom and self-government.

Harry S. Truman
Speech, Alexandria, Virginia
February 22, 1950

Freedom has never been an abstract idea to us here in the United States. It is real and concrete. It means not only political and civil rights; it means much more. It means a society in which man has a fair chance. It means an opportunity to do useful work. It means the right to an education. It means protection against economic hardship.

Harry S. Truman
Address, Independence, Missouri
November 6, 1950

Freedom is still expensive. It still costs money. It still costs blood. It still calls for courage and endurance, not only in soldiers, but in every man and woman who is free and who is determined to remain free.

Harry S. Truman
Speech, Washington, D.C.
July 4, 1951

America is best described by one word, freedom.

Dwight D. Eisenhower
Sixth annual message, Congress
January 9, 1958

In the long history of the world, only a few generations have been granted the role of defending freedom in its hour of maximum danger. I do not shrink from that responsibility—I welcome it. I do not believe that any of us would exchange places with any other people or any other generation. The energy, the faith, the devotion which we bring to this endeavor will light our country and all who serve it—and the glow from that fire can truly light the world.

John F. Kennedy
Inaugural address
January 20, 1961

Let every nation know, whether it wishes us well or ill, that we shall pay any price, bear any burden, meet any hardship, support any friend, oppose any foe to assure the survival and the success of liberty.

John F. Kennedy
Inaugural address
January 20, 1961

We know what works: Freedom works. We know what's right: Freedom is right. We know how to secure a more just and prosperous life for man on earth: through free markets, free speech, free elections and the exercise of free will unhampered by the state.

George Bush
Inaugural Address
January 20, 1989

Ironically, on the 200th anniversary of our Bill of Rights, we find free speech under assault throughout the United States, including on some college campuses. The notion of political correctness has ignited controversy across the land. And although the movement arises from the laudable desire to sweep away the debris of racism and sexism and hatred it replaces old prejudices with new ones. It declares certain topics off-limits, certain expressions off-limits, even certain gestures off-limits. What began as a crusade for civility has soured into a cause of conflict and even censorship. Disputants treat sheer force—getting their foes punished or expelled, for instance, as a substitute for the power of ideas.

George Bush
Commencement speech, University of Michigan
May 4, 1991

Friends

Let them come—let the whole hundred come on—I would resign the Presidency or lose my life sooner than I would desert my friend [Cabinet member Major John] Eaton or be forced to do an act that my conscience may disapprove.

Andrew Jackson
Told by Major Samuel Bradford to W. T. Barry
c. 1831

You know little of Andrew Jackson if you suppose him capable of consenting to . . . a humiliation of his friends by his enemies.

Andrew Jackson
Comment, rejecting the resignation of Martin Van
    Buren as Secretary of State
c. 1831

In this job I am not worried about my enemies. I can take care of them. It is my friends who are giving me trouble.

Warren G. Harding
Cited in Arthur Bernon Tourtellot, *The Presidents on
    the Presidency*

You must act in your friend's interest whether it pleases him or not; the object of love is to serve, not to win.

Woodrow Wilson
Baccalaureate address
May 9, 1907

[Alger] Hiss was learning what many people in politics had learned before him: those he thought were his best friends turned out to be the heaviest cross he had to bear.

Richard Nixon
Six Crises
1962

Future

I like the dreams of the future better than the history of the past.

Thomas Jefferson
Letter, John Adams
1816

But if your [America's] past is limited, your future is boundless.

Franklin Pierce
Inaugural address
March 4, 1853

I have no fears for the future of our country. It is bright with hope.

Herbert Hoover
Inaugural address
March 4, 1929

The only limit to our realization of tomorrow will be our doubts of today.

Franklin D. Roosevelt
Draft, Jefferson Day address (last written by F.D.R.)
April 13, 1945

We don't propose, like some people, to meet today's problems by saying they don't exist, and tomorrow's problems by wishing that tomorrow wouldn't come.

Harry S. Truman
Speech, Kansas City, Missouri
September 29, 1949

If anyone tells you that America's best days are behind her, they're looking the wrong way.

George Bush
State of the union address
January 29, 1991

G

James A. Garfield

Garfield has shown that he is not possessed of the backbone of an angleworm.

Ulysses S. Grant
Comment, Adam Badeau
1867

He is the ideal candidate because he is the ideal self-made man.

Rutherford B. Hayes
Cited in Richard Kenin and Justin Wintle, *The Dictionary of Biographical Quotations*
1880

Who of us, having heard him here or elsewhere speaking upon a question of great national concern, can forget the might and majesty, the force and directness, the grace and beauty of his utterances.

William McKinley
Cited in Richard Kenin and Justin Wintle, *The Dictionary of Biographical Quotations*
1880

Generals

It is unfortunate that heaven has not set its stamp on the forehead of those whom it has qualified for military achievement, that it has left us to draw for them in a lottery of so many blanks to a prize, and where the blank is to be manifested only by the public misfortunes.

Thomas Jefferson
Letter, John Armstrong
February 8, 1813

The creator has not thought proper to mark those in the forehead who are of stuff to make good generals. We are first, therefore, to seek them blindfold, and let them learn the trade at the expense of great losses.

Thomas Jefferson
Letter, General Baily
February 1813

The successful warrior is no longer regarded as entitled to the first place in the temple of fame.

William Henry Harrison
Letter, Simon Bolívar
September 27, 1829

From Caesar to Cromwell, and from Cromwell to Napoleon, . . . history presents the same solemn warning—beware of elevating to the highest civil trust the commander of your victorious armies.

James Buchanan
Speech, Greensburg, Pennsylvania
October 7, 1852

Only those generals who gain successes can set up dictators. What I now ask of you is military success, and I will risk the dictatorship.

Abraham Lincoln
Letter, Major-General J. Hooker
January 26, 1863

I didn't fire him [General MacArthur] because he was a dumb son of a bitch, although he was, but that's not against the law for generals. If it was, half to three-quarters of them would be in jail.

Harry S. Truman
Cited in Merle Miller, *Plain Speaking*

93

Germany

America . . . is the prize amateur nation of the world. Germany is the prize professional nation.

Woodrow Wilson
Speech, officers of the fleet
August 1917

The idea of dethroning the Hapsburgs and the Hohenzollerns makes me weary.

Warren G. Harding
New York Times
1917

On the morning of December 11 the Government of Germany, pursuing its course of world conquest, declared war against the United States. The long-known and the long-expected has thus taken place. The forces endeavoring to enslave the entire world now are moving toward this hemisphere. Never before has there been a greater challenge to life, liberty and civilization. Delay invites great danger. United effort by all of the peoples of the world who are determined to remain free will insure a world victory of the forces of justice and of righteousness over the forces of savagery and barbarism. Italy has declared war against the United States. I therefore request the Congress to recognize a state of war between the United States and Germany, and between the United States and Italy.

Franklin D. Roosevelt
War message, Congress
December 11, 1941

I hear it said that West Berlin is militarily untenable. And so, in fact, was Stalingrad. Any dangerous spot is tenable if men—brave men—will make it so.

John F. Kennedy
Speech, Berlin crisis
July 25, 1961

Those who threaten to unleash the forces of war on a dispute over West Berlin should recall the words of the ancient philosopher: "A man who causes fear cannot be free from fear."

John F. Kennedy
Speech, Berlin crisis
July 25, 1961

Government

Those who bear equally the burdens of government should equally participate of its benefits.

Thomas Jefferson
Address, Lord Dunmore
1775

Mankind when left to themselves, are unfit for their own Government.

George Washington
Letter, Henry Lee
October 31, 1786

The natural progress of things is for liberty to yield and government to gain ground.

Thomas Jefferson
Letter, Edward Carrington
May 27, 1788

What is the meaning of government? An institution to make people do their duty. A government leaving it to a man to do his duty, or not, as he pleases, would be a new species of government, or rather no government at all.

James Madison
Debates, Virginia Convention
June 14, 1788

Justice is the end of government. It is the end of civil society. It ever has been and ever will be pursued until it be obtained, or until liberty be lost in the pursuit.

James Madison
Federalist, LI
1788

But what is government itself, but the greatest of all reflections on human nature? If men were angels, no government would be necessary. If angels were to govern men, neither external nor internal controls on government would be necessary.

James Madison
Federalist, LI
1788

A good government implies two things: fidelity to the object of government, which is the happiness of the people; secondly, a knowledge of the means by which that object can be best attained.

James Madison
Federalist, LXII
1788

No government of human device and human administration can be perfect; . . . that which is the least imperfect is therefore the best government.

James Madison
Cited in Saul K. Padover, ed., *The Complete Madison: His Basic Writings*

It is substantially true, that virtue or morality is a necessary spring of popular government.

George Washington
Farewell address
September 17, 1796

The very idea of the power and the right of the people to establish government presupposes the duty of every individual to obey the established government. . . . [Remember] especially that for the efficient management of your common interests in a country so extensive as ours a government of as much vigor as is consistent with the perfect security of liberty is indispensable. Liberty itself will find in such a government, with powers properly distributed and adjusted, its surest guardian.

George Washington
Farewell address
September 17, 1796

It is not denied that there may be cases in which a respect to the general principles of liberty, the essential rights of the people, or the overruling sentiments of humanity, might require a government, whether new or old, to be treated as an illegitimate despotism.

James Madison
Letter, Thomas Jefferson
May 13, 1798

A wise and frugal government, which shall restrain men from injuring one another, shall leave them otherwise free to regulate their own pursuits of industry and improvement, and shall not take from the mouth of labor the bread it has earned. This is the sum of good government, and this is necessary to close the circle of our felicities.

Thomas Jefferson
First inaugural address
March 4, 1801

That government is the strongest of which every man feels himself a part.

Thomas Jefferson
Letter, H. D. Tiffin
1807

While all other sciences have advanced, that of government is at a standstill—little better understood, little better practiced now than three or four thousand years ago.

John Adams
Letter, Thomas Jefferson
July 9, 1813

The question before the human race is whether the God of nature shall govern the world by his own laws, or whether priests and kings shall rule it by fictitious miracles.

John Adams
Letter, Thomas Jefferson
June 20, 1815

The great object of . . . civil government is the improvement of the condition of those who are parties to the social compact.

John Quincy Adams
First annual message, Congress
December 6, 1825

All power in human hands is liable to be abused. In Governments independent of the people, the rights and interests of the whole may be sacrificed to the views of the Government. In Republics, where . . . the majority govern, a danger to the minority arises from . . . a sacrifice of their rights to the interests . . . of the majority. No form of government, therefore, can be a perfect guard against the abuse of power.

James Madison
Letter, Thomas Ritchie
December 18, 1825

As long as our Government is administered for the good of the people, and is regulated by their will; as long as it secures to us the rights of persons and of property, liberty of conscience and of the press, it will be worth defending.

Andrew Jackson
First inaugural address
March 4, 1829

There are no necessary evils in government. Its evils exist only in its abuses. If it would confine itself to equal protection, and, as Heaven does its rains, shower its favors alike on the high and the low, the rich and the poor, it would be an unqualified blessing.

Andrew Jackson
Veto, Bank Bill
July 10, 1832

To frame a complete system of government . . . [is] an attempt as absurd as to build a tree or manufacture an opinion.

Martin Van Buren
Inquiry into the origin and course of political parties in the United States

I believe and I say it is true Democratic feeling, that all the measures of Government are directed to the purpose of making the rich richer and the poor poorer.

William Henry Harrison
Speech
October 1, 1840

A decent and manly examination of the acts of Government should be not only tolerated, but encouraged.

William Henry Harrison
Inaugural address
March 4, 1841

Sir, I wish you to understand the true principles of the government. I wish them carried out. I ask nothing more.

William Henry Harrison
Comment, on his deathbed
1841

Restraint, restraint . . . this Federal Government is nothing but a system of restraints from beginning to end.

James Buchanan
Cited in Philip S. Klein, *President James Buchanan: A Biography*
c. 1844

The goal to strive for is a poor government but a rich people.

Andrew Johnson
c. 1845

The legitimate object of government is to do for a community of people whatever they need to have done, but cannot do at all, or cannot so well do, for themselves, in their separate and individual capacities.

Abraham Lincoln
"Fragment on Government"
July 1, 1854

Perpetuity is implied, if not expressed, in the fundamental law of all national governments. It is safe to assert that no government proper ever had a provision in its organic law for its own termination.

Abraham Lincoln
First inaugural address
March 4, 1861

I am for this government above all earthly possessions and if it perish I do not want to survive it. I am for it though slavery should be struck from existence—I say, in the face of Heaven, Give me my Government and let the Negro go.

Andrew Johnson
Comment, soldiers in camp
1862

It is not always in the power of governments to enlarge or restrict the scope of moral results which follow the policies that they may deem it necessary for the public safety from time to time to adopt.

Abraham Lincoln
Open Letter, working men of Manchester, England
January 19, 1863

It has long been a grave question whether any government, not too strong for the liberties of its people, can be strong enough to maintain its existence in great emergencies.

Abraham Lincoln
Open Letter
November 10, 1864

The Theory of government changes with general progress.

Ulysses S. Grant
Second inaugural address
March 4, 1883

Good government, and especially the government of which every American citizen boasts, has for its objects the protection of every person within its care in the greatest liberty consistent with the good order of society, and his perfect security in the least possible diminution for public needs.

Grover Cleveland
Message, Congress
December 6, 1886

The government is us; we are the government, you and I.

Theodore Roosevelt
Speech, Asheville, North Carolina
December 5, 1905

We have passed beyond the times of . . . the laissez-faire school which believes that the government ought to do nothing but run a police force.

William Howard Taft
Speech, Milwaukee, Wisconsin
September 17, 1909

There is no indispensable man. The Government will not collapse and go to pieces if any one of the gentlemen who are seeking to be entrusted with its guidance should be left at home.

Woodrow Wilson
1912

Government is merely an attempt to express the conscience of everybody, the average conscience of the nation, in the rules that everybody is commanded to obey. That is all it is.

Woodrow Wilson
Speech, Washington, D.C.
January 29, 1915

No man ever saw a government. I live in the midst of the government of the United States, but I never saw the government of the United States. Its personnel extends through all the nations, and across the seas, and into every corner of the world.

Woodrow Wilson
Speech, Pittsburgh, Pennsylvania
January 29, 1916

The firm basis of government is justice, not pity.

Woodrow Wilson
First inaugural address
March 4, 1913

The whole art and practice of government consists, not in moving individuals, but in moving masses.

Woodrow Wilson
Speech, Atlantic City, New Jersey
September 8, 1916

Our most dangerous tendency is to expect too much of government, and at the same time do for it too little.

Warren G. Harding
Inaugural address
March 4, 1921

You cannot extend the mastery of the government over the daily working life of a people without at the same time making it the master of the people's souls and thoughts.

Herbert Hoover
American Individualism
1922

The government of the United States is a device for maintaining in perpetuity the rights of the people, with the ultimate extinction of all privileged classes.

Calvin Coolidge
Address, Philadelphia, Pennsylvania
September 25, 1924

I came to have a good working knowledge of the practical side of government. I understood that it consisted of restraints which the people had imposed upon themselves in order to promote the common welfare.

Calvin Coolidge
The Autobiography of Calvin Coolidge
1929

Every time the government is forced to act, we lose something in self-reliance, character and initiative.

Herbert Hoover
Speech
1929

Our government is not the master but the creature of the people. The duty of the State toward the citizens is the duty of a servant to its master. The people have created it; the people, by common consent, permit its continual existence.

Franklin D. Roosevelt
Speech, New York State Legislature
August 28, 1931

The highest form of self-government is the voluntary cooperation within our people.

Herbert Hoover
Fourth annual message, Congress
December 6, 1932

The American form of government [is] a three horse team provided by the Constitution to the American people so that their field might be plowed. The three horses are, of course, the three branches of government—the Congress, the Executive and the Courts. . . . Those who have intimated that the President of the United States is trying to drive the team, overlook the simple fact that the President of the United States, as Chief Executive, is himself one of the three horses.

Franklin D. Roosevelt
Fireside chat
March 9, 1937

Every segment of our population, and every individual, has a right to expect from his government a Fair Deal.

Harry S. Truman
Speech, Congress
September 6, 1945

The basis of effective government is public confidence.

John F. Kennedy
Campaign speech prepared for delivery in Dallas, Texas
November 22, 1963

When there is a lack of humor in government, the morals of the whole people are poisoned.

Herbert Hoover
Quoted in the *New York Times* magazine
August 9, 1964

Government is not an enemy of the people. Government is the people themselves.

Lyndon B. Johnson
Speech, University of New Mexico, Albuquerque, New Mexico
October 28, 1964

If government is to serve any purpose it is to do for others what they are unable to do for themselves.

Lyndon B. Johnson
Remarks, Internal Revenue Service
1966

The people are fed up with government. They think it doesn't work. And they are right.

Richard Nixon
Reader's Digest
April 1972

The challenge for us in Government is to be worthy of [the people]—to make Government a help, not a hindrance to our people in the challenging days ahead.

Ronald Reagan
State of the union address
January 25, 1983

Does Government have a place? Yes. Government is part of the nation of communities—not the whole, just a part. And I don't hate government. A government that remembers that the people are its master is a good and needed thing.

George Bush
Acceptance speech, Republican Convention
August 18, 1988

Government Ownership and Regulation

Bear in mind that you may labor and toil, in the whirl and excitement of business, to build new warehouses, and add to the city's wealth and to your own, but that, while you thus build, ignorant, negligent, or corrupt men among your lawmakers can easily and stealthily pull down. Political duty and selfish interests lead in the same direction, and a neglect of this duty will, I believe, bring a sure punishment.

Grover Cleveland
Evacuation Day Celebration, New York, New York
November 26, 1883

I do not believe in government ownership of anything which can with propriety be left in private hands, and in particular I should most strenuously object to government ownership of the railroads.

Theodore Roosevelt
Speech, Raleigh, North Carolina
October 19, 1905

Under government ownership corruption can flourish just as rankly as under private ownership.

Theodore Roosevelt
Letter, Lincoln Steffens
June 1908

It is a false liberalism that interprets itself into the government operation of commercial business. Every step of bureaucratizing of the business of our country poisons the very roots of liberalism—that is, political equality, free speech, free assembly, free press, and equality of opportunity. It is the road not to more liberty, but to less liberty.

Herbert Hoover
Speech, New York, New York, on rugged individualism
October 22, 1928

Commercial business requires a concentration of responsibility. Self-government requires decentralization and many checks and balances to safeguard liberty. Our Government to succeed in business would need to become in effect a despotism. There at once begins the destruction of self-government.

Herbert Hoover
Speech, New York, New York
October 22, 1928

It is just as important that business keep out of government as that government keep out of business.

Herbert Hoover
Speech, New York, New York
October 22, 1928

I am firmly opposed to the Government entering any business the major purpose of which is competition with our citizens.

Herbert Hoover
Message, Senate, Veto, Muscle Shoals Bill
March 3, 1931

I hesitate to contemplate the future of our institutions, of our government, and of our country if the preoccupation of its officials is to be no longer the promotion of justice and equal opportunity but is to be devoted to barter in the markets. That is not liberalism, it is degeneration.

Herbert Hoover
Veto, Muscle Shoals Bill
March 3, 1931

The moment the Government participates, it becomes a competitor with the people. As a competitor it becomes at once a tyranny in whatever direction it may touch.

Herbert Hoover
Fourth annual message, Congress
December 6, 1932

Government enterprise is the most inefficient and costly way of producing jobs.

Richard Nixon
The Memoirs of Richard Nixon
1978

Ulysses S. Grant

He is a scientific Goth, resembling Alaric, destroying the country as he goes and delivering the people over to starvation. Nor does he bury his dead, but leaves them to rot on the battlefields.

John Tyler
Letter, Sterling Prince
June 7, 1864

When Grant once gets possession of a place, he holds on to it as if he had inherited it.

Abraham Lincoln
Letter, General Benjamin Butler
June 22, 1864

I can't spare the man; he fights.

Abraham Lincoln
Cited in Richard Kenin and Justin Wintle, *The Dictionary of Biographical Quotations*

Great Britain

There seems to be a direct and formal design on foot [by Great Britain] to enslave all America. . . . The first step that is intended seems to be an entire subversion of the whole system of our fathers, by the introduction of canon and feudal law into America.

John Adams
"Dissertation on the Canon and the Feudal Law"
August 1765

The thought that we might be driven to the sad Necessity of breaking our Connection with G[reat] B[ritain] exclusive of the Carnage & Destruction which it was easy to see must attend a separation, always gave me a great deal of grief. And even now, I would chearfully retire from public life forever, renounce all Chance for Profits or Honours from the public, nay I would chearfully contribute my little Property to obtain Peace and Liberty. But all these must go and my life too before I can surrender the Right of my Country to a Free Constitution.

John Adams
Letter, Abigail Adams
October 7, 1775

The sun of her glory is fast descending to the horizon.

Thomas Jefferson
"Notes on Virginia"
1782

England is a nation which nothing but views of interest can govern.

Thomas Jefferson
Letter, James Madison
1785

Great Britain's governing principles are conquest, colonialization, commerce, monopoly.

Thomas Jefferson
Letter, William Carmichael
1790

The day that France takes possession of New Orleans . . . we must marry ourselves to the British fleet and nation.

Thomas Jefferson
1802

A pirate spreading misery and ruin over the face of the ocean.

Thomas Jefferson
Letter, Walter Jones
1810

England presents a singular phenomenon of an honest people whose constitution, from its nature, must render their government forever dishonest.

Thomas Jefferson
Letter, James Ronaldson
1810

As for France and England, with all their preeminence in science, the one is a den of robbers, and the other of pirates. And if science produces no better fruits than tyranny, murder, rapine and destitution of national morality, I would rather wish our country to be ignorant, honest and estimable, as our neighboring savages are.

Thomas Jefferson
Letter, John Adams
January 21, 1812

I consider [the English] government as the most flagitius which has existed since the days of Philip of Macedon, whom they make their model. It is not only founded in corruption itself, but insinuates the same poison into the bowels of every other, corrupts its councils, nourishes factions, stirs up revolutions, and places its own happiness in fomenting commotions and civil wars among others, thus rendering itself truly the *hostis humani generis*.

Thomas Jefferson
Letter, John Adams
1816

The extremes of opulence and of want are more remarkable, and more constantly obvious, in this country than in any other that I ever saw.

John Quincy Adams
Diary
November 8, 1816

Youth at the prow, and pleasure at the helm.

Martin Van Buren
Comment, on England under the new queen, 18-year-old Victoria
December 1837

War is a blessing compared with national degredation. . . . To prevent war with England a bold and undaunted front must be exposed. England with all her boast dare not go to war.

Andrew Jackson
Letter, James Polk, Oregon dispute
May 2, 1845

I remarked to him that the only way to treat John Bull was to look him straight in the eye . . . if Congress faltered or hesitated in their course, John Bull would immediately become arrogant and more grasping in his demands . . . such had been the history of the British nation in all their contests with other powers for the last two hundred years.

James K. Polk
The Diary of James K. Polk
January 4, 1846

An Englishman who was wrecked on a strange shore and wandering along the coast came to a gallows with a victim hanging on it, and fell down on his knees and thanked God that he at last beheld a sign of civilization.

James Garfield
Speech, House of Representatives
June 15, 1870

England and the United States are natural allies, and should be the best of friends.

Ulysses S. Grant
Personal Memoirs of U.S. Grant
1885

The trouble is that when you sit around a table with a Britisher he usually gets 80 percent of the deal and you get what's left.

Franklin D. Roosevelt
Cited in John Morton Blum, *From the Morgenthau Diaries*, vol. I

In the dark days and darker nights when England stood alone—and most men save Englishmen despaired of England's life—he mobilized the English language and sent it into battle. The incandescent quality of his words illuminated the courage of his countrymen.

John F. Kennedy
Speech, conferring honorary citizenship on Winston Churchill
April 9, 1963

H

Happiness

Our greatest happiness . . . does not depend
on the condition of life in which chance
has placed us, but is always the result of a
good conscience, good health, occupation
and freedom in all just pursuits.

Thomas Jefferson
"Notes on Virginia"
1782

He is happiest of whom the world says
least, good or bad.

Thomas Jefferson
Letter, John Adams
1786

It is neither wealth nor splendor, but
tranquility and occupation, which give
happiness.

Thomas Jefferson
Letter, Mrs. A. S. Marks
1788

Warren G. Harding

He has a bungalow mind.

Woodrow Wilson
Cited in Thomas A. Bailey, *Woodrow Wilson and the
    Great Betrayal*

Benjamin Harrison

My chances of going to the moon and of
donning a silk gown at the hands of
President Harrison are about equal.

William Howard Taft
Letter, Alphonso Taft
August 24, 1889

William Henry Harrison

Harrison comes in upon a hurricane; God
grant he may not go out upon a wreck!

John Quincy Adams
Diary, vol. 1
Cited in Richard Kenin and Justin Wintle, *The Dic-
    tionary of Biographical Quotations*

[An] active but shallow mind, a political
adventurer not without talents but self-
sufficient, vain and indiscreet.

John Quincy Adams
Cited in Richard Kenin and Justin Wintle, *The Dic-
    tionary of Biographical Quotations*

The President is the most extraordinary
man I ever saw. He does not seem to realize
the vast importance of his elevation. . . . He
is as tickled with the Presidency as a young
man with a new bonnet.

Martin Van Buren
Cited in A. Steinberg, *The First Ten*

History

We can no longer say there is nothing new
under the sun. For this whole chapter in
the history of man is new.

Thomas Jefferson
Letter, Doctor Joseph Priestly
March 21, 1801

History, in general, only informs us what
bad government is.

Thomas Jefferson
Letter, John Norvell
June 14, 1807

[I prefer] the dreams of the future better than the history of the past.

Thomas Jefferson
Letter, John Adams
August 1, 1816

To write history requires a whole life of observation, of inquiry, of labor and correction. Its materials are not to be found among the ruins of a decayed memory.

Thomas Jefferson
Letter, Doctor J. B. Stuart
May 10, 1817

A morsel of genuine history is a thing so rare as to be always valuable.

Thomas Jefferson
Letter, John Adams
1817

The public history of all countries, and all ages, is but a sort of mask, richly colored. The interior working of the machinery must be foul.

John Quincy Adams
Diary
November 9, 1822

Man is fed with fables through life, and leaves it in the belief he knows something of what has been passing, when in truth he has known nothing but what has passed under his own eye.

Thomas Jefferson
Letter, Thomas Cooper
1823

It is a base untruth to say that happy is the nation that has no history. Thrice happy is the nation that has a glorious history.

Theodore Roosevelt
Speech, Chicago, Illinois
April 10, 1899

The history of free men is never really written by chance but by choice—their choice.

Dwight D. Eisenhower
Speech, Pittsburgh, Pennsylvania
October 9, 1956

Let us resolve to be masters, not the victims, of our history, controlling our own destiny without giving way to blind suspicions and emotions.

John F. Kennedy
Speech, University of Maine, Orono, Maine
October 1963

History makes the man more than the man makes history.

Richard Nixon
The Memoirs of Richard Nixon
1978

Communism held history captive for years, and it suspended ancient disputes and it suppressed ethnic rivalries, nationalistic aspirations and old prejudices. As it has dissolved, suspended hatreds have sprung to life . . . . this revival of history ushers in a new era teeming with opportunities and perils . . . .

George Bush
Address to the United Nations
September 23, 1991

Honesty

The first of qualities for a great statesman is to be honest. And if it were possible that this opinion were an error, I should rather carry it with me to my grave than to believe that a man cannot be a statesman without being dishonest.

John Adams
Letter, William Eustis, Boston, Massachusetts
June 22, 1809

To believe all men honest would be folly. To believe none so, is something worse.

John Quincy Adams
Letter, William Eustis, Boston Massachusetts
June 22, 1809

Men are disposed to live honestly, if the means of doing so are open to them.

Thomas Jefferson
Letter, M. de Marbois
1817

No public man can be just a little crooked.

Herbert Hoover
Cited in Bruce Bohle, *The Home Book of American Quotations*

Herbert Hoover

Herbert Hoover is certainly a wonder, and I wish we could make him president.

Franklin D. Roosevelt
Comment, Josephus Daniels
c. 1918

That man has offered me unsolicited advice for six years, all of it bad.

Calvin Coolidge
Comment
c. 1929

As for Mr. Hoover . . . I hold him in very high regard. I think he is a great American and will some day be so recognized even by the people who have defamed him.

Harry S. Truman
Comment, Admiral Lewis Strauss
1948

Hope

There is nothing . . . in this world so inspiring as the possibilities that lie locked up in the head and breast of a young man.

James Garfield
Cited in John M. Taylor, *Garfield of Ohio: The Available Man*

Hope has become the secret weapon of the forces of liberation.

Harry S. Truman
Address, Joint Session of Congress
April 16, 1945

Unfortunately, many Americans live on the outskirts of hope—some because of their poverty, and some because of their color, and all too many because of both.

Lyndon B. Johnson
State of the union address
January 8, 1964

We have discovered that every child who learns, and every man who finds work, and every sick body that is made whole—like a candle added to an altar—brightens the hope of all the faithful.

Lyndon B. Johnson
Inaugural address
January 20, 1965

The future holds little hope for any government where the present holds no hope for the people.

Lyndon B. Johnson
Speech, signing of Immigration Bill, Liberty Island, New York, New York
October 3, 1965

Millions of our neighbors are without work. It is up to us to see they are not without hope.

Ronald Reagan
State of the union address
January 25, 1983

Yet, to hope is to believe in humanity; and in its future. Hope remains the highest reality, the age-old power; hope is at the root of all the great ideas and causes that have bettered the lot of humankind across the centuries.

Ronald Reagan
Speech, United Nations General Assembly, New York, New York
September 22, 1986

I refuse to be part of a generation that celebrates the death of communism abroad with the loss of the American dream at home.

Bill Clinton
Campaign Address
October 3, 1991

I

Ideas

He who receives an idea from me, receives instruction himself without lessening mine; as he who lights his taper at mine receives light without darkening mine.

Thomas Jefferson
Cited in Bruce Bohle, *The Home Book of American Quotations*

Integrity of views more than their soundness, is the basis of esteem.

Thomas Jefferson
Letter, Elbridge Gerry
April 22, 1800

The great warriors of the world.

James A Garfield
Cited in Eugene E. Brussell, *Dictionary of Quotable Definitions*

You cannot stop the spread of an idea by passing a law against it.

Harry S. Truman
Address, Swedish Pioneer Centennial Association, Chicago, Illinois
June 4, 1948

Ignorance

I think it is Montaigne who has said, that ignorance is the softest pillow on which a man can rest his head. I am sure it is true as to everything political, and shall endeavor to estrange myself to everything of that character.

Thomas Jefferson
Letter, Edmund Randolph
February 3, 1794

If a state expects to be ignorant and free, in a state of civilization, it expects what never was and never will be.

Thomas Jefferson
Letter, Colonel Charles Yancey
January 6, 1816

Thomas Jefferson said no nation can be both ignorant and free. Today no nation can be both ignorant and great.

Lyndon B. Johnson
State of the union address
January 4, 1965

Immigrants and Immigration

Freedom of emigration is favorable to morals.

James Madison
National Gazette
November 19, 1791

The Alien bill proposed in the Senate is a monster that must forever disgrace its parents.

James Madison
Letter, Thomas Jefferson
May 20, 1798

I have no hostility to foreigners. . . . Having witnessed their deplorable condition in the old country, God forbid I should add to their sufferings by refusing them an asylum in this.

Millard Fillmore
Speech, Newburgh, New York
June 1856

There is no danger of having too many immigrants of the right kind.

Theodore Roosevelt
Annual message, Congress
December 5, 1905

There can be no fifty-fifty Americanism in this country. There is room here for only one-hundred percent Americanism.

Theodore Roosevelt
Speech, Saratoga, New York
July 19, 1918

They saw this star of the West rising over the peoples of the world, and they said, "That is the star of hope and the star of salvation. We will set our footsteps towards the West, and join that body of men whom God has blessed with the vision of liberty."

Woodrow Wilson
Speech, Des Moines, Iowa
September 6, 1919

Remember always that all of us, and you and I especially, are descended from immigrants and revolutionists.

Franklin D. Roosevelt
Speech, Daughters of the American Revolution,
    reported in *New York Times*
April 28, 1938

[W]e are—one and all—immigrants or sons and daughters of immigrants.

Dwight D. Eisenhower
State of the union address
February 20, 1953

Over the years the ancestors of all of us—some 42 million human beings—have migrated to these shores. The fundamental, long-time American attitude has been to ask not where a person comes from but what are his personal qualities. On this basis men and women migrated from every quarter of the globe. By their hard work and their enormously varied talents they hewed a great nation out of a wilderness. By their dedication to liberty and equality, they created a society reflecting man's most cherished ideas.

Lyndon B. Johnson
Message, Congress
January 13, 1965

From this day forth those wishing to immigrate to America shall be admitted on the basis of their skills and their close relationship to those already here. This is a simple test, and it is a fair test. Those who can contribute most to this country—to its growth, to its strength, to its spirit—will be the first that are admitted to this land.

Lyndon B. Johnson
Speech, signing Immigration Bill, Liberty Island,
    New York
October 3, 1965

Impeachment

Experience has already shown that the impeachment the Constitution has provided is not even a scarecrow.

Thomas Jefferson
Letter, Spencer Roane
1819

I have come to the conclusion that the public interest is no longer served by repetition of my previously expressed belief that on the basis of all the evidence known to me and to the American people, the President [Richard Nixon] is not guilty of an impeachable offense.

Gerald Ford
Speech
August 5, 1974

Independence

Nothing short of independence, it appears to me, can possibly do. A peace on other terms would, if I may be allowed the expression, be a peace of war.

George Washington
Letter, John Banister
April 21, 1778

If ever there was a holy war, it was that which saved our liberties and gave us independence.

Thomas Jefferson
Letter, J. W. Eppes
1813

Our forefathers brought with them the germ of Independence in the principle of self-taxation.

James Madison
Letter, John Adams
August 7, 1818

Independence forever!

John Quincy Adams
Comment, on his deathbed
July 4, 1826

Individualism

I am of a sect by myself, as far as I know.

Thomas Jefferson
Letter, Ezra Stiles
1819

Our individualism is in our very nature. It is based on conviction born of experience.

Herbert Hoover
American Individualism
1922

When the war closed . . . we were challenged with a peace-time choice between the American system of rugged individualism and a European philosophy of diametrically opposed doctrines—doctrines of paternalism and state socialism.

Herbert Hoover
Speech, New York, New York
October 22, 1928

We cannot expect that all nations will adopt like systems, for conformity is the jailer of freedom and the enemy of growth.

John F. Kennedy
Address, United Nations General Assembly
September 25, 1961

We will have differences. Men of different ancestries, men of different tongues, men of different environments, men of different geographies do not see everything alike. If we did we would all want the same wife—and that would be a problem, wouldn't it!

Lyndon B. Johnson
Speech, Washington, D.C.
February 11, 1964

Industry

I am glad that [Massachusetts] has stretched forth her iron arms to the great West and to the Canadas.

Millard Fillmore
Speech, New England
1851

Slavery exists. It is black in the South, and white in the North.

Andrew Johnson
Speech, Nashville, Tennessee
January 8, 1856

The busy hum of industry is heard on all sides, and the worshippers in this temple have laid upon its altars their choicest offerings for the admiration of the world.

Millard Fillmore
Speech, Buffalo, New York
June 27, 1862

Yes, we are going to invest in America. This administration is determined to encourage the creation of capital, capital of all kinds. Physical capital; everything from our farms and factories to our workshops and production lines, all that is needed to produce and deliver quality goods and services. Intellectual capital: the source of ideas that spark tomorrow's products. And of course, our human capital: the talented work force that we'll need to compete in the global market.

George Bush
State of the union address
January 31, 1990

Internal Improvements

These ponds! Lake Erie, and Lake Ontario, and Lake Huron, and even Lake Superior, cannot be taken under the care of the constitution. . . . I believe the constitution is not a salt water animal. . . . It can live as well in fresh as in salt water.

Millard Fillmore
Protesting President Polk's veto of river and harbor
    improvements in the Great Lakes area
Buffalo Express
October 2, 1846

The extravagant expenditure of public money is an evil not to be measured by the value of that money to the people who are taxed for it.

Chester A. Arthur
Veto, River and Harbor Bill
August 1, 1882

International Organizations

A steadfast concert for peace can never be maintained except by a partnership of democratic nations. No autocratic government could be trusted to keep faith within it or observe its covenants.

Woodrow Wilson
Message, Congress
April 2, 1917

A general association of nations must be formed under specific covenants for the purpose of affording mutual guarantees of political independence and territorial integrity to great and small states alike.

Woodrow Wilson
Address, Congress
January 8, 1918

If the League of Nations means that we will have to go to war every time a Jugoslav wishes to slap a Czecho-slav in the face, then I won't follow them.

Theodore Roosevelt
Comment, his doctor
1918

I have come to fight a cause and that cause is greater than the U.S. Senate!

Woodrow Wilson
Cross country tour to create support for ratification of the Covenant of the League of Nations
September 1919

And the glory of the Armies and Navies of the United States is gone like a dream in the night, and there ensues upon it, in the suitable darkness of the night, the nightmare of dread which lay upon the nations before this war came; and there will come sometime, in the vengeful Providence of God, another struggle in which, not a few hundred thousand fine men from America will have to die, but as

many millions as are necessary to accomplish the final freedom of the peoples of the world.

Woodrow Wilson
Speech, St. Louis, Missouri
September 5, 1919

My soul yearns for peace. My heart is anguished by the sufferings of war. My spirit is eager to serve. My passion is for justice over force. My hope is in the great court.

Warren G. Harding
Speech, St. Louis, Missouri
1923

The more I have seen of the conduct of our foreign relations the more I am convinced that we are better off out of the League.

Calvin Coolidge
The Autobiography of Calvin Coolidge
1929

We have the right to say that there shall not be an organization of world affairs which permits us no choice but to turn our countries into barracks unless we are to be vassals of some conquering empire.

Franklin D. Roosevelt
Hands Off the Western Hemisphere speech, Pan-American Day
April 14, 1939

I suggest the United Nations should be reorganized without the communist nations in it.

Herbert Hoover
Speech, Newspaper Publishers Association
April 1950

But in the creation of the League itself, the Allied Powers made sure that they would surrender nothing, change nothing. They did it by securing effective control of the Council by certain permanent members from the Great Powers and the requirement of unanimous vote on major issues.

Herbert Hoover
The Memoirs of Herbert Hoover: Years of Adventure 1874-1920
1951

Our strength and our hope is the United Nations, and I see little merit in the impatience of those who would abandon this imperfect world instrument because they dislike our imperfect world.

John F. Kennedy
State of the union address
January 29, 1961

The members of the United Nations must be aligned on the side of justice rather than injustice, peace rather than aggression, human dignity rather than subjugation....
What harms the Charter harms peace.

Ronald Reagan
Speech, United Nations General Assembly, New York, New York
September 26, 1983

The founders of the United Nations expected that member nations would behave and vote as individuals after they had weighed the merits of an issue—rather like a great, global town meeting. The emergence of blocks and the polarization of the United Nations undermine all that this organization initially valued.

Ronald Reagan
Speech, United Nations General Assembly, New York, New York
September 26, 1983

What is at stake is more than one small country [Kuwait]; it is a big idea—a new world order where diverse nations are drawn together in a common cause to achieve the universal aspirations of mankind: peace and security, freedom and the rule of law. Such is a world worthy of our struggle and worthy of our children's future.

George Bush
State of the union address
January 29, 1991

Isolationism

Against the insidious wiles of foreign influence . . . the jealousy of a free people ought to be *constantly* awake. . . . But that jealousy, to be useful, must be impartial,

else it becomes the instrument of the very influence to be avoided, instead of a defense against it.

George Washington
Farewell address
September 17, 1796

[Are we] to sit down in our isolation and recognize no obligation?

William McKinley
Speech, Piedmont Park, Atlanta, Georgia
1898

From the time of the Mexican War up to 1898 we had lived by ourselves in a spirit of isolation.

William McKinley
Comment, Charles Dawes and George Cortelyou
1899

We have learned that we cannot live alone, at peace; that our well-being is dependent on the well-being of other nations, far away. We have learned that we must live as men *and* not as ostriches, not as dogs in the manger.

Franklin D. Roosevelt
Fourth inaugural address
January 20, 1945

Isolationism is the road to war. Worse than that, isolationism is the road to defeat in war.

Harry S. Truman
Address, St. Louis, Missouri
June 10, 1950

There can be no such thing as Fortress America. If ever we were reduced to the isolationism implied by that term we would occupy a prison, not a fortress.

Dwight D. Eisenhower
State of the union address
January 9, 1959

This is a fact: Strength in the pursuit of peace is no vice; isolation in the pursuit of security is no virtue.

George Bush
State of the union message
January 28, 1992

J

Andrew Jackson

I feel much alarmed at the prospect of seeing General Jackson President. He is the most unfit man I know for such a place.

Thomas Jefferson
Cited in Eugene E. Brussell, *Dictionary of Quotable Definitions*

A barbarian who cannot write a sentence of grammar and can hardly spell his own name.

John Quincy Adams
Comment, Josiah Quincy, president of Harvard, on refusing to confer an honorary doctor of laws on Andrew Jackson
June 1833

Incompetent both by his ignorance and by the fury of his passions. . . . He will be surrounded and governed by incompetent men, whose ascendancy over him will be secured by their servility and who will bring to the Government of the nation nothing by their talent for intrigue.

John Quincy Adams
Cited in Richard Kenin and Justin Wintle, *The Dictionary of Biographical Quotations*

Never could it have been said with as much truth that heaven and earth and the other place too are raised to defeat him.

Martin Van Buren
Letter, John Van Buren
February 10, 1834

The Gen'l is in fine health and rampant spirits. If Louis Philippe were in striking distance he would hold his throne by a brittle tenure.

Martin Van Buren
Letter, William C. Rives
December 3, 1834

Mr. Douglas, I desire you to remember that no Democrat ever yet differed from an Administration of his own choice without being crushed.

Mr. President, I wish you to remember that General Jackson is dead!

Exchange between James Buchanan and Stephen Douglas, White House
December 3, 1858

An overwhelming proportion of the material power of the Nation was against him. The great media for the dissemination of information and the molding of public opinion fought him. Haughty and sterile intellectualism opposed him. Hollow and outworn traditionalism shook a trembling finger at him—all but the people of the United States.

Franklin D. Roosevelt
Jackson Day Address
January 8, 1936

113

Japan

I should hang my head in shame if I were capable of discriminating against a Japanese general or admiral, statesman, philanthropist or artist, because he and I have different shades of skin.

Theodore Roosevelt
Comment
1904

My most cherished hope is that after Japan joins the Nazis in utter defeat, neither my country nor yours [England] need ever again summon its sons and daughters from their peaceful pursuits to face the tragedies of battle.

Dwight D. Eisenhower
Speech, London, England
June 12, 1945

The United States can get out of Japanese waters, but others will still fish there.

Richard Nixon
Comment, Chou En-lai
February 1972

Thomas Jefferson

Jefferson thinks he shall . . . get a Reputation of a humble, modest, meek man, wholly without ambition or vanity. He may even have deceived himself into this Belief. But if a Prospect opens, the World will see and he will feel, that he is as ambitious as Oliver Cromwell though no soldier.

John Adams
Letter, John Quincy Adams
January 3, 1794

His genius is of the old French school. It conceives better than it combines.

John Quincy Adams
Diary
November 23, 1804

You should remember that Jefferson was but a boy to me. I was at least ten years older than him in age and more than twenty years older than him in politics.

John Adams
Letter, Banjamin Rush
October 25, 1809

I held levees once a week, that all my time might not be wasted by idle visits. Jefferson's whole eight years was a levee.

John Adams
Letter, Benjamin Rush
December 25, 1811

His talents were of the highest order, his ambition transcendent, and his disposition to intrigue irrepressible.

John Quincy Adams
Parties in the United States
c. January 1822

It may be said of him as has been said of others that he was a "walking library," and what can be said of but few such prodigies, that Genius of Philosophy ever walked hand in hand with him.

James Madison
Letter, Samuel Harrison Smith
November 1826

If not an absolute atheist, he had no belief in a future existence. All his ideas of obligation or retribution were under no stronger guarantee than the laws of the land and the opinions of the world. The tendency of this condition upon a mind of great compass and powerful resources is to produce insincerity and duplicity, which were his besetting sins through life.

John Quincy Adams
Diary
January 11, 1831

He saw the gross inconsistency between the principles of the Declaration of Independence and the fact of negro slavery, and he could not, or would not, prostitute the faculties of his mind to the vindication of that slavery which from his soul he abhorred. Mr. Jefferson had not the spirit of martyrdom. He would have introduced a flaming denunciation of slavery into the Declaration of Independence, but the discretion of his colleagues struck it out.

John Quincy Adams
Diary
January 27, 1831

His success through a long life, and especially from his entrance upon the office of Secretary of State under Washington until he reached the Presidential Chair, seems, to my imperfect vision, a slur upon the moral government of the world.

John Quincy Adams
Diary
July 29, 1836

The principles of Jefferson are the definitions and axioms of free society.

Abraham Lincoln
Letter, H. L. Pierce
April 6, 1859

The immortality of Jefferson does not lie in any one of his achievements, but in his attitude toward mankind.

Woodrow Wilson
Speech, Washington, D.C.
April 13, 1916

The trouble with us is that we talk about Jefferson but do not follow him. In his theory that the people should manage their government, and not be managed by it, he was everlastingly right.

Calvin Coolidge
The Autobiography of Calvin Coolidge
1929

John Adams and Thomas Jefferson were political enemies, but they became fast friends. And when they passed away on the same day, the last words of one of them was, "The country is safe. Jefferson still lives." And the last words of the other was, "John Adams will see that things go forward."

Harry S. Truman
Informal remarks, Quincy, Massachusetts
October 28, 1948

I think it's the most extraordinary collection of talent, of human knowledge, that has ever been gathered together at the White House—with the possible exception of when Thomas Jefferson dined alone.

John F. Kennedy
At a White House dinner for Nobel Prize winners
April 29, 1962

Andrew Johnson

I would impeach him because he is such an infernal liar.

Ulysses S. Grant
Comment, Senator Henderson
1868

Lyndon Johnson

Above all Johnson wanted to be loved—to earn not only the approval but also the affection of every American.

Richard M. Nixon
The Memoirs of Richard Nixon
1978

I think Lyndon Johnson died of a broken heart, physically and mentally. He was an enormously able and proud man. He desperately wanted, and expected, to be a great President. He drove himself to outdo his predecessor.

Richard Nixon
The Memoirs of Richard Nixon
1978

Seeking both guns and butter is a policy that works only in the very short term. I think that Johnson belatedly came to understand this, because through the four years of my first term I cannot recall an instance when he urged me to go forward with any of his Great Society programs.

Richard Nixon
The Memoirs of Richard Nixon
1978

I knew that Johnson would soon be bitterly disappointed by the ingratitude of those he tried to help. His Great Society programs spawned a new constituency of government, dependents who would always demand more than he could give. Johnson was a man who needed praise, but he would get precious little of it from them.

Richard Nixon
The Memoirs of Richard Nixon
1978

Lyndon Johnson . . . seemed unable to carry on a conversation without nudging or poking or even shaking the other person.

Richard Nixon
The Memoirs of Richard Nixon
1978

Judiciary

It is better to toss up cross and pile in a cause than to refer it to a judge whose mind is warped by any motive whatever, in that particular case. But the common sense of twelve honest men gives a still better chance of just decision than the hazard of cross and pile.

Thomas Jefferson
Notes on Virginia
1782

Man is not made to be trusted for life, if secured against all liability to account.

Thomas Jefferson
Letter, Adamantios Korais
Mid-1780s

These decisions [of federal judges] nevertheless become law by precedent, sapping by little and little the foundations of the Constitution, and working its change by construction before anyone has perceived that this humble and helpless worm has been busily employed in consuming its substance.

Thomas Jefferson
Letter, Adamantios Korais
Mid-1780s

The judiciary of the United States is the subtle corps of sappers and miners constantly working underground to undermine the foundations of our confederate fabric.

Thomas Jefferson
After retiring from office
1809

Knowing that religion does not furnish grosser bigots than law, I expect little from old judges.

Thomas Jefferson
Letter, Thomas Cooper
1810

Our judges are as honest as other men, and not more so. They have, with others, the same passions for party, for power, and the privilege of their corps.

Thomas Jefferson
Letter, William Charles Jarvis
1820

This member of government was at first considered as the most harmless of all its organs. But it has proved that the power of declaring what law is, *ad libitum*, by sapping and mining, slying, and without alarm, the foundations of the Constitution, can do what open force would not dare to attempt.

Thomas Jefferson
Letter, Edward Livingston
1825

I told [John Marshall] it was law logic—an artificial system of reasoning, exclusively used in the courts of justice, but good for nothing anywhere else.

John Quincy Adams
Cited in Clifton Fadiman and Charles van Doran, *The American Treasury*

An ark of future safety which the Constitution placed beyond the reach of public opinion . . .

Martin Van Buren
Inquiry into the Origin and Course of Political Parties in the United States

I may not know much about law, but I do know one can put the fear of God into judges.

Theodore Roosevelt
Remark on his attack on judicial excesses, William Henry Harbaugh
1912

It is right—wholly right—to prosecute criminals. But that is not enough, for there is the immense added task for working for the elimination of present and future crime by getting rid of evil social conditions which breed crime. Good government can prevent a thousand crimes for every one it punishes.

Franklin D. Roosevelt
Speech
November 4, 1938

Our chief justices have probably had more profound and lasting influence on their times and on the direction of the nation than most presidents have had.

Richard Nixon
Television broadcast
May 21, 1969

The law is not the private property of lawyers, nor is justice the exclusive province of judges and juries.

Jimmy Carter
Cited in *Dallas Times Herald*
April 26, 1978

The one thing that I do seek are judges that will interpret the law and not write the law.

Ronald Reagan
Washington, D.C.
June 23, 1986

Justice

A certain degree of impartiality, or the appearance of it, is necessary in the most despotic Governments. In republics this may be considered as the vital principle of the administration.

James Madison
Letter, Edmund Pendleton
October 20, 1788

The administration of justice is the firmest pillar of government.

George Washington
Letter
1789

Equal and exact justice to all men, . . . freedom of religion, freedom of the press, freedom of person under the protection of the habeas corpus; and trial by juries impartially selected,—these principles form the bright constellation which has gone before us.

Thomas Jefferson
First inaugural address
March 4, 1801

The sword of the law should never fall but on those whose guilt is so apparent as to be pronounced by their friends as well as foes.

Thomas Jefferson
Letter, Sarah Mease
March 1801

I believe that justice is instinct and innate, that the moral sense is as much a part of our constitution as that of feeling, seeing, or hearing.

Thomas Jefferson
Letter, John Adams
1816

The severest justice may not always be the best policy.

Abraham Lincoln
Message, Congress
July 17, 1862

A jury too frequently has at least one member more ready to hang the panel than to hang the traitor.

Abraham Lincoln
Letter, Erastus Corning et al
June 12, 1863

I have always found that *mercy bears richer fruits than strict justice.*

Abraham Lincoln
Washington, D.C.
1865

I must make a clear, firm and accurate statement of the facts as to Southern outrages, and reiterate the sound opinions I have long held on the subject. What good people demand is exact justice, equality before the law, perfect freedom of political speech and action and no denial of rights to any citizen on account of color or race—the same to colored as to whites.

Rutherford B. Hayes
Diary
October 26, 1878

Justice and goodwill will outlast passion.

James A. Garfield
Letter accepting nomination for presidency
July 12, 1880

The equal and exact justice of which we boast, as the underlying principle of our institutions, should not be confined to the relations of our citizens to each other. The government itself is under bond to the American people that, in the exercise of its functions and powers, it will deal with the body of our citizens in a manner scrupulously honest and fair, and absolutely just. It is agreed that American citizenship shall be the only credential necessary to justify the claim of equality before the law, and that no condition in life shall give rise to discrimination in the treatment of the people by their government.

Grover Cleveland
Fourth annual message, Congress
December 3, 1888

Justice has nothing to do with expediency. It has nothing to do with any temporary standard whatever. It is rooted and grounded in the fundamental instincts of humanity.

Woodrow Wilson
Speech, Washington, D.C.
February 26, 1916

We have learned that social injustice is the destruction of justice itself.

Herbert Hoover
American Individualism
1922

The friendless, the weak, the victims of prejudice and public excitement are entitled to the same quality of justice and fair play that the rich, the powerful, the well-connected, and the fellow with pull, thinks he can get.

Harry S. Truman
Speech, Attorney General's Conference, Washington, D.C.
February 15, 1950

Justice means a man's hope should not be limited by the color of his skin.

Lyndon Johnson
State of the union address
January 12, 1966

And I see something happening in our towns and in our neighborhoods. Sharp lawyers are running wild. Doctors are afraid to practice medicine. And some moms and pops won't even coach Little League any more. We must sue each other less— and care for each other more.

George Bush
Acceptance speech, Republican Convention
August 20, 1992

K

John F. Kennedy

The greatest leader of our time has been struck down by the foulest deed of our time. . . . No words are sad enough to express our determination to continue the forward thrust of America that he began.

Lyndon B. Johnson
First address to Congress after John F. Kennedy's burial
November 27, 1962

It is not for us to know how many great things he might have accomplished had he been spared the assassin's hand, but of this we are certain—he lived long enough and well enough, to rekindle our spirit, to renew our faith, and reaffirm our commitment as a people to all the great purposes for which this Nation was created.

Lyndon B. Johnson
Speech, Fredericksburg, Texas, Memorial services marking the second anniversary of the assassination of President Kennedy
November 22, 1965

Kennedy had two principal political liabilities. In my judgment one was only apparent—his Catholicism; the other was real—his lack of experience.

Richard Nixon
The Memoirs of Richard Nixon
1978

His [Kennedy's] hands were thrust in his jacket pockets, but his head was bowed and his usually jaunty walk seemed slow. At that moment I felt empathy for a man who had to face up to a bitter tragedy [Bay of Pigs] that was not entirely his fault but was nonetheless his inescapable responsibility.

Richard Nixon
The Memoirs of Richard Nixon
1978

Korea

The attack upon Korea makes it plain beyond all doubt that Communism has passed beyond the use of subversion to conquer independent nations and will now use armed invasion and war.

Harry S. Truman
Statement, start of Korean War
June 27, 1950

It must be clear to everyone that the United States cannot—and will not—sit idly by and await for foreign conquest. The only question is: When is the best time to meet the threat and how?

Harry S. Truman
Speech to nation, recalling General Douglas MacArthur
April 11, 1951

In the simplest terms, what we are doing in Korea is this: We are trying to prevent a third world war.

Harry S. Truman
Speech to nation, recalling General Douglas MacArthur
April 16, 1951

I left Korea impressed by the courage and endurance of its people, and by the strength and intelligence of Syngman Rhee. I also gave much thought to Rhee's insight about the importance of being unpredictable in dealing with the Communists.

Richard Nixon
The Memoirs of Richard Nixon
1978

L

Labor

Take not from the mouth of labor the bread it has earned.

Thomas Jefferson
Inaugural address
March 4, 1801

If we except the light and the air of heaven, no good thing has been or can be enjoyed by us without having first cost labor. And inasmuch as most good things are produced by labor, it follows that all such things of right belong to those whose labor has produced them. But it has so happened, in all ages of the world, that some have labored, and others have without labor enjoyed a large proportion of the fruits. This is wrong, and should not continue. To secure to each laborer the whole product of his labor, or as nearly as possible, is a worthy object of any good government.

Abraham Lincoln
"Fragments of a Tariff Discussion"
December 1, 1847

There is no permanent class of hired laborers among us. Twenty-five years ago, I was a hired laborer. The hired laborer of yesterday, labors on his own account to-day; and will hire others to labor for him to-morrow.

Abraham Lincoln
Meeting, Springfield, Illinois
1852

I am glad to see that a system of labor prevails in New England under which laborers CAN strike when they want to, where they are not obliged to work under all circumstances, and are not tied down and obliged to labor whether you pay them or not!

Abraham Lincoln
Speech, New Haven, Connecticut
1859

The workingmen are the basis of all governments, for the plain reason that they are more numerous.

Abraham Lincoln
Speech, Cincinnati, Ohio
February 12, 1861

Labor is prior to, and independent of, capital. Capital is only the fruit of labor, and could never have existed if labor had not first existed. Labor is the superior of capital, and deserves much the higher consideration.

Abraham Lincoln
First annual message, Congress
December 3, 1861

The main highway and surest passport to honesty and useful distinction will soon be through the harvest field and the workshop.

Andrew Johnson
Letter, Judge, accompanying a coat that Johnson had cut for him, as Governor of Tennessee
Cited in Eric L. McKitrick, "Andrew Johnson, Outsider," in Eric L. McKitrick, *Andrew Johnson: A Profile*

Now, "every man has a right if he sees fit to quarrel with his own bread and butter, but he has no right to quarrel with the bread and butter of other people." Every man has a right to determine for himself the value of his own labor, but he has no right to determine for other men the value of their labor.

Rutherford B. Hayes
Diary
August 5, 1877

May that God who has so long blessed us as a Nation . . . long preserve to us that intelligent, thrifty and cheerful body of workmen that was our strength in war and is our guarantee of social order in time of peace.

Benjamin Harrison
Speech, Indianapolis, Indiana
October 6, 1888

We cannot afford in America to have any discontented classes, and if fair wages are paid for fair work we will have none.

Benjamin Harrison
Speech, Massillon, Ohio
October 13, 1890

For labor a short day is better than a short dollar.

William McKinley
Letter, Henry Cabot Lodge
September 8, 1900

No man should receive a dollar unless that dollar has been fairly earned. Every dollar received should represent a dollar's worth of service rendered—not gambling in stocks, but service rendered.

Theodore Roosevelt
Speech, Milwaukee, Wisconsin
October 14, 1912

We cannot afford to let any group of citizens, any individual citizens, live or labor under conditions which are injurious to the common welfare. Industry must submit to such public regulation as will make it a means of life and health, not of death or inefficiency.

Theodore Roosevelt
Speech, Chicago, Illinois
August 8, 1912

There is no right to strike against the public peace by anybody, anywhere, any time.

Calvin Coolidge
Reply to Samuel Gompers's request that the Boston Police Commissioner be removed by Coolidge, then Governor of Massachusetts, for requesting State Troops to break the Boston Police Strike
1919

Nothing will contribute so much to American industrial stability and add so much to American industrial happiness as the abolition of the twelve-hour working day and the seven-day working week.

Warren G. Harding
Speech, steel leaders, White House
May 1923

Nothing has been further from the purpose of the present Administration than any thought of destroying the right of either labor or capital to organize.

Warren G. Harding
Speech, Helena, Montana
June 29, 1923

No business which depends for its existence on paying less than living wages to its workers has any right to continue in this country.

Franklin D. Roosevelt
Statement
June 16, 1933

Unemployment is not a chronic disease of a free system. It is a disease of governmental interference with that system.

Herbert Hoover
Republican Convention
1940

It's like the old Kipling saying about "Judy O'Grady an' the Colonel's Lady." They [business and labor] are both under the same thing.

Franklin D. Roosevelt
Speech, Business Advisory Council and Labor Representatives, White House
December 1941

Production for war is based on men and women—the human hands and brains which we collectively call labor.

Franklin D. Roosevelt
State of the union address
January 6, 1942

Labor is the best customer management has: and management is the source of labor's livelihood. Both are wholly dependent on each other; and the country in turn is dependent on each other.

Harry S. Truman
Radio address
October 30, 1945

Today too many Americans in country clubs and fashionable resorts are repeating, like parrots, the phrase "labor must be kept in its place." It is time that all Americans realize that the place of labor is side by side with the businessman and with the farmer, and not one degree lower.

Harry S. Truman
Labor Day address, Detroit, Michigan
September 6, 1948

[I am] disturbed by what seems to be becoming habit in this country, to adopt certain theories that Marx advanced. One is that there is inevitably a bitter and implacable warfare between the man that works and the man that hires him.

Dwight Eisenhower
News conference
1959

Our society cannot tolerate a situation where a man cannot work unless somebody else dies.

Lyndon B. Johnson
Speech, Knoxville, Tennessee
May 7, 1964

We are not interested in black power and we are not interested in white power. But we are interested in American democratic power, with a small "d." We believe that the citizen, regardless of his race or his religion or color, ought to be armed with the right to have a job at decent wages.

Lyndon B. Johnson
News conference, LBJ Ranch
July 5, 1966

No dramatic challenge is more crucial than providing stable, permanent jobs for all Americans who want to work.

Ronald Reagan
State of the union address
January 25, 1983

Law

Numberless have been the systems of iniquity contrived by the great for the gratification of this passion in themselves; but in none of them were they ever more successful than in the invention and establishment of the canon and the feudal law.

John Adams
"Dissertation on the Canon and the Feudal Law"
August 1765

There seems to be a direct and formal design on foot [by Great Britain] to enslave all America. . . . The first step that is intended seems to be an entire subversion of the whole system of our fathers, by the introduction of canon and feudal law into America.

John Adams
"Dissertation on the Canon and the Feudal Law"
August 1765

The law no passion can disturb. . . . On the one hand, it is inexorable to the cries and lamentations of the prisoner; on the other, it is deaf, deaf as an adder, to the clamours of the populace.

John Adams
Defense of British soldiers on trial after the Boston
    Massacre
1770

The people at large are governed much by custom. To acts of legislation or civil authority they have either been taught to yield a willing obediance, without reasoning about their propriety; on those of military power, whether immediate or derived originally from another source, they have ever looked with a jealous and suspicious eye.

George Washington
Letter, President of the Continental Congress
December 14, 1777

That the laws of every country ought to be executed, cannot be denied. That force must be used if necessary cannot be denied. Can any government be established, that will answer any purpose whatever, unless force be provided for executing its laws?

James Madison
Virginia Convention
June 14, 1788

It is not only vain, but wicked, in a legislator to frame laws in opposition to the laws of nature, and to arm them with the terrors of death. This is truly creating crimes in order to punish them.

Thomas Jefferson
"Notes on the Crimes Bill"
1779

Laws made by common consent must not be trampled on by individuals.

George Washington
Letter, Colonel Vanneter
1781

Ignorance of the law is not excuse in any country. If it were, the laws would lose their effect, because it can always be pretended.

Thomas Jefferson
Letter, M. Limozin
December 22, 1787

No society can make a perpetual constitution, or even a perpetual law.

Thomas Jefferson
Letter, James Madison
September 6, 1789

The execution of the laws is more important than the making of them.

Thomas Jefferson
Letter, Abbé Arnond
1789

No man has a natural right to commit aggression on the equal rights of another, and this is all from which the laws ought to restrict him; every man is under the natural duty of contributing to the necessities of society, and this is all the laws should enforce on him; and no man having a natural right to be the judge between himself and another, it is his natural duty to submit to the umpirage of an impartial third.

Thomas Jefferson
Letter, F. W. Gilmor
1816

Laws are made for men of ordinary understanding, and should therefore be construed by the ordinary rules of common sense. Their meaning is not to be sought for in metaphysical subtleties, which may make anything mean everything or nothing, at pleasure.

Thomas Jefferson
Letter, William Johnson
1823

I told [John Marshall] it was law logic—an artificial system of reasoning, exclusively used in courts of justice, but good for nothing anywhere else.

John Quincy Adams
Cited by Clifton Fadiman, *The American Treasury*

The laws of the United States must be executed. I have no discretionary power on the subject.

Andrew Jackson
Proclamation to the People of South Carolina
December 10, 1832

Let every man remember that to violate the law is to trample on the blood of his father, and to tear the charter of his own and his children's liberty.

Abraham Lincoln
Address, Young Men's Lyceum, Springfield, Illinois
January 27, 1837

I acknowledge no master but the law.

James Buchanan
c. 1858

Follow law, and forms of law, as far as convenient.

Abraham Lincoln
Instructions to Grant
October 21, 1862

I know no method to secure the repeal of bad or obnoxious laws so effective as their stringent execution.

Ulysses S. Grant
Inaugural address
March 4, 1869

After an existence of nearly twenty years of almost innocuous desuetude these laws are brought forth.

Grover Cleveland
Message, regarding the Tenure of Office Act
March 1, 1886

It is the great thought of our country that men shall be governed as little as possible, but full liberty shall be given to individual effort, and that the restraints of law shall be reserved for the turbulent and disorderly.

Benjamin Harrison
Speech, Galesburg, Illinois
October 8, 1889

The law, the will of the majority expressed in orderly, constitutional methods, is the only king to which we bow.

Benjamin Harrison
Speech, Topeka, Kansas
October 10, 1890

It is difficult to make our material condition better by the best of laws, but it is easy enough to ruin it by bad laws.

Theodore Roosevelt
Speech, Providence, Rhode Island
August 23, 1902

No man is above the law and no man is below it; nor do we ask any man's permission when we require him to obey it.

Theodore Roosevelt
Message, Congress
1904

The only thing that has ever distinguished America among the nations is that she has shown that all men are entitled to the benefits of the law.

Woodrow Wilson
Address, New York, New York
December 14, 1906

The two great evils in the execution of our criminal laws today are sentimentality and technicality.

Theodore Roosevelt
Message, Congress
1908

American industry is not free, as once it was free; American enterprise is not free; the man with only a little capital is finding it harder to get into the field, more and more impossible to compete with the big fellow. Why? Because the laws of this country do not prevent the strong from crushing the weak.

Woodrow Wilson
The New Freedom
1912-1913 speeches

We live in a stage of politics, where legislators seem to regard the passage of laws as much more important than the results of their enforcement.

William Howard Taft
The President and His Powers
1916

Someone has said, "Let me make the ballads of the country, and I care not who makes the laws." One might also say, paraphrasing this, "Let any one make the laws of the country, if I can construe them."

William Howard Taft
The President and His Powers
1916

We often . . . find the law more honored in the breach than in the observance.

William Howard Taft
The President and his Powers
1916

You will see that international law is revolutionized by putting morals into it.

Woodrow Wilson
address, Pueblo, Colorado
1919

One with the law is a majority.

Calvin Coolidge
Acceptance speech, Republican National
    Convention
July 27, 1920

Men speak of natural rights, but I challenge anyone to show where in nature any rights existed or were recognized until there was established for their declaration and protection a duly promulgated body of corresponding laws.

Calvin Coolidge
Acceptance speech, Republican National
    Convention
July 27, 1920

The observance of the law is the greatest solvent of public ills.

Calvin Coolidge
Acceptance speech, Republican National
    Convention
July 27, 1920

I do not feel that any one ever really masters the law, but it is not difficult to master the approaches to the law, so that given a certain state of facts it is possible to know how to marshall practically all the legal decisions which apply to them.

Calvin Coolidge
The Autobiography of Calvin Coolidge
1929

If the law is upheld only by government officials, then all law is at an end.

Herbert Hoover
Message, Congress
1929

The worst evil of disregard for some law is that it destroys respect for all law.

Herbert Hoover
Inaugural address
March 4, 1929

You see, unfortunately, in spite of what some people say, the President of the United States is more or less bound by the law.

Franklin D. Roosevelt
To Brazil
November 7, 1939

We cannot subscribe one law for the weak, another law for the strong; one law for those opposing us, another for those allied with us. There can be only one law—or there shall be no peace.

Dwight D. Eisenhower
Campaign speech, Philadelphia, Pennsylvania
November 1, 1956

A foundation of our American way of life is our national respect for law.

Dwight D. Eisenhower
Speech, on the situation in Little Rock, Arkansas
September 24, 1957

If a beachhead of cooperation may push back the jungles of suspicion, let both sides join in creating a new endeavor—not a new balance of power, but a new world of law, where the strong are just and the weak secure and the peace preserved.

John F. Kennedy
Inaugural address
January 20, 1961

A town that can't support one lawyer can always support two.

Lyndon B. Johnson
Comment, swearing-in ceremony of U.S. Attorney
    General Nicholas Katzenbach and Deputy
    Attorney General Ramsey Clark, Washington,
    D.C.
February 13, 1965

Law is the greatest human invention. All the rest give him mastery over his world, but law gives him mastery over himself.

Lyndon B. Johnson
Speech, Conference on World Peace through Law,
    Washington, D.C.
September 16, 1965

Law is not the soothing keeper of the status quo. Law is an instrument in the battle for the hopes of man.

Lyndon B. Johnson
Speech, Conference on World Peace through Law,
    Washington, D.C.
September 16, 1965

If about 90 percent of the laws that are passed by Congress and the state legislatures each year were lost on the way to the printer, and if all the people in the bureaus went fishing, I don't think they would be missed for quite a while.

Ronald Reagan
Speech, Annual Dinner, 77th Congress of American
    Industry, National Association of Manufacturers,
    New York, New York
December 8, 1972

I deeply believe in equal justice for all Americans, whatever their station or former station. The law, whether human or divine, is no respecter of persons, but the law is a respecter of reality.

Gerald Ford
Proclamation of Pardon for Richard Nixon
September 9, 1974

Leadership

If you would preserve your reputation, or that of the state over which you preside, you must take a straightforward determined course; regardless of the applause or censure of the populace, and of the forebodings of that dastardly and designing crew who, at a time like this, may be expected to clamor continually in your ears.

Andrew Jackson
To Governor William Blount
1813

The practical statesman . . . has to look at things as they are, to take things as he finds them, to supply deficiencies and to prune excesses as far as in him lies.

John Tyler
First annual message, Congress
December 7, 1841

He who hid his talent in a napkin and added nothing to it was condemned as unfaithful, when called upon to give an account of his stewardship.

Grover Cleveland
Speech, Jewelers Association Annual Dinner
November 21, 1890

It's harder for a leader to be born in a palace than to be born in a cabin.

Woodrow Wilson
Speech, Denver, Colorado
October 7, 1912

It's a terrible thing to look over your shoulder when you are trying to lead—and find no one there.

Franklin D. Roosevelt
Comment, friend
1937

A good leader can't get too far ahead of his followers.

Franklin D. Roosevelt
1940

I would rather persuade a man to go along, because once he has been persuaded he will stick. If I scare him, he will stay just as long as he is scared, and then he is gone.

Dwight D. Eisenhower
On working with Congress
November 15, 1956

You do not lead by hitting people over the head—that's assault, not leadership.

Dwight D. Eisenhower
October 10, 1970

This is a government by stalemate.

Jimmy Carter
Comment, on the Ford administration, the first Ford-
    Carter debate, Philadelphia, Pennsylvania
September 23, 1976

The president ought to be a powerful force for progress. But right now I know how President Lincoln felt when Gen. McClellan wouldn't attack in the Civil War. He asked him, "If you're not going to use your army, may I borrow It?" And so I say, George Bush, if you won't use your power to help America, step aside. I will.

Bill Clinton
Acceptance Speech, Democratic National Convention
July 16, 1992

Legislation

It is a misfortune, inseparable from human affairs, that public measures are rarely investigated with that spirit of moderation which is essential to a just estimate of their real tendency to advance or obstruct the public good.

James Madison
Federalist, XXXVII
January 11, 1788

The executive in our government is not the sole, it is scarcely the principal object of my jealousy. The tyranny of the legislatures is the most formidable dread at present and will be for many years. That period of the executive will come in its turn, but it will be at a remote period.

Thomas Jefferson
Letter, James Madison
1789

The people are not qualified to legislate. With us, therefore, they only chose the legislators.

Thomas Jefferson
Letter, Abbé Arnond
1789

It may be safely assumed as an axiom in the government of states that the greatest wrongs inflicted upon a people are caused by unjust and arbitrary legislation.

Andrew Johnson
Fourth annual message, Congress
December 19, 1868

Legislation can neither be wise nor just which seeks the welfare of a single interest at the expense and to the injury of many and varied interests.

Andrew Johnson
Veto of the Tariff Act
February 22, 1869

Every measure should stand or fall on its own merits. This should be the fundamental principle in legislation.

Rutherford B. Hayes
Diary
March 27, 1879

The practice of annexing general legislation to appropriation has become a serious abuse. Every measure should stand on its own bottom.

Rutherford B. Hayes
Diary
April 2, 1879

Congressional legislation often confers on those who comply with its conditions property rights or valuable privileges.

William Howard Taft
The President and His Powers
1916

The world is not going to be saved by legislation, and is really benefited by an occasional two years of respite from the panacea and magic that many modern schools of politicians seems to think are to be found in the words, "Be it enacted."

William Howard Taft
The President and His Powers
1916

A system in which we may have an enforced rest from legislation for two years is not bad.

William Howard Taft
The President and His Powers
1916

Pretty raw, some of these bills. I don't like 'em. But what can I do? The Organization wants them.

Warren G. Harding
Comment, H. F. Alderfer
c. 1920

I learned a great while ago that a proposal for legislation, or even the introduction of a bill that was not in accordance with sound policy wouldn't need any active opposition from the executive, in order to prevent its adoption. . . . Congress will look after it.

Calvin Coolidge
Press conference
December 1923

Liberalism

I suppose I must be a "progressive," which I take to be one who insists on recognizing the facts, adjusting policies to facts and circumstances as they arise.

Woodrow Wilson
Speech, New York, New York
January 29, 1911

It is a false liberalism that interprets itself into the government operation of commercial business. Every step of bureaucratizing of the business of our country poisons the very roots of liberalism—that is, political equality, free speech, free assembly, free press, and equality of opportunity. It is the road not to more liberty, but to less liberty.

Herbert Hoover
Speech, New York, New York, on rugged
   individualism
October 22, 1928

Liberalism is a force truly of the spirit proceeding from the deep realization that economic freedom cannot be sacrificed if political freedom is to be preserved.

Herbert Hoover
Speech, New York, New York
October 31, 1932

Men who are going about the country announcing that they are liberals because of the government in business are not liberals, they are reactionaries of the United States.

Herbert Hoover
Madison Square Garden, New York, New York
1932

In every single case before the rise of totalitarian governments there had been a period dominated by economic planners. . . . They might be called the totalitarian liberals. They were the spiritual fathers of the New Deal.

Herbert Hoover
Republican Convention
1940

If being a liberal means federalizing everything, then I'm no liberal. If being a conservative means turning back the clock, denying problems that exist, then I'm no conservative.

Richard Nixon
Referring to speeches made in 1965, *The Memoirs of
   Richard Nixon*
1978

Liberty

The God who gave us life gave us liberty at the same time.

Thomas Jefferson
"The Rights of British America"
1774

The natural progress of things is for liberty to yield and government to gain ground.

Thomas Jefferson
Letter, Edward Carrington
1788

Liberty may be endangered by the abuses of liberty as well as the abuses of power.

James Madison
Federalist, LXIII
1788

Liberty, when it begins to take root, is a plant of rapid growth.

George Washington
To James Madison
March 2, 1788

It is a melancholy reflection that liberty should be equally exposed to danger whether the Government have too much or too little power.

James Madison
Letter, Thomas Jefferson
October 17, 1788

The preservation of the sacred fire of liberty and the destiny of the republican model of government are justly considered, perhaps, as *deeply*, as *finally*, staked on the experiment intrusted to the hands of the American people.

George Washington
First inaugural address
April 30, 1789

The ground of liberty is to be gained by inches.

Thomas Jefferson
To Reverend Charles Clay
January 27, 1790

The numbers of men in all ages have preferred ease, slumber, and good cheer to liberty, when they have been in competition.

John Adams
To Samuel Adams, New York, New York
October 18, 1790

It is of infinite importance to the cause of liberty to ascertain the degree of it which will consist with the purposes of society. An error on one side may be as fatal as on the other.

James Madison
To Philip Mazzei
December 19, 1791

Liberty and order will never be *perfectly* safe, until a trespass on the constitutional provisions for either, shall be felt with the same keenness that resents an invasion of the dearest rights, until every citizen shall be an Argus to espy, and an Aegeon to avenge, the unhallowed deed.

James Madison
National Gazette
January 19, 1792

The class of citizens who provide at once their own food and their own raiment . . . are the best basis of public liberty, and the strongest bulwark of public safety.

James Madison
National Gazette
March 29, 1792

The ball of liberty is not so well in motion that it will roll round the globe.

Thomas Jefferson
Letter, Tench Coxe
1795

Perhaps it is a universal truth that the loss of liberty at home is to be charged to provisions against danger, real or pretended, from abroad.

James Madison
To Thomas Jefferson
May 13, 1799

It behooves every man who values liberty of conscience for himself, to resist invasions of it in the case of others.

Thomas Jefferson
Letter, Doctor Benjamin Rush
1803

Liberty, according to my metaphysics, is an intellectual quality; an attribute that belongs not to fate nor chance.

John Adams
Letter, John Taylor
April 15, 1814

I would define liberty to be a power to do as we would be done by.

John Adams
To J. H. Tiffany
March 31, 1819

Timid men prefer the calm of despotism to the boisterous sea of liberty.

Thomas Jefferson
Cited in George Seldes, *The Great Quotations*

The proposition that people are the best keepers of their own liberties is not true.

John Adams
Cited by Clifton Fadiman, *The American Treasury*

Strait is the gate and narrow is the way that leads to liberty, and few nations, if any, have found it.

John Adams
To Richard Rush
May 14, 1821

Let us not be unmindful that liberty is power, that the nation blessed with the largest portion of liberty must in proportion to its numbers be the most powerful nation upon earth.

John Quincy Adams
1821

See to the government. See that the government does not acquire too much power. Keep a check on your rulers. Do this, and liberty is safe.

William Henry Harrison
"Log Cabin" campaign meeting
1840

In the pursuit of happiness, liberty is indispensable to the exercise of [man's] faculties. Were his hands given him to be manacled or tied? Were his feet given him to be fettered or cramped into impotence? How absurd do these questions appear to you; and yet read the history of your race and see how they have been manacled, and fettered and cramped, till their limbs have been disabled, by torture, to the purposes for which they were given them by their Maker.

John Quincy Adams
An oration delivered before the Cincinnati Astronomical Society
November 10, 1843

The march of free government on this continent must not be trammelled by the intrigues and selfish interests of European powers. Liberty must be allowed to work out its natural results; and these will, ere long, astonish the world.

James Buchanan
Letter, John Slidell
November 10, 1845

The shepherd drives the wolf from the sheep's throat, for which the sheep thanks the shepherd as his liberator, while the wolf denounces him for the same act. . . . Plainly the sheep and the wolf are not agreed upon a definition of liberty.

Abraham Lincoln
Speech, Baltimore, Maryland
April 18, 1864

The world has never had a good definition of the word liberty.

Abraham Lincoln
Speech, Baltimore, Maryland
April 18, 1864

Liberty has never come from the government. Liberty has always come from the subjects of the government. The history of liberty is the history of resistance. The history of liberty is a history of the limitation of governmental power, not the increase of it.

Woodrow Wilson
Speech, New York, New York
September 9, 1912

Liberty does not consist, my fellow citizens, in mere declarations of the rights of man. It consists in the translation of those declarations into definite actions.

Woodrow Wilson
Speech
July 4, 1914

I have always in my own thought summed up individual liberty, and business liberty, and every other kind of liberty, in the phrase that is common in the sporting world, "A free field and no favor."

Woodrow Wilson
Speech, Washington, D.C.
January 29, 1915

The prolific soil of individual liberty produces not only magnificent blossoms but noxious weeds, and we have grown a lot of thistles.

Herbert Hoover
Cited in Eugene Lyons, *Herbert Hoover: A Biography*

I am not for a return of that definition of liberty under which for many years a free people were being gradually regimented into the service of the privileged few.

Franklin D. Roosevelt
Fireside chat
September 30, 1934

Those, who would give up essential liberty to purchase a little temporary safety, deserve neither liberty nor safety.

Franklin D. Roosevelt
Message, Congress
January 7, 1941

Liberty does not make all men perfect nor all society secure. But it has provided more solid progress and happiness and decency for more people than any other philosophy of government in history.

Harry S. Truman
Radio address after the signing of the terms of unconditional surrender by Japan
September 1, 1945

Let every nation know, whether it wishes us well or ill, that we shall pay any price, bear any burden, meet any hardship, support any friend, oppose any foe to assure the survival and the success of liberty.

John F. Kennedy
Inaugural address
January 20, 1961

Liberty without learning is always in peril and learning without liberty is always in vain.

John F. Kennedy
Speech, Vanderbilt University, Nashville, Tennessee
May 1963

Life

Life is the art of avoiding pain.

Thomas Jefferson
Letter, Maria Cosway
October 12, 1786

A noble life, crowned with heroic death, rises above and outlives the pride and pomp and glory of the mightiest empire of the earth.

James A. Garfield
Speech, House of Representatives
December 9, 1858

I wish to preach, not the doctrine of ignoble ease, but the doctrine of the strenuous life.

Theodore Roosevelt
Speech, Chicago, Illinois
April 10, 1899

Abraham Lincoln

Mr. Lincoln has come and gone. . . . He has been raising a respectable pair of dark-brown whiskers, which decidedly improve his looks, but no appendage can ever render him remarkable for beauty.

James A. Garfield
Letter, Mrs. Garfield
February 16, 1861

God gave us Lincoln and Liberty; let us fight for both.

Ulysses S. Grant
February 22, 1863

Whereas our country has become one great house of mourning, where the head of the family has been taken away . . . I recommend my fellow citizens then to assemble in their respective places of worship, there to unite in solemn service to Almighty God in memory of the good man who has been removed, so that all shall be occupied at the same time in contemplation of his virtues and in sorrow for his sudden and violent end.

Andrew Johnson
A Proclamation of Mourning
April 25, 1865

He always showed a generous and kindly spirit toward the Southern people, and I never heard him abuse an enemy.

Ulysses S. Grant
Personal Memoirs
1886

The civil war called for a president who had faith in time, for his country as well as himself; who could endure the impatience of others and abide his time.

Benjamin Harrison
Views of an Ex-President
1901

Lincoln was a very normal man with very normal gifts, but all upon a great scale, all knit together in loose and natural form, like the great frame in which he moved and dwelt.

Woodrow Wilson
Speech, Chicago, Illinois
February 2, 1909

I have not made any speech *only* on the Liberty Loan, because while I may not share any other quality with Abraham Lincoln, I do share his lack of intimate acquaintance with finance.

Theodore Roosevelt
Letter, Herbert Hoover
1917

M

Majority

Great innovations should not be forced on slender majorities.

Thomas Jefferson
Cited in *The Penguin Dictionary of Political Quotations*

On a candid examination of history, we shall find that turbulence, violence, and abuse of power, by the majority trampling on the rights of the minority, have produced factions and commotions which, in republics, have, more frequently than any other cause, produced despotism.

James Madison
Letter, Thomas Jefferson
February 4, 1790

In governments, where the will of the people prevails, the danger of injustice arises from the interest, real or supposed, which a majority may have in trespassing on that of the minority.

James Madison
To Thomas Cooper
March 23, 1824

Man

The bulk of mankind are schoolboys through life.

Thomas Jefferson
"Notes on a Money Unit"
1784

Vain man! Mind your own business! Do no wrong! Do all the good you can! Eat your canvas-back ducks! Drink your Burgundy! Sleep your siesta, when necessary, and trust in God.

John Adams
Letter, Thomas Jefferson
March 14, 1820

What a Bedlamite is man.

Thomas Jefferson
Letter, John Adams
1821

William McKinley

He [Mark Hanna] has advertised McKinley as if he were a patent medicine.

Theodore Roosevelt
Cited in Margaret Leach, *In the Days of McKinley*
c. 1896

McKinley has no more backbone than a chocolate eclair.

Theodore Roosevelt
On McKinley's reluctance to enter the war with Spain
1898

Mercy and Clemency

Too much lenity will be cruelty.

James Monroe
Letter, John Quincy Adams
June 26, 1820

In charity to all mankind, bearing no malice or ill-will to any human being, and even compassioning those who hold in bondage their fellow-men, not knowing what they do.

John Quincy Adams
Letter, A. Bronson Alcott
July 30, 1838

It would be judicious to act with magnanimity towards a prostrate foe.

Zachary Taylor
Letter, R. C. Wood
September, 28, 1846

On principle, I dislike an oath which requires a man to swear he *has not* done wrong. It rejects the Christian principle of forgiveness on terms of repentance. I think it is enough if the man does no wrong *hereafter*.

Abraham Lincoln
Letter, Edwin M. Stanton, on Loyalty Oath proposed
    by Cabinet
February 5, 1864

I have always found that *mercy bears richer fruits than strict justice*.

Abraham Lincoln
Washington, D.C.
1865

With malice toward none, with charity for all, with firmness in the right as God gives us to see the right, let us strive on to finish the work we are in, to bind up the nation's wounds, to care for him who shall have borne the battle and for his widow and his orphan, to do all which may achieve and cherish a just and lasting peace among ourselves and with all nations.

Abraham Lincoln
Second inaugural address
March 4, 1865

Go home and you shall be unmolested while you obey the laws in force at the place where you reside.

Ulysses S. Grant
Appomattox, Virginia
April 1865

Pardon no man who is not provided with employment, or the means of subsistance.

Rutherford B. Hayes
Diary
April 2, 1876

There are no historic or legal precedents to which I can turn in this matter, none that precisely fit the circumstances of a private citizen who has resigned the Presidency of the United States. But it is common knowledge that serious allegations and accusations hang like a sword over our former President's head, threatening his health as he tries to reshape his life, a great part of which was spent in the service of this country and by the mandate of its people.

Gerald Ford
Proclamation of Pardon of Richard Nixon
September 8, 1974

Middle East

We encouraged him [the Shah] to hang firm and to count on our backing.

Jimmy Carter
Diary, when the Shah of Iran was deciding his future
November 2, 1978

The difference between our goal and the Soviet goal in the Middle East is very simple but fundamental. *We* want peace. *They* want the Middle East.

Richard Nixon
The Memoirs of Richard Nixon
1978

Since the United States could not stand idly by and watch Israel being driven into the sea, the possibility of a direct U.S.-Soviet confrontation was uncomfortably high. It was like a ghastly game of dominoes, with a nuclear war waiting at the end.

Richard Nixon
On P.L.O. attempt to overthrow King Hussein in
    September 15, 1970, *The Memoirs of Richard
    Nixon*
1978

I don't have any feelings that the Shah or we would be better off with him playing tennis several hours a day in California instead of in Acapulco.

Jimmy Carter
Diary
July 27, 1979

I resolved to do everything possible to get out of the negotiating process.

Jimmy Carter
Diary, during a Middle East peace negotiation
March 14, 1979

Begin wanted to keep two things; the peace with Egypt—and the West Bank.

Jimmy Carter
Keeping Faith
1982

Minority

All, too, will bear in mind this sacred principle, that though the will of the majority is in all cases to prevail, that will to be rightful must be reasonable; that the minority possess their equal rights, which equal law must protect, and to violate would be oppression.

Thomas Jefferson
First inaugural address
March 4, 1801

That the majority should govern is a general principle controverted by none, but they must govern according to the Constitution, and not according to an undefined and unrestrained discretion, whereby they may oppress the minority.

James K. Polk
Fourth annual message, Congress
December 5, 1848

One great object of the Constitution in conferring upon the President a qualified negative upon the legislation of Congress was to protect minorities from injustice and oppression by majorities.

James K. Polk
Fourth annual message, Congress
December 5, 1848

I have scant patience with this talk of the tyranny of the majority. The only tyrannies from which men, women, and children are suffering in real life are the tyrannies of minorities [the coal trust, the water-power trust, the meat-packing trust].

Theodore Roosevelt
Speech, Carnegie Hall, New York, New York
March 20, 1912

It is because in their hours of timidity the Congress becomes subservient to the importunities of organized minorities that the President comes more and more to stand as the champion of the rights of the whole country.

Calvin Coolidge
The Autobiography of Calvin Coolidge
1929

The moment a mere numerical superiority by either states or voters in this country proceeds to ignore the needs and desires of the minority, and for their own selfish purpose or advancement, hamper or oppress that minority, or [keep] them in any way from equal privileges and equal rights—that moment will mark the failure of our constitutional system.

Franklin D. Roosevelt
Radio address
March 2, 1930

Moderation

The middle of the road is all of the usable surface. The extremes, right and left, are in the gutters.

Dwight D. Eisenhower
New York Times
November 10, 1963

I, who preached moderation to everyone, never practiced it myself. I didn't have ulcers; I gave them to the people who worked for me.

Lyndon B. Johnson
Commenting on his recovery from a heart attack
    suffered on July 2, 1955
Cited in Bruce Bohle, *The Home Book of American
    Quotations*

Extremism in the pursuit of the Presidency is an unpardonable vice. Moderation in the affairs of the nation is the highest virtue.

Lyndon B. Johnson
Speech, New York, New York
October 31, 1964

Monarchy

You are afraid of the one, I, of the few. . . . You are apprehensive of monarchy, I, of aristocracy.

John Adams
Letter, Thomas Jefferson
December 6, 1787

I am no king killer, merely because they are kings. Poor creatures! They know no better; they sincerely and conscientiously believe that God made them to rule the world. I would not, therefore, behead them, or send them to St. Helena to be treated like Napoleon; but I would shut them up like the man in the mask, feed them well, and give them as much finery as they please, until they could be converted to right reason and common sense.

John Adams
Letter, Thomas Jefferson
August 15, 1823

In other forms of government where the people are not regarded as composing the sovereign power, it is easy to perceive that the safeguard of the empire consists chiefly in the skill by which the monarch can wield the bigoted acquiescence of his Subjects.

Andrew Jackson
Rough draft of inaugural address
March 1829

Money

It is not a custom with me to keep money to look at.

George Washington
Letter, John Custis
January 20, 1780

Money, and not morality, is the principle of commercial nations.

Thomas Jefferson
Letter, John Langdon
1810

If you earn $10—save a little of it. If you earn $100, save more. The difference between spending all and saving something is the difference between misery and happiness.

Rutherford B. Hayes
Speech, Hampton Institute, Virginia
1878

We cannot gamble with anything so sacred as money.

William McKinley
Speech, Niles, Ohio
1891

That which we call money, my fellow citizens, and with which values are measured and settlements made, must be as true as the hours of labor which the man who toils is required to give.

William McKinley
Speech, McKinley and Hobart Club of Knoxville, Pennsylvania
August 1896

Good money never made times hard.

William McKinley
Speech in defense of the gold standard
1896

I believe in the tight fist and the open mind—a tight fist with money and an open mind to the needs of America.

Lyndon B. Johnson
Speech, ceremony marking the 10th anniversary of the Government Employees Incentive Awards Act, Constitution Hall, Philadelphia, Pennsylvania
December 4, 1964

Monopoly

It is better to abolish monopolies in all cases than not to do it in any.

Thomas Jefferson
Letter, James Madison
1788

Where a trust becomes a monopoly the state has an immediate right to interfere.

Theodore Roosevelt
Message, New York State Legislature
January 1, 1900

This country would not be a land of opportunity, America would not be America, if the people were shackled with government monopolies.

Calvin Coolidge
Acceptance speech
August 14, 1924

James Monroe

He is a man whose soul might be turned wrong side outwards, without discovering a blemish to the world.

Thomas Jefferson
Letter, W. T. Franklin
1786

There behold him for a term of eight years, strengthening his country for defence by a system of combined fortifications, military and naval, sustaining her rights, her dignity and honor abroad; soothing her dissentions, and conciliating her acerbities at home; controlling by firm although peaceful policy the hostile spirit of the European Alliance against Republican South America, exhorting by the mild compulsion of reason, the shores of the Pacific from the stipulated acknowledgement of Spain; and leading back the imperial autocrat of the North, to his lawful boundaries, from his hastily asserted dominion over the Southern Ocean. This strengthening and consolidating the federative edifice of his country's Union, till he was entitled to say, like Augustus Caesar of his imperial city, that he had found her built of brick and left her constructed of marble.

John Quincy Adams
Cited in Richard Kenin and Justin Wintle, *The Dictionary of Biographical Quotations*

A mind, anxious and unwearied in the pursuit of truth and right, patient of inquiry, patient of contradiction, courteous even in the collision of sentiment, sound in its ultimate judgements, and firm in its final conclusions.

John Quincy Adams
Eulogy, cited in Richard Kenin and Justin Wintle, *The Dictionary of Biographical Quotations*

Mr. Monroe is a very remarkable instance of a man whose life has been a continued series of the most extraordinary good fortune, who has never met with any known disaster, has gone through a splendid career of public service, has received more pecuniary reward from the public than any other man since the existence of the nation, and is now dying, at the age of 72, in wretchedness and beggary.

John Quincy Adams
April 27, 1831

Monroe Doctrine

We consider the interests of Cuba, Mexico and ours as the same, and that the object of both must be to exclude all European influence from this hemisphere.

Thomas Jefferson
Letter, W. C. C. Claiborn
October 1808

American continents are no longer subjects for European colonial establishments.

John Quincy Adams
c. 1821

We should consider any attempt [by the European powers] to extend their system to any portion of this hemisphere as dangerous to our peace and safety. With the existing colonies or dependencies of any European Power we have not interfered, and shall not interfere. But with the governments who have declared their independence, and maintained it, . . . we could not view any interposition for the purpose of oppressing them, or controlling, in any other manner, their destiny, by any European Power, in any other light than as the manifestation of an unfriendly disposition towards the United States.

James Monroe
Message, Congress
December 2, 1823

The United States, sincerely desirous of preserving relations of good understanding with all nations, cannot in silence permit any European interference on the North American continent, and should any such interference be attempted will be ready to resist it at any and all hazards.

James K. Polk
First annual message, Congress
December 2, 1845

It is well known to the American people and to all nations that this government has never interfered with the relations subsisting between other governments. We have never made ourselves parties to their wars or their alliances; we have not sought their territories by conquest; we have not mingled with parties in their domestic struggles; and believing our own form of government to be the best, we have never attempted to propagate it by intrigues, by diplomacy, or by force. We may claim on this continent a like exemption from European interference.

James K. Polk
First annual message, Congress
December 2, 1845

The rights, security, and repose of this Confederacy reject the idea of interference or colonization on this side of the ocean by any foreign power beyond present jurisdiction as utterly inadmissable.

Franklin Pierce
Inaugural address
March 4, 1853

Hereafter no territory on this continent shall be regarded as subject of transfer to a European power.

Ulysses S. Grant
Speech, Senate, on Dominican Republic
May 31, 1870

The United States will not consent that any European power shall control the Railroad or Canal across the Isthmus of Central America. With due regards to the rights and wishes of our sister republics in the Isthmus, the United States will insist that this passage way shall always remain under American control.

Rutherford B. Hayes
Diary
February 7, 1880

There is a homely adage which runs, "Speak softly and carry a big stick; you will go far." If the American nation will speak softly and yet build and keep at a pitch of the highest training a thoroughly efficient navy, the Monroe Doctrine will go far.

Theodore Roosevelt
Address, Minnesota State Fair
September 2, 1901

If a nation shows that it knows how to act with decency in industrial and political matters, if it keeps order and pays its obligations, then it need fear no interference from the United States. . . . Brutal wrongdoing, or an impotence which results in a general loosening of the ties of civilizing society, may finally require intervention by some civilizing nation; and in the Western Hemisphere the United States cannot ignore this duty.

Theodore Roosevelt
Roosevelt Corollary to the Monroe Doctrine, Letter
    read by Elihu Root at Cuban anniversary dinner,
    New York, New York
May 20, 1904

Perhaps I am the only person in high authority amongst all the peoples of the world who is at liberty to speak and hold nothing back. I am speaking as an individual, and yet I am speaking also, of course, as the responsible head of a great government, and I feel confident that I have said what the people of the United States would wish me to say . . . I am proposing, as it were, that the nations should with one accord adopt the doctrine of President Monroe as the doctrine of the world: that no nation should seek to extend its polity over any other nation or people, but that every people should be left free to determine its own polity, its own way of development, unhindered, un-threatened, unafraid, the little along with the great and powerful.

Woodrow Wilson
Address to the Senate, Peace Without Victory
January 22, 1917

If former President Eisenhower had under-stood the Monroe Doctrine, we would not have any trouble in Cuba today.

Harry S. Truman
Statement
October 14, 1962

Morals

It is substantially true, that virtue or morality is a necessary spring of popular government.

George Washington
Farewell address
September 1796

In a free government the demand for moral qualities should be made superior to that of talents.

Andrew Jackson
Rough draft of inaugural address
March 1829

It is not always in the power of governments to enlarge or restrict the scope of moral results which follow the policies that they may deem it necessary for the public safety from time to time to adopt.

Abraham Lincoln
Reply, Working Men of Manchester, England
January 19, 1863

Point to your immense fortunes, if you will; point to your national growth and prosperity; boast of the day of practical politics, and discard as obsolete all senti-ment and all conception of morality and patriotism in public life, but do not for a moment delude yourselves into the belief that you are navigating in the safe course marked out by those who launched and blessed the Ship of State.

Grover Cleveland
Speech, Southern Society of New York, Washington's Birthday
February 22, 1890

If I cannot retain my moral influence over a man except by occasionally knocking him down, if that is the only basis upon which he will respect me, then for the sake of his soul I have got occasionally to knock him down.

Woodrow Wilson
Speech
May 15, 1916

You will see that international law is revolutionized by putting morals into it.

Woodrow Wilson
Address, Pueblo, Colorado
1919

Here in America, where the tablets of human freedom were first handed down, their sacred word has been flouted. Today the stern task is before the Republican party to restore the Ark of that Covenant to the temple in Washington.

Herbert Hoover
Republican Convention, Cleveland, Ohio
1932

We have always known that heedless self-interest was bad morals; we know now that it is bad economics.

Franklin D. Roosevelt
Second inaugural address
January 20, 1937

The strength of our society does not rest in the silos of our missiles nor lie in the vaults of our wealth—for neither arms nor silver are gods before which we kneel. The might of America lies in the morality of our purposes and their support by the will of the people of the United States.

Lyndon B. Johnson
Commencement address, Howard University, Washington, D.C.
June 4, 1965

We Americans do not believe in moral double-bookkeeping.

Lyndon B. Johnson
Speech, swearing in of Nicholas deB. Katzenbach as under secretary of state, White House
October 3, 1966

N

Native Americans

If either party, cherokees, friendly creeks, or whites, takes property of the Red Sticks [Creeks], the property belongs to those who take it.

Andrew Jackson
Orders, attack on Creek village
1813

Listen. . . . The United States would have been justified by the Great Spirit, had they taken all the land of the nation. . . . Listen—the truth is, the great body of the Creek chiefs and warriors did not respect the power of the United States—they thought we were an insignificant nation—that we would be overpowered by the British. . . . They were fat with eating beef—they wanted flogging. . . . We bleed our enemies in such cases to give them their senses.

Andrew Jackson
Comments, Big Warrior, Creek chief
c. 1814

I am but one man. I am the voice of my people. Whatever their hearts are, that I talk. I want no more war. I want to be a man. My skin is red; my heart is a white man's heart; but I am a Modoc. I am not afraid to die. I will not fall on the rocks. When I die, my enemies will be under me. Your soldiers began on me when I was asleep on Lost River. They drove us to these rocks, like a wounded deer.

Andrew Jackson
Cited in Dee Brown, *Bury My Heart at Wounded Knee*

They [native Americans] have claims on the magnanimity and, I may add, on the justice of this nation which we must all fill. We should become their real benefactors; we should perform the office of their Great Father, the endearing title which they emphatically give to the Chief Magistrate of our Union.

James Monroe
Second inaugural address
March 4, 1821

Toward the aborigines of the country no one can indulge a more friendly feeling than myself. . . . [However] the waves of population and civilization are rolling westward, and we now propose to acquire the countries occupied by the red men of the South and West by a fair exchange.

Andrew Jackson
1830

Have you not enough Indians to expel from the land of their fathers? Are you not large and unwieldly enough already?

John Quincy Adams
Speech, House of Representatives, arguing against annexation of Texas
May 18, 1836

In your relations with the Indian tribes, you never declare war, although you do make and break treaties with them, whenever [it] happens to suit the purposes of the President and the majority of both houses of Congress.

John Quincy Adams
Speech, House of Representatives
May 18, 1836

A system which looks to the extinction of a race is too horrible for a nation to adopt without entailing upon itself the wrath of all Christendom and engendering in the citizen a disregard of human life and the rights of others, dangerous to society. I see no substitute for such a system, except in placing all the Indians on large reservations, as rapidly as it can be done, and giving them absolute protection there.

Ulysses S. Grant
First annual message, Congress
December 6, 1869

Let all our dealings with the Red man be characterized by justice and good faith, and let there be the most liberal provision for his physical wants, for education in its widest sense, and for religious instruction and training. To do all this will cost money, but like all money well expended it is wise economy.

Rutherford B. Hayes
Diary
July 1, 1878

If by reason of the intrigues of the Whites or from any cause Indian wars come then let us correct the errors of the past. Always the Numbers and prowess of the Indians have been underrated.

Rutherford B. Hayes
Diary
July 1, 1878

Navy

The most sincere neutrality is not a sufficient guard against the depredations of nations at war. To secure a respect to a neutral flag requires a naval force organized and ready to vindicate it from insult or agression.

George Washington
Address, Congress
December 7, 1796

It is no part of our policy to create and maintain a navy able to cope with that of other great powers of the world.

Chester A. Arthur
Message, Congress
December 4, 1883

It can never be doubted that the good will be delivered by this Nation, whose Navy believes in the tradition of "Damn the torpedoes; full speed ahead!"

Franklin D. Roosevelt
Speech, Washington, D.C., Navy Day
October 27, 1941

Negotiations

The nature of foreign negotiations requires caution and their success must often depend on secrecy. . . . The necessity of such caution and secrecy was one cogent reason for vesting the power of making treaties in the President. . . . To admit, then, a right in the House of Representatives to demand and to have . . . all the papers respecting a negotiation with a foreign power would be to establish a dangerous precedent.

George Washington
Message, House of Representatives
March 30, 1796

In conference rooms, as in courts, it is necessary that both sides enter upon the discussion in good faith, assuming that substantial justice will accrue to both; and it is customary that they leave their arms outside the room where they confer.

Franklin D. Roosevelt
Message, Adolph Hitler, appealing for peace in Europe
April 14, 1939

The weakest must come to the conference table with the same confidence as do we. . . . That table, though scarred by many past frustrations, cannot be abandoned for the certain agony of the battle-field.

Dwight D. Eisenhower
Farewell address
January 17, 1961

So let us begin anew—remembering on both sides that civility is not a sign of weakness, and sincerity is always subject to proof. Let us never negotiate out of fear. But let us never fear to negotiate.

John F. Kennedy
First inaugural address
January 20, 1961

But I am not going to destroy the world by throwing my weight around without achieving something for it. I am going to do as the Good Book says. . . . I am going to say to all the leaders of the world, "Come, now, let us reason together."

Lyndon B. Johnson
Speech, "Salute to President Johnson" Dinner,
    Cleveland, Ohio
October 8, 1964

I believe in building bridges but we should build only our end of the bridge.

Richard Nixon
Lakeside speech, Bohemian Grove, California
July 1967

Let me be quite blunt. Our fighting men are not going to be worn down. Our mediators are not going to be talked down. And our allies are not going to be let down.

Richard Nixon
Broadcast speech on Vietnam War negotiations
May 14, 1969

It's certainty versus the uncertainty that weakens, not our actual bargaining position so much.

Richard Nixon
The Memoirs of Richard Nixon
1978

Neutrality

We ought to lay it down, as a first principle and a maxim never to be forgotten, to maintain an entire neutrality in all future European wars.

John Adams
Autobiography
September 1775

Our form of government, inestimable as it is, exposes us, more than any other, to the insidious intrigues and pestilent influence of foreign nations. Nothing but our inflexible neutrality can preserve us.

John Adams
Letter, *The Boston Patriot*
C. 1809

A virtuous people may and will confine themselves within the limit of a strict neutrality; but it is not in their power to behold a conflict so vitally important to their neighbors without the sensibility and sympathy which naturally belong to such a case.

James Monroe
Third annual message, Congress
December 7, 1819

If a system of universal and permanent peace would be established, or if in war the belligerent parties would respect the rights of neutral powers, we should have no occasion for a navy or an army. . . .
The history of all ages proves that this cannot be presumed; on the contrary, that at least one half of every century, in ancient as well as modern times, has been consumed in wars, and often of the most general and desolating character.

James Monroe
Speech, House of Representatives
January 30, 1824

And as to the rights of neutral powers, it is sufficient to appeal to our own experiences to demonstrate how little regard will be paid to them whenever they come into conflict with the interests of the powers at war while we rely on the justice of our own Cause and Argument alone.

James Monroe
Speech, House of Representatives
January 30, 1824

The right of search is the right of war of the belligerent toward the neutral.

James Monroe
Speech, Senate, on Spanish relations with South
    America
May 21, 1824

We have to . . . eschew intermeddling with the national policy and the domestic repose of other governments, and to repel it from our own.

Franklin Pierce
Second annual message, Congress
December 4, 1854

Whereas information has been received by me that sundry persons . . . are preparing . . . to participate in military operations in Nicaragua: Now, I, Franklin Pierce, President of the United States, do warn all persons against connecting themselves with any such enterprise or undertaking, as being contrary to their duty as good citizens and to the laws of their country and threatening the peace of the United States.

Franklin Pierce
Proclamation
December 8, 1855

The basis of neutrality . . . is not indifference; it is not self-interest. The basis of neutrality is sympathy for mankind. It is fairness, it is good will, at bottom. It is impartiality of spirit and of judgment.

Woodrow Wilson
Speech, Associated Press, New York, New York
April 20, 1915

Armed neutrality is ineffectual at best . . . it is practically certain to draw us into the war without either the rights or the effectiveness of belligerents.

Woodrow Wilson
Speech, Joint Session of both houses of Congress,
    Declaration of War against Germany
April 2, 1917

We must realize that there is no easy way out. We either get out, surrender on the installment plan through neutralization, or we find a way to win.

Richard Nixon
Speech, Sales Executive Club of New York
January 26, 1965

Richard Nixon

Do you realize the responsibility I carry? I'm the only person standing between Nixon and the White House.

John F. Kennedy
Comment, Arthur Schlessinger, Jr., cited in *A Thousand Days*

Mr. Nixon may be very experienced in kitchen debates. So are a great many other married men I know.

John F. Kennedy
Speech, Alexandria, Virginia
August 24, 1960

I wonder when he put his finger under Mr. Khrushchev's nose whether he was saying, "I know you are ahead of us in rockets, Mr. Khrushchev, but we are ahead of you in color television." I would just as soon look at black and white television and be ahead of them in rockets.

John F. Kennedy
Speech, Pittsburgh, Pennsylvania
October 10, 1960

He was very shy, a loner in many respects, and he seemed to prefer dealing with paperwork than dealing with people.

Gerald Ford
A Time to Heal
1979

Most of us have hidden flaws or personality quirks that seldom come to the surface. . . . In Nixon's case, that flaw was pride. A terribly proud man, he detested weakness in other people.

Gerald Ford
A Time to Heal
1979

Making up his mind and then pretending that his options were still open—that was a Nixon trait that I'd have occasion to witness again.

Gerald Ford
A Time to Heal
1979

O

Opinion

The opinions of men are not the object of civil government, nor under its jurisdiction.

Thomas Jefferson
Virginia Statute of Religious Freedom
1779

Every difference of opinion is not a difference of principle. We have called by different names brethren of the same principle. We are all Republicans, we are all Federalists. If there be any among us who would wish to dissolve this Union or to change its republican form, let them stand undisturbed as monuments of the safety with which error of opinion may be tolerated where reason is left free to combat it.

Thomas Jefferson
First inaugural address
March 4, 1801

Most men are not scolded out of their opinion.

Martin Van Buren
Comment
1803

There is no more fundamental axiom of American freedom than the familiar statement: In a free country we punish men for the crimes they commit but never for the opinions they have.

Harry S. Truman
Message, House of Representatives, veto of McCarran Act
September 22, 1950

Our house is large, and it is open. It is open to all, those who agree and those who dissent.

Lyndon B. Johnson
Speech, Washington, D.C.
June 24, 1965

Opinion and protest are the life breath of democracy—even when it blows heavy.

Lyndon B. Johnson
Speech, ceremony honoring the Presidential Scholars, the White House
June 7, 1966

Opportunity

I believe also in the American opportunity which puts the starry sky above every boy's head, and sets his foot upon a ladder which he may climb until his strength gives out.

Benjamin Harrison
Speech, Tippecanoe Club of Marion County, Ohio
July 4, 1888

My country owes me no debt. It gave me, as it gives every boy and girl, a chance.

Herbert Hoover
Comment, after nomination as Republican candidate
    for president
June 1928

We must open the doors of opportunity. But we also must equip our people to walk through those doors.

Lyndon B. Johnson
Address, National Urban League Conference,
    Washington, D.C.
December 10, 1964

P

Parties

I am not a federalist, because I never submitted the whole system of my opinions
to the creed of any party of men whatever,
in religion, in philosophy, in politics or in
anything else, where I was capable of
thinking for myself. Such an addiction is
the last degradation of a free and moral
agent. If I could not go to heaven but with a
party, I would not go there at all.

Thomas Jefferson
Letter, Francis Hopkinson
March 13, 1789

No! The real fault is, that the president has
not influence enough, and is not independent enough. Parties will not allow
him to act [like] himself.

John Adams
Letter, E. Randolph
February 11, 1790

Let me now . . . warn you in the most
solemn manner against the baneful effects
of the spirit of party . . . . It serves always to
distract the public councils and enfeebles
the public administration. It agitates the
community with ill-founded jealousies
and false alarms; kindles the animosity of
one part against another; foments
occasionally riot and insurrection. It
opens the door to foreign influence and
corruption. . . . A fire not to be quenched, it
demands a uniform vigilance to prevent its
bursting into flame, lest, instead of warm-
ing, it should consume.

George Washington
Farewell address
September 17, 1796

If any one entertains the idea, that, because I am a President of three [electoral]
votes only, I am in the power of a party,
they shall find I am no more so than the
Constitution forces upon me.

John Adams
Letter, U. Forrest
May 13, 1799

I . . . cannot cease to consider all the individuals of both parties as my
countrymen.

John Quincy Adams
Letter, William Plumer
August 16, 1809

The President has, or ought to have, the
whole nation before him, and he ought to
select the men best qualified and most
meritorious for offices at this own
responsibility, without being shackled by
any check by law, constitution, or institution. Without this unrestrained liberty, he
is not a check upon the legislative power
nor either branch of it. Indeed, he must be
the slave of the party that brought him in.

John Adams
Letter, J. Quincy
February 18, 1811

When and where were ever found, or will
be found, sincerity, honesty, or veracity, in
any sect or party in religion, government,
or philosophy?

John Adams
Letter, Thomas Jefferson
June 20, 1815

No free Country has ever been without parties, which are a natural offspring of Freedom.

James Madison
Note on his suffrage speech at the Constitutional Convention of 1787
c. 1821

This party [the Whigs] contains in itself the seeds of its own destruction, if they are permitted to germinate and bring forth their natural fruit.

James Buchanan
Letter, Doctor Edward C. Gazzam
December 11, 1840

The true spirit of liberty, although devoted, persevering, bold, and uncompromising in principle, that secured is mild and tolerant and scrupulous as to the means it employs, whilst the spirit of party, assuming to be that of liberty, is harsh, vindictive, and intolerant, and totally reckless as to the character of the allies which it brings to the aid of its cause.

William Henry Harrison
Inaugural address
March 4, 1841

If I occupy the White House, I must be untrammelled & unpledged, so as to be president of the nation & not of a party.

Zachary Taylor
Letter, son-in-law
1848

The party lash and the fear of ridicule will overawe justice and liberty.

Abraham Lincoln
Speech, Bloomington, Indiana
May 19, 1856

Being an errand boy to one hundred and fifty thousand people tires me so by night I am ready for bed instead of soirees.

Rutherford B. Hayes
Letter, Sophia Hayes
January 28, 1866

I found a kind of party terrorism pervading and oppressing the minds of our best men.

James A. Garfield
Letter, J. D. Cox
April 8, 1871

He serves his party best who serves the country best.

Rutherford B. Hayes
Inaugural address
March 4, 1877

All free governments are party governments.

James Garfield
Speech, House of Representatives
January 18, 1878

I left this great Country prosperous and happy, and the party of my choice strong, victorious and united. In serving my country I served the Party.

Rutherford B. Hayes
Diary
December 29, 1881

Let us exalt patriotism and moderate our party contentions. Let those who would die for the flag on the field of battle give a better proof of their patriotism and a higher glory to their country by promoting fraternity and justice.

Benjamin Harrison
Inaugural address
March 4, 1889

Party honesty is party expediency.

Grover Cleveland
Interview, *New York Commercial Advertiser*
September 19, 1889

Party faithlessness is party dishonor.

Grover Cleveland
Speech, Business Men's Democratic Association, New York, New York
January 8, 1892

The people will visit with quick revenge the party which betrays them.

Grover Cleveland
Speech, Business Men's Democratic Association, New York, New York
January 8, 1892

I can no longer be called the President of a party; I am now the President of the whole people.

William McKinley
Cited in Arthur Bernon Tourtellot, *The Presidents on the Presidency*

I am afraid I am a constant disappointment to my party. The fact of the matter is, the longer I am President the less of a party man I seem to become.

William Howard Taft
Cited in Arthur Bernon Tourtellot, *The Presidents on the Presidency*

When I think of the number of men who are looking to me as the representative of a party, with the hope for all varieties of the salvage from the things they are struggling in the midst of, it makes me tremble. It makes me tremble not only with a sense of inadequacy and weakness, but as if I were shaken by the very things that are shaking them and, if I seem circumspect, it is because I am so diligently trying not to make any colossal blunders.

Woodrow Wilson
Speech, National Press Club
March 20, 1914

In these recent years the average American seldom thinks of Jefferson and Jackson as Democrats or of Lincoln and Theodore Roosevelt as Republicans; he labels each one of them according to his attitude toward the fundamental problems that confronted him as President, when he was active in the affairs of government.

Franklin D. Roosevelt
Political address
January 8, 1936

May cooperation be permitted and be the mutual aim of those who, under the concepts of our Constitution, hold to differing political faiths; so that all may work for the good of our beloved country and Thy glory. Amen.

Dwight D. Eisenhower
Inaugural address
January 20, 1953

Patience

It has been my observation in life that, if one will only exercise the patience to wait, his wants are likely to be filled.

Calvin Coolidge
The Autobiography of Calvin Coolidge
1929

The older I get, the more wisdom I find in the ancient rule of taking first things first—a process which often reduces the most complex human problems to manageable proportions.

Dwight D. Eisenhower
Readers Digest
December 1963

Patriotism

It [patriotism] must be aided by a prospective interest or some reward. For a time, it may of itself push men into action, to bear much, to encounter difficulties. But it will not endure unassisted by interest.

George Washington
Quoted by Ronald Reagan, Speech, U.S. Military Academy, West Point, New York
May 27, 1981

I never was . . . much of John Bull. But I was John Yankee and such I shall live and die.

John Adams
Letter, James Warren
August 4, 1778

I must avow to your Majesty I have no attachment but to my own country.

John Adams
Comment, King George III, on being presented as minister to Court of St. James
1785

Merchants are the least virtuous citizens and possess the least of the *amor patriae*.

Thomas Jefferson
Letter, M. de Meunier
1786

Guard against the postures of pretended patriotism.

George Washington
Farewell address
September 17, 1796

National honor is national property of the highest value.

James Monroe
First inaugural address
March 4, 1817

The individual owes the exercise of all his faculties to the service of his country.

John Quincy Adams
Letter, Francis Calley Gray
August 3, 1818

The patriotic impulses of the popular heart . . .

Franklin Pierce
Third annual message, Congress
December 31, 1855

It is no time now to inquire by whose fault or folly this state of things has been produced. . . . [Rather] let every man stand to his post, and . . . let posterity . . . find our skeleton and armour on the spot where duty required us to stand.

Millard Fillmore
Speech, Buffalo, New York, four days after Beauregard fired on Fort Sumter
April 16, 1861

He who takes the oath to-day to preserve, protect, and defend the Constitution of the United States only assumes the solemn obligation which every patriotic citizen—on the farm, in the workshop, in the busy marts of trade, and everywhere—should share with him.

Grover Cleveland
Inaugural address
March 4, 1885

Impatience is not patriotism.

William McKinley
Comment, Charles G. Dawes, on war with Spain
June 1899

The man who loves other countries as much as his own stands on a level with the man who loves other women as much as he loves his own wife.

Theodore Roosevelt
The Works of Theodore Roosevelt
1910

Patriotism is easy to understand in America. It means looking out for yourself by looking out for your country.

Calvin Coolidge
Speech, Northampton, Massachusetts
May 30, 1923

We would rather die on our feet than live on our knees.

Franklin D. Roosevelt
1939

As men do not live by bread alone, they do not fight by armaments alone.

Franklin D. Roosevelt
Four Freedoms Speech
January 6, 1941

Now the trumpet summons us again—not as a call to bear arms, though arms we need—not as a call to battle, though embattled we are—but a call to bear the burden of a long twilight struggle year in and year out . . .—a struggle against the common enemies of man: tyranny, poverty, disease and war itself.

In the long history of the world, only a few generations have been granted the role of defending freedom in its hour of maximum danger. I do not shrink from this responsibility—I welcome it. . . . The energy, the faith, the devotion which we bring to this endeavor will light our country and all who serve it—and the glow from that fire can truly light the world.

And so, my fellow Americans: ask not what your country can do for you—ask what you can do for your country.

John F. Kennedy
Inaugural address
January 20, 1961

Let us put an end to self-inflicted wounds. Let us remember that our national unity is a most priceless asset. Let us deny our adversaries the satisfaction of using Vietnam to pit American against American.

Gerald Ford
Address, Congress, on Southeast Asia
April 10, 1975

Flag burning is wrong. Protection of the flag, a unique national symbol, will in no way limit the opportunity nor the breadth of protest available in the exercise of free speech rights. I believe the importance of this issue compels me to call for a constitutional amendment.

George Bush
Speech
June 27, 1989

Peace

There is nothing so likely to produce peace as to be well prepared to meet an enemy.

George Washington
Letter, Elbridge Gerry
January 29, 1780

Whatever enables us to go to war, secures our peace.

Thomas Jefferson
Letter, James Monroe
July 11, 1790

Observe good faith and justice toward all nations. Cultivate peace and harmony with all. . . . The nation which indulges toward another an habitual hatred or an habitual fondness is in some degree a slave. It is a slave to its animosity or to its affection, either of which is sufficient to lead it astray from its duty and its interest.

George Washington
Farewell address
December 17, 1796

Tranquility is the old man's milk.

Thomas Jefferson
Letter, Edward Rutledge
June 24, 1797

Such will be a great lesson of peace; teaching men that what they cannot take by an election, neither can they take by a war; teaching all the folly of being the beginners of war.

Abraham Lincoln
Message, Congress
July 4, 1861

Peace does not appear so distant as it did. I hope it will come soon, and come to stay; and so come as to be worth the keeping in all future time. It will then have been proved that, among free men, there can be no successful appeal from the ballot to the bullet; and that they who take such appeal are sure to lose their case, and pay the cost.

Abraham Lincoln
Letter, James C. Conkling
Summer 1863

Peace and universal prosperity—its sequence—with economy of administration, will lighten the burden of taxation while it constantly reduces the national debt. Let us have peace.

Ulysses S. Grant
Presidential acceptance speech
May 29, 1868

My policy is trust—peace, and to put aside the bayonet.

Rutherford B. Hayes
Diary
March 14, 1877

The long peace that has lulled us into a sense of fancied security may at any time be disturbed.

Chester A. Arthur
Message, Congress, in appeal to build up the navy
March 26, 1884

With capability for war on land and on sea unexcelled by any nation in the world, we are smitten by the love of peace.

Benjamin Harrison
Speech, San Francisco, California
May 1, 1891

The United States is not a country to which peace is necessary.

William McKinley
On impending war with Spain
1895

Peace is preferable to war in almost every contingency.

William McKinley
Inaugural address
March 4, 1897

We do not admire the man of timid peace.

Theodore Roosevelt
Speech, Chicago, Illinois
April 10, 1899

There must be no scuttle policy.

William McKinley
Repudiating suggestion of a premature peace in the Philippines (response to formal notification for his renomination for the presidency), Canton, Ohio.
July 1900

Peace is generally good in itself, but it is never the highest good unless it comes as the handmaid of righteousness; and it becomes a very evil thing if it serves merely as a mask for cowardice and sloth, or as an instrument to further the ends of despotism or anarchy.

Theodore Roosevelt
Nobel Peace Prize Speech, Christiana, Norway
1910

There is a price which is too great to pay for peace, and that price can be put in one word. One cannot pay the price of self-respect.

Woodrow Wilson
Speech, Des Moines, Iowa
February 1, 1916

The professional pacifist is merely a tool of the sensual materialist who has no ideals, whose shrivelled soul is wholly absorbed in automobiles, and the movies, and money making, and in the policies of the cash register and the stock ticker, and the life of fatted ease.

Theodore Roosevelt
Speech, Kansas City, Missouri
May 30, 1916

It must be peace without victory.

Woodrow Wilson
Speech, Senate
January 22, 1917

Only a peace between equals can last.

Woodrow Wilson
Speech, Senate
January 22, 1917

The program of the world's peace, therefore, is our program; and that program, the only possible program, as we see it, is this:

Open covenants of peace, openly arrived at, after which there shall be no private international understandings of any kind but diplomacy shall proceed always frankly and in the public view.

Woodrow Wilson
Speech, Congress (The Fourteen Points)
January 8, 1918

There must be, there shall be the commanding voice of a conscious civilization against armed warfare.

Warren G. Harding
Unknown soldier's burial on Armistice Day
November 12, 1921

One hundred million, frankly, want less of armament and none of war!

Warren G. Harding
Arms Limitation Conference, Continental Memorial
    Hall, Washington, D.C.
November 13, 1921

In my own judgement the most important service that I rendered to peace was the voyage of the battle fleet around the world.

Theodore Roosevelt
Autobiography
1926

There isn't any short cut to peace. There is no short cut to any other salvation. I think we are advised it has to be worked out with fear and trembling.

Calvin Coolidge
Press conference
November 25, 1927

We can make war but we do not and cannot make peace in Europe.

Herbert Hoover
After Munich
c. 1939

The issue is really whether our civilization is to be dragged into the tragic vortex of unending militarism punctuated by periodic wars, or whether we shall be able to maintain the ideal of peace, individuality and civilization as the fabric of our lives.

Franklin D. Roosevelt
Hands Off the Western Hemisphere speech, Pan-
    American Day
April 15, 1939

The work, my friends, is peace more than an end of this war—an end to the beginning of all wars, yes, and end, forever, to this impractical, unrealistic settlement of differences between governments by the mass killing of peoples.

Franklin D. Roosevelt
Draft of Jefferson Day Address (last written by F.D.R.)
April 13, 1945

There is only one reason why we cannot afford failures. When we fail to live together in peace, the failure touches not us alone, but the cause of democracy itself in the whole world. That we must never forget.

Harry S. Truman
Remarks, Wendell Wilkie Awards for Journalism
February 28, 1947

We have learned the hard way that peace is best at home and abroad with our neighbors. We have fought two world wars within a generation. We have found that the victor loses in total war as well as the vanquished.

Harry S. Truman
Speech, Mexico City
March 3, 1947

I don't believe in peace at any price—no honest man does. But I don't believe that because peace is difficult that war is inevitable.

Harry S. Truman
Rear platform remarks, Elkhart, Indiana
October 26, 1948

It takes only one nation to make war. But it takes two or more to make peace.

Harry S. Truman
Remarks, Hartford, Connecticut
October 27, 1948

Peace is more the product of our day-to-day living than of a spectacular program, intermittently executed.

Dwight D. Eisenhower
Speech, Columbia University, New York, New York
March 23, 1950

Our goal must not be peace in our time, but peace for all time.

Harry S. Truman
Galesburg, Illinois
May 8, 1950

America, with its skill in organization and the valor of its sons, could win great wars. But it could not make lasting peace.

Herbert Hoover
The Memoirs of Herbert Hoover: Years of Adventure, 1874-1920
1951

We can well afford to pay the price of peace. Our only alternate is to pay the terrible cost of war.

Harry S. Truman
Quote Magazine
August 5, 1951

Peace is my passion.

Dwight D. Eisenhower
Speech, Cincinnati, Ohio
September 22, 1952

[Peace] signifies more than the stilling of guns, easing the sorrow of war. More than escape from death, it is a way of life. More than a haven for the weary, it is a hope for the brave.

Dwight D. Eisenhower
First inaugural address
January 20, 1953

The worst to be feared and the best to be expected can be simply stated. The worst is atomic war. The best would be this: a life of perpetual fear and tension; a burden of arms draining the wealth and labor of all peoples. . . . Every gun that is made, every warship launched, every rocket fired, signifies, in the final sense, a theft from those who hunger and are not fed, those who are cold and are not clothed.

Dwight D. Eisenhower
The Chance for Peace Speech, Washington, D.C.
April 16, 1953

Occasional pages of history do record the faces of the "Great Destroyers" but the whole book of history reveals mankind's never-ending quest for peace, and mankind's God-given capacity to build.

Dwight D. Eisenhower
Speech to the United Nations (Atoms for Peace Program)
December 8, 1953

It is not enough to take this weapon [the atomic bomb] out of the hands of soldiers. It must be put into the hands of those who will know how to strip its military casing and adapt it to the arts of peace.

Dwight D. Eisenhower
Address to the United Nations (Atoms for Peace Program)
December 8, 1953

The quest for peace is the statesman's most exacting duty.

Dwight D. Eisenhower
Statement on Disarmament presented at the Geneva Conference (Open Skies Proposal)
July 21, 1955

When we get to the point, as we one day will, that both sides know that in any outbreak of general hostilities, regardless of the element of surprise, destruction will be both reciprocal and complete, possibly we will have sense enough to meet at the conference table with the understanding that the era of armaments has ended and the human race must conform its actions to this truth or die.

Dwight D. Eisenhower
Letter, publisher
1956

Indeed, I think that people want peace so much that one of these days governments had better get out of the way and let them have it.

Dwight D. Eisenhower
London television interview
September 1959

Peace and freedom do not come cheap, and we are destined . . . to live out most if not all of our lives in uncertainty and challenge and peril.

John F. Kennedy
Speech, University of North Carolina, Chapel Hill, North Carolina
October 12, 1961

Arms alone are not enough to keep the peace. It must be kept by men.

John F. Kennedy
State of the union address
January 11, 1962

If we cannot now end our differences, at least we can help make the world safe for diversity.

John F. Kennedy
Speech on disarmament, American University, Washington, D.C.
June 10, 1963

And is not peace, in the last analyses, basically a matter of human rights—the right to live out our lives without fear of devastation—the right to breathe air as nature provided it—the right of future generations to a healthy existence?

John F. Kennedy
Speech, American University, Washington, D.C.
June 1963

My fervent prayer is to be a President who can make it possible for every boy in this land to grow to manhood by loving his country—instead of dying for it.

Lyndon B. Johnson
Speech, Washington, D.C.
March 24, 1964

Now let us use that force and all our resources and all our skills in the great cause of a just and lasting peace.

Harry S. Truman
Address on returning from Potsdam, Reader's Digest
November 1965

Peace is not merely the absence of war. It is that climate in which man may be liberated from the hopelessness that imprisons his spirit.

Lyndon B. Johnson
Speech, lighting of the nation's Christmas Tree, the White House
December 17, 1965

Uneasy is the peace that wears the nuclear crown.

Lyndon B. Johnson
Speech, site of the Atomic Energy Commission's National Reactor Testing Station, Arco, Idaho
August 26, 1966

The greatest honor history can bestow is the title of peacemaker. This honor now beckons America. . . . If we succeed, generations to come will say of us now living that we mastered our moment, that we helped make the world safe for mankind. This is our summons to greatness.

Richard Nixon
Inaugural address
January 20, 1969

Let's get them all a little pregnant.

Richard Nixon
Comment, Soviet Premier Leonid Brezhnev,
    Moscow, concerning congressional support for
    détente
June 27, 1974

Peace is a process requiring mutual
restraint and practical arrangements.

Gerald Ford
Helsinki, Finland
August 1, 1975

We have a common interest in survival.

Jimmy Carter
Speech, American Newspaper Publishers Conven-
    tion, New York, New York, on SALT II
April 25, 1979

The American concept of peace goes well
beyond the absence of war. We foresee a
flowering of economic growth and individual liberty in a world at peace.

Ronald Reagan
Speech, National Press Club, Washington, D.C.
November 18, 1981

Peace is not the absence of conflict, but the
ability to cope with conflict by peaceful
means.

Ronald Reagan
Eureka College, Eureka, Illinois
May 9, 1982

The Bible tells us there will be a time for
peace. But, so far in this century, mankind
has failed to find it.

Ronald Reagan
Speech, United Nations, Special Session on Disarma-
    ment, New York, New York
June 17, 1982

Our foreign policy, as President
Eisenhower once said, is not difficult to
state. We are for peace, first, last and
always.

Ronald Reagan
Speech, United Nations, Special Session on Disarma-
    ment, New York, New York
June 17, 1982

America has no territorial ambitions. We
occupy no countries and we have built no
walls to lock our people in. Our commitment [to peace] is as strong today as it ever
was.

Ronald Reagan
Speech, United Nations, Special Session on Disarma-
    ment, New York, New York
June 17, 1982

We can't afford to believe we will never be
threatened. There have been two world
wars in my lifetime. We didn't start them
and, indeed, did everything to avoid being
drawn into them. But we were ill-prepared
for both—had we been better prepared,
peace might have been preserved.

Ronald Reagan
Speech, Washington, D.C.
March 23, 1983

I have become more and more deeply convinced that the human spirit must be
capable of rising above dealing with other
nations and human beings by threatening
their existence.

Ronald Reagan
Speech, Washington, D.C.
March 23, 1983

Would it not be better to save lives than to
avenge them? Are we not capable of
demonstrating our peaceful intentions by
applying all our abilities and our ingenuity
to achieving a truly lasting stability?

Ronald Reagan
Speech, Washington, D.C.
March 23, 1983

Out of billions of people who inhabit this
planet, why, some might ask, should the
death of several hundred shake the world
so profoundly? Why should the death of a
mother flying toward a reunion with her
family or the death of a scholar heading
toward new pursuits of knowledge matter
so deeply? Why are nations who lost no
citizens in the tragedy so angry? The
reason rests on our assumptions about
civilized life and the search for peace. The
confidence that allows a mother or a
scholar to travel to Asia or Africa or Europe
or anywhere else on this planet may be

only a small victory in humanity's struggle for peace. Yet what is peace if not the sum of such small victories?

Ronald Reagan
Speech, United Nations General Assembly, on the downing of the Korean airliner by the Soviet Union
September 15, 1983

The keys to personal fulfillment, national development, human progress and world peace are freedom and responsibility for individuals, and cooperation among nations.

Ronald Reagan
Speech, Annual Joint Meeting of Governors of the World Bank and International Monetary Fund, Washington, D.C.
September 27, 1983

Peace follows in freedom's path and conflicts erupt when the will of the people is denied.

Ronald Reagan
State of the union address
February 2, 1986

Peace is more than just the absence of war. True peace is justice, true peace is freedom. And true peace dictates the recognition of human rights.

Ronald Reagan
Speech, United Nations General Assembly, New York, New York
September 22, 1986

People

All governments depend upon the good will of the people.

John Adams
Letter, E. C. E. Genet
May 15, 1770

An individual, thinking himself injured, makes more noise than a state.

Thomas Jefferson
Letter, Georgia delegates, Congress
December 22, 1785

I am persuaded that the good sense of the people will always be found to be the best army.

Thomas Jefferson
Letter, Edward Carrington
1787

The people are the only sure reliance for the preservation of our liberty.

Thomas Jefferson
Letter, James Madison
1787

The people are the only censors of their governors, and even their errors will tend to keep these to the true principles of their institutions. To punish these errors too severely would be to suppress the only safeguards of the public liberty.

Thomas Jefferson
Letter, Edward Carrington
1787

The proposition that people are the best keepers of their own liberties is not true.

John Adams
Cited by Clifton Fadiman, *The American Treasury*

It is essential to liberty that the government in general should have a common interest with the people.

James Madison
Federalist LXIII
1788

If a member of the Executive or Legislature does wrong, the day is never far distant when the people will remove him.

Thomas Jefferson
Letter, S. Kercheval
1816

All authority belongs to the people.

Thomas Jefferson
Letter, Spencer Roane
1821

All power is inherent in the people.

Thomas Jefferson
Letter, John Cartwright
1824

The people need friends. They have a great deal to bear.

Andrew Johnson
Cited in Kenneth M. Stamp, "Andrew Johnson: The Last Jacksonian," in Eric L. McKitrick, *Andrew Jackson: A Profile*

All the powers of government, in free countries, emanate from the people: all organized and operative power exists by delegation from the people.

John Quincy Adams
"Life of James Monroe," a eulogy
August 25, 1831

The people are the sovereigns, they can alter and amend.

Andrew Jackson
Letter, General John Coffee
December 14, 1832

May God serve the country; for it is evident the people will not.

Millard Fillmore
Letter, Henry Clay
November 11, 1844

I am too old a soldier to murmur against such high authority as [the people].

Zachary Taylor
Letter, J. S. Allison
April 12, 1848

I think very much of the people, as an old friend said he thought of a woman. He said when he lost his first wife, who had been a great help to him in his business, he thought he was ruined—that he could never find another to fill her place. At length, however, he married another . . . and that his opinion now was that *any woman would do well that was done well by.*

Abraham Lincoln
Speech, Bloomington, Illinois
November 21, 1860

Why should there not be a patient confidence in the ultimate justice of the people? Is there any better or equal hope in the world?

Abraham Lincoln
Inaugural address
March 4, 1861

That this nation, under God, shall have a new birth of freedom; and that government of the people, by the people and for the people shall not perish from the earth.

Abraham Lincoln
Gettysburg Address
November 19, 1863

Humble as I am, plebian as I may be deemed, permit me in the presence of this brilliant assemblage to enunciate the truth that courts and cabinets, the President and his advisers, derive their power and their greatness from the people.

Andrew Johnson
Speech, Senate chamber, on being sworn in as vice president
March 4, 1865

The people under our system, like the king in a monarchy, never dies.

Martin Van Buren
Inquiry into the Origin and Course of Political Parties
1867

I shall on all subjects have a policy to recommend, but none to enforce against the will of the people.

Ulysses S. Grant
Inaugural address
March 5, 1869

The wildest delusions of paper money, the crudest theories of taxation, the passions and prejudices that find expression in the senate and house, were first believed and discussed at the firesides of the people, on the corners of the streets, and in the caucuses and conventions of political parties.

James Garfield
"A Century of Congress," *Atlantic*
1877

I am not liked as a President by the politicians in office, in the press, or in Congress. But I am content to abide the judgment—the sober second thought—of the people.

Rutherford B. Hayes
Diary
March 1, 1878

All free governments are managed by the combined wisdom and folly of the people.

James A. Garfield
Letter
April 21, 1880

To lose faith in the intelligence of the people is a surrender and an abandonment of the struggle. To arouse their intelligence, and free it from darkness and delusion, gives assurance of speedy and complete victory.

Grover Cleveland
Fourth annual message, Congress
1888

Ours is not a government which operates well by its own momentum. It is so constructed that it will only yield its best results when it feels the constant pressure of the hands of the people.

Grover Cleveland
Speech, Fellowship Club, New York, New York
May 14, 1889

The intrigues of monarchy which taint the individual character of the subject; the splendor which dazzles the popular eye and distracts the attention from abuses and stifles discontent; and schemes of conquest and selfish aggrandizement which makes a selfish people, have no legitimate place in our national life. Here the plain people of the land are the rulers.

Grover Cleveland
Speech, Thurman Birthday Banquet, Columbus, Ohio
November 13, 1890

Every thoughtful and patriotic man has at times been disappointed by the apparent indifference and demoralization of the people.

Grover Cleveland
Speech, Thurman Birthday Banquet, Columbus, Ohio
November 13, 1890

We draw our Presidents from the people. It is a wholesome thing for them to return to the people. I came from them. I wish to be one of them again.

Calvin Coolidge
The Autobiography of Calvin Coolidge
1929

It is only governments that are stupid, not the masses of people.

Dwight D. Eisenhower
Speech
July 25, 1954

Trust the people—this is the crucial lesson of history.

Ronald Reagan
Speech, Joint meeting of the Board of Governors of the World Bank and International Monetary Fund, Washington, D.C.
September 27, 1983

Persuasion

There is a homely adage which runs, "Speak softly and carry a big stick."

Theodore Roosevelt
Speech, Minnesota State Fair
September 2, 1901

I would rather persuade a man to go along, because once he has been persuaded he will stick. If I scare him, he will stay just as long as he is scared, and then he is gone.

Dwight D. Eisenhower
On working with Congress
November 15, 1956

The principal power the President has is to bring people in and try to persuade them to do what they ought to do without persuasion. That's what I spent most of my time doing. That's what the powers of the Presidency amount to.

Harry S. Truman
Quote Magazine
March 21, 1965

Philippines

If old [Commodore George] Dewey had just sailed away when he smashed that Spanish fleet, what a lot of trouble he would have saved us.

William McKinley
Comment, H. H. Kohlsaat, on the Philippines, a few weeks after the armistice
1898

I walked the floor of the White House night after night until midnight, and I am not ashamed to tell you, gentlemen, that I went down on my knees and prayed Almighty God for light and guidance more than one night. And one night late it came to me this way—I don't know how it was, but it came . . . that there was nothing left for us to do but to take them all, and to educate the Filipinos, and uplift them and civilize them. . . . And then I went to bed, and went to sleep, and slept soundly, and the next morning I sent for the chief engineer of the War Department [map-maker], and I told him to put the Philippines on the map of the United States, and there they are, and there they will stay while I am President.

William McKinley
Comment, General Missionary Committee of the
    Methodist Episcopal Church
1898

I have no light or knowledge not common to my countrymen. I do not prophesy. The present is all-absorbing to me. But I cannot bound my vision by the blood-stained trenches around Manila,—where every red drop, whether from the veins of an American soldier or a misguided Filipino, is anguish to my heart,—but the broad range of future years, when . . . [that people's] children and children's children shall for ages hence bless the American republic because it emancipated and redeemed their fatherland, and set them in the pathway of the world's best civilization.

William McKinley
Speech, Banquet of the Home Market Club, Boston,
    Massachusetts
February 16, 1899

And one of the best things we ever did was to insist upon taking the Philippines and not a coaling station or an island, for if we had done the latter we would have been the laughing stock of the world. And so it has come to pass that in a few short months we have become a world power.

William McKinley
Comments, Charles Dawes and George Cortelyou
1899

I have been criticized a good deal about the Philippines, but don't deserve it. The truth is I didn't want the Philippines, and when they came to us, as a gift from the Gods, I did not know what to do with them.

William McKinley
Comments, Philippine problem
1899

The Philippines form our heel of Achilles. They are all that makes the present situation with Japan dangerous.

Theodore Roosevelt
Letter, William Howard Taft
July 1907

The people of the Philippines are now revitalizing their democratic traditions.

Ronald Reagan
Message, Congress, on presidency of Corazon Aquino
March 14, 1986

Franklin Pierce

A small politician, of low capacity and mean surroundings, proud to act as the servile tool of men worse than himself but also stronger and abler. He was ever ready to do any work the slavery leaders set to him, and to act as their attorney in argument in its favor,—to quote [Thomas Hart] Benton's phrase, with "undaunted mendacity, moral callosity [and] mental obliquity."

Theodore Roosevelt
Life of Thomas Hart Benton
1887

He's got the best picture in the White House, Franklin Pierce, but being President involves a little bit more than just winning a beauty contest, and he was another one that was a complete fizzle. . . . Pierce didn't know what was going on, and even if he had, he wouldn't of known what to do about it.

Harry S. Truman
Cited in Merle Miller, *Plain Speaking: An Oral Biog-*
    raphy of Harry S. Truman

Politics and Politicians

Political contests are necessary sometimes, as well as military, to afford exercise and practice, and to instruct in the art of defending liberty and property.

James Madison
Letter, William Bradford, Jr.
January 24, 1774

When I was young, and addicted to reading, I had heard about dancing on the points of metaphysical needles; but, by mixing in the world, I found the points of political needles finer and sharper than the metaphysical ones.

John Adams
Diary
November 18, 1782

In all political societies, different interests and parties arise out of the nature of things, and the great art of politicians lies in making them checks and balances to each other.

James Madison
National Gazette
January 23, 1792

From the situation where I now am [the Presidency], I see a scene of ambition beyond all my former suspicions or imaginations; an emulation which will turn our government topsy-turvy. Jealousies and rivalries have been my theme, and checks and balances as their antidotes till I am ashamed to repeat the words; but they never stared me in the face in such horrid forms as at present. I see how the thing is going. At the next Election England will set up Jay or Hamilton, and France, Jefferson, and all the corruption of Poland will be introduced; unless the American spirit should rise and say, we will have neither John Bull or Louis Baboon.

John Adams
Letter, Abigail Adams
March 17, 1797

Brutus and Cassius were conquered and slain, Hampden died in the field, Sidney on the scaffold, Harrington in jail, etc. This is cold comfort. Politics are an ordeal path among red-hot ploughshares. Who then would be a politician for the pleasure of running about barefoot among them? Yet somebody must.

John Adams
Letter, James Warren
Undated

Politics is such a torment that I would advise everyone I love not to mix with it.

Thomas Jefferson
Letter, Martha Jefferson Randolph
1800

Politics, like religion, holds up the torches of martyrdom to the reformers of error.

Thomas Jefferson
Letter, James Ogilvie
April 4, 1811

I have labored with holy zeal to rid this devoted state [New York] of a Junta which sits like the nightmare upon her. . . . We have scotched the snake, not killed it.

Martin Van Buren
Letter, Gorham Worthy
June 1, 1820

I hope, Judge, you are now satisfied that there is such a thing in politics as killing a man too *dead.*

Martin Van Buren
Comment, Rofer Skinner
November 1824

There is nothing so deep and nothing so shallow which political enmity will not turn to account.

John Quincy Adams
Diary
August 19, 1822

From the practices of artful and unprincipled men I have heretofore suffered much.

James Monroe
Letter, John Calhoun
March 16, 1828

Is it possible to be anything in this country without being a politician?

Martin Van Buren
Comment, law partner
1828

His idol controls him as much as the shewman does his puppets.

Andrew Jackson
Letter, W. B. Lewis
June 26, 1830

Be firm in politics, but avoid giving personal offense.

James Buchanan
Letter, Maria Yates
January 3, 1831

I find that remark, "'Tis distance lends enchantment to the view" is no less true of the political than of the natural world.

Franklin Pierce
Letter
1832

Fellow citizens: I presume you all know who I am—Abraham Lincoln. I have been solicited by many friends to become a candidate for the legislature. My politics are short and sweet, like an old lady's dance. I am in favor of a national bank. I am in favor of the internal improvement system and a high protective tariff. These are my sentiments and political principles. If elected I shall be thankful. If not, it will be all the same.

Abraham Lincoln
After defeat for seat in Illinois legislature
1832

More than sixty years of active intercourse with the world has made political movement to me as much a necessity of life as the atmospheric air.

John Quincy Adams
Diary
1840

I will die the moment I give up public life.

John Quincy Adams
Comment, wife, Louisa
1847

[The Tennessee Legislature] had parted my garments and for my vesture are casting lots.

Andrew Johnson
House Journal, Tennessee Legislature
1851-1852

This struggle and scramble for office, for a way to live without work, will finally test the strength of our institutions.

Abraham Lincoln
Letter, W. H. Herndon
1861

In politics I am growing indifferent. I would like it, if I could now return to my planting and books at home.

Rutherford B. Hayes
Diary
April 11, 1876

Tolerance is an admirable intellectual gift; but it is of little worth in politics. Politics is a war of *causes*; a joust of principles.

Woodrow Wilson
University of Virginia Magazine
March 1880

When politicians play the game of politics, they must play gamely, regardless of the umpire.

Warren G. Harding
The Star
January 22, 1908

The most successful politician is he who says what everybody is thinking most often and in the loudest voice.

Theodore Roosevelt
Cited in M. Cohen and M. J. Cohen, *Penguin Dictionary of Modern Quotations*

Kings and such like are just as funny as politicians.

Theodore Roosevelt
Cited in John Dos Passos, *Mr. Wilson's War*

The cure for bad politics is the same as the cure for tuberculosis. It is living in the open.

Woodrow Wilson
Speech, Minneapolis, Minnesota
September 18, 1912

I am a man of peace, and I don't want to fight. But . . . even a rat in a corner will fight.

William Howard Taft
Campaign speech, Hyattsville, Maryland
May 1912

Publicity is one of the purifying elements of politics. . . . Nothing checks all the bad practices of politics like public exposure. . . . An Irishman, seen digging around the wall of a house, was asked what he was doing. He answered, "Faith, I am letting the dark out of the cellar." Now, that's exactly what we want to do.

Woodrow Wilson
Speech
1912

I think that in public affairs stupidity is more dangerous than knavery, because harder to fight and dislodge.

Woodrow Wilson
Fortnightly Review
February 1913

The great curse of public life is that you are not allowed to say all the things that you think. Some of my opinions about some men are extremely picturesque, and if you could only take a motion picture of them, you would think it was Vesuvious in eruption.

Woodrow Wilson
Speech, New York, New York
January 27, 1916

Politics I conceive to be nothing more than the science of the ordered progress of society along the lines of the greatest usefulness and convenience to itself.

Woodrow Wilson
Speech, Washington, D.C.
January 6, 1916

We're in the Big League now, boys. We're going to play ball.

Warren G. Harding
Said, according to legend, to a group of political
    friends just after his election as president
1921

I very soon learned that making fun of people in a public way was not a good method to secure friends, or likely to lead to much advancement, and I have scrupulously avoided it.

Calvin Coolidge
The Autobiography of Calvin Coolidge
1929

There is only one form of political strategy in which I have any confidence, and that is to try to do the right thing and sometimes be able to succeed.

Calvin Coolidge
The Autobiography of Calvin Coolidge
1929

Do you know, I've never really grown up? It's a hard thing for me to play this game. In politics, one must meet people, and that's not easy for me.

Calvin Coolidge
Comment, Frank W. Stearns
Donald R. McCoy, Calvin Coolidge: The Quiet
    President

He may be an S.O.B., but he's our S.O.B.

Franklin D. Roosevelt
Comment

A Radical is a man with both feet planted firmly in the air. . . . A Conservative is a man with two perfectly good legs who, however, has never learned to walk. . . . A Reactionary is a somnambulist walking backward.

Franklin D. Roosevelt
Radio speech
October 26, 1939

I have just made some additions to my Kitchen Cabinet, which I shall pass on to my successor in case the Cow should fall down when she goes over the moon. . . . I have appointed a Secretary of Semantics—a most important post. He is to furnish me with 40 to 50 dollar words. Tell me how to say yes and no in the same sentence without a contradiction. He is to tell me the combination of words that will put me against inflation in San Francisco and for it in New York.

Harry S. Truman
Memorandum
December 1947

Any good politician with nerve and *a program that is right* can win in the face of the stiffest opposition.

Harry S. Truman
Memoirs
1948

A politician is a man who understands government. Usually, if he understands it well enough and has made a reputation, as he should have, he will wind up—when he is dead—by being called a statesman. You have to have your own definition of what to call things political. It depends altogether on what your own viewpoint is. If you are for it, it is statesmanlike. If you are against it, it is purely low politics.

Harry S. Truman
News conference
February 23, 1950

History shows that when the Executive and Legislative Branches are politically in conflict, politics in Washington runs riot. In these conditions, the public good goes begging while politics is played for politics' sake. Meanwhile, in the eyes of the world, we appear divided in council and uncertain in purpose.

Dwight D. Eisenhower
To the secretary of defense
May 17, 1954

The best way to reduce his [Senator Joe McCarthy's] influence to the proper proportion is to take him on as part of the [Eisenhower] team.

Richard Nixon
1953

I don't pretend to be a philospher. I'm just a politician from Missouri and proud of it.

Harry S. Truman
Quote Magazine
October 23, 1955

A politician is a man who understands government, and it takes a politician to run a government. A statesman is a politician who's been dead ten or fifteen years.

Harry S. Truman
Cited in *New York World Telegram and Sun*
April 12, 1958

I grow to despise political expediency more every day.

Dwight D. Eisenhower
Comment, Paul Hoffman
June 23, 1958

How dreadful it is that cheap politicians can so pillory an honorable man.

Dwight D. Eisenhower
Comment, Ann Whitman, on demands that Sherman
    Adams be forced out of the administration.
September 16, 1958

I seldom think of politics more than eighteen hours a day.

Lyndon B. Johnson
Speech, Texas
1958

But in politics, victory is never total.

Richard Nixon
Six Crises
1962

Acts of . . . thoughtfulness are so rare in political life that they have a meaning far beyond the ballot box.

Richard Nixon
Six Crises
1962

In politics . . . not speaking out can be another way of speaking out.

Richard Nixon
Six Crises
1962

A professional politician's first duty is to appeal to the forces that unite us, and to channel the forces that divide us into paths where a democratic solution is possible. It is our obligation to resolve issues—not create them.

Lyndon B. Johnson
Life
November 19, 1963

Politics is like football. If you see daylight, go through the hole.

John F. Kennedy
Comment, Pierre Salinger
Cited in Bruce Bohle, *The Home Book of American
    Quotations*

In the service, when a man gives you his word, his word is binding. In politics, you never know.

Dwight D. Eisenhower
Comment, William Scranton
June 7, 1964

Frequently in my life I have had to settle for progress short of perfection. I have done so because—despite cynics—I believe that half a loaf *is* better than none. But my acceptance has always been conditioned upon the premise that the half-loaf is a step towards the full loaf—and that if I go on working, the day of the full loaf will come.

Lyndon B. Johnson
A Time for Action
1964

Our political philosophies, I have found, are the sum of our life experiences.

Lyndon B. Johnson
A Time for Action
1964

I believe there is always a national answer to each national problem, and, believing this, I do not believe that there are necessarily two sides to every question.

Lyndon B. Johnson
A Time for Action
1964

It is a curious fact that when we get sick we want an uncommon doctor. If we have a construction job, we want an uncommon engineer. When we get into a war, we dreadfully want an uncommon admiral and an uncommon general. Only when we get into politics are we content with the common man.

Herbert Hoover
New York Times
October 21, 1964

If you're in politics and you can't tell when you walk into a room who's for you and who's against you, then you're in the wrong line of work.

Lyndon B. Johnson
Cited in B. Mooney, *The Lyndon Johnson Story*

We politicians are just like lawyers who get together for a drink after fighting each other like hell in the courtroom.

Lyndon B. Johnson
Comment, Richard Nixon, Gridiron Dinner, Washington, D.C.
March 12, 1966

The search for a scapegoat is the easiest of all hunting expeditions.

Dwight D. Eisenhower
At Ease: Stories I Tell Friends
1967

Politics is a very hard game. Winston Churchill once pointed out that politics is even more difficult than war. Because in politics you die many times; in war you die only once.

Richard Nixon
Letter, Thomas Eagleton
August 2, 1972

It is a very sad commentary that an individual can be bruised and battered and maligned and libeled and then become expendable. But in politics I fear that is the case.

Richard Nixon
The Memoirs of Richard Nixon
1972

Often a consensus develops, sometimes no more than a shared instinct, that the burden of the wounded must be removed in order for the rest to survive.

Richard Nixon
The Memoirs of Richard Nixon
1972

James K. Polk

He is sold soul and body to that grim idiot, half albino, half negro, the compound of democracy and of slavery, which, by the slave representation in Congress, rules and ruins the Union.

John Quincy Adams
Cited in Richard Kenin and Justin Wintle, *The Dictionary of Biographical Quotations*

Polk's appointments all in all are the most damnable set that was ever made by any President since the government was organized. . . . He has a set of interested parasites about him, who flatter him until he does not know himself. He seems to be acting on the principle of hanging an old friend for the purpose of making two new ones. . . . There is one thing I will say . . . *I never betrayed a friend or [was] guilty of the black sin of ingratitude. Mr. Polk cannot say as much.*

Andrew Jackson
Cited in Eric L. McKitrick, *Andrew Jackson: A Profile*

Poverty

A certain degree of misery seems inseparable from a high degree of populousness.

James Madison
Letter, Thomas Jefferson
June 19, 1786

Ignorance and vice bred poverty which was as immutable as the seasons.

Martin Van Buren
Letter, Edward Livingston
November 22, 1831

The poor are to be relieved. And not only their physical, but their moral and intellectual wants are to be provided for. And all this is to be done for the worthy poor, because they are poor and worthy, and not because they profess any creed, or religious belief. A common humanity is the only necessary credential.

Grover Cleveland
Speech, laying of the corner stone of the Fitch Institute of Buffalo, New York
May 10, 1882

The gulf between employers and the employed is constantly widening, and classes are rapidly forming, one comprising the very rich and powerful, while in another are found the toiling poor.

Grover Cleveland
Fourth annual message, Congress
December 3, 1888

He mocks the people who proposes that the government shall protect the rich and that they in turn will care for the laboring poor.

Grover Cleveland
Fourth annual message, Congress
December 3, 1888

Abolish plutocracy if you would abolish poverty.

Rutherford B. Hayes
Diary
February 16, 1890

Business underlies everything in our national life, including our spiritual life. Witness the fact that in the Lord's Prayer the first petition is for daily bread. No one can worship God or love his neighbor on an empty stomach.

Woodrow Wilson
Speech, New York, New York
1912

Hunger does not breed reform; it breeds madness, and all the ugly distempers that make an ordered life impossible.

Woodrow Wilson
Address, Congress
November 11, 1918

I know very well what it means to awake in the night and realize that the rent is coming due, wondering where the money is coming from with which to pay it.

Calvin Coolidge
The Autobiography of Calvin Coolidge
1929

We in America today are nearer to the final triumph over poverty than ever before in the history of any land.

Herbert Hoover
Just before the crash
c. 1929

Any retreat—and this should be underscored—from our American philosophy of constantly increasing standards of living becomes a retreat into perpetual unemployment and the acceptance of a cesspool of poverty for some large part of our people.

Herbert Hoover
Speech, bankers
1930s

The reconstruction of children is more precious than factories and bridges.

Herbert Hoover
Radio broadcast from Egypt
c. 1940

People who are hungry and out of a job are the stuff of which dictatorships are made.

Franklin D. Roosevelt
Message, Congress
January 11, 1944

If a free society cannot help the many who are poor, it cannot save the few who are rich.

John F. Kennedy
Inaugural address
January 20, 1961

The war against hunger is truly mankind's war of liberation.

John F. Kennedy
Speech, opening of World Food Congress
June 4, 1963

There is inherited wealth in this country and also inherited poverty.

John F. Kennedy
Address, Amherst College, Amherst, Massachusetts

Unfortunately, many Americans live on the outskirts of hope—some because of their poverty, some because of their color, and all too many because of both. Our task is to help replace their despair with opportunity.

Lyndon B. Johnson
State of the union address, opening the War on
    Poverty
January 8, 1964

This administration here and now declares an unconditional war against poverty.

Lyndon B. Johnson
State of the union address
January 8, 1964

The war against poverty will not be won here in Washington. It must be won in the field, in every private home, in every public office, from the courthouse to the White House.

Lyndon B. Johnson
State of the union address
January 8, 1964

We have never lost sight of our goal: an America in which every citizen shares all the opportunities of his society, in which every man has a chance to advance his welfare to the limit of his capacities. We have come a long way toward this goal. We still have a long way to go. The distance which remains is the measure of the great unfinished work of our society. To finish that work I have called for a national war on poverty: Our objective: total victory.

Lyndon B. Johnson
Message, Congress
March 16, 1964

Let those who are well-fed, well-clothed, and well-housed never forget and never overlook those who live on the outskirts of hope.

Lyndon B. Johnson
Telephone remarks, Convention of the Plasterer's
    Union, Philadelphia, Pennsylvania
August 31, 1964

Giving a man a chance to work and feed his family and provide for his children does not destroy his initiative. Hunger destroys initiative. Ignorance destroys initiative. A cold and indifferent government destroys initiative.

Lyndon B. Johnson
Speech, Dedication, Airport, Morgantown, West
    Virginia
September 20, 1964

Poverty has many roots, but the tap root is ignorance.

Lyndon B. Johnson
Speech, Congress
January 12, 1965

Human hunger is no longer an inevitable fact of life—its elimination is within our grasp.

Lyndon B. Johnson
Statement, Food For Peace Program
March 27, 1965

A guarantee of a job is useless to a child who drops out of school in the eighth grade. The promise of a new skill is useless to a man who doesn't believe in the future. A new classroom is useless to a child whose stomach is so empty that he cannot study, or whose eyes cannot recognize what he sees.

Lyndon B. Johnson
Remarks, reception for participants in a planning session for the White House Conference "To Fulfill These Rights"
November 16, 1965

I know what it is to teach children who are listless and tired because they are hungry—and realize the difference a decent meal can make in the lives and attitudes of school children.

Lyndon B. Johnson
Comments, signing the Child Nutrition Act, The White House
October 11, 1966

Poverty is a very high price to pay for wisdom. Men ought to be able to build bridges of understanding between themselves and out of better stuff than their common poverty.

Lyndon B. Johnson
Speech, Pocatello, Idaho
August 26, 1966

To be poor is to be without an advocate—in dealing with a landlord, a creditor, or a government bureaucrat. It is to be subjected to the hostility or indifference of society, without redress.

Lyndon B. Johnson
Message, Congress
March 14, 1967

We have launched a war on poverty—not to give away the taxpayer's hard-earned treasure, but to help every citizen discover the treasure of his own ability; to help him get a job and become a taxpayer, not a tax-eater.

Lyndon B. Johnson
Speech, Democratic Party Dinner, Austin, Texas
June 16, 1967

If I became dictator of the world I'd give all the poor a cottage and birth-control pills—and I'd make damn sure they didn't get one if they didn't take the other!

Lyndon B. Johnson
Cited in *Atlantic Monthly*
September 1973

It's difficult to believe that people are starving in this country because food isn't available. . . . I find it difficult also to find any cases of starvation and undernourishment.

Ronald Reagan
Press conference, Washington, D.C.
June 11, 1986

Power

The jaws of power are always open to devour, and her arm is always stretched out, if possible, to destroy the freedom of thinking, speaking, and writing.

John Adams
"Dissertation on the Canon and the Feudal Law"
August 1765

Nip the shoots of arbitrary power in the bud, is the only maxim which can ever preserve the liberties of any people.

John Adams
"Novanglus," in the Boston *Gazette*
February 6, 1775

One precedent in favor of power is stronger than an hundred against it.

Thomas Jefferson
Notes on Virginia
1782

Neither philosophy, nor religion nor morality, nor wisdom, nor interest will ever govern nations or parties against their vanity, their pride, their resentment or revenge, or their avarice or ambition. Nothing but force and power and strength can restrain them.

John Adams
Letter, Thomas Jefferson
October 9, 1787

It will not be denied that power is of an encroaching nature, and that it ought to be effectually restrained from passing the limits assigned to it.

James Madison
Federalist XLVII
1788

It is weakness rather than wickedness which renders men unfit to be trusted with unlimited power.

John Adams
"A Defence of the Constitutions of Government of
   the United States of America"
1787-1788

[Absolute power is] tyranny, delirious tyranny.

John Adams
"A Defence of the Constitutions of Government of
   the United States of America"
1787-1788

But every project has been found no better than committing the lamb to the custody of the wolf, except that one which is called *balence of power.*

John Adams
Letter, Roger Sherman
July 18, 1789

Power naturally grows. Why? Because human passions are insatiable.

John Adams
Letter, Roger Sherman
July 18, 1789

Where an excess of power prevails, property of no sort is duly respected. No man is safe in his opinions, his person, his faculties or his possessions.

James Madison
National Gazette
March 29, 1792

I have never been able to conceive how any rational being could propose happiness to himself from the exercise of power over others.

Thomas Jefferson
Letter, A. L. C. Destutt de Tracy
January 26, 1811

Let us not be unmindful that liberty is power, that the nation blessed with the largest portion of liberty must in proportion to its numbers be the most powerful nation upon earth.

John Quincy Adams
1821

All power in human hands is liable to be abused.

James Madison
Letter, Thomas Ritchie
December 18, 1825

What a perversion of the natural order of things! . . . To make power the primary and central object of the social system, and Liberty but its satellite.

James Madison
National Gazette
December 20, 1825

There is nothing more corrupting, nothing more destructive of the noblest and finest feelings of our nature, than the exercise of unlimited power. The man who, in the beginning of such a career, might shudder at the idea of taking away the life of a fellow-being, might soon have his conscience so scarred by the repetition of crime, that the agonies of his murdered victims might become music to his soul, and the drippings of his scaffold afford "blood enough to swim in." History is full of such examples.

William Henry Harrison
Letter, Simon Bolívar
September 27, 1829

Republics can commit no greater error than to adopt . . . any feature in their systems of government which may be calculated to create or increase the love of power in the bosoms of those to whom necessity obliges them to commit the management of their affairs.

William Henry Harrison
Inaugural address
March 4, 1841

When this corrupting passion [power] once takes possession of the human mind, like the love of gold it becomes insatiable. It is the never-dying worm in his bosom, grows with his growth and strengthens with the declining years of its victim.

William Henry Harrison
Inaugural address
March 4, 1841

As a matter of fact and experience, the more power is divided the more irresponsible it becomes.

Woodrow Wilson
1885

He is . . . more powerful because he is vindictive and not restrained by conscience.

Rutherford B. Hayes (on Senator Roscoe Conkling,
   New York Republican boss)
Diary
c. 1878

They talk of my power: my power vanishes into thin air the instant that my fellow citizens who are straight and honest cease to believe that I represent them and fight for what is straight and honest; that is all the strength I have.

Theodore Roosevelt
Speech, Binghamton, New York
October 24, 1910

It is fine to feel one's hand guiding great machinery.

Theodore Roosevelt
Cited in Edmund Morris, *The Rise of Theodore
   Roosevelt*

When we resist . . . concentration of power, we are resisting the powers of death, because concentration of power is what always precedes the destruction of human liberties.

Woodrow Wilson
Address, New York Press Club
May 9, 1912

The history of liberty is the history of the limitation of governmental power, not the increase of it.

Woodrow Wilson
September 9, 1912

But . . . the intoxication of power rapidly sobers off in the knowledge of its restrictions and under the prompt reminder of an ever-present and not always considerate press, as well as the kindly suggestions that not infrequently come from [Congress].

William Howard Taft
Speech, Lotus Club, New York, New York
November 16, 1912

Power consists in one's capacity to link his will with the purpose of others, to lead by reason and a gift of cooperation.

Woodrow Wilson
Letter, Mary A. Hulbert
September 21, 1913

Mankind is looking now for freedom of life, not for equipoises of power.

Woodrow Wilson
Address, Senate (Peace Without Victory)
January 22, 1917

Is the present war a struggle for a just and secure peace, or only for a new balance of power?

Woodrow Wilson
Speech, Senate (Peace Without Victory)
January 22, 1917

There must be, not a balance of power, but a community of power; not organized rivalries, but an organized common peace.

Woodrow Wilson
Address, Senate (Peace Without Victory)
January 22, 1917

I suppose I am the most powerful man in the world, but great power doesn't mean much except great limitations.

Calvin Coolidge
Letter, his father
January 1, 1926

They [people in high office] are always surrounded by worshippers. They are constantly, and for the most part sincerely, assured of their greatness.

Calvin Coolidge
The Autobiography of Calvin Coolidge
1929

They [powerful people] live in an artificial atmosphere of adulation and exaltation which sooner or later impairs their judgment. They are in grave danger of becoming careless and arrogant.

Calvin Coolidge
The Autobiography of Calvin Coolidge
1929

I should like to have it said of my first Administration that in it the forces of selfishness and of lust for power met their match. . . . I should like to have it said of my second Administration that in it these forces met their master.

Franklin D. Roosevelt
Speech, New York, New York
October 31, 1936

In the past, those who foolishly sought power by riding the back of the tiger ended up inside.

John F. Kennedy
Inaugural address
January 20, 1961

Precedent

As the first of everything, in our situation, will serve to establish a Precedent, it is devoutly wished on my part, that these precedents may be fixed on true principles.

George Washington
Letter, James Madison
May 15, 1789

Precedents once established are so much positive power.

James Madison
Virginia Assembly
January 23, 1799

Mere precedent is a dangerous source of authority.

Andrew Jackson
Veto, Bank Renewal Bill
July 10, 1832

The people have thought proper to invest him [the president] with the most honorable, responsible, and dignified office in the world; and the individual, however unworthy, now holding this exalted position, will take care, so far as in him lies, that their rights and prerogatives shall never be violated in his person, but shall pass to his successors unimpaired by the adoption of a dangerous precedent.

James Buchanan
Special Message, House
March 28, 1860

Prejudice

The moment a person forms a theory, his imagination sees in every object only the traits that favor that theory.

Thomas Jefferson
Letter, Charles Thompson
September 20, 1787

All bigotries hang to one another.

Thomas Jefferson
Letter, John Adams
1814

Your sect by it's [*sic*] sufferings has furnished a remarkable proof of the universal spirit of religious intolerance, inherent in every sect, disclaimed by all while feeble, and practised by all when in power. Our laws have applied the only antidote to this vice, protecting our religious as they do our civil rights by putting all on an equal footing. But more remains to be done.

Thomas Jefferson
Letter, Mordecai Noah, Jewish diplomat
1818

Sectionalism and race prejudice . . . are the only two enemies America has any cause to fear.

Rutherford B. Hayes
Speech, Hampton Institute, Virginia
1880

How few can say sincerely with Dr. Haygood, "Our brother in black."

Rutherford B. Hayes
Letter, B. T. Tanner
February 20, 1883

The prejudices of generations are not like marks upon the blackboard, that can be rubbed out with a sponge. These are more like the deep glacial lines that the years have left in the rock; but the water, when that surface is exposed to its quiet, gentle, and perpetual influence, wears even these out, until the surface is smooth and uniform.

Benjamin Harrison
Speech, Brattleboro, Vermont
August 27, 1891

I should hang my head in shame if I were capable of discriminating against a Japanese general or admiral, statesman, philanthropist or artist, because he and I have different shades of skin.

Theodore Roosevelt
Comment, John Roosevelt
1904

There are a great many hyphens left in America. For my part, I think the most un-American thing in the world is a hyphen.

Woodrow Wilson
Speech, St. Paul, Minnesota
September 9, 1919

Anti-semitism is a noxious weed that should be cut out. It has no place in America.

William Howard Taft
Speech
1920

The idea behind this discriminatory policy [of quotas] was, to put it baldly, that Americans with English or Irish names were better people and better citizens than Americans with Italian or Greek or Polish names.

Harry S. Truman
Veto, McCarran-Walter Immigration Act
June 25, 1952

The time to shake off this dead weight of past mistakes is now.

Harry S. Truman
Veto, McCarran-Walter Immigration Act
June 25, 1952

It is not just the Negro, but really all of us, who must overcome the crippling legacy of bigotry and injustice.

Lyndon B. Johnson
Message, Congress
March 15, 1965

There is no Negro problem. There is no Southern problem. There is no Northern problem. There is only an American problem.

Lyndon B. Johnson
Message, Congress
March 15, 1965

Much of the Negro community is buried under a blanket of history and circumstance. It is not a lasting solution to lift just one corner of that blanket. We must stand on all sides and we must raise the entire cover if we are to liberate our fellow citizens.

Lyndon B. Johnson
Commencement address, Howard University, Washington, D.C.
June 4, 1965

The stories of our Nation and of the American Negro are like two great rivers. Welling up from that tiny Jamestown spring they flow through the centuries along divided channels. When pioneers subdued a continent to the need of man, they did not tame it for the Negro. When the Liberty Bell rang out in Philadelphia, it did not toll for the Negro. When Andrew Jackson threw open the doors of democracy, they did not open for the

Negro. It was only at Appomattox, a century ago, that an American victory was also a Negro victory. And the two rivers—one shining with promise, the other dark-stained with oppression—began to move toward one another.

Lyndon B. Johnson
Speech, Signing of Voting Rights Act, Capitol
  Rotunda
August 6, 1965

Negro Americans comprise 22 percent of the enlisted men in our Army combat units in Viet-Nam—and 22 percent of those who have lost their lives in battle there. We fall victim to a profound hypocrisy when we say that they cannot buy or rent dwellings among citizens they fight to save.

Lyndon B. Johnson
Message, Congress
April 28, 1966

As a Southerner, it makes me feel angry when I see them [the Ku Klux Klan] with a Confederate battle flag, because I remember Judah P. Benjamin, who was Secretary of State; he was a Jew. And I remember General Pat Cleburne of Arkansas, who died in battle not far from this very spot, and General Beauregard of Louisiana—brave men. Both were Catholics. . . . And sometimes when I see the raising of a cross, and I remember that the One who was crucified taught us to have faith, to hope, and not to hate but to love one another.

Jimmy Carter
Speech, Tuscumbia, Alabama
September 1, 1980

Presidency

I must heartily wish the choice to which you allude [his election to the presidency] may not fall on me. . . . If I should conceive myself in a manner constrained to accept, I call Heaven to witness that this very act would be the greatest sacrifice of my personal feelings and wishes that I ever have been called upon to make.

George Washington
Letter, Benjamin Lincoln
October 26, 1788

I bade adieu to Mount Vernon, to private life, and to domestic felicity, and with a mind oppressed with more anxious and painful sensations than I have words to express, set out for New York . . . with the best disposition to render service to my country in obedience to its calls, but with less hope of answering its expectations.

George Washington
Diaries of George Washington
April 16, 1789

My movements to the chair of government will be accompanied by feelings not unlike those of a culprit who is going to the place of his execution.

George Washington
Letter
1789

Among the vicissitudes incident to life no event could have filled me with greater anxiety than that of which the notification was transmitted of your order. . . . On the one hand, I was summoned by my country . . . from a retreat which I had chosen with the fondest predilection . . . as the asylum of my declining years. . . . On the other hand, the magnitude and the difficulty of the trust to which the voice of my country called me . . . could not but overwhelm with despondence one who . . . ought to be peculiarly conscious of his own deficiencies. . . . All I dare hope is that if . . . I have been too much swayed . . . by an affectionate sensibility to this transcendent proof of the confidence of my fellow citizens . . . my error will be palliated by the motives which mislead me, and its consequences be judged by my country with some share of the partiality in which they originated.

George Washington
First inaugural address
April 30, 1789

So much is expected, so many untoward circumstances may intervene, in such a new and critical situation, that I feel an insuperable diffidence in my own abilities. I feel, in the execution of the duties of my arduous Office, how much I shall stand in need of the contenance and aid of every friend to myself, of every friend to the

Revolution, and of every lover of good Government.

George Washington
Letter, E. Rutledge
May 5, 1789

My political conduct in nominations, even if I was influenced by principle, must be exceedingly circumspect and proof against just criticism, for the eyes of Argus are upon me, and no slip will pass unnoticed that can be improved into a supposed partiality for friends or relatives.

George Washington
Letter, Bushrod Washington
July 27, 1789

I suffered every attack that was made upon my Executive conduct . . . to pass unnoticed while I remained in public office, well knowing that if the general tenor of it would not stand the test of investigation, a newspaper vindication would be of little avail.

George Washington
Letter, W. Gordon
October 15, 1789

The powers of the Executive of the U. States are more definite, and better understood perhaps than those of almost any other Country; and my aim has been, and will continue to be, neither to stretch, nor relax from them in any instance whatever, unless imperious circumstances shd. render the measure indispensable.

George Washington
Letter, Alexander Hamilton
July 2, 1794

I envy you the Society of your Farm but another year and one Month may make me the Object of Envy.

John Adams
Letter, Thomas Jefferson
January 31, 1796

No man will ever bring out of the Presidency the reputation which carries him into it.

Thomas Jefferson
Letter, Edward Rutledge
1796

I have no ambition to govern men. It is a painful and thankless office.

Thomas Jefferson
Letter, John Adams
1796

But it must astonish others who know that the Constitution allows the President ten days to deliberate on each Bill that is brought before him that he should be allowed by the Legislature less than half that time to consider all the business of the Session; and in some instances, scarcely an hour to [resolve] the most important. But as the scene is closing, with me, it is of little avail now to let it be with murmurs.

George Washington
Letter, J. Trumbull
March 1797

The second office of the government is honorable and easy; the first is but a splendid misery.

Thomas Jefferson
Letter, Elbridge Gerry
1797

I have no idea that I shall be chosen President a second time; thought this is not to be talked of. The business of the office is so oppressive that I shall hardly support it two years longer.

John Adams
Letter, Abigail Adams
February 22, 1799

The danger is that the indulgence and attachments of the people will keep a man in the chair after he becomes a dotard, that reelection through life shall become habitual, and election for life follow that.

Thomas Jefferson
Early in his second administration, announcing that he would not be a candidate for a third term

I am tired of an office where I can do no more good than many others, who would be glad to be employed in it. To myself, personally, it brings nothing but unceasing drudgery and daily loss of friends.

Thomas Jefferson
Letter, John Dickinson
January 13, 1807

Had I been chosen President again, I am certain I could not have lived another year.

John Adams
To the *Boston Patriot*
1809

In all great and essential measures he [the president] is bound by his honor and his conscience, by his oath to the Constitution, as well as his responsibility to the public opinion of the nation, to act his own mature and unbiased judgement, though unfortunately, it may be in direct contradiction to the advice of all his ministers. This was my situation in more than one instance.

George Washington
To the *Boston Patriot*
1809

The executive powers lodged in the Senate are the most dangerous to the Constitution, and to liberty, of all the powers in it. The people then, ought to consider the President's office as the indispensable guardian of their rights. I have ever, therefore, been of the opinion, that the electors of [the] President ought to be chosen by the people at large.

John Adams
To the *Boston Patriot*
1809

Five weeks more will relieve me from a drudgery to which I am no longer equal, and restore me to a scene of tranquility, amidst my family and friends, more congenial to my age and natural inclinations.

John Adams
Letter, James Monroe
January 1809

I am for responsibilities at short periods, seeing neither reason nor safety in making public functionaries independent of the nation for life, or even for long terms of years. On this principle I prefer the Presidential term of four years, to that of seven years, which I myself had at first suggested, annexing to it, however, ineligibility forever after; and I wish it were now annexed to the 2d quadrennial election of President.

Thomas Jefferson
Letter, J. Martin
September 20, 1813

A President can declare war and can conclude peace without being hurled from his chair.

John Adams
Letter, W. S. Smith
February 22, 1815

I left my country in peace and harmony with all the world . . . I left navy yards, fortifications, frigates, timber, naval stores, manufactures of canon and arms, and a treasury full of five millions of dollars. This was all done . . . against perpetual oppositions, clamors and reproaches, such as no other President ever had to encounter. . . . For this I was turned out of office, degraded and disgraced by my country.

John Adams
Letter, James Lloyd
March 31, 1815

And they talked a great deal about "the dignity" of the office of President, which I do not find that any other persons, public or private, regards very much.

John Adams
Letter, Thomas Jefferson
April 19, 1817

If that office [the presidency] was to be the prize of cabal and intrigue, of purchasing newspapers, bribing by appointments, or bargaining for foreign missions, I had no ticket in that lottery. Whether I had the qualities necessary for a President of the United States was, to say the very least, very doubtful to myself. But that I had no talents for obtaining the office by such means was perfectly clear.

John Quincy Adams
Memoirs
February 25, 1821

No man who ever held the office of President would congratulate a friend on obtaining it. He will make one man ungrateful, and a hundred men his enemies, for every office he can bestow.

John Adams
Letter, Josiah Quincy
February 14, 1825

In truth, though I occupy a very high position, I am the hardest working man in this country.

James K. Polk
Inaugural address
March 4, 1824

Had I been disposed to take advantage of my country a thousand opportunities had before presented themselves, in which I might have made an immense profit, and escaped detection.

James Monroe
Letter, General Jackson
July 3, 1825

I can scarcely conceive a more harassing, wearying, teasing condition of existence. It literally renders life burdensome. What retirement will be I cannot realize, but have formed no favorable anticipation. It cannot be worse than this perpetual motion and crazing cares. The weight grows heavier from day to day.

John Quincy Adams
Diary
March 5, 1827

I can with truth say mine is a situation of dignified slavery.

Andrew Jackson
Letter, T. R. J. Chester
November 30, 1829

No one knows, and few conceive, the agony of mind that I have suffered from the time that I was made by circumstances, and not by my volition, a candidate for the Presidency till I was dismissed from that station by failure of my re-election.

John Quincy Adams
Diary
November 7, 1830

The duty of the Executive is a plain one ... the laws will be executed and the Union preserved by all the constitutional and legal means he is invested with.

Andrew Jackson
Letter, Joel R. Poinsett
November 7, 1832

If he [the president] speaks to Congress, it must be in the language of truth.

Andrew Jackson
Letter, Martin Van Buren
October 27, 1834

Some folks are silly enough as to have formed a plan to make a President of the United States out of this Clerk and Clodhopper.

William Henry Harrison
Letter, Stephen Van Rensselaer
1836

I returned [from Washington] with barely ninety dollars in my pocket, [Bacon] for my family and corn and oats for the stock to buy, the new roof on my house just rebuilt leaking and to be repaired.

Andrew Jackson
Letter
March 17, 1837

The President himself is not more than a representative of public opinion at the time of his election; and as public opinion is subject to great and frequent fluctuations, he *must* accommodate his policy to them; or the people will speedily give him a successor.

John Quincy Adams
Jubilee of the Constitution
1839

I represent the executive authority of the people of the United States, and it is in their name, whose mere agent and servant I am, and whose will declared in their fundamental law I dare not, even were I inclined, to disobey, that I protest against every attempt to break down the undoubted constitutional power of this department without a solemn amendment of that fundamental law.

John Tyler
Protest to the House of Representatives
August 30, 1842

[Candidacy for president] seems to me too visionary to require a serious answer. Such an idea never entered my head, nor is it likely to enter the head of any sane person.

Zachary Taylor
Letter, his brother
June 11, 1846

[I] can truly say that I feel more interest in the recovery of your wound, & in the termination of this war . . . than I do of being president of the U. States.

Zachary Taylor
Letter, Jefferson Davis
July 27, 1847

I do not care a fig about the office.

Zachary Taylor
Letter, J. R. Ingersoll
August 3, 1847

No candidate for the Presidency ought ever to remain in the cabinet. He is an unsafe adviser.

James K. Polk
The Diary of James K. Polk
February 21, 1848

With me it is exceptionally true that the Presidency is "no bed of roses."

James K. Polk
The Diary of James K. Polk
March 4, 1849

You have summoned me in my weakness; you must sustain me by your strength.

Franklin Pierce
Inaugural address
March 4, 1853

It is a relief to feel that no heart but my own can know the personal regret and bitter sorrow over which I have been borne to a position so suitable for others rather than desirable for myself.

Franklin Pierce
Inaugural address, referring to the recent death of his son, Benjamin, on January 6, 1853
March 4, 1853

When the Constitution makers of France strove to reconcile the first Napoleon to an abridgement of his immediate power by proposing to confer upon him authority to direct what should be done after his decease he promptly refused the offer for the reason that a dead man was nothing in respect to power whatever or whoever he may have been when alive. The same may be said of a President whom a few short months will dispossess of his station in obedience to the decree of the People.

Martin Van Buren
Autobiography of Martin Van Buren
1854

Nobody has ever expected me to become president. In my poor, lean, lank face nobody has ever seen that any cabbages were sprouting.

Abraham Lincoln
Second campaign speech against Stephen Douglas
July 17, 1858

It is a national disgrace that our Presidents, after having occupied the highest position in the country, should be cast adrift, and, perhaps, be compelled to keep a corner grocery for subsistence.

Millard Fillmore
Letter, a party committee
October 12, 1858

I must, in candor, say I do not think myself fit for the Presidency.

Abraham Lincoln
Letter, T. J. Pickett
April 1859

I am now in my 69th year & am heartily tired of my position as President. I shall leave it in the beginning of March, 1861, should a kind Providence prolong my days until that period, with much greater satisfaction than when entering on the duties of the office.

James Buchanan
Letter, Mrs. J. K. Polk
September 19, 1859

Only events and not a man's exertions in his own behalf, can make a President.

Abraham Lincoln
c. 1859

After all, he [the president] is no more than the chief executive officer of the Government. His province is not to make but to execute the laws.

James Buchanan
Fourth annual message, Congress (on secession)
December 3, 1860

I have been selected to fill an important office for a brief period, and am now, in your eyes, invested with an influence which will soon pass away; but should my administration prove to be a very wicked one, or what is more probable, a very foolish one, if you, the people, are true to yourselves and the Constitution, there is but little harm I can do, thank God.

Abraham Lincoln
Speech, Lawrenceburg, Indiana
February 28, 1861

If you are as happy, my dear sir, on entering this house as I am in leaving it and returning home, you are the happiest man in this country.

James Buchanan
Letter, Abraham Lincoln
March 4, 1861

You have heard about the man tarred and feathered and ridden out of town on a rail? A man in the crowd asked him how he liked it, and his reply was that if it wasn't for the honor of the thing, he would much rather walk.

Abraham Lincoln
Reply to a friend who asked how it felt to be president
c. 1862

I desire to conduct the affairs of this administration that if at the end, when I come to lay down the reins of power, I have lost every other friend on earth, I shall at least have one friend left, and that friend shall be down inside of me.

Abraham Lincoln
Reply, Missouri Committee of Seventy
1864

In the language of the lamented but immortal [Henry] Clay: "I had rather be right than be President."

Millard Fillmore
Speech, Albany, New York

What is the Presidency worth to me if I have no country?

Abraham Lincoln
Washington, D.C.
1864

I may not have made as great a President as some other man, but I believe I have kept these discordant elements together as well as anyone could.

Abraham Lincoln
Letter, Leonard Swett

I shall go just so fast and only so fast as I think I'm right and the people are ready for the step.

Abraham Lincoln
Letter, H. Maynard

I fail . . . to find in the Constitution of the United States the authority given to the House of Representatives . . . to enquire of the Executive . . . an account of his discharge of his appropriate and purely executive offices, acts, and duties either as to when, where, or how performed.

Ulysses S. Grant
Speech, House of Representatives, in reference to executive acts
May 4, 1876

Now that the flush of gratification upon the nomination is about to end, I begin to prefer the independence of a private citizen. If the result leaves me so, I will be the most contented defeated Presidential candidate, having any prospects, that was ever voted for.

Rutherford B. Hayes
Letter, General Randolph P. Buckland, Diary
August 13, 1876

The Boston Post says, 1. Hayes will, during the absence of Mrs. Hayes, be acting President.

Rutherford B. Hayes
Letter, Mrs. Hayes

With good health & great opportunities, may I not hope to confer great and lasting benefits on my Country! I mean to try. Let me be kind and considerate in treatment of the unfortunate who crowd my doorway, and firm and conscientious in dealing with the temptors.

Rutherford B. Hayes
Diary
October 4, 1877

This reminds me of my feeling at the great moment of my life, when I heard I was nominated at Cincinnati. I felt a sense of responsibility—a sobered feeling—It was my feeling that with soundness of judgment, with a cheerful and elastic temper, with firmness, with an honest purpose to do right, and with some experience in affairs I could do well in the place.

Rutherford B. Hayes
Diary
April 28, 1878

This laborious, anxious, slavish life . . .

Rutherford B. Hayes
Diary
June 6, 1879

Well I am heartily tired of this life of bondage, responsibility and toil.

Rutherford B. Hayes
Diary
June 6, 1879

The strain [of the presidency] is hard to bear. It grows harder as time passes.

Rutherford B. Hayes
Diary
July 26, 1879

I have so long and so often seen the evil effects of the presidential fever upon my associates and friends that I am determined it shall not seize upon me.

James A. Garfield
Diary
February 1880

I am casting about me to find someone who will help to enliven the solitude which surrounds the Presidency. The unfortunate incumbent of that office is the most isolated man in America.

James A. Garfield
Letter, John Hay
1881

Nobody ever left the Presidency with less regret, less disappointment, fewer heartburnings, or more general content with the result of his term (in his own heart, I mean), than I do.

Rutherford B. Hayes
Letter, G. M. Bryan
January 1, 1881

That the White House will be left *"willingly"* by both Mrs. Hayes and myself is perfectly true. We have upon the whole enjoyed our four years here. But the responsibility, the embarrassments, the heart breaking sufferings which we can't relieve, the ever present danger of scandals and crimes among those we are compelled to trust, and a thousand other draw backs to our satisfaction and enjoyment by which we are constantly surrounded leave us no place for regret upon retiring from this conspicuous scene to the freedom, independence and safety of our obscure and happy home.

Rutherford B. Hayes
Diary
January 16, 1881

Tonight I am a private citizen. Tomorrow, I shall be called to assume new responsibilities and, on the day after, the broadside of the world's wrath will strike.

James A. Garfield
Speech, Wormley Hotel, Washington, D.C.
March 3, 1881

I have never had presidential fever, not even for a day . . . and I would thank God were I today a free lance in the House or the Senate.

James A. Garfield
Speech, Wormley Hotel, Washington, D.C.
March 3, 1881

I am wholly unfit for this sort of work.

James A. Garfield
Journal
March 16, 1881

It had better be known in the outset whether the President is the head of the government, or the registering clerk of the Senate.

James A. Garfield
Letter, Whitelaw Reid
March 30, 1881

Presidents in the past have always been better than their adversaries have predicted.

Rutherford B. Hayes
Diary
July 26, 1881

A President's usefulness is measured, not by efficiency, but by calendar months. It is reckoned that if he be good at all he will be good for four years. A Prime Minister must keep himself in favor of the majority, a President need only keep alive.

Woodrow Wilson
1885

It seems to me I am as much consecrated to a service, as the religionist who secludes himself from all that is joyous in life and devotes himself to a sacred mission.

Grover Cleveland
Letter, W. E. Bissell
June 25, 1885

The office of President has not, to me personally, a single allurement.

Grover Cleveland
Letter, W. E. Bissell
June 25, 1885

I believe I shall buy or rent a house near here where I can go and be away from this cursed constant grind.

Grover Cleveland
Letter, W. E. Bissell
June 25, 1885

Franklin, I hope you never become President.

Grover S. Cleveland
Comment, to the boy Franklin D. Roosevelt
Cited by Clifton Fadiman, *The American Treasury*

They might just as well call me His Transparency for all I care.

Theodore Roosevelt
Cited in Edmund Morris, *The Rise of Theodore Roosevelt*

The People of the United States have one and all a sacred mission to perform, and your President, not more surely than any other citizen who loves his country, must assume part of the responsibility of the demonstration to the world of the success of popular government. No man can hide his talent in a napkin, and escape the condemnation which his slothfulness deserves, or evade the stern sentence which his faithfulness invites.

Grover Cleveland
Speech, Harvard College, Cambridge, Massachusetts
November 9, 1886

The executive power is large because not defined in the Constitution. The real test has never come because the Presidents have, down to the present, been conservative, or what might be called conscientious, men, and have kept within limited range. . . . But if a Napoleon ever became President, he could make the executive almost what he wished to make it.

Rutherford B. Hayes
Comment, C. Ellis Stevens
September 30, 1889

It has always seemed to me that, beyond the greatness of the office and the supreme importance of its duties and responsibilities, the most impressive thing connected with the Presidency is the fact that after its honor has been relinquished, and after its labor and responsibility are past, we simply see that a citizen whom the people had selected from their ranks to do their bidding for a time and to be their agent in the discharge of public duty, has laid aside the honor and the work of the highest office in the world and has returned again to the people, to resume at their side the ordinary duties which pertain to everyday citizenship.

Grover Cleveland
Speech at Sandwich, Massachusetts
July 25, 1891

What an impressive thing it is to assume tremendous responsibilities.

William McKinley
To Grover Cleveland
March 4, 1897

I have also an idea that the Presidency is preeminently the people's office.

Grover Cleveland
Regarding a fourth renomination
March 9, 1892

Two presidents or three, with equal powers, would as surely bring disaster as three generals of equal rank and command in a single army. I do not doubt that this sense of single and personal responsibility to the people has strongly held our Presidents to responsibility a good conscience, and to a high discharge of their great duties.

Benjamin Harrison
This Country of Ours
1897

A man who is endowed for the presidency will know how to be President, in fact as well as in name, without any fussy self-assertion.

Benjamin Harrison
This Country of Ours
1897

There is only a door—one that is never locked—between the President's office and what are not very accurately called his private apartments. . . . For everyone else in the public service there is an unroofed space between the bedroom and the desk.

Benjamin Harrison
This Country of Ours
1897

It is a rare piece of good fortune during the early months of an administration if the President gets one wholly uninterrupted hour at his desk each day. His time is so broken up into bits that he is often driven to late night work, or to set up a desk in his bedroom, when preparing a message or other paper requiring unbroken attention.

Benjamin Harrison
This Country of Ours
1897

[The presidency demands:] the constitution of an athlete, the patience of a mother, the endurance of the early Christian.

Woodrow Wilson
Cited in Bill Adler, *Presidential Wit from Washington to Johnson*

I would be the happiest man in America if I could go out of office in 1901.

William McKinley
Comments, James Boyle and George Cortelyou
1900

I am of course in a perfect whirl of work and have every kind of worry and trouble—but that's what I am here for and down at bottom I enjoy it after all.

Theodore Roosevelt
Letter, Kermit Roosevelt
December 4, 1902

Of course political life in a position such as this is one long strain on the temper, one long experiment of checking one's own impulses with an iron hand and learning to subordinate one's own desires to what some hundreds of associates can be forced or cajoled or led into desiring.

Theodore Roosevelt
Letter, Maria K. Storer
December 8, 1902

I am President of all the people of the United States, and my business is to see fair play among all men, capitalists or wageworkers, whether they conduct their private business as individuals or as members of organizations.

Theodore Roosevelt
Letter, G. B. Cortelyou
July 13, 1903

But even a President has feelings.

Theodore Roosevelt
Letter, J. W. Wadsworth, Jr.
June 29, 1904

It [the presidency] is especially the office related to the people as individuals, in no general, local, or other combination.

Grover Cleveland
Presidential Problems
1904

For the very reason I believe in being a strong President and making the most of the office and using it without regard to the little, snarling men who yell about executive usurpation, I also believe that it is not a good thing that any one man should hold it too long.

Theodore Roosevelt
Letter, W. W. Sewell
June 25, 1908

If I were now presiding in the Supreme Court of the United States, I should feel entirely at home, but with the troubles of selecting a Cabinet . . . I feel just a bit like a fish out of water. . . . My wife is the politician and she will be able to meet all these issues.

William Howard Taft
Letter, friend, few weeks after his election as
   president
1908

While President, I have *been* President emphatically.

Theodore Roosevelt
Comment after leaving office

I am President now, and tired of being kicked around.

William Howard Taft
Comment, Chief Usher Irwin Hood Hoover
1908

Well, now I'm in the White House, I'm not going to be pushed around any more.

William Howard Taft
Inauguration day, to his wife
March 4, 1909

I have come to the conclusion that the major part of the work of a president is to increase the gate receipts of expositions and fairs and bring tourists into the town.

William Howard Taft
Cited in Arthur Bernon Tourtellot, *The Presidents on
   the Presidency*

I'll be damned if I am not getting tired of this. It seems to be the profession of a President simply to hear other people talk.

William Howard Taft
Cited in Arthur Bernon Tourtellot, *The Presidents on
   the Presidency*

No other President ever enjoyed the Presidency as I did.

Theodore Roosevelt
Letter, G. O. Trevelyan
September 10, 1909

I took the canal zone and let Congress debate, and while the debate goes on the canal does also.

Theodore Roosevelt
Speech, Berkeley, California
March 23, 1911

To me there is something fine in the American theory that a private citizen can be chosen by the people to occupy a position as great as that of the mightiest monarch, and to exercise a power which may for the time being surpass that of Czar, Kaiser, or Pope, and that then, after having filled this position, the man shall leave it as an unpensioned private citizen, who goes back into the ranks of his fellow citizens with entire self-respect, claiming nothing save what on his own individual merits he is entitled to receive.

Theodore Roosevelt
To G. O. Trevelyan
October 1, 1911

The President cannot make clouds to rain and cannot make the corn to grow, he cannot make business good; although when these things occur, political parties do claim some credit for the good things that have happened in this way.

William Howard Taft
The President and his Powers
1916

We have had Presidents who felt the public pulse with accuracy, who played their parts upon the political stage with histrionic genius and commanded the people almost as if they were an army and the President their Commander-in-Chief.

William Howard Taft
The President and his Powers
1916

The more I succeed in directing things the more I am depended on for leadership and expected to do everything, make all parts straight and carry every plan to its completion.

Woodrow Wilson
To M. Poindexter
May 22, 1918

I am very happy in the Senate and much prefer to remain there. I do not believe I could be happy as President. I don't want it.

Warren G. Harding
Comment, Samuel G. McClure
1920

My God, this is a hell of a job!

Warren G. Harding
Told to William Allen White, *Autobiography of William Allen White*

I am a man of limited talents, from a small town. I do not seem to grasp that I am President.

Warren G. Harding
Cited in Vic Fredericks, *The Wit and Wisdom of the Presidents*

I knew this job would be too much for me.

Warren G. Harding
Cited in Arthur Bernon Tourtellot, *The Presidents on the Presidency*

Oftentimes, as I sit here, I don't seem to grasp that I am President.

Warren G. Harding
Cited in Arthur Bernon Tourtellot, *The Presidents on the Presidency*

It's hell! No other word can describe it.

Warren G. Harding
To Senator Frank Brandegee
1921

Frankly, being President is rather an unattractive business unless one relishes the exercise of power. That is a thing which has never greatly appealed to me.

Warren G. Harding
Letter to a friend
1921

The presidential office is not a rosewater affair. This is an office in which a man must put on his war paint.

Woodrow Wilson
Woodrow Wilson: Life and Letters
1927

I do not choose to run for President in 1928.

Calvin Coolidge
August 2, 1927

I never dreamed such loneliness and desolation of the heart possible. . . . The very magnitude and fatefulness of the task I have every day to face dominates me and holds me steady to my duty. Nothing less great, I imagine, could.

Woodrow Wilson
1927-1935

It has become the custom in our country to expect all Chief Executives, from the President down, to conduct activities analogous to an entertainment bureau. No occasion is too trivial for its promoters to invite them to attend and deliver an address.

Calvin Coolidge
Autobiography of Calvin Coolidge
1929

Perhaps one of the most important accomplishments of my administration has been minding my own business.

Calvin Coolidge
News conference
March 1, 1929

This is not a showman's job. I will not step out of character.

Herbert Hoover
Cited in Theodore G. Joslin, *Hoover Off the Record*
c. 1929

In the discharge of the duties of the office there is one rule of action more important than all others. It consists of never doing anything that someone else can do for you.

Calvin Coolidge
The Autobiography of Calvin Coolidge
1929

I was convinced in my own mind that I was not qualified to fill the exalted office of President.

Calvin Coolidge
The Autobiography of Calvin Coolidge
1929

It is a great advantage to a President, and a major source of safety to the country, for him to know that he is not a great man.

Calvin Coolidge
The Autobiography of Calvin Coolidge
1929

But a President cannot, with success, constantly appeal to the country. After a time he will get no response.

Calvin Coolidge
The Autobiography of Calvin Coolidge
1929

A President should not only not be selfish, but he ought to avoid the appearance of selfishness.

Calvin Coolidge
The Autobiography of Calvin Coolidge
1929

It is difficult for men in high office to avoid the malady of self-delusion.

Calvin Coolidge
The Autobiography of Calvin Coolidge
1929

Like the glory of a morning sunrise, it can only be experienced—it cannot be told.

Calvin Coolidge
The Autobiography of Calvin Coolidge
1929

It costs a great deal to be president.

Calvin Coolidge
The Autobiography of Calvin Coolidge
1929

A few hair shirts are part of the mental wardrobe of every man. The President differs only from other men in that he has a more extensive wardrobe.

Herbert Hoover
Speech, Washington, D.C.
December 14, 1929

No one can occupy the high office of President and be other than completely confident of the future of the United States. Perhaps as to no other place does the cheerful courage and power of a confident people reflect as to his office.

Herbert Hoover
October 1930

I think the American public wants a solemn ass as a President and I think I'll go along with them.

Calvin Coolidge
To Ethel Barrymore, cited in *Time*
May 16, 1955

I thought I could swing it.

Calvin Coolidge
Cited in Arthur Bernon Tourtellot, *The Presidents on the Presidency*

The first requisites of a President of the United States are intellectual honesty and sincerity.

Herbert Hoover
Addresses on the American Road, 1933-1966

Presidents do make mistakes, but the immortal Dante tells us that divine justice weighs the sins of the cold-blooded and the sins of the warm-hearted in different scales.

Franklin D. Roosevelt
Speech
June 27, 1936

I decided the best thing to do was to go home and get as much rest as possible and face the music.

Harry S. Truman
Diary (on learning that F.D.R. had died, and that Truman would be the next president)
April 12, 1945

Boys, if you ever pray, pray for me now.

Harry S. Truman
Comments, to reporters
April 13, 1945

When you get to be President, there are all those things, the honors, the twenty-one gun salutes, all those things. You have to remember it isn't for you. It's for the Presidency.

Harry S. Truman
Comment, Merle Miller, *Plain Speaking*

I would rather have a Medal of Honor than be President of the United States.

Harry S. Truman
Comments on presenting the medal
March 27, 1946

There are only two occasions when Americans respect privacy, especially in Presidents. Those are prayer and fishing.

Herbert Hoover
New York Herald Tribune
May 19, 1947

If you don't have a sense of humor, you're in a hell of a fix when you are President of the United States.

Harry S. Truman
Cited in *Quote* magazine
October 5, 1947

Being a President is like riding a tiger. A man has to keep on riding or be swallowed.

Harry S. Truman
Memoirs
1948

It's almost impossible for a man to be President of the United States without learning something.

Harry S. Truman
Cited in *Quote* magazine
August 4, 1948

In my opinion eight years as president is enough and sometimes too much for any man to serve in that capacity. There is a lure in power. It can get into a man's blood just as gambling and lust for money have been known to do.

Harry S. Truman
Memorandum
April 16, 1950

The President hears a hundred voices telling him that he is the greatest man in the world. He must listen carefully indeed to hear the one voice that tells him he is not.

Harry S. Truman
Cited in Caroline Thomas Harnsberger, *Treasury of Presidential Quotations*

I have served my time. . . . I don't want to be carried out of the White House in a pine box.

Harry S. Truman
Cited in *Quote* magazine
July 27, 1952

Just as I believe that every President is president of all the people, there is no such thing as a president of the Republicans, there is no such thing as a president of the Democrats.

Dwight D. Eisenhower
Speech, Governors Conference
August 4, 1953

Now look, this idea that all wisdom is in the President . . . that's baloney . . . . no one has a monopoly on the truth and on the facts that affect this country.

Dwight D. Eisenhower
1953

I probably long ago used up my time; but you know, there is one thing about being President, it is hard to tell him to sit down.

Dwight D. Eisenhower
Speech, Governors Conference
August 4, 1953

If ever for a second time [1956] I should show any signs of yielding to persuasion to run, please call in the psychiatrist—or even better, the sheriff.

Dwight D. Eisenhower
To Milton Eisenhower
December 11, 1953

The nakedness of the battlefield when the soldier is all alone in the smoke and the clamor and the terror of war is comparable to the loneliness—at times—of the Presidency. These are the times when one man must conscientiously, deliberately, prayerfully, scrutinize every argument, every proposal, every prediction, every alternative, every probable outcome of his action and then—all alone—make a decision.

Dwight D. Eisenhower
Political address
November 4, 1960

Maybe the country would have been better off if I had been a concert pianist.

Harry S. Truman
Cited in *Quote* magazine
July 1, 1962

The President . . . is rightly described as a man of extraordinary powers. Yet it is also true that he must wield these powers under extraordinary limitations—and it is these limitations which so often give the problem of choice its complexities and even poignancy. Lincoln, Franklin Roosevelt once remarked, "was a sad man because he couldn't get it all at once. And nobody can." Every President must endure a gap between what he would like and what is possible.

John F. Kennedy
Inaugural address
January 20, 1961

When we got into office, the thing that surprised me most was to find that things were just as bad as we'd been saying they were.

John F. Kennedy
Speech, honoring Kennedy's 44th birthday
May 27, 1961

To paraphrase the old saying, "Good news is no news." So the kind of news a president usually gets is bad. But it is more important that there is a lot of good news, too, which does not immediately cross a president's desk. One must remember to keep a balance, to maintain a broad perspective and to refuse to be overwhelmed by bad news.

John F. Kennedy
Cited in *Parade*
April 8, 1962

I know when things don't go well, they like to blame the President, and that is one of the things Presidents are paid for.

John F. Kennedy
Press conference
June 15, 1962

The American presidency is a formidable, exposed, and somewhat mysterious institution. It is formidable because it represents the point of ultimate decision in the American political system. It is exposed because decision cannot take place in a vacuum. . . . And it is mysterious because the essence of ultimate decision remains impenetrable to the observer—often, indeed, to the decider himself.

John F. Kennedy
Foreword to Theodore Sorensen's *Decision-Making in the White House*
1963

Of course, we can't all be Winston Churchills. We can't all be President. I found that out.

Richard Nixon
New York Times
June 15, 1963

The Presidency of this Nation is no place for a timid soul or a torpid spirit. It is the one place where a petty temper and a narrow view can never reside.

Lyndon B. Johnson
Speech, Democratic Party Dinner, Miami Beach, Florida
February 27, 1964

I know of nothing in the President's job that is more important than being accountable to the people.

Lyndon B. Johnson
News conference, State Department
February 29, 1964

My White House job pays more than public school systems but the tenure is less certain.

Lyndon B. Johnson
Comments, presenting the award to the Teacher of the Year for 1963, Washington, D.C.
May 4, 1964

A President's hardest task is not to *do* what is right, but to *know* what is right.

Lyndon B. Johnson
State of the union address
January 5, 1965

I do not want to be the President who built empires or sought grandeur or extended dominion. I want to be the President who helped the poor find their own way and who protected the right of every citizen to vote in every election. I want to be the President who helped end hatred among his fellow men.

Lyndon B. Johnson
Speech in support of legislation giving blacks the vote
   in the South
1965

As we stood together in the Oval Office, he [Lyndon Johnson] welcomed me into a club of very exclusive membership, and he made a promise to adhere to the cardinal rule of that membership: stand behind those who succeed you.

Richard Nixon
Washington, D.C.
November 1968

Former Presidents of the United States are like British kings; they have great responsibility but no power.

Richard Nixon
Comment, Chou En-lai
February 1972

I must get away from the thought of considering the office at any time a burden.

Richard Nixon
Diary
December 24, 1972

I guess it just proves that in America anyone can be President.

Gerald Ford
Cited in Richard Reeves, *A Ford Not a Lincoln*

I am acutely aware that you have not elected me as your President by your ballots, and so I ask you to confirm me as your President with your prayers.

Gerald Ford
Inaugural address
August 9, 1974

If you have not chosen me by secret ballot, neither have I gained office by any secret promises.

Gerald Ford
Inaugural address
August 9, 1974

Only eight months ago, when I last stood here, I told you I was a Ford, not a Lincoln. Tonight I say I am still a Ford, but I am not a Model T.

Gerald Ford
Address, Congress
August 12, 1974

To the limits of my strength and ability, I will be the President of black, brown, red and white Americans, of old and young, of women's liberationists and male chauvinists and all the rest of us in between, of the poor and the rich, of native sons and new refugees, of those who work at lathes or at desks or in mines or in the fields, or of Christians, Jews, Moslems, Buddhists and Atheists, if there really are any Atheists after what we have been through.

Gerald Ford
Address, Congress
August 12, 1974

You know, the President of the United States is not a magician who can wave a wand or sign a paper that will instantly end a war, cure a recession, or make a bureaucracy disappear.

Gerald Ford
Acceptance speech, Republican Convention, Kansas
   City, Missouri
August 19, 1976

To me the Presidency and Vice Presidency were not prizes to be won but a duty to be done.

Gerald Ford
Acceptance speech, Republican Convention, Kansas
   City, Missouri
August 19, 1976

I discovered how isolated from the reality of American life a President can feel in the White House. For all its cosmopolitan self-confidence, Washington is a parochial city preoccupied by politics and gossip—which at times in Washington are the same thing. Like other Presidents before and after me, I felt the need to get out of the White House and out of Washington in order to keep some sense of perspective.

Richard Nixon
The Memoirs of Richard Nixon
1978

I have a lot of problems on my shoulders but, strangely enough, I feel better as they pile up. My main concern is propping up the people around me who tend to panic (and who might possibly have a better picture of the situation than I do!).

Jimmy Carter
Diary
July 31, 1980

A president must be many things. He must be a shrewd protector of America's interests, and he must be an idealist who leads those who move for a freer and more democratic planet. And he must see to it that government intrudes as little as possible in the lives of the people; and yet remember that it is right and proper that a nation's leader take an interest in the nation's character. And he must be able to define—and lead—a mission.

George Bush
Acceptance speech, Republican Convention
August 18, 1988

Press

But none of the means of information are more sacred, or have been cherished with more tenderness and care by the settlers of America, than the press.

John Adams
Dissertation on the Canon and the Feudal Law
1765

Be not intimidated, therefore, by any terrors, from publishing with the utmost freedom whatever can be warranted by the laws of your country; nor suffer yourselves to be wheedled out of your liberty by any pretenses of politeness, delicacy, or decency. These, as they are often used, are but three different names for hypocrisy, chicanery, and cowardice.

John Adams
Dissertation on the Canon and the Feudal Law
1765

Let us dare to read, think, speak and write.

John Adams
Dissertation on the Canon and the Feudal Law
1765

Our liberty depends on the freedom of the press, and that cannot be limited without being lost.

Thomas Jefferson
Letter, Colonel Edward Carrington
1787

Were it left to me to decide whether we should have a government without newspapers, or newspapers without government, I should not hesitate a moment to prefer the latter.

Thomas Jefferson
Letter, Colonel Edward Carrington
January 16, 1787

My great wish is to go on in a strict but silent performance of my duty; to avoid attracting notice, and to keep my name out of the newspapers.

Thomas Jefferson
Letter, Francis Hopkinson
January 11, 1789

No government ought to be without censors, and, where the press is free, no one ever will.

Thomas Jefferson
Letter, George Washington
1792

To the press alone, chequered as it is with abuses, the world is endebted for all the triumphs which have been gained by reason and humanity over error and oppression.

Thomas Jefferson
Virginia and Kentucky Resolutions
1799

The printers can never leave up in a state of perfect rest and union of opinion. They would be no longer useful and would have to go the plow.

Thomas Jefferson
Letter, Elbridge Gerry
March 1801

Newspapers serve to carry off noxious vapors and smoke.

Thomas Jefferson
Letter, Tadeuz Kosciusko
April 1802

It is a melancholy truth, that a suppression of the press could not more completely deprive the nation of its benefits than is done by its abandoned prostitution to falsehood.

Thomas Jefferson
Letter, John Norvell
June 11, 1807

The man who never looks into a newspaper is better informed than he who reads them, inasmuch as he who knows nothing is nearer the truth than he whose mind is filled with falsehoods and errors.

Thomas Jefferson
Letter, John Norvell
June 11, 1807

If I am to judge by the newspapers and pamphlets that have been printed in America for twenty years past, I should think that both believed me the meanest villain in the world.

John Adams
Letter, Benjamin Rush
August 28, 1811

If M. de Becourt's book be false in its facts, disprove them; if false in its reasoning, refute it. But, for God's sake, let us freely hear both sides, if we choose it.

Thomas Jefferson
Letter, Dufief, Philadelphia bookseller
1814

Where the press is free and every man able to read, all is safe.

Thomas Jefferson
Letter, Charles Yancey
1816

If a nation expects to be ignorant and free, in a state of civilization, it expects what never was and never will be.

Thomas Jefferson
Letter, Colonel Charles Yancey
1816

Advertisements contain the only truths to be relied on in a newspaper.

Thomas Jefferson
Letter, Nathaniel Macon
1819

They [journalists] are a sort of assassins who sit with loaded blunderbusses at the corner of streets and fire them off for hire or for sport at any passenger they select.

John Quincy Adams
Diary
September 7, 1820

I had read but one newspaper and that . . . more for its advertisements than its news.

Thomas Jefferson
Letter, Charles Pinckney
1820

The press is the best instrument for enlightening the mind of man, and improving him as a rational, moral, and social being.

Thomas Jefferson
Letter, M. Coray
1823

Could it be so arranged that every newspaper, when printed on one side should be handed over to the press of an adversary, to be printed on the other, thus presenting to every reader both sides of every question, truth would always have a fair chance. But such a remedy is ideal.

James Madison
Letter, N. P. Trist
April 23, 1828

Golden shackles, by whomsoever or by whatever pretense imposed, are as fatal to it as the iron bonds of despotism. The presses in the necessary employment of the Government should never be used "to clear the guilty or to varnish crime."

William Henry Harrison
Inaugural address
March 4, 1841

Congress lives in the blaze of "that fierce light which beats against the throne." The press and the telegraph will to-morrow morning announce at a million breakfast tables what has been said and done in Congress to-day.

James Garfield
"A Century of Congress," *Atlantic*
1877

The main point is that the President has so few supporters in Congress and among the newspapers.

Rutherford B. Hayes
Diary
March 12, 1878

When the [New York] Tribune can say, "The President has the courtesy of a Chesterfield and the firmness of a Jackson," (!) I must be prepared for the reactionary counterblast.

Rutherford B. Hayes
Diary
July 1, 1879

I would honor the man who would give to his country a good newspaper.

Rutherford B. Hayes
Speech, Baltimore, Maryland
February 12, 1881

If it were not for the reporters, I would tell you the truth.

Chester A. Arthur
Speech, Union League Club, Delmonico's, New
    York, New York
February 11, 1881

Ah, you really must excuse me. I make it a habit not to talk politics with you gentlemen of the press. . . . I dislike very much to open a newspaper in the morning and find a column or so of a conversation in which I have taken part the day before.

Chester A. Arthur
August 4, 1883

The Man with the Muck-rake is set forth as the example of him whose vision is fixed on carnal instead of spiritual things . . . the man who never does anything else, who never speaks or writes, save of his feats with the muck-rake, speedily becomes, not a help to society, not an incitement to good, but one of the most potent forces for evil.

Theodore Roosevelt
Speech, Gridiron Club dinner
January 1906

Don't worry over what the newspapers say. I don't. Why should anyone else? I told the truth to the newspaper correspondents—but when you tell the truth to them they are at sea.

William Howard Taft
Letter, Marion DeVries
August 12, 1909

If we wish to contribute $50,000,000 to the education of the country, I can find a great deal better method of doing it than by the circulation of Collier's Weekly and Everybody's Magazine.

William Howard Taft
Letter, Otto T. Bannard
March 2, 1910

In our country, I am inclined to think that almost, if not quite, the most important profession is that of the newspaper man, including the man of the magazines, especially the cheap magazines, and the weeklies.

Theodore Roosevelt
Speech, Milwaukee, Wisconsin
September 7, 1910

The more I see of the Czar, the Kaiser, and the Mikado, the better I am content with democracy, even if we have to include the American newspapers as one of its assets—liability would be a better term.

Theodore Roosevelt
Letter, Henry Cabot Lodge
June 16, 1905

A revered President, long since dead, once told me that there . . . never would be a President who could satisfy the press until he was twenty years dead.

Herbert Hoover
Speech, Gridiron Club, Washington, D.C.
December 12, 1931

Freedom of conscience, of education, of speech, of assembly are among the very fundamentals of democracy and all of them would be nullified should freedom of the press ever be successfully challenged.

Franklin D. Roosevelt
Letter, W. H. Hardy
September 4, 1940

I am amazed, sometimes, when I find that some of you disagree with me. When I consider how you disagree among yourselves, I am somewhat comforted. I begin to think that maybe I'm all right after all!

Harry S. Truman
Address, American Society of Newspaper Editors
April 17, 1948

When you read what the press had to say about Washington, Jefferson, and Lincoln, and the other Presidents, you would think that we never had a decent man in the office since the country began.

Harry S. Truman
Special Conference with Editors of Business and
    Trade Papers
April 23, 1948

I have found nothing but a desire to dig at the truth . . . and be open-handed and forthright about it.

Dwight D. Eisenhower
First press conference
February 17, 1953

Now that all the members of the press are so delighted I lost, I'd like to make a statement. . . . As I leave you, I want you to know—just think how much you'll be missing. You won't have Richard Nixon to kick around any more because, gentlemen, this is my last press conference.

Richard Nixon
After his defeat in the 1962 California gubernatorial
    race
Washington Post
November 8, 1962

Thomas Jefferson pointed out that no government ought to be without censors. I can assure you, where the press is free, none will ever be needed.

Lyndon Johnson
Speech, Presentation of the William Randolph Hearst
    Foundation Journalism Awards, the White House
May 11, 1964

The media are far more powerful than the president in creating public awareness and shaping public opinion, for the simple reason that the media always have the last word.

Richard Nixon
The Memoirs of Richard Nixon
1978

Principle

Temporary deviations from fundamental principles are always more or less dangerous. When the first pretext fails, those who become interested in prolonging the evil will rarely be at a loss for other pretexts.

James Madison
Letter, Caleb Wallace
August 23, 1785

We will make converts day by day; we will grow strong by the violence and injustice of our adversaries. And, unless truth be a mockery and justice a hollow lie, we will be in the majority after a while, and then the revolution which we will accomplish will be none the less radical from being the result of pacific measures. The battle of freedom is to be fought out on principle.

Abraham Lincoln
Speech
May 19, 1856

Treat the Negro as a citizen and a voter, as he is and must remain, and soon parties will be divided not on the color line but on principle.

Ulysses S. Grant
Annual message, Congress
December 1874

To stand upon the ramparts and die for our principles is heroic, but to sally forth to battle and win for our principles is something more than heroic.

Franklin D. Roosevelt
Speech nominating Alfred E. Smith for president
June, 1928

It would be better that the [Republican] party go down in defeat, the banner of principle flying, than to win by pussyfooting.

Herbert Hoover
Speech, Philadelphia, Pennsylvania
1936

A man who has never lost himself in a cause bigger than himself has missed one of life's mountaintop experiences. Only in losing himself does he find himself.

Richard Nixon
Six Crises
1962

Progress

A railroad! It would frighten horses, put the owners of public vehicles out of business, break up inns and taverns, and be a monopoly generally.

Andrew Johnson
Speech, Tennessee Legislature
1835

Our great American experiment has demonstrated that the people will of their own initiative take care of progress if the Government can remove abuse and help put the signs on the road, stimulation to all of which is part of the job of Presidents.

Herbert Hoover
Letter, G. O. Trevelyan
October 1, 1911

Substantial progress toward better things can rarely be taken without developing new evils requiring new remedies.

William Howard Taft
The President and His Powers
1916

Progress of the nation is the sum of progress of its individuals.

Herbert Hoover
American Individualism
1922

The slogan of progress is changing from the full dinner pail to the full garage.

Herbert Hoover
Speech, New York, New York
October 22, 1928

If I had permitted my failures, or what seemed to me at the time a lack of success, to discourage me I cannot see any way in which I would ever have made progress.

Calvin Coolidge
The Autobiography of Calvin Coolidge
1929

The test of our progress is not whether we add more to the abundance of those who have too much; it is whether we provide enough for those who have too little.

Franklin D. Roosevelt
Second inaugural address
January 20, 1937

Let us once again transform the American Continent into a vast crucible of revolutionary ideas and efforts, a tribute to the power of the creative energies of free men and women, an example to all the world that liberty and progress walk hand in hand.

John F. Kennedy
Proposal, The Alliance for Progress
March 13, 1961

Let us once again awaken our American revolution until it guides the struggles of people everywhere—not with an imperialism of force and fear but the rule of courage and freedom and hope for the future of man.

John F. Kennedy
Proposal, The Alliance for Progress
March 13, 1961

Our motto is what it has always been—progress yes, tyranny no.

John F. Kennedy
Proposal, The Alliance for Progress
March 13, 1961

Frequently in my life I have had to settle for progress short of perfection. I have done so because—despite cynics—I believe that half a loaf *is* better than none. But my acceptance has always been conditioned upon the premise that the half-loaf is a step towards the full loaf—and that if I go on working, the day of the full loaf will come.

Lyndon B. Johnson
A Time for Action
1964

Propaganda

Dark alleys of inspired propaganda. . .

Herbert Hoover
Speech
December 16, 1935

I can at least take satisfaction that liquidation by propaganda is not as fatal as that by machine gun in a muffled cellar.

Herbert Hoover
On attempts by Moscow press to discredit the ARA
1958

Property

Political contests are necessary sometimes, as well as military, to afford exercise and practice, and to instruct in the art of defending liberty and property.

James Madison
Letter, William Bradford, Jr.
January 24, 1774

The balance of power in a society accompanies the balance of property in land.

John Adams
Letter, James Sullivan
May 26, 1776

Whenever there is, in any country, uncultivated land and unemployed poor, it is clear that the laws of property have been so far expended as to violate natural right.

Thomas Jefferson
Letter, James Madison
1785

I have no doubt but that the misery of the lower classes will be found to abate wherever the Government assumes a freer aspect, & the laws favor a subdivision of property.

James Madison
Letter, Thomas Jefferson
June 19, 1786

So strong is this propensity of mankind to fall into mutual animosities, that where no substantial occasion presents itself, the most frivolous and fanciful distinctions have been sufficient to kindle their unfriendly passions and excite their most violent conflicts. . . . But the most common and durable source of factions has been the various and unequal distribution of property.

James Madison
Federalist, X
1787

Those who hold and those who are without property have ever formed distinct interests in society. Those who are creditors, and those who are debtors, fall under a like discrimination. A landed interest, a manufacturing interest, a mercantile interest, a moneyed interest, with many lesser interests, grow up of necessity in civilization and divide them into different classes, actuated by different sentiments and views.

James Madison
Federalist, X
1787

Government is instituted to protect property of every sort. . . . This being the end of government, that alone is a *just* government, which *impartially* secures to every man, whatever is his *own*.

James Madison
National Gazette
March 29, 1792

I believe in shaping the ends of government to protect property as well as human welfare. Normally, and in the long run, the ends are the same; but whenever the alternative must be faced, I am for men and not for property.

Theodore Roosevelt
The New Nationalism
1910

What I am interested in is having the government of the United States more concerned about human rights than about property rights. Property is an instrument of humanity; humanity isn't an instrument of property.

Woodrow Wilson
Speech, Minneapolis, Minnesota
September 18, 1912

Next to the right of liberty, the right of property is the most important individual right guaranteed by the Constitution and the one which, united with that of personal liberty, has contributed more to the growth of civilization than any other institution established by the human race.

William Howard Taft
Popular Government: Its Essence, Its Permanence
    and Its Perils
1913

Property can be paid for; the lives of peaceful and innocent people cannot be.

Woodrow Wilson
Address to the Joint Session of the Two Houses of
    Congress, Declaration of War against Germany
April 2, 1917

Property is not . . . an object in itself, but . . . a useful instrument in stimulating the initiative of the individual.

Herbert Hoover
American Individualism
1922

But the possession of property carries the obligation to use it in a larger service.

Calvin Coolidge
The Autobiography of Calvin Coolidge
1929

Public

Uninvited strangers fell like public finance into two categories. Some were taxes and others, bounties.

James Madison
Comment, Harriet Martineau
1834

The office of the President is generally esteemed a very high and dignified position, but really I think the public would not so regard it if they could look in occasionally and observe the kind of people by whom I am often annoyed.

James K. Polk
Diaries
October 19, 1848

They do not want much; they get but little, and I must see them.

Abraham Lincoln
Comment, Senator Henry Wilson
c. 1863

If these people want to see me, why shouldn't I see them?

Warren G. Harding
Inaugural reception
March 1921

Well, many times I only say "yes" or "no," and even that winds *them* up for twenty minutes more.

Calvin Coolidge
Comment, Bernard Baruch
1924

You have to stand every day three or four hours of visitors. Nine-tenths of them want something they ought not to have. If you keep dead-still they will run down in three or four minutes. If you even cough or smile they will start up all over again.

Calvin Coolidge
To Herbert Hoover
1928

Public Office

The ordinary affairs of a nation offer little difficulty to a person of any experience, but the gift of office is the dreadful burthen which oppresses him.

Thomas Jefferson
Letter, Governor James Sullivan
March 3, 1808

A public life ought to be a perpetual sacrifice of resentments.

John Quincy Adams
Debate
1835-1836

It is difficult for men in high office to avoid the malady of self-delusion. They are always surrounded by worshippers. They are constantly, and for the most part sincerely, assured of their greatness.

Calvin Coolidge
The Autobiography of Calvin Coolidge
1929

Public Opinion

Public opinion, the fear of losing the public confidence, apprehensive of censure by the press, make all men in power conservative and safe.

Rutherford B. Hayes
Diary
October 22, 1876

Real political issues cannot be manufactured by the leaders of political parties. The real political issues of the day declare themselves, and come out of the depths of that deep which we call public opinion.

James Garfield
Speech, Boston, Massachusetts
September 10, 1878

Lincoln said in his homely way that he wanted "to take a bath in public opinion." I think I have a right to take a bath before I do much talking.

James Garfield
Letter, Burke A. Hinsdale
November 17, 1880

There is little danger to the public weal from the tyranny or reckless character of a President who is not sustained by the people.

William Howard Taft
The President and His Powers
1916

A government can be no better than the public opinion that sustains it.

Franklin D. Roosevelt
Speech, Washington, D.C.
January 8, 1936

Although publicly I continued to ignore the raging antiwar controversy. . . . I knew, however, that after all the protests and the Moratorium, American public opinion would be seriously divided by any military escalation of the war.

Richard Nixon
The Memoirs of Richard Nixon
1978

Public Service

Our mission among the nations of the earth, and our success in accomplishing the work God has given the American people to do, require of those intrusted with the making and execution of our laws perfect devotion, above all other things, to the public good.

Grover Cleveland
Fourth annual message, Congress
December 1888

I always made my living practicing law up to the time I became Governor, without being dependent on any official salary. This left me free to make my own decisions in accordance with what I thought was the public good. We lived where we did that I might better serve the people.

Calvin Coolidge
The Autobiography of Calvin Coolidge
1929

R

Radicals

Mad-caps among the old democrats who think nothing-wise that is not violent and flatter themselves that they merit Knighthood by assailing everything that is memorable in old institutions.

Martin Van Buren
Letter, John King
October 1821

Only radicals have accomplished anything in a great crisis.

James Garfield
Diary
December 16, 1876

[Extremists] are not progressives; they are political emotionalists or neurotics.

William Howard Taft
Speech, condemning advocates of direct popular government, New York, New York
February 12, 1912

I tell you the so-called radicalism of our times is simply the effort of nature to release the generous energies of our people.

Woodrow Wilson
The New Freedom
1912-1913 speeches

Ronald Reagan

Reagan was, "Aw, shucks, this and that. I'm a grandfather, and . . . I love peace," etc.

Jimmy Carter
Diary, the night after his televised debate with Ronald Reagan
October 28, 1980

He was one of the few political leaders I have ever met whose public speeches revealed more than his private conversations.

Gerald Ford
A Time to Heal
1982

There is a man here who has earned a lasting place in our hearts and in our history. President Reagan, on behalf of our nation, I thank you for the wonderful things you have done for America.

George Bush
Inaugural Address
January 20, 1989

Rebellion and Revolution

This is the most magnificent movement of all.

John Adams
On the Boston Tea Party
1773

The people should never rise without doing something to be remembered, something notable and striking. This destruction of the tea is so bold, so daring, so firm, intrepid, and inflexible, and it must have so important consequences, and so lasting, that I cannot but consider it as an epoch in history.

John Adams
Diary, on the Boston Tea Party
December 17, 1773

My creed has been formed on usheathing the sword at Lexington.

Thomas Jefferson
Letter, Virginia delegates to Congress
August 1774

The most sensible and jealous people are so little attentive to government that there are no instances of resistance until repeated, multiplied oppressions have placed it beyond a doubt that their rulers had formed settled plans to deprive them of their liberties; not to oppress an individual or a few, but to break down the fences of a free constitution, and deprive the people at large of all share in the government, and are the checks by which it is limited.

John Adams
"Novanglus"
1774-1775

When it is said that if we are not subject to the supreme authority of parliament, Great Britain will make us so, all other laws and obligations are given up, and recourse is had . . . to the law of brickbats and balls.

John Adams
"Novanglus"
1774-1775

Our cause is just. Our union is perfect. Our internal resources are great, and, if necessary, foreign assistance is undoubtedly attainable. . . . The arms we have been compelled by our enemies to assume we will, in defiance of every hazard, with unabating firmness and perseverance, employ for the preservation of our liberties; being with one mind resolved to die free men rather than live slaves.

Thomas Jefferson
Declaration of the Causes of Taking Up Arms
July 6, 1775

Rebellion to tyrants is obedience to God.

Thomas Jefferson
Motto on his seal

We hold these truths to be self-evident, that all men are created equal, that they are endowed by their Creator with certain unalienable Rights, that among these are Life, Liberty and the pursuit of Happiness. That to secure these rights, Governments are instituted among Men, deriving their just powers from the consent of the governed. That whenever any Form of Government becomes destructive of those ends, it is the Right of the People to alter or abolish it, and to institute a new Government, laying its foundation on such principles and organizing its power in such form, as to them shall seem most likely to effect their Safety and Happiness.

Thomas Jefferson
Declaration of Independence
July 4, 1776

The time is now near at hand which must probably determine whether Americans are to be freemen or slaves; whether they are to have any property they can call their own; whether their houses and farms are to be pillaged and destroyed, and themselves consigned to a state of wretchedness from which no human efforts will deliver them. The fate of unborn millions will now depend, under God, on the courage and conduct of this army. Our cruel and unrelenting enemy leaves us only the choice of a brave resistance, or the most abject submission. We have, therefore, to resolve to conquer or die.

George Washington
Speech, American troops before the Battle of Long Island
July 1776

Our cause is noble, it is the cause of mankind! And the danger to it is to be apprehended from ourselves.

George Washington
Letter, friend
March 31, 1779

It is an observation of one of the profoundest inquirers into human affairs that a revolution of government is the strongest proof that can be given by a people of their virtue and good sense.

John Adams
Diary
1786

If the happiness of the mass of mankind can be secured at the expense of a little tempest now and then, or even of a little blood, it will be a precious purchase.

Thomas Jefferson
Letter, Ezra Stiles
1786

A little rebellion, now and then, is a good thing, and as necessary in the political world as storms in the physical. . . . It is a medicine necessary for the sound health of government.

Thomas Jefferson
Letter, James Madison
January 30, 1787

The spirit of resistance to government is so valuable on certain occasions, that I wish it to be always kept alive. It will often be exercised when wrong but better so than not to be exercised at all. I like a little rebellion now and then. It is like a storm in the atmosphere.

Thomas Jefferson
Letter, Abigail Adams
February 22, 1787

The tree of liberty must be refreshed from time to time with the blood of patriots and tyrants. It is its natural manure.

Thomas Jefferson
Letter, William Stevens Smith
November 13, 1787

And what country can preserve its liberties, if its rulers are not warned from time to time, that this people preserve the spirit of resistance? Let them take arms. The remedy is to set them right as to facts, pardon and pacify them. What signify a few lives lost in a century or two?

Thomas Jefferson
Letter, Colonel William S. Smith
1787

God forbid we should ever be twenty years without such a rebellion.

Thomas Jefferson
Letter, Colonel William S. Smith
1787

We are not to expect to be translated from despotism to liberty in a featherbed.

Thomas Jefferson
Letter, Lafayette
1790

If there be a principle that ought not to be questioned within the United States, it is that every nation has a right to abolish an old government and establish a new one. This principle . . . is the only lawful tenure by which the United States hold their existence as a nation.

James Madison
To "Pacificus"
April 22, 1793

Have I not been employed in mischief all my days? Did not the American Revolution produce the French Revolution? And did not the French Revolution produce all the calamities and desolations to the human race and the whole globe ever since? My conscience was clear as a crystal glass, without a scruple or a doubt.

John Adams
Letter, Josiah Quincy
February 9, 1811

But what do we mean by the American Revolution? Do we mean the American war? The Revolution was effected before the war commenced. The Revolution was in the minds and hearts of the people; a change in their religious sentiments of their duties and obligations.

John Adams
Letter, T. H. Niles
February 13, 1818

The right of resisting oppression is a natural right.

Andrew Jackson
Letter, General John Coffee
December 14, 1832

Any people anywhere being inclined and having the power, have the right to rise up and shake off the existing government, and form a new one that suits them better. This is a most valuable, a most sacred right—a right which we hope and believe is to liberate the world.

Abraham Lincoln
Speech, House of Representatives, in reply to
    President Polk on Mexico
1848

Let us remember that revolutions do not always establish freedom. Our own free institutions were not the offspring of our Revolution. They existed before.

Millard Fillmore
Third annual message, Congress
December 5, 1852

Be not deceived. Revolutions do not go backward. The founder of the Democratic party declared that *all* men were created equal.

Abraham Lincoln
Speech, Bloomington, Indiana
May 19, 1856

The right of revolution is an inherent one.

Ulysses S. Grant
Personal Memoirs of U.S. Grant
1885-1886

We stand in the presence of a revolution—not a bloody revolution; America is not given to the spilling of blood—but a silent revolution, whereby America will insist upon recovering in practice those ideals which she has always professed, upon securing a government devoted to the general interest and not the special interests.

Woodrow Wilson
The New Freedom
1912-1913 speeches

The seed of revolution is repression.

Woodrow Wilson
Seventh annual message, Congress
December 2, 1919

One hundred and eighty-one years ago, our forefathers started a revolution that still goes on.

Dwight D. Eisenhower
Time
October 6, 1956

We dare not forget today that we are heirs of that first revolution. Let the word go forth from this time and place, to friend and foe alike, that the torch has been passed to a new generation of Americans—born in this century, tempered by war, disciplined by a hard and bitter peace, proud of our ancient heritage—and unwilling to witness or permit the slow undoing of those human rights to which this nation has always been committed today at home and around the world.

John F. Kennedy
First inaugural address
January 20, 1961

Let us once again transform the American Continent into a vast crucible of revolutionary ideas and efforts, a tribute to the power of the creative energies of free men and women, an example to all the world that liberty and progress walk hand in hand.

John F. Kennedy
Proposed for the Alliance for Progress
March 13, 1961

Let us once again awaken our American revolution until it guides the struggles of people everywhere—not with an imperialism of force and fear but the rule of courage and freedom and hope for the future of man.

John F. Kennedy
Proposal for The Alliance for Progress
March 13, 1961

Reconstruction

If a State is to be nursed until it again gets strength, it must be nursed by its friends, not smothered by its enemies.

Andrew Johnson
Speech
c. 1866

Our victories subjected the insurgents to legal obedience, not to the yoke of an arbitrary despotism.

Andrew Johnson
Veto, First Reconstruction Bill
March 2, 1867

If in the exercise of the constitutional guaranty that Congress shall secure to every State a republican form of government, universal suffrage for blacks as well as whites is a sine qua non, the work of reconstruction may as well begin in Ohio as in Virginia, in Pennsylvania as in North Carolina.

Andrew Johnson
Veto, Second Reconstruction Bill
March 23, 1867

Personal freedom, property, and life, if assailed by the passion, the prejudice, or the rapacity of the ruler, have no security whatever.

Andrew Johnson
Third annual message, Congress, on reconstruction and military rule
December 3, 1867

Reform

The hole and patch should be commensurate.

Thomas Jefferson
Letter, James Madison
1787

[I rang the] peal of the party tocsin in the ears of those who glorified the "Era of Good Feelings."

Martin Van Buren
The Autobiography of Martin Van Buren
1822

The most healing of medicines, unduly administered, becomes the most deadly of poisons.

John Quincy Adams
Speech, House of Representatives
December 1831

The reform should be thorough, radical, and complete.

Rutherford B. Hayes
"The Republican Campaign," *New York Times*, advocating civil service reform
July 10, 1876

Opportunity for safe, careful, and deliberate reform is now offered; and none of us should be unmindful of a time when an abused and irritated people . . . may insist upon a radical and sweeping rectification of their wrongs.

Grover Cleveland
Annual message
December 6, 1887

In the track of reform are often found the dead hopes of pioneers and the despair of those who fell in the march.

Grover Cleveland
Letter, Massachusetts Tariff Reform League
December 24, 1888

Promises of redress and benefit are held up to their [the people's] sight, "like Dead Sea fruits, that tempt the eye but turn to ashes on the lips."

Grover Cleveland
Speech, Buffalo, New York
May 12, 1891

It does not at all follow because abuses exist that it is the concern of the Federal Government to attempt their reform.

Calvin Coolidge
Cited in Arthur Bernon Tourtellot, *The Presidents on the Presidency*

Every reform movement has a lunatic fringe.

Theodore Roosevelt
Speech
1913

We find that often the difference between political machines and a party organization for reform is only determined by the question, "Is it for you or against you.?"

William Howard Taft
The President and His Powers
1916

The remedies in America are not revolution. They are, except for peace and war, mostly jobs of marginal repairs around a sound philosophy and a stout heart.

Herbert Hoover
Cited in the *New York Times*
August 9, 1964

Regionalism

As the President in the Administration of the government, I hope to be man enough not to know one citizen of the United States from another, nor one section from another.

Abraham Lincoln
Reply, Delegation
March 5, 1861

If I am ever President of this country again, I shall be President of the whole country, and not of any set of men or class in it.

Grover Cleveland
Cited in Arthur Bernon Tourtellot, *The Presidents on the Presidency*

While those who fought, and who have so much to forgive, lead in the pleasant ways of peace, how wicked appear the traffic in sectional hate and the betrayal of patriotic sentiment!

Grover Cleveland
Letter, reunion of Union and ex-Confederate soldiers held at Gettysburg, Pennsylvania
July 2, 1887

Religion

Religious bondage shackles and debilitates the mind, and unfits it for every noble enterprise.

James Madison
Letter, William Bradford, Jr.
January 24, 1774

It does me no injury for my neighbor to say there are twenty gods, or no God. It neither picks my pocket nor breaks my leg.

Thomas Jefferson
Notes on Virginia
1782

Is uniformity obtainable? Millions of innocent men, women, and children, since the introduction of Christianity, have been burnt, tortured, fined, imprisoned; yet we have not advanced an inch toward uniformity. What has been the effect of coercion? To make one half the world fools, and the other half hypocrites. To support roguery and error all over the earth . . .

Thomas Jefferson
Notes on Virginia
1782

Every man, conducting himself as a good citizen, and being accountable to God alone for his religious opinions, ought to be protected in worshipping the Deity according to the dictates of his own conscience.

George Washington
Letter, United Baptist Chamber of Virginia
May 1789

A German ambassador once told me, "he could not bear St. Paul, he was so severe against fornication." On the same principle these philosophers cannot bear a God, because he is just.

John Adams
Letter, F. A. Vanderkemp
March 3, 1804

The government of the United States of America is not in any sense founded on the Christian religion,—as it has itself no character of enmity against the law, religion or tranquility of Musselmen.

John Adams
Letter, Benjamin Rush
August 28, 1811

If thinking men would have the courage to think for themselves, and to speak what they think, it would be found they do not differ in religious opinions as much as is supposed.

Thomas Jefferson
Letter, John Adams
1813

The question before the human race is whether the God of nature shall govern the world by his own laws, or whether priests and kings shall rule it by fictitious miracles.

John Adams
Letter, Thomas Jefferson
June 20, 1815

I never told my own religion nor scrutinized that of another. I never attempted to make a convert, nor wished to change another's creed. I have ever judged of another's religion by their lives . . . for it is in our lives and not from our words, that our religion must be read.

Thomas Jefferson
Letter, Mrs. M. H. Smith
August 6, 1816

The Ten Commandments and the Sermon on the Mount contain my religion.

John Adams
Letter, Thomas Jefferson
November 4, 1816

[I have] ever regarded the freedom of religious opinions & worship as equally belonging to every sect & the secure enjoyment of it as the best human provision for bringing all either into the same way of thinking, or into . . . mutual charity.

James Madison
Letter, Mordecai M. Noah
May 15, 1818

The experience of the United States is a happy disproof of the error so long rooted in the unenlightened minds of well-meaning Christians, as well as in the corrupt hearts of the persecuting usurpers, that without a legal incorporation of religious and civil polity, neither could be supported. A mutual independence is found most friendly to practical Religion, to social harmony, and to political prosperity.

James Madison
Letter, F. L. Schaeffer
December 3, 1821

We are teaching the world the great truth that Gov[ernments] do better without Kings and Nobles than with them. The merit will be doubled by the other lesson that Religion flourishes in greater purity, without than with the aid of Gov[ernment].

James Madison
Letter, Edward Livingston
July 19, 1822

We, on our side, are praying to Him to give us victory, because we believe we are right; but those on the other side pray Him, too, for victory, believing they are right. What must He think of us?

Abraham Lincoln
To the Reverend Byron Sunderland, chaplain of the Senate
1862

Both read the same Bible, and pray to the same God; and each invokes His aid against the other.

Abraham Lincoln
Inaugural address
April 4, 1864

Declare church and state forever separate and distinct; but each free within their proper spheres.

Ulysses S. Grant
Seventh annual message, Congress
December 7, 1875

Free government is the political expression of a deeply felt religious faith.

Dwight D. Eisenhower
Speech, Abilene, Kansas, reported in *Time*
June 16, 1952

In a very Christian way, as far as I'm concerned, he can go to hell.

Jimmy Carter
Comment on the Reverend Jerry Falwell, cited in *Newsweek*
September 22, 1986

America does not need a religious war. It needs reaffirmation of the values that for most of us are rooted in our religious faith.

Bill Clinton
Address, Notre Dame University
Spetember 11, 1992

Republican Party

Republicans are for both the man and the dollar, but in case of conflict the man before the dollar.

Abraham Lincoln
Letter, H. L. Pierce
April 6, 1859

I am glad to meet the tired and faithful soldiers, "the Old Guard" of the Republican Party.

Chester A. Arthur
Speech, New York, New York
June 13, 1880

I am a dead statesman, but a living and rejuvenated Republican.

Benjamin Harrison
Speech, Michigan Club Banquet, Detroit, Michigan
February 22, 1888

Shall we not insist that what is true of those who fought to destroy the country shall be true of every man who fought for it, or loved it, like that black man of the South did—that to belong to Abraham Lincoln's party shall be respectable and reputable everywhere in America?

Benjamin Harrison
Speech, Michigan Club Banquette, Detroit, Michigan
February 22, 1888

The Republican party. . . . The first assembly that sounded in its camp was a call to sacrifice, and not to spoils.

Benjamin Harrison
Speech, Marquette Club Banquette, Chicago, Illinois
March 20, 1888

The emancipation of a race, brought about as an incident of war under the proclamation of the first Republican President, has forever immortalized the party that accomplished it.

Benjamin Harrison
Speech, Marquette Club Banquette, Chicago, Illinois
March 20, 1888

It is the only political party organized in America that has its "Book of Martyrs."

Benjamin Harrison
Speech, Marquette Club Banquette, Chicago, Illinois
March 20, 1888

The Republican party has walked in the light of the Declaration of Independence. It has lifted the shaft of patriotism upon the foundation laid at Bunker Hill. It has made the more perfect union secure by making all men free.

Benjamin Harrison
Speech, Notification Committee representing the Republican National Convention, upon receiving the Republican nomination for the presidency, Indianapolis, Indiana
July 4, 1888

The Republican party did not organize for spoils; it assembled about an altar of sacrifice and in a sanctuary beset with enemies. You have not forgotten our early battle cry—"Free speech, a free press, free schools and free Territories." We have widened the last word: it is now "a free Nation."

Benjamin Harrison
Speech, Indianapolis, Indiana
August 7, 1888

Our own party leaders did not realize that I was able to hold the Republican party in power only because I insisted on a steady advance, and dragged them along with me.

Theodore Roosevelt
Comment
1909

The Republican party would have died of dry-rot if we had not made this fight.

Theodore Roosevelt
Speech, Worcester, Massachusetts
May 4, 1912

They are a trifle better than the corrupt and lunatic wild asses of the desert who seem most influential in democratic councils, under the lead of that astute, unprincipled and physically cowardly demagogue Wilson; but they are a sorry lot.

Theodore Roosevelt
Written communication, describing Republicans who nominated Charles Evans Hughs as their presidential candidate in 1916
1916

[The Republican party should become] the Party of sane, constructive radicalism, just as it was under Lincoln.

Theodore Roosevelt
Comment, Republican senators and representatives
1918

I have often wondered what a so-called liberal Republican thinks. On election year they call him out and pat him on the back, and send him around over the country to make speeches in support of a platform that he doesn't believe in—and just as soon as the election year is over, they put him back in the doghouse, and he votes with the Democrats for the rest of the time.

Harry S. Truman
Remarks, Young Democrats Dinner
May 14, 1948

Herbert Hoover once ran on the slogan: "Two cars in every garage." Apparently the Republican candidate this year is running on the slogan: "Two families in every garage."

Harry S. Truman
Speech, in reference to Dewey
July 1948

A sound government to the Republican is the kind of government where the President makes nice while the Vice-President snarls.

Harry S. Truman
Quote Magazine
November 2, 1958

When a leader is in the Democratic party he's a boss; when he's in the Republican party he's a leader.

Harry S. Truman
Speech, Columbia University, New York, New York
April 28, 1959

We had an interesting convention at Los Angeles and we ended with a strong Democratic platform which we called "The Rights of Man." The Republican platform has also been presented. I do not know its title, but it has been referred to as "The Power of Positive Thinking."

John F. Kennedy
Speech, New York, New York
September 14, 1960

I am going to always, when I am dealing with the Republicans, do like I do when I am dealing with other people in the world. I am going to keep my guard up and my hand out.

Lyndon B. Johnson
Remarks, editors and broadcasters attending a national Conference on Foreign Policy, the White House
April 21, 1964

I urged my audiences to be Lincoln Republicans: liberal in their concern for people and conservative in their respect for the rule of law.

Richard Nixon
The Memoirs of Richard Nixon, referring to speeches made in 1965
1978

Resignation

Disbandment has no terror.

Zachary Taylor
Letter, Thomas Jesup
June 18, 1820

This desk of mine is one at which a man may die, but from which he cannot resign.

Dwight D. Eisenhower
Cited in Parade
April 8, 1962

Tonight I would like to give my answer to those who have suggested that I resign. I have no intention whatever of walking away from the job I was elected to do. As long as I am physically able, I am going to continue to work sixteen to eighteen hours a day for the cause of real peace abroad, and for the cause of prosperity without inflation and without war at home.

Richard Nixon
Speech, Washington, D.C.
November 7, 1973

In the past few days . . . it has become evident to me that I no longer have a strong enough political base in the Congress to justify continuing. . . . As long as there was such a base, I felt strongly that it was necessary to see the constitutional process through to its conclusion, that to do otherwise would be unfaithful to the spirit of precedent for the future. But with the disappearance of that base, I now believe that the constitutional purpose has been served, and there is no longer a need for the process to be prolonged. Therefore, I shall resign the presidency effective at noon tomorrow.

Richard Nixon
Speech, White House
August 8, 1974

Retirement

Not unconscious in the outset of the inferiority of my qualifications, experience in my own eyes . . . has strengthened the motives to diffidence of myself; and every day the increasing weight of years admonishes me more and more that the shade of retirement is as necessary to me as it will be welcome. . . . I have the consolation to believe that, while choice and prudence invite me to quit the political scene, patriotism does not forbid it.

George Washington
Farewell address
September 17, 1796

I have taken final leave [of politics]. I think little of them and say less. I have given up newspapers in exchange for Tacitus and Thucydides, for Newton and Euclid, and I find myself much happier.

Thomas Jefferson
Letter, John Adams
January 21, 1812

After the long and laborious service in which I have been engaged, and in the most difficult conjunctions to which our country has been exposed, it is my earnest desire to cherish tranquillity in my retirement.

James Monroe
Letter, General Roger Jones
1826

If a Chief Magistrate has any power of restraint while in office, it must cease after his retirement.

James Monroe
Letter, S. Southerd
February 8, 1831

I want relaxation from business and rest, but where can I get rest; I fear not on this earth.

Andrew Jackson
Letter, Martin Van Buren
June 6, 1833

I am heartily rejoiced that my term is so near its close. I will soon cease to be a servant and will become a sovereign.

James K. Polk
The Diary of James K. Polk
February 13, 1849

It is better to wear out than rust out.

Millard Fillmore
Letter, Hugh Maxwell
March 19, 1855

I dare not go to Washington [lest] I am publically attacked for interfering.

Millard Fillmore
Letter, W. W. Corcoran
October 12, 1858

My dear sir, if you are as happy in entering the White House as I shall feel on returning to Wheatland [Pennsylvania], you are a happy man indeed.

James Buchanan
Comment, Abraham Lincoln, on Lincoln's
    inauguration
March 4, 1861

An old man, weary with the cares of state, has come to lay his bones among you.

Andrew Johnson
Comment, H. H. Ingersall
March 1869

That the White House will be left *"willingly"* by both Mrs. Hayes and myself is perfectly true. We have upon the whole enjoyed our four years here. But the responsibility, the embarrassments, the heart breaking sufferings which we can't relieve, the ever present danger of scandals and crimes among those we are compelled to trust, and a thousand other drawbacks to our satisfaction and enjoyment by which we are constantly surrounded leave us no place for regret upon retiring from this conspicuous scene to the freedom, independence and safety of our obscure and happy home.

Rutherford B. Hayes
Diary
January 16, 1881

The escape from bondage into freedom is grateful indeed to my feelings. . . . The burden, even with my constitutional problems, has not been a light one. *I am glad to be a freedman.*

Rutherford B. Hayes
Letter, W. H. Smith
March 29, 1881

Well, there doesn't seem anything else for an ex-President to do but go into the country and raise big pumpkins.

Chester A. Arthur
Comment, George Bliss, *New York Herald*
November 19, 1886

I always answer them that there will be one ex-President about whom they need not give themselves the slightest concern . . . and I add that they need waste no sympathy on me—that I have had the best time of any man of my age in all the world, and that I have enjoyed myself in the White House more than I have ever known any other President to enjoy himself, and that I am going to enjoy myself thoroughly when I leave the White House.

Theodore Roosevelt
Letter, Ted Roosevelt
October 27, 1908

Ha, ha! *You* are making up your Cabinet. *I* in a lighthearted way have spent the morning testing the rifles for my African trip. Life has compensation.

Theodore Roosevelt
Letter, William Howard Taft
December 31, 1908

[Let retiring presidents] expire under the anaesthetic effects of the debates.

William Howard Taft
Speech, Lotus Club, New York, New York
November 16, 1912

I am having rather more trouble in getting out of the White House than I had getting in.

Calvin Coolidge
Press conference, Washington, D.C., on leaving the
      White House after Hoover's election
1928

I am now in the army of unemployed presidents. But it is a very small army.

Harry S. Truman
Cited in *Quote* magazine
February 1, 1953

Right

What is right and what is practicable are two different things.

James Buchanan
Comment
1860

I have tried so hard to do the right.

Grover Cleveland
May 12, 1912

Right must be based upon the common strength, not upon the individual strength, of the nations upon whose concert peace will depend.

Woodrow Wilson
Speech, Senate
January 22, 1917

The right thing to do never requires any subterfuge, it is always simple and direct.

Calvin Coolidge
The Autobiography of Calvin Coolidge
1929

Rights

If we cannot secure all our rights, let us secure what we can.

Thomas Jefferson
Letter, James Madison
1789

As a man is said to have a right to his property, he may be equally said to have a property to his rights.

James Madison
March 29, 1792

Nothing then is unchangeable but the inherent and unalienable rights of man.

Thomas Jefferson
1824

All eyes are opened or opening to the rights of man. The general spread of the lights of science has already opened to every view the palpable truth, that the mass of mankind has not been born with saddles on their backs, nor a favored few booted and spurred, ready to ride them legitimately, by the grace of God.

Thomas Jefferson
Letter, R. C. Weightman
June 24, 1826

The rights of man as the foundation of just Government had long been understood; but the superstructures projected had been sadly defective.

James Madison
Letter, Nicholas P. Trist
February 15, 1830

Where is your law which says the mean and low, and the degraded, shall be deprived of the right of petition? . . . Where in the land of the freemen was the right of petition ever placed on the exclusive basis of morality and virtue? Petition is supplication. It is entreaty. It is prayer. And where is the degree of vice or immorality which shall deprive the citizen of the right to supplicate for a boon or to pray for mercy?

John Quincy Adams
Speech, House of Representatives, defending his
    right to introduce a petition from slaves for the
    abolition of slavery in the District of Columbia.
January 1837

It is now true that this is God's Country, if equal rights—a fair start and an equal chance in the race of life are everywhere secured to all.

Rutherford B. Hayes
Diary
July 25, 1880

The community that by concert, open or secret, among its citizens denies a portion of its members their plain rights under the law has severed the only safe bond of social order and prosperity. The evil works, from a bad center, both ways.

Benjamin Harrison
Inaugural address
March 4, 1889

But we cannot forget that we are . . . by the force of circumstances the responsible spokesmen of the rights of humanity, and that we cannot remain silent while those rights seem in process of being swept utterly away in the maelstrom of this terrible war.

Woodrow Wilson
Address, Congress
April 19, 1916

No peace can last, or ought to last, which does not recognize and accept the principle that governments derive all their just powers from the consent of the governed, and that no right anywhere exists to hand peoples from sovereignty to sovereignty as if they were property.

Woodrow Wilson
Speech, Senate (Peace without Victory)
January 22, 1917

We are glad . . . to fight thus . . . for the rights of nations great and small and the privilege of men everywhere to choose their way of life and of obedience.

Woodrow Wilson
Address, Joint session of the two houses of Congress,
    Declaration of War against Germany
April 2, 1917

The government of the United States is a device for maintaining in perpetuity the rights of the people, with the ultimate extinction of all privileged classes.

Calvin Coolidge
Speech, Philadelphia, Pennsylvania
September 25, 1924

If we are to continue to be proud that we are Americans there must be no weakening of the codes by which we have lived; by the right to meet your accuser face to face, if you have one; by your right to go to church or the synagogue or even the mosque of your own choosing; by your right to speak your mind and be protected in it.

Dwight D. Eisenhower
Speech
November 23, 1953

They [the Founding Fathers] proclaimed to all the world the revolutionary doctrine of the divine rights of the common man. That doctrine has ever since been the heart of the American faith.

Dwight D. Eisenhower
Speech, Columbia University, New York, New York
May 31, 1954

The same revolutionary beliefs for which our forebears fought are still at issue around the globe—the belief that the rights of man come not from the generosity of the state but from the hand of God.

John F. Kennedy
Inaugural address
January 20, 1961

No state can be regarded as permanent over the rights of individuals. Individual rights are supreme.

Ronald Reagan
Speech, Annual Joint Meeting of Governors of the World Bank and International Monetary Fund, Washington, D.C.
September 27, 1983

Franklin D. Roosevelt

[A] chameleon on plaid.

Herbert Hoover
Cited in James MacGregor Burns, *Roosevelt: The Lion and the Fox*

He was the only person I ever knew—anywhere—who was never afraid. God, how he could take it for us all.

Lyndon B. Johnson
Cited in James MacGregor Burns, *Roosevelt: The Lion and the Fox*

Theodore Roosevelt

He is the most dangerous man of the age.

Woodrow Wilson
Cited in Edmund Morris, *The Rise of Theodore Roosevelt*

And then he clenched his fist and said, "Sometimes I wish I could be President and Congress too." Well, I suppose if the truth were told, he is not the only President that has that idea.

Franklin D. Roosevelt
Speech, Dallas, Texas
June 12, 1936

Ruling Elite

Rulers are no more than attorneys, agents, and trustees, for the people.

John Adams
Dissertation on the Canon and the Feudal Law
August 1765

If anybody thinks that kings, nobles, priests are good conservators of the public happiness, send him [to Europe].

Thomas Jefferson
Letter, George Wythe
August 13, 1786

Since the general civilization of mankind, I believe there are more instances of the abridgement of the freedom of the people, by gradual and silent encroachments of those in power, than by violent and sudden usurpations.

James Madison
Virginia Convention
June 20, 1788

Many of our rich men have not been content with equal protection and equal benefits, but have besought us to make them richer by act of Congress.

Andrew Jackson
Veto, Bank Bill
July 10, 1832

It is to be regretted that the rich and powerful too often bend the acts of government to their selfish purposes.

Andrew Jackson
Veto, Bank Renewal Bill
July 10, 1832

I believe and I say it in true Democratic feeling, that all the measures of Government are directed to the purpose of making the rich richer and the poor poorer.

William Henry Harrison
Speech
October 1, 1840

Some day I will show the stuck-up aristocrats who is running the country. . . . A cheap purse-proud set they are, not half as good as the man who earns his bread by the sweat of his brow.

Andrew Johnson
Cited in Eric L. McKitrick, "Andrew Johnson, Outsider," in Eric L. McKitrick, *Andrew Johnson: A Profile*

The aristocracy based on $3,000,000,000 of property in slaves . . . has disappeared; but an aristocracy, based on over $2,500,000,000 of national securities, has arisen in the Northern states . . . . We have all read history, and is it not certain, that of all aristocracies mere wealth is the most odious, rapacious, and tyrannical?

Andrew Johnson
Speech, Cited in Kenneth M. Stampp, "Andrew Johnson: the Last Jacksonian," in Eric L. McKitrick, *Andrew Johnson: A Profile*

Our country is "ours" for the purpose of securing through its means justice, happiness, and prosperity to all—not for the purpose of permitting the selfish and designing to be enriched at the expense of their fellow-countrymen.

Grover Cleveland
Speech, Jewelers' Association Annual Dinner, New York, New York
November 21, 1890

We do not intend that this Republic shall ever fail as those republics of olden times failed, in which there finally came to be a government by classes, which resulted either in the poor plundering the rich or in the rich . . . exploiting the poor.

Theodore Roosevelt
Speech, Union League Club of Philadelphia, Pennsylvania
January 1905

Russia

I cannot but think . . . that the future growth of Russia and the stability of the British ascendancy are not a little overrated. Without a civilization of the hordes nominally extending the Russian dominion over so many latitudes and longitudes, they will add little to her real force, if they do not detract from it.

James Madison
Letter, Richard Rush
November 20, 1821

Russia seems at present the great bug-bear of the European politicians on the land, as the British Leviathan is on the water.

James Madison
Letter, Richard Rush
November 20, 1821

It is most appropriate that a people whose storehouses have been so lavishly filled with all the fruits of the earth by the gracious favor of God should manifest their gratitude by large gifts to his suffering children in other lands.

Benjamin Harrison
Speech, Senate and House, on the famine in Russia
January 5, 1892

For the people of Russia the people of the United States have ever entertained friendly feelings, which have now been greatly deepened by the knowledge that, actuated by the same lofty motives, the two Governments and peoples are co-operating to bring to a successful termination the conflict now raging for human liberty and a universal acknowledgement of those principles of right and justice which should direct all governments.

Woodrow Wilson
Address, Washington, D.C.
July 5, 1917

Twenty million people are starving. Whatever their politics, they shall be fed.

Herbert Hoover
Speech, on food relief to Russia, Washington, D.C.
August 1921

Our government offers no objection to the carrying on of commerce by our citizens with the people of Russia. Our government does not propose, however, to enter into relations with another regime which refuses to recognize the sanctity of international obligations. I do not propose to barter away for the privilege of trade any of the cherished rights of humanity. I do not propose to make merchandise of any American principle.

Calvin Coolidge
Message, Congress
December 6, 1923

I would rather have implanted the love of the American flag in the hearts of millions than to have added to the American Navy all the battleships that the Atlantic could float.

Herbert Hoover
Speech on food aid to Russia
1923

I don't know a good Russian from a bad Russian. I can tell a good Frenchman from a bad Frenchman. I can tell a good Italian from a bad Italian. I know a good Greek when I see one. But I don't understand the Russians.

Franklin D. Roosevelt
Comment, Francis Perkins

If, on the other side of the Iron Curtain, a backward civilization with a second-rate production plant can develop the power to frighten us all out of our wits, then we, without potential power can, through work, intelligence and courage, build any countering force that may be necessary.

Dwight D. Eisenhower
Comment, William Draper, special representative to NATO
March 16, 1953

No one should ever use his strength to put another in the position where he in effect has an ultimatum. For us to argue who is the stronger misses the point. If war comes, we both lose.

Richard Nixon
Comment, Nikita Khrushchev
"Kitchen Debate," Moscow
1959

I know something about Mr. Khrushchev, whom I met a year ago in the Senate Foreign Relations Committee, and I know something about the nature and history of his country, which I visited in 1939. Mr. Khrushchev himself, it is said, told the story about the Russian who began to run through the Kremlin, shouting, "Khrushchev is a fool. Khrushchev is a fool." He was sentenced, he said, to twenty-three years in prison, three for insulting the Party Secretary, and twenty for revealing a state secret.

John F. Kennedy
Speech, Pikesville, Maryland
September 16, 1960

Tell him, if he doesn't mind, we'll shake hands.

John F. Kennedy
Comment, interpreter, first meeting with Premier Khrushchev, Vienna
June 4, 1961

We seek peace as an end in itself. They seek victory.

Richard Nixon
Lakeside Speech, Bohemian Grove, California
July 1967

We shouldn't have any illusions that it will do any good or make any difference, but it is good to let them [the Russians] know that we're not as big fools as the requirements of diplomacy may sometimes make us seem.

Richard Nixon
Comment, Henry Kissinger
October 20, 1969

I have never said that the Soviets are "good guys." What I have always said is that we should not enter into unnecessary confrontations with them.

Richard Nixon
Speech, bipartisan leadership meeting
October 25, 1973

If the Soviet Union and the United States can reach an agreement so that our astronauts can fit together the most intricate scientific equipment, work together and shake hands 137 miles out in space, we as statesmen have an obligation to do as well on earth.

Gerald Ford
Speech, Helsinki Conference
August 1, 1975

I don't believe . . . that the Yugoslavs consider themselves dominated by the Soviet Union. I don't believe that the Rumanians consider themselves dominated by the Soviet Union. I don't believe that the Poles consider themselves dominated by the Soviet Union.

Gerald Ford
Ford vs. Carter, the second debate
October 6, 1976

There is no Soviet domination of Eastern Europe and there never will be any under Ford Administration.

Gerald Ford
Ford vs. Carter, the second debate
October 6, 1976

At the Cabinet meeting this morning Zbig [Zbigniew Brzezinski, national security adviser] made an interesting comment that under Lenin the Soviet Union was like a religious revival, under Stalin like a prison, under Khrushchev like a circus, and under Brezhnev like the U.S. Post Office.

Jimmy Carter
Diary
November 7, 1977

During the transition period [Henry] Kissinger and I developed a new policy for dealing with the Soviets . . . we decided to link progress in such areas of Soviet concern as strategic arms limitation and increased trade with progress in areas that were important to us—Vietnam, the Mideast, and Berlin. This concept became known as linkage.

Richard Nixon
The Memoirs of Richard Nixon
1978

The defense needs of the Soviet Union hardly call for maintaining more combat divisions in East Germany today than were in the whole allied invasion force that landed in Normandy on D-Day.

Ronald Reagan
Speech, National Press Club, Washington, D.C.
November 18, 1981

[The Soviets] have offered to trade us an apple for an orchid. We don't do that in our country.

John F. Kennedy
Speech
1982

The United States rejects as false and misleading the views of the world as divided between the empires of East and West. We reject it on factual grounds. The United States does not head any bloc of subservient nations nor do we desire to. What is called the West is a free alliance of governments, most of whom greatly value their independence. What is called the East is an empire directed from the center, which is Moscow.

Ronald Reagan
Speech, United Nations, New York, New York
September 26, 1983

The Soviets take the long view—to dominate the strategic sea lanes and chokepoints around the world.

Ronald Reagan
Speech, United Nations, New York, New York
September 26, 1983

S

Scandals

If Albert Fall [secretary of the interior during the Teapot Dome scandal] isn't an honest man, I'm not fit to be President of the United States.

Warren G. Harding
Comment, Albert D. Lasker, Washington, D.C.
April 1922

If there is any guilt it will be punished; if there is any civil liability, it will be enforced; if there is any fraud, it will be revealed; if there are any contracts which are illegal, they will be canceled.

Calvin Coolidge
New York Herald Tribune, on Teapot Dome scandal
January 27, 1924

There are only three purgatories to which people can be assigned: to be damned by one's fellows; to be damned by the courts; to be damned in the next world. I want these men to get all three without probation.

Calvin Coolidge
Comment, Herbert Hoover, regarding the scandals under the Harding administration
1924

I do not propose to sacrifice any innocent man for my own welfare, nor do I propose to retain in office any unfit man for my own welfare.

Calvin Coolidge
On Teapot Dome scandal
1924

We did get something—a gift. . . . It was a little cocker spaniel dog in a crate . . . sent all the way from Texas. Black and white spotted. And our little girl, Tricia, the six-year-old, named it Checkers. And you know the kids love that dog and I just want to say this right now, that regardless of what they say about it, we're going to keep it.

Richard Nixon
Denying use of a slush fund from California backers during Checkers Speech
September 23, 1952

What really hurts in matters of this sort [the Watergate break-in] is not the fact that they occur, because overzealous people in campaigns do things that are wrong. What really hurts is if you try to cover it up.

Richard Nixon
Press conference
August 29, 1972

The President's losses [have] got to be cut on the cover-up deal.

Richard Nixon
Comment, Charles Colson, White House, Watergate tapes
1972

That's why for your immediate thing you've got no choice with [Watergate defendant E. Howard] Hunt but the 120 [$120,000 bribe money] or whatever it is. Right? Would you agree that it's a buy-time thing, you better damn well get that done, but fast?

Richard Nixon
Comment, John Dean, White House, Watergate tapes
March 21, 1973

Perjury is an awful hard rap to prove.

Richard Nixon
Comment, John Dean, White House, Watergate tapes
March 21, 1973

Just be damned sure you say I don't remember; I can't recall, I can't give any honest answer to that that I can recall.

Richard Nixon
Comment, John Dean, H. R. Haldeman, White
    House, Watergate tapes
March 21, 1973

And you handled it just right. You contained it.

Richard Nixon
Comment, John Dean, White House, Watergate tapes
March 21, 1973

I condemn any attempts to cover-up in this case, no matter who is involved.

Richard Nixon
Press conference
April 17, 1973

There can be no whitewash in the White House.

Richard Nixon
TV address on the Watergate scandal
April 30, 1973

Should have destroyed the tapes after April 30, 1973.

Richard Nixon
Note on bedside pad, Bethesda Naval Hospital
July 19, 1973

Some people . . . will say that Watergate demonstrates the bankruptcy of the American political system. I believe precisely the opposite is true. Watergate represented a series of illegal acts and bad judgments by a number of individuals. It was the system that has brought the facts to light and that will bring those guilty to justice. . . . It is essential now that we place our faith in the system.

Richard Nixon
Reader's Digest
July 1973

I welcome this kind of examination, because people have got to know whether or not their President is a crook. Well, I am not a crook. I have earned everything I have got.

Richard Nixon
Press conference, Washington, D.C.
November 18, 1973

[Watergate is] the thinnest scandal in American history.

Richard Nixon
Comment, Rabbi Baruch Korff
May 13, 1974

If these charges on Watergate were true, nobody would have to ask me to resign—I wouldn't serve for one month. But I know they are not true, therefore I will stay here and do the job I was elected to do as well as I can and let the constitutional process make the final verdict.

Richard Nixon
Comment, Rabbi Baruch Korff
May 13, 1974

I have come to the conclusion that the public interest is no longer served by repetition of my previously expressed belief that on the basis of all evidence known to me and to the American people, the President [Richard Nixon] is not guilty of an impeachable offense.

Gerald Ford
Speech
August 5, 1974

My fellow Americans, our long national nightmare [Watergate] is over. Our Constitution works. Our great Republic is a government of laws and not of men.

Gerald Ford
Inaugural address
August 9, 1974

For a long time our American citizens have been excluded, sometimes misled, sometimes have been lied to. This is not compatible with the purpose of our nation.

Jimmy Carter
On Nixon, Ford administrations, first Ford-Carter
    debate, Philadelphia, Pennsylvania
September 23, 1976

What we were elected to do we are going to do, and let others wallow in Watergate.

Richard Nixon
Speech, White House
July 23, 1976

When the President does it, that means it is not illegal.

Richard Nixon
TV interview, David Frost
May 20, 1977

In fact, I had known some of the details of the cover-up before March 21 [1973], and when I did become aware of their implications, instead of exerting presidential leadership aimed at uncovering the cover-up, I embarked upon an increasingly desperate search for ways to limit the damage to my friends, my administration, and to myself.

Richard Nixon
The Memoirs of Richard Nixon
1978

I was faced with having to fire my friends for things that I myself was a part of, things that I could not accept as morally or legally wrong, no matter how much that opened me to charges of cynicism and amorality. There had been no thievery or venality. We had all simply wandered into a situation unthinkingly, trying to protect ourselves from what we saw as a political problem. Now, suddenly, it was like a Rorschach ink [blot]; others, looking at our actions, pointed out a pattern that we ourselves had not seen.

Richard Nixon
The Memoirs of Richard Nixon, on asking for resignations of Robert Haldeman and John Ehrlichman in the wake of the Watergate scandal
1978

We did not—repeat—did not trade weapons or anything else for hostages—nor will we.

Ronald Reagan
Presidential address
November 13, 1986

I'm afraid that I let myself be influenced by others' recollections, not my own. . . . The only honest answer is to state that try as I might, I cannot recall anything whatsoever about whether I approved an Israeli sale in advance or whether I approved replenishment of Israeli stocks around August of 1985. My answer therefore and the simple truth is, "I don't remember—period."

Ronald Reagan
Letter, Tower Commission
February 20, 1987

But I draw a difference between our dealing with people that are not terrorist and shipping arms to terrorists.

Ronald Reagan
Comment, Robert McFarlane
Tower Commission Report, cited in Newsweek
March 9, 1987

A few months ago I told the American people I did not trade arms for hostages. My heart and my best intentions still tell me that is true, but the facts and the evidence tell me it is not.

Ronald Reagan
Speech, Washington, D.C.
1987

There ain't no smoking gun.

Ronald Reagan
On allegations of his involvement in the Iran-contra scandal, Newsweek
June 29, 1987

Secession

This is all that we want . . . to nullify the nullifiers.

Andrew Jackson
Letter, Martin Van Buren
November 18, 1832

Their object is disunion. But be not deceived by names. Disunion by armed force is treason. Are you really ready to incur its guilt?

Andrew Jackson
Proclamation to the People of South Carolina
December 10, 1832

I consider, then, the power to annul a law of the United States, *assumed by one State*, uncompatible with the existence of the Union, contradicted expressly by the letter of the Constitution, unauthorized by its spirit, inconsistent with every principle on which it was founded, and destructive of the great object for which it was formed.

Andrew Jackson
Proclamation to the People of South Carolina
December 10, 1832

Can anyone of common sense believe the absurdity that a faction of any state, or a state, has a right to secede and destroy this union and the liberty of our country with it, or nullify the laws of the Union; then indeed is our Constitution a rope of sand; under such I would not live.

Andrew Jackson
Letter, General John Coffee
December 14, 1832

The laws of the United States must be executed. For any state to disregard these laws, is disunion; and disunion by armed force is treason.

Andrew Jackson
When South Carolina rejected Tariff of 1832

The right of the people of a single State to absolve themselves at will and without the consent of the other States from their most solemn obligations, and hazard the liberties and happiness of the millions composing this Union, cannot be acknowledged.

Andrew Jackson
Special Message, Congress
January 16, 1833

For my own part, I know only my country, my whole country, and nothing but my country.

Millard Fillmore
Speech, New York, New York
June 23, 1856

Secession is hell-born and hell-bound.

Andrew Johnson
Speech, Tennessee
1860

The Union was designed to be perpetual. . . . Its framers never intended . . . the absurdity of providing for its own destruction.

James Buchanan
Cited in Philip Klein, *President James Buchanan: A Biography*

All for which the slave States have ever contended, is to be let alone and permitted to manage their domestic institutions in their own way.

James Buchanan
Fourth annual message, Congress (on secession)
December 3, 1860

In order to justify secession as a constitutional remedy, it must be on the principle that the Federal Government is a mere voluntary association of States, to be dissolved at pleasure by any one of the contracting parties. If this be so, the Confederacy is a rope of sand, to be penetrated and dissolved by the first adverse wave of public opinion in any of the States.

James Buchanan
Fourth annual message, Congress (on secession)
December 3, 1860

Let us look the danger fairly in the face. Secession is neither more nor less than revolution.

James Buchanan
Fourth annual message, Congress
December 3, 1860

The central idea of secession is the essence of anarchy.

Abraham Lincoln
First inaugural address
March 4, 1861

It is safe to assert that no government proper ever had a provision in its organic law for its own termination.

Abraham Lincoln
First inaugural address
March 4, 1861

The first necessity that is upon us, is of proving that popular government is not an absurdity. We must settle this question now—whether in a free government the minority have the right to break it up whenever they choose. If we fail, it will go far to prove the incapability of the people to govern themselves.

Abraham Lincoln
Comment, John Hay
April 1861

Security

These three objectives—the security of the home, the security of livelihood, and the security of social insurance—are, it seems to me, a minimum of the promise that we can offer to the American people.

Franklin D. Roosevelt
Message, Congress
June 8, 1934

If all Americans want is security they can go to prison. They'll have enough to eat, a bed and a roof over their heads. But if an American wants to preserve his dignity and his equality as a human being, he must not bow his neck to any dictatorial government.

Dwight D. Eisenhower
Speech, Galveston, Texas
December 1949

Even if security from the cradle to the grave could eliminate the risks of life, it would be a dead hand on the creative spirit of our people.

Herbert Hoover
West Branch, Iowa
August 10, 1954

Too often, the demands of prosperity and security are viewed as competitors when, in fact, they are complementary, natural and necessary allies.

Ronald Reagan
Speech, Annual Meeting of Governors of the World Bank and International Monetary Fund, Washington, D.C.
September 27, 1984

Senate

You are apprehensive of monarchy; I, of aristocracy. I would therefore have given more power to the President and less to the Senate.

John Adams
Letter, Thomas Jefferson
November 16, 1787

The only remedy [for corruption] is to throw the rich and the proud into one group, in a separate assembly, and there tie their hands; if you give them scope with the people at large or their representatives, they will destroy *all equality and liberty, with the consent and acclamations of the people themselves.*

John Adams
A Defence of the Constitutions of the Government of the United States of America
1787-1788

"Mischief has been done by the Senate of U.S." I have known and felt more of this mischief, than Washington, Jefferson and Madison altoge[the]r. But this has been all caused by the constitutional Power of the Senate in Executive Business, which ought to be immediately, totally and eternally abolished.

John Adams
Letter, Thomas Jefferson
November 14, 1813

The legislative and executive authorities are too much blended together. While the Senate of the United States has a negative on all appointments to office, we can never have a national President. In spite of his own judgment, he must be the President, not the tool, of a party.

John Adams
Letter, R. Rush
May 11, 1821

If the censures of the Senate be submitted to by the President, the confidence of the people in his ability and virtue and the character and usefulness of his Administration will soon be at an end, and the real power of the Government will fall into the hands of a body holding their offices for long terms, not elected by the people and not to them directly responsible.

Andrew Jackson
Protest to the Senate
April 15, 1834

[I will] receive no message from those damned scoundrels [senators].

Andrew Jackson
National Intelligencer
March 5, 1835

Nothing is more certain than that the tenure of the Senate, was meant as an obstacle to the instability, which not only history, but the experience of our Country, had shewn to be the besetting infirmity of popular Governments.

James Madison
March 1836

I would rather have the vindication of my State by electing me to my old seat in the Senate of the United States than to be monarch of the grandest empire on earth. For this I live, and will never die content without.

Andrew Johnson
Comment, to former aide Reeves
1872

I go into the unknown and the untried; and I have this premonition that the Senate is composed of old men whose ideas and opinions are crystallized into fixed and well-nigh unchangeable forms and they are much less likely to be impressed by anything that may be said to them than are the members of the House. Furthermore, a decided majority of all my associates who have gone from the House to the Senate have been measurably lost in its silence.

James Garfield
Letter, Burke Hinsdale, after Republican nomination
for Senate
1879

This brings on the contest at once and will settle the question whether the President is registering clerk of the Senate or the Executive of the United States.

James Garfield
Letter, friend, (on submission of William Robertson's name to the Senate for collector of the New York Customhouse)
1881

[I had hoped] the Senators might change their minds, or that the people might change the Senate; instead of which they changed me.

William Howard Taft
Comment, cited in Paolo E. Coletta, *The Presidency of William Howard Taft*

I have come to fight a cause and that cause is greater than the U.S. Senate.

Woodrow Wilson
Speech, cross-country tour to create support for ratification of the Covenant of The League of Nations
September 1919

It may seem that [senatorial] debate is endless, but there is scarcely a time when it is not informing, and, after all, the power to compel due consideration is the distinguishing mark of a deliberative body.

Calvin Coolidge
The Autobiography of Calvin Coolidge
1929

At first I intended to become a student of the Senate rules and I did learn much about them, but I soon found out that the Senate had but one fixed rule, subject to exceptions of course, which was to the effect that the Senate would do anything it wanted to do whenever it wanted to do it.

Calvin Coolidge
Autobiography of Calvin Coolidge
1929

If the Senate has any weaknesses it is because the people have sent to that body men lacking the necessary ability and character to perform the proper functions.

Calvin Coolidge
Autobiography of Calvin Coolidge
1929

Thank God she doesn't have to be confirmed by the Senate.

Herbert Hoover
Comment on the birth of his granddaughter
c. 1929

Anything that is sent up to the Senate and House with my name on it will quiver a couple of times and then turn over and die.

Harry S. Truman
Comment, Clark M. Clifford, suggesting the Truman Formula be renamed the Marshall Plan
Cited in *New York Times*
June 5, 1987

Slander

Defamation is becoming a necessity of life; inasmuch as a dish of tea in the morning or evening cannot be digested without that stimulant.

Thomas Jefferson
Letter, John Norvell
June 11, 1807

The murderer only takes the life of the parent and leaves his character as a goodly heritage to his children, whilst the slanderer takes away his goodly reputation and leaves him a living monument to his children's disgrace.

Andrew Jackson
Note
August, 1837

Never sue for assault or slander, settle them cases yourself.

Andrew Jackson
Cited in Vic Fredericks, *The Wit and Wisdom of the Presidents*

Slavery

There is not a man living who wishes more sincerely than I do to see a plan adopted for the abolition of slavery. But there is only one proper way and effectual mode by which it can be accomplished, and that is by legislative authority.

George Washington
Letter, Robert Morris
April 12, 1786

I never mean, unless some particular circumstance should compel me to it, to possess another slave by purchase, it being among my first wishes to see some plan adopted by which slavery in this country may be abolished.

George Washington
Letter, John Francis Mercer
September 10, 1786

This abomination must have an end. And there is a superior bench reserved in Heaven for those who hasten it.

Thomas Jefferson
Letter, Edward Rutledge
July 14, 1787

It is to be hoped that by expressing a national disapprobation of this trade we may destroy it, and make ourselves free from reproaches, and our posterity from the imbecility ever attendant on a country filled with slaves.

James Madison
Speech, House of Representatives
May 13, 1789

The abolition of slavery must be gradual, and accomplished with much caution and circumspection.

John Adams
Letter, George Churchman and Jacob Lindley
January 24, 1801

It is the law of nature between master and servant that the servant shall spoil or plunder the master.

John Quincy Adams
Diary
December 17, 1810

The turpitude, the inhumanity, the cruelty, and the infamy of the African commerce in slaves have been so impressively represented to the public by the highest powers of eloquence that nothing that I can say would increase the just odium in which it is and ought to be held. Every measure of prudence, therefore, ought to be assumed for the eventual total extirpation of slavery from the United States.

John Adams
Letter, T. Robert J. Evans
June 8, 1819

No evil can result from its [slavery's] inhibition more pernicious than its toleration.

Martin Van Buren
Written communication
January 4, 1820

Slavery is the great and foul stain upon the North American Union.

John Quincy Adams
Diary
January 10, 1820

It is, in truth, all perverted sentiment—mistaking labor for slavery and dominion for freedom.

John Quincy Adams
Diary
March 3, 1820

This momentous question, like a firebell in the night, awakened and filled me with terror. I considered it at once as the knell of the Union.

Thomas Jefferson
Letter, John Adams, on the Missouri Compromise,
    extending slavery
April 22, 1820

Our opinions agree as to the evil, moral, political, and economical, of slavery.

James Madison
Letter, Francis Corbin
November 26, 1820

That nature's God commands the slave to
    rise,
And on the oppressor's head to break his
    chain. Roll, years of promise,
rapidly roll round,
Till not a slave shall on this earth be found.

John Quincy Adams
Written while president
1825-1829

It's in slavery that are to be found all the embarrassments of the present and the fears of the future.

John Quincy Adams
Comment, Alexis de Tocqueville
1831

I have heard it declared by the gentleman from Georgia [A. S. Clayton] that the species of the population he alluded to [slaves] constituted the *machines of the South*. Now those *machines* have twenty-odd Representatives in this hall, Representatives elected not by *machines*, but by those who own them. Is there any such representation in any other portion of the Union? Have the manufacturers asked for representation on their *machines*? Their looms and factories have no vote in Congress, but the *machines* of the South have more than twenty Representatives on this floor.

John Quincy Adams
Speech, House of Representatives
February 4, 1833

For aught I know, ere long any member who should dare to raise his voice on abolition of slavery will be expelled from this House. Sir, I am ready to be that member whenever the House shall come to that decision.

John Quincy Adams
Speech, House of Representatives
January 9, 1837

No man is good enough to govern another man without that other's consent.

Abraham Lincoln
Speech, Springfield, Illinois
January 1837

Such is the condition of things in these shambles of human flesh that I cannot now expose the whole horrible transaction but at the hazard of my life.

John Quincy Adams
Diary, on threats to his life for his antislavery
    position
1837

I do believe slavery to be a sin before God, and that is the reason and the only unsurmountable reason why we should not annex Texas to this Union.

John Quincy Adams
Speech, House of Representatives
February 1838

Four-fifths of whom [the members of the House who were committed to slavery] would crucify me if their votes could erect the cross; forty members, representatives of the free, in the league of slavery, . . . would break me on the wheel; and four-fifths of the other hundred and twenty are either so cold or so lukewarm that they are ready to desert me at the first scintillation of indiscretion on my part.

John Quincy Adams
January 1840

I see where the shoe pinches, Mr. Speaker. It will pinch *more* yet. I'll deal out to the gentlemen a diet that they will find it hard to digest. If before I get through every slaveholder, slave trader and slave breeder on this floor does not get material for better reflection, it shall be no fault of mine!

John Quincy Adams
Speech, House of Representatives
January 1842

By the laws of nature and nature's God, man cannot be the property of man.

John Quincy Adams
Address to his constituents
September 17, 1842

If slavery must go by blood and war, let war come.

John Quincy Adams
Speech, House of Representatives
February 4, 1843

Holders of slaves often delude themselves, by assuming that the test of property is human law. The soul of one man cannot by human law be made the property of another. The owner of a slave is the owner of a living corpse; but he is not the owner of the man.

John Quincy Adams
Speech, Bangor, Maine
July 4, 1843

So far as Slavery is concerned, we of the south must throw ourselves on the constitution & defend our rights under [it] to the last, & when arguments will no longer suffice, we will appeal to the sword, if necessary to do so. I will be the last to yield one inch.

Zachary Taylor
Letter, Jefferson Davis
July 27, 1847

The result of leaving the slavery question an open one, to be agitated by ambitious political aspirants and gamblers and their friends, will be to produce an organization of parties upon geographical lines, which must prove dangerous to the harmony if not the existence of the Union itself.

James K. Polk
The Diary of James K. Polk
July 28, 1848

The agitation of the slavery question is mischievous and wicked, and proceeds from no patriotic motive by its authors. It is a mere political question on which demagogues and ambitious politicians hope to promote their own prospects for political promotion. And this they seem willing to do even at the hazard of disturbing the harmony if not dissolving the Union itself.

James K. Polk
The Diary of James K. Polk
December 22, 1848

As labor is the common burden of our race, so the effort of some to shift their share of the burden on to the shoulders of others is the great durable curse of the race.

Abraham Lincoln
Fragment
c. July 1854

I believe that involuntary servitude, as it exists in different States of this Confederacy, is recognized by the Constitution. I believe that it stands like any other admitted right.

Franklin Pierce
Inaugural address
March 4, 1853

If the Negro is a man, why then my ancient faith teaches me that "all men are created equal," and that there can be no moral right in connection with one man's making a slave of another.

Abraham Lincoln
Speech, Peoria, Illinois
October 16, 1854

This declared indifference, but, as I must think, real, covert zeal, for the spread of slavery, I cannot but hate. I hate it because of the monstrous injustice of slavery itself. I hate it because it deprives our republican example of its just influence in the world, enables the enemies of free institutions with plausibility to taunt us as hypocrites, causes the real friends of freedom to doubt our sincerity, and especially because it forces so many good men amongst ourselves into an open war with the very fundamental principles of civil liberty, criticizing the Declaration of Independence, and insisting that there is no right principle of action but self-interest.

Abraham Lincoln
Reply, Senator Douglas, Peoria, Illinois
October 16, 1854

Slavery is founded on the selfishness of man's nature—opposition to it on his love of justice. These principles are in eternal antagonism; and when brought into collision so fiercely as slavery extension brings them, shocks and throes and convulsions must ceaselessly follow.

Abraham Lincoln
Speech, Peoria, Illinois
October 16, 1854

Let us revere the Declaration of Independence; let us continue to obey the Constitution and the laws; let us keep step to the music of the Union. Let us draw a cordon, so to speak, around the slave States, and the hateful institution [slavery], like a reptile poisoning itself, will perish by its own infamy.

Abraham Lincoln
Speech, Bloomington, Indiana
May 19, 1856

Those arguments that are made, that the inferior race is to be treated with as much allowance as they are capable of enjoying; that as much is to be done for them as their condition will allow, what are these arguments? They are the arguments that kings have made for enslaving the people in all the ages of the world.

Abraham Lincoln
Campaign speech, Senate race
1858

As I would not be a *slave*, so I would not be a *master*. Whatever differs from this, to the extent of the difference, is no democracy.

Abraham Lincoln
"Fragment on Slavery"
August 1, 1858

I have no purpose, either directly or indirectly, to interfere with the institution of slavery in the States where it exists. I believe I have no lawful right to do so, and I have no inclination to do so. I have no purpose to introduce political and social equality between the white and black races. There is a physical difference between the two, which, in my judgment, will probably forever forbid their living together upon the footing of perfect equality, and inasmuch as it becomes a necessity that there must be a difference, I, as well as Judge Douglas, am in favor of the race to which I belong having the superior position.

Abraham Lincoln
Reply, Stephen Douglas, Debate, Ottawa, Illinois
August 21, 1858

Can the people of a United States Territory, in any lawful way, against the wish of any citizen of the United States, exclude slavery from its limits prior to the formation of a State constitution?

Abraham Lincoln
The Lincoln-Douglas debates, the second joint debate, Freeport, Illinois
August 27, 1858

If the Supreme Court of the United States shall decide that States cannot exclude slavery from their limits, are you in favor of acquiescing in, adopting, and following such decision as a rule of political action?

Abraham Lincoln
The Lincoln-Douglas debates, the second joint debate, Freeport, Illinois
August 27, 1858

There is vigor enough in slavery to plant itself in a new country even against unfriendly legislation. It takes not only law, but the *enforcement* of law to keep it out. That is the history of this country upon the subject.

Abraham Lincoln
The Lincoln-Douglas debates, the third joint debate, Lincoln's reply to Douglas, Jonesboro, Illinois
September 15, 1858

If there be a man here among us who does not think the institution of slavery is wrong in any one of the aspects of which I have spoken, he is misplaced, and ought not to be among us.

Abraham Lincoln
The Lincoln-Douglas debates, the seventh joint debate, Alton, Illinois
October 15, 1858

Has anything ever threatened the existence of this Union save and except this very institution of slavery?

Abraham Lincoln
The Lincoln-Douglas debates, the seventh joint debate, Alton, Illinois
October 15, 1858

He [Stephen Douglas] may say he don't care whether an indifferent thing [slavery] is voted up or down, but he must logically have a choice between a right thing and a wrong thing.

Abraham Lincoln
The Lincoln-Douglas debates, the seventh joint debate, Alton, Illinois
October 15, 1858

That is the real issue. That is the issue that will continue in this country when these poor tongues of Judge Douglas and myself shall be silent. It is the eternal struggle between these two principles—right and wrong—throughout the world. They are the two principles that have stood face to face from the beginning of time, and will ever continue to struggle. The one is the common right of humanity, and the other is the divine right of kings.

Abraham Lincoln
The Lincoln-Douglas debates, the seventh joint debate, Alton, Illinois
October 15, 1858

In the right to eat the bread, which his own hand earns, he, the Negro, is my equal and the equal of Judge Douglas, and the equal of every living man.

Abraham Lincoln
The Lincoln Douglas debates
1858

This is a world of compensation; and he who would be no slave must consent to have no slave. Those who deny freedom to others deserve it not for themselves; and, under a just God, cannot long retain it.

Abraham Lincoln
Letter, H. L. Pierce
April 6, 1859

All for which the slave States have ever contended, is to be let alone and permitted to manage their domestic institutions in their own way.

James Buchanan
Fourth annual message, Congress (on secession)
December 3, 1860

There is no possible compromise on [slavery]. . . . On that point hold firm, as with a chain of steel.

Abraham Lincoln
Letter, E. B. Washburne
December 13, 1860

Away with slavery, the breeder of Aristocrats. Up with the Stars and Stripes, symbol of free labor and free men.

Andrew Johnson
1861

In *giving* freedom to the *slave*, we *assure* freedom to the *free*.

Abraham Lincoln
The Emancipation Proclamation
January 1, 1863

I never, in my life, felt more certain that I was doing right, than I do in signing this paper. But I have been receiving calls and shaking hands since nine o'clock this morning, till my arm is stiff and numb. Now this signature is one that will be closely examined, and if they find my hand trembled they will say, "he had some compunctions." But anyway, it's going to be done.

Abraham Lincoln
Signing of The Emancipation Proclamation
January 1, 1863

And I hereby enjoin upon the people so declared to be free to abstain from all violence, unless in necessary self-defence; and I recommend to them that, in all cases when allowed, they labor faithfully for reasonable wages.

Abraham Lincoln
The Emancipation Proclamation
January 1, 1863

And I further declare and make known, that such persons of suitable condition [freed slaves], will be received into the armed services of the United States to garrison forts, positions, stations, and other places, and to man vessels of all sorts in said service.

Abraham Lincoln
The Emancipation Proclamation
January 1, 1863

If slavery is not wrong, nothing is wrong.

Abraham Lincoln
Letter, A. G. Hodges
April 4, 1864

I never knew a man who wished himself to be as slave. Consider if you know any *good* thing that no man desires for himself.

Abraham Lincoln
Written in an album at a Sanitary Commission Fair
1864

Slavery is dead, and you must pardon me if I do not mourn over its dead body.

Andrew Johnson
Speech, Nashville, Tennessee
1864

We shall never know why slavery dies so hard in this Republic . . . till we know why Sin is long-lived and Satan is immortal.

James A. Garfield
Speech, Congress
1864

Whenever I hear any one arguing for slavery, I feel a strong impulse to see it tried on him personally.

Abraham Lincoln
Speech, Indiana Regiment
March 17, 1865

The white race and the black race of the South have hitherto lived together under the relation of master and slave—capital owning labor. . . . Capital, it is true, has more intelligence, but labor is never so ignorant as not to understand its own interests, not to know its own value.

Andrew Johnson
Veto, Civil Rights Act
March 27, 1866

To the race more favored by our laws I would say, withhold no legal privilege of advancement to the new citizen.

Ulysses S. Grant
Message, Congress, in reference to the 15th
    Amendment
March 30, 1870

My countrymen, . . . fifty years hence our children will not be divided in their opinions concerning our controversies; they will surely bless their fathers—and their fathers' God—that the Union was preserved; that slavery was overthrown, and that both races were made equal before the law. We may hasten on, we may retard, but we cannot prevent the final reconciliation.

James A. Garfield
Inaugural address
March 4, 1881

A grossly anarchistic and un-American form of evil.

Theodore Roosevelt
The Life of Thomas Hart Benton
1887

Shall the prejudices and paralysis of slavery continue to hang upon the skirts of progress?

Benjamin Harrison
Inaugural address
March 4, 1889

All those fires of industry which I saw through the South were lighted at the funeral pyre of slavery.

Benjamin Harrison
Speech, Veterans, San Francisco, California
May 1, 1891

I will not be a party to any treaty that makes anybody a slave; now that is all there is to it.

Dwight D. Eisenhower
Press conference
June 30, 1954

Three and a half centuries ago the first Negroes arrived at Jamestown. They did not arrive in brave ships in search of a home for freedom. They did not mingle fear and joy, in expectation that in this New World anything would be possible to a man strong enough to reach for it. They came in darkness and they came in chains.

Lyndon B. Johnson
Speech, signing of Voting Rights Act, Capitol Rotunda
August 6, 1965

Socialism

Nothing has spread socialistic feeling in this country more than the automobile. . . . They are the picture of the arrogance of wealth with all its independence and carelessness.

Woodrow Wilson
1906

The adoption of a logical and extreme Socialistic system would spell sheer destruction; it would produce grosser wrong and outrage, fouler immorality than any existing system. But this does not mean that we may not with great advantage adopt certain of the principles proposed by some given set of men who happen to call themselves Socialists.

Theodore Roosevelt
Speech, Sorbonne
April 23, 1910

Socialism proposes no adequate substitute for the motive of enlightened selfishness that today is at the basis of all human labor and effort, enterprise and new activity.

William Howard Taft
Popular Government
1913

Social Security and Welfare

I have considered the pension list of the republic a roll of honor.

Grover Cleveland
Veto Message, Congress
July 5, 1888

When I say I believe in a square deal I do not mean . . . it[s] possible to give every man the best hand. If the cards do not come to any man, or if they do come, and he has not the power to play them, that is his affair. All I mean is that there shall not be any crookedness in the dealing.

Theodore Roosevelt
Speech, Dallas, Texas
April 5, 1906

Modern society cannot survive with the defense of Cain, "Am I my brother's keeper?"

Herbert Hoover
Speech, Relief Drive
October 18, 1931

The Federal government must and shall quit this business of relief.

Franklin D. Roosevelt
Message, Congress
January 4, 1935

Social security must be built upon a cult of work, not a cult of leisure.

Herbert Hoover
Speech
June 16, 1935

The challenge of the next half-century is whether we have the wisdom to use wealth to enrich and elevate our national life—and to advance the quality of American civilization—for in your time we have the opportunity to move not only toward the rich society and the powerful society, but upward toward the Great Society.

Lyndon B. Johnson
Speech, University of Michigan, Ann Arbor, Michigan
May 22, 1964

The great society is a place where men are more concerned with the quality of their goals than the quantity of their goods.

Lyndon B. Johnson
Speech, University of Michigan, Ann Arbor, Michigan
May 22, 1964

We must open the doors of opportunity. But we also must equip our people to walk through those doors.

Lyndon B. Johnson
Address, National Urban League Conference, Washington, D.C.
December 10, 1964

I do not believe that the Great Society is the ordered, changeless, and sterile battalion of the ants. It is the excitement of becoming, trying, probing, failing, resting, and trying again.

Lyndon B. Johnson
Inaugural address
January 20, 1965

The Great Society is not a welfare state—nor is it a spending state. Its object is to give the individual identity and self-esteem—not to impose upon him any oppressive paternalism. Further, the Great Society seeks not to raise the costs of government but to reduce for the individual—and the Nation—the costs of obsolescence, waste, and neglect wherever such may exist in our national life.

Lyndon B. Johnson
Speech, National Industrial Conference Board, Sheraton-Park Hotel, Washington, D.C.
February 17, 1965

A great nation is one which breeds a great people. A great people flower not from wealth and power, but from a society which spurs them to the fullness of their genius.

Lyndon B. Johnson
State of the union address
January 12, 1966

The great society leads us along three roads—growth and justice and liberation.

Lyndon B. Johnson
State of the union address
January 12, 1966

I want to be remembered as one who spent his whole life trying to get more people more to eat and more to wear, to live longer, to have medicine and have attention, nursing, hospitals, and doctors' care when they need it, and to have their children have a chance to go to school and carry out really what the Declaration of Independence says, "All men are created equal."

Lyndon B. Johnson
Speech, signing the Medicare Extension Bill, San Antonio, Texas
April 8, 1966

The Great Society was created by liberal academics and bureaucrats steeped in the myths of the New Deal. When its theoretical high-mindedness ran up against the self-interested tough-mindedness of the people it was intended to serve, there was certain to be conflict.

Richard Nixon
The Memoirs of Richard Nixon
1978

In the past two decades, we have created hundreds of new programs to provide personal assistance. Many of these programs may have come from a good heart, but not all have come from a clear head.

Ronald Reagan
Speech, Washington, D.C.
September 24, 1981

South America

A virtuous people may and will confine themselves within the limit of a strict neutrality; but it is not in their power to behold a conflict so vitally important to their neighbors without the sensibility and sympathy which naturally belong to such a case.

James Monroe
Third annual message, Congress, on Spanish
   relations with South America
December 7, 1819

In regard to the stipulation proposed as the condition of the ratification of the treaty [with Spain], that the United States shall abandon the right to recognize the revolutionary Colonies in South America or to form other relations with them when in their judgment it may be just and expedient to do so, it is manifestly so repugnant to the honor and even to the independence of the United States that it has been impossible to discuss it.

James Monroe
Message to the Senate and House of Representatives
   on Spain
May 9, 1820

The revolution which has severed the colonies of Spanish America from European thraldom, and left them to form self-dependent governments as members of the society of civilized nations, is among the most important events in modern history

John Quincy Adams
Speech, Washington, D.C.
May 27, 1823

In regard to the American Republics . . . it has been my constant aim strictly to observe all the obligations of political friendship and of good neighborhood.

Franklin Pierce
Third annual message, Congress
December 31, 1855

If you are content, I am not, that the nations of Europe shall absorb nearly the entire commerce of these near sister republics that lie to the south of us. It is naturally in large measure ours—ours by neighborhood, ours by nearness of access, ours by that sympathy that binds a hemisphere without a king.

Benjamin Harrison
Speech, Galveston, Texas
April 18, 1891

There is no calamity which a great nation can invite which equals that which follows from a supine submission to wrong and injustice, and the consequent loss of national self-respect and honor, beneath which are shielded and defended a people's safety and greatness.

Grover Cleveland
Message, Congress, on Venezuela
December 17, 1895

The relations of good neighbors.

Herbert Hoover
On goodwill tour of Latin America
1929

To our sister republics south of our border, we offer a special pledge—to convert our good words into good deeds—in a new alliance for progress—to assist free men and free governments in casting off the chains of poverty. But this peaceful revolution of hope cannot become the prey of hostile powers. Let all our neighbors know that we shall join with them to oppose aggression or subversion anywhere in the Americas. And let every other power know that this hemisphere intends to remain the master of its own house.

John F. Kennedy
Inaugural address
January 20, 1961

The Western Hemisphere does not belong to any one of us—we belong to the Western Hemisphere.

Ronald Reagan
Speech, Organization of American States
February 24, 1982

Space, Science and Technology

Let both sides seek to invoke the wonders of science instead of its terrors. Together let us explore the stars, conquer the deserts, eradicate disease, tap the ocean depths and encourage the arts and commerce.

John F. Kennedy
Inaugural address
January 20, 1961

This is the greatest week in the history of the world since the creation.

Richard Nixon
Comment, Mankind's first landing on the moon.
July 24, 1969

Nuclear weapons are an expression of one side of our character. But there is another side. The same rocket technology that delivers nuclear warheads has also taken us peacefully into space. From that perspective, we see our earth as it really is—a small and fragile and beautiful globe, the only home we have. We see no barriers of race or religion or country. We see the essential unity of our species and our planet; and with faith and common sense that bright vision will ultimately prevail.

Jimmy Carter
Farewell address, Washington, D.C.
January 14, 1981

To many of us now, computers, silicon chips, cybernetics and all the other innovations of the dawning high technology age are as mystifying as the workings of the combustion engine must have been when the first Motel T rattled down Main Street, U.S.A. But, as surely as America's pioneer spirit made us the industrial giant of the twentieth century, the same pioneer spirit today is opening up another vast opportunity—the frontier of high technology.

Ronald Reagan
State of the union address
January 25, 1983

Up until now we have increasingly based our strategy of deterrence upon the threat of retaliation. But what if free people could live secure in the knowledge that their security did not rest upon the threat of instant United States retaliation to deter a Soviet attack; that we could intercept and destroy strategic ballistic missiles before they reached our own soil or that of our allies?

Ronald Reagan
Speech proposing Strategic Defense Initiative program, Washington, D.C.
March 3, 1983

A security shield can one day render nuclear weapons obsolete and free mankind from the prison of nuclear terror. America met one historic challenge and went to the moon. Now, America must meet another—to make our strategic defense real for all the citizens of Planet Earth.

Ronald Reagan
State of the union address
February 2, 1986

Speech

Amplification is the vice of the modern orator. Speeches measured by the hour die by the hour.

Thomas Jefferson
Letter, David Harding
April 20, 1824

I speak by right, and not by permission. I will never tamely . . . submit to yield a right . . . guaranteed by the Constitution. . . . I would as willingly be the slave of one master as of a thousand.

Millard Fillmore
Speech fighting a gag order in the House of Representatives
March 1840

Whatever may be said against the chewing of tobacco, this at least can be said of it, that it gives a man time to think between sentences.

Woodrow Wilson
Presidential campaign
1912

I have always been among those who believed that the greatest freedom of speech was the greatest safety, because if a man is a fool, the best thing to do is encourage him to advertise the fact by speaking.

Woodrow Wilson
Speech, Institute of France, Paris
May 10, 1919

I have noticed that nothing I never said ever did me any harm.

Calvin Coolidge
Congressional Record

To permit freedom of expression is primarily for the benefit of the majority, because it protects criticism, and criticism leads to progress.

Harry S. Truman
Message, House of Representatives, veto of
   McCarran Act
September 22, 1950

We need not fear the expression of ideas—we do need to fear their suppression.

Harry S. Truman
Message, House of Representatives, veto of
   McCarran Act
September 22, 1950

We live . . . in a sea of semantic disorder in which old labels no longer faithfully describe. Police states are called "people's democracies." Armed conquest of free people is called "liberation."

Dwight D. Eisenhower
State of the union address
January 7, 1960

State

And when the harvest from the fields, the cattle from the hills, and the ores of the earth shall have been weighed, counted, and valued, we will turn from them all to crown with the highest honor the State that has most promoted education, virtue, justice, and patriotism among the people.

Benjamin Harrison
Inaugural address
March 4, 1889

Character is the only secure foundation of the state.

Calvin Coolidge
Speech, New York, New York
February 12, 1924

For a man not to recognize the truth, not to be obedient to law, not to render allegiance to the State, is for him to be at war with his own nature, to commit suicide.

Calvin Coolidge
The Autobiography of Calvin Coolidge
1929

States' Rights

Rest assured, that our population require the curb more than the rein.

James Buchanan
Speech, House of Representatives, against
   Bankruptcy Bill
March 1821

Save the state and let the nation save itself.

Martin Van Buren
Letter, A. C. Flagg
1828

A State in a condition of duress would be *presumed* to speak as an individual manacled and in prison might be presumed to be in the enjoyment of freedom. Far better to say to the States boldly and frankly, Congress wills and submission is demanded.

John Tyler
Veto, bill establishing District of Columbia bank
   with state branches
August 16, 1841

Having never been States either in substance or in name outside of the Union, whence this magical omnipotence of "State rights," asserting a claim of power to lawfully destroy the Union itself?

Abraham Lincoln
Message, Congress, Special Session
July 4, 1861

Stock Market

Men are not justified in deliberately making a profit on the losses of other people.

Herbert Hoover
On the public investigation of the Stock Exchange
March 4, 1932

There is no moral difference between gambling at cards and . . . gambling in the stock market.

Theodore Roosevelt
Special message, Congress
January 31, 1908

This is purely a stock market thing, and there are no indicators out there of recession or hard times at all.

Ronald Reagan
Press conference, after biggest single price drop in the history of the stock market
October 22, 1987

Success

My whole life has been a succession of disappointments. I can scarcely recollect a single instance of success to anything that I ever undertook. Yet, with fervent gratitude toward God, I confess that my life has been equally marked by great and signal success which I neither aimed at nor anticipated.

John Quincy Adams
Diary
August 9, 1833

The melancholy thing in our public life is the insane desire to get higher.

Rutherford B. Hayes
Letter, editor
April 10, 1875

But I am in no way elated. I prefer success. But I am clear that for our happiness failure is to be preferred.

Rutherford B. Hayes
Diary, awaiting decision by the Electoral Commission on the 1876 presidential election
January 31, 1876

Galloway wrote of Samuel Adams: "He drinks little, eats temperately, thinks much, and is most indefatigable in the pursuit of his objects." This description can still be fittingly applied to all men who deserve and achieve success anywhere, but especially in public life.

James Garfield
"A Century of Congress," Atlantic
1877

Honors to me now are not what they once were.

Chester A. Arthur
Comments, friends, during the last seven years of his life, at the height of his political success

My success so far has only been won by absolute indifference to my future career.

Theodore Roosevelt
Comment, reporter
April 29, 1884

My progress had been slow and toilsome, with little about it that was brilliant, or spectacular, the result of persistent and painstaking work, which gave it a foundation that was solid.

Calvin Coolidge
The Autobiography of Calvin Coolidge
1929

If I had permitted my failures, or what seemed to me at the time a lack of success, to discourage me I cannot see any way in which I would ever have made progress.

Calvin Coolidge
The Autobiography of Calvin Coolidge
1929

Recognition of the falsity of material wealth as the standard of success goes hand in hand with the abandonment of the false belief that public office and high political position are to be valued only by the standards of pride of place and personal profit.

Franklin D. Roosevelt
First inaugural address
March 4, 1933

I have no expectation of making a hit every time I come to bat.

Franklin D. Roosevelt
Reader's Digest
January 1934

I was a lousy football player, but I remember Chief Newman, our coach, saying that "There's one thing about Nixon, he plays every scrimmage as though the championship were at stake."

Richard Nixon
Saturday Evening Post
July 12, 1958

Success is not a harbor but a voyage with its own perils to the spirit. The game of life is to come up a winner, to be a success, or to achieve what we set out to do. Yet there is always the danger of failing as a human being. The lesson that most of us on this voyage never learn, but can never quite forget, is that to win is sometimes to lose.

Richard Nixon
Cited in *The American Idea of Success*

[College football coach Wallace] Newman used to say, "Show me a good loser, and I'll show you a loser." He also said, "When you lose get mad—but get mad at yourself, not your opponent." There is no way I can adequately describe Chief Newman's influence on me.

Richard Nixon
The Memoirs of Richard Nixon
1978

Supreme Court

It is a very dangerous doctrine to consider the judges as the ultimate arbiters of all constitutional questions. It is one which would place us under the despotism of an oligarchy.

Thomas Jefferson
Letter, W. C. Jarvis
1820

John Marshall has made his decision; now let him enforce it.

Andrew Jackson
Cited in Horace Greely, *The American Conflict*

But we found that in general the women judges and lawyers qualified to be nominated for the Supreme Court were too liberal to meet the strict constructionist criterion I had established.

Richard Nixon
The Memoirs of Richard Nixon
1978

I do not believe the United States Senate will succumb to allowing the special interests to choose Supreme Court nominees.

Ronald Reagan
Speech, Washington, D.C., days before Senate Judiciary voted not to confirm Robert H. Bork to the Supreme Court
September 30, 1987

T

William Howard Taft

I am the seventh son of a seventh daughter
and I have clairvoyant powers. I see a man
weighing three hundred and fifty pounds.
There is something hanging over his head.
I cannot make out what it is. . . . At one
time it looks like the presidency, then
again it looks like the chief justiceship.

Theodore Roosevelt
Offering a choice to William Howard Taft
1908

Taft is utterly hopeless as a leader. I fear
that he has just enough strength to keep
with him the people of natural inertia.

Theodore Roosevelt
Letter, Ted Roosevelt
Summer 1909

You call me a megalomaniac—I call you a
Serpent's tooth.

Theodore Roosevelt
Comment, William Howard Taft

A flub-dub with a streak of the second-rate
and the common in him . . .

Theodore Roosevelt
Written communication
August 1911

[A President who] meant well but meant
well feebly.

Theodore Roosevelt
Cited in Richard Kenin and Justin Wintle, *The Dictionary of Biographical Quotations*
1912

Tariff

Every yard of cloth imported here makes a
demand for one yard less of American
fabrication. Let England take care of
herself. Let France look after her own interests. Let Germany take care of her own
people; but in God's name let America
look after America.

William McKinley
Speech, Boston, Massachusetts
1888

The United States should adopt a protective tariff of such a character as will help
the struggling industries of Europe to get
on their feet.

Warren G. Harding
Comment, Bruce Bliven
c. 1921

When domestic markets are closed to the
exports of others, it is no longer free trade.
When governments subsidize their
manufacturers and farmers so that they
can dump goods in other markets, it is no
longer free trade. When governments
permit counterfeiting or copying of
American products, it is stealing our future and it is no longer free trade. When
governments assist their exporters in ways
that violate international laws then the
playing field is no longer level and there is
no longer free trade. When governments
subsidize industries for commercial

advantage and underwrite costs, placing an unfair burden on competitors, that is not free trade.

Ronald Reagan
Speech, business and congressional leaders, Washington, D.C.
September 23, 1985

Taxes

We have always understood it to be a grand and fundamental principle of the constitution that no freeman should be subject to any tax to which he has not given his own consent, in person or by proxy.

John Adams
Instructions of the Town of Braintree to their representative (in opposition to the Stamp Act)
1765

A just security to property is not afforded by that government under which unequal taxes oppress one species of property and reward another species; where arbitrary taxes invade the domestic sanctuaries of the rich, and excessive taxes grind the faces of the poor.

James Madison
National Gazette
March 29, 1792

Our forefathers brought the germ of Independence in the principle of self-taxation.

James Madison
National Gazette
March 29, 1792

It may be the pleasure and pride of an American to ask, what farmer, what mechanic, what laborer, ever sees a taxgatherer of the United States?

Thomas Jefferson
Second inaugural address
March 4, 1805

To impose taxes when the public exigencies require them is an obligation of the most sacred character. . . . To dispense with taxes when it may be done with perfect safety is equally the duty of their representatives.

James Monroe
First annual message, Congress
December 21, 1817

My idea is that Congress have an unlimited power to raise money, and that in its appropriation they have a discretionary power, restricted only by the duty to appropriate it to purposes of common defense and of general, not local, national, not State, benefit.

James Monroe
View on the subject of Internal Improvements, veto of Cumberland Road Bill
1822

The wisdom of man never yet contrived a system of taxation that would operate with perfect equality.

Andrew Jackson
Proclamation to the People of South Carolina
December 10, 1832

To require the people to pay taxes to the Government merely that they may be paid back again is sporting with the substantial interests of the country.

Andrew Jackson
Paper
c. December 1836

The revenue of the country, levied almost insensibly to the taxpayer, goes on from year to year, increasing beyond either the interests or the prospective wants of the Government.

Franklin Pierce
First annual message, Congress
December 5, 1853

We now pride ourselves upon having given freedom to 4,000,000 of the colored race; it will then be our shame that 40,000,000 of people, by their own toleration of usurpation and profligacy, have suffered themselves to become enslaved, and merely exchanged slave owners for new taskmasters in the shape of bondholders and taxgatherers.

Andrew Johnson
Fourth annual message, Congress
December 9, 1868

If someone were to ask to-day, "What is the matter with the United States?" I am sure we would hear some Democratic friend respond, "Its people are oppressed and impoverished by tariff taxation."

Benjamin Harrison
Speech, Indianapolis, Indiana
September 18, 1888

True democracy . . . seeks to lighten the burdens of life in every home and to take from the citizen for the cost of government the lowest possible tribute.

Grover Cleveland
Speech, Reception, Democratic Club, New York,
    New York
April 27, 1889

No injunction is permitted to suspend the agony of an unwilling taxpayer and permit him to withold the money pending the deliberation of a court.

William Howard Taft
The President and His Powers
1916

That the government takes up to 50 percent of the profits from professional earnings or business transactions, while the individual takes all the risks, is intensely discouraging to initiative.

Herbert Hoover
Memo, President Harding
1921

I can't make a damn thing out of this tax problem. I listen to one side and they seem right, and then—God!—I talk to the other side and they seem just as right, and here I am where I started. I know somewhere there is a book that will give me the truth, but hell! I couldn't read the book.

Warren G. Harding
c. 1921

The power to tax is the power to destroy. . . . A government which lays taxes on the people not required by urgent public necessity and sound public policy is not a protector of liberty, but an instrument of tyranny.

Calvin Coolidge
Speech, Washington, D.C.
June 30, 1924

I have in mind that the taxpayers are the stockholders of the business corporation of the United States, and that if this business is showing a surplus of receipts the taxpayer should share therein in some material way that will be of immediate benefit.

Calvin Coolidge
Congressional Record, 68th Congress, 1st session,
    Part 1
March 4, 1923-March 3, 1925

Taxes have grown up like topsy in this country.

Franklin D. Roosevelt
Remarks, Conference of Mayors
November 19, 1935

Here is my principle: Taxes shall be levied according to ability to pay. That is the only American principle.

Franklin D. Roosevelt
Campaign address, Worcester, Massachusetts
October 21, 1936

In 1790, the nation which had fought a revolution against taxation without representation discovered that some of its citizens weren't much happier about taxation with representation.

Lyndon B. Johnson
Speech, U.S. Coast Guard Academy, New London,
    Connecticut
June 3, 1964

There are 116 taxes in a suit of clothes each one of us is wearing, 151 on the bread we had for dinner tonight. There are 100 taxes on an egg and I don't think the chicken put them there; someplace between the hen and the table they crept in.

Ronald Reagan
Speech, Annual Dinner, 77th Congress of American
    Industry, National Association of Manufacturers,
    New York, New York
December 8, 1972

The present tax structure is a disgrace to this country; it's just a welfare program for the rich.

Jimmy Carter
The first Ford-Carter debate, Philadelphia,
    Pennsylvania
September 23, 1976

I am against the big tax spender and for the little taxpayer.

Gerald Ford
Acceptance speech, Republican nomination
August 19, 1976

More than any single thing, high rates of taxation destroy incentive to earn, to save, to invest. And they cripple productivity, lead to deficit financing and inflation, and create unemployment.

Ronald Reagan
Five-Year Economic Program for United States, Let's Get America Working Again, International Business Council
September 9, 1980

The "tax and tax, spend and spend" policies of the last few decades lead only to economic disaster. Our Government must return to the tradition of living within our means and must do it now.

Ronald Reagan
Speech, Washington, D.C.
September 24, 1981

If I could paraphrase a well-known statement by Will Rogers that he never met a man he didn't like—I'm afraid we have some people around here who never met a tax they didn't hike.

Ronald Reagan
Speech, Washington, D.C.
July 27, 1981

The number of votes available to the sponsors of a tax bill [are] almost exactly proportional to the number of loopholes added to the legislation.

Jimmy Carter
Keeping Faith
1982

I will not ask you to try to balance the budget on the backs of the American taxpayers. . . . I promised the American people to bring their tax rates down and keep them down. . . . Tonight I'm urging the American people: Seize these new opportunities to produce, to save, to invest, and together we'll make this economy a mighty engine of freedom, hope and prosperity again.

Ronald Reagan
State of the union address
January 26, 1982

What tax increases . . . actually reduce is economic growth—by discouraging savings, investment and consumption.

Ronald Reagan
Speech, Annual Joint Meeting of the Board of Governors of the World Bank and International Monetary Fund
September 9, 1983

We cannot and we will not accept tax reform that is a tax increase in disguise. True reform must be an engine of productivity and growth and that means a top personal rate no higher than 35 percent. True reform must be truly fair and that means raising personal exemptions to $2,000. True reform means a tax system that at long last is pro-family, pro-jobs, pro-future, and pro-America.

Ronald Reagan
State of the union address
February 2, 1986

I'm the one who will not raise taxes . . . . And my opponent won't rule out raising taxes. But I will and the Congress will push me to raise taxes, and I'll say no, and they'll push, and I'll say no, and they'll push again and I'll say to them, read my lips, no new taxes.

George Bush
Acceptance speech, Republican Convention
August 18, 1988

Zachary Taylor

He is evidently a weak man and has been made giddy with the idea of the Presidency. He is most ungrateful, for I have promoted him, as I now think, beyond his deserts, and without reference to his politics. I am now satisfied that he is a narrow-minded, bigoted partisan, without resources and wholly unqualified for the command he holds.

James K. Polk
The Diary of James K. Polk
November 21, 1846

General Taylor is, I have no doubt, a well-meaning old man. He is, however, un-educated, exceedingly ignorant of public affairs, and, I should judge, of very ordinary capacity. He will be in the hands of others, and must rely wholly upon his Cabinet to administer the government.

James K. Polk
The Diary of James K. Polk
March 5, 1849

Terrorism

This last few months has not been an easy time for any of us. As we meet tonight, it has never been more clear that the State of the Union depends on the state of the world. . . . At this time in Iran 50 Americans are still held captive, innocent victims of terrorism and anarchy.

Jimmy Carter
State of the union address
January 23, 1980

The fate of the hostages [held in the U.S. Embassy in Iran] is too important to the hostages, their families and to our country to make it a political football.

Jimmy Carter
Speech, Orlando, Florida, in response to Ronald Reagan's criticism of Carter's handling of the hostage crisis.
October 21, 1980

Let terrorists beware that when the rules of international behavior are violated, our policy will be one of swift and effective retribution.

Ronald Reagan
Speech, Washington, D.C.
January 27, 1981

Our evidence is direct, it is precise, it is irrefutable.

Ronald Reagan
Speech, Washington, D.C., on Libya's sponsorship of the terrorist bombing of the La Belle discotheque in West Berlin
April 14, 1986

Europeans who remember history understand better than most that there is no security, no safety, in the appeasement of evil. It must be the core of Western policy that there be no sanctuary for terror, and to sustain such a policy, free men and free nations must unite and work together.

Ronald Reagan
Speech, Washington, D.C., on foreign relations with Libya
April 14, 1986

For us to ignore, by inaction, the slaughter of American civilians and American soldiers, whether in nightclubs or airline terminals, is simply not in the American tradition. When our citizens are abused or attacked anywhere in the world, on the direct orders of a hostile regime, we will respond, so long as I'm in this Oval Office. Self-defense is not only our right, it is our duty.

Ronald Reagan
Speech, Washington, D.C., on foreign relations with Libya
April 14, 1986

America will never watch passively as our innocent citizens are murdered by those who would do our country harm. We are slow to wrath and hesitant to use the military power available to us. By nature, we prefer to solve problems peacefully. But . . . no one can kill Americans and brag about it. No one.

Ronald Reagan
Speech, International Forum of the United States Chamber of Congress, Washington, D.C., in reference to the American attack on Libya the week before
April 23, 1986

Time

We wish the people to have an opportunity of testing their [elected officials'] conduct, not by the feelings of temporary excitement but by that sober second thought which is never wrong.

Martin Van Buren
Letter
1821

Time and the virtue of the people will bring all right.

Martin Van Buren
Letter, Silas Wright
February 20, 1833

Trade and Commerce

The spirit of commerce . . . is incompatible with that purity of heart and greatness of soul which is necessary for an happy republic.

John Adams
Letter, Mercy Warren
April 16, 1776

A perfect system [of trade] is the system which would be my choice.

James Madison
Letter, James Monroe
August 7, 1785

But you know that commerce, luxury, and avarice have destroyed every republican government.

John Adams
Letter, Benjamin Rush
September 27, 1808

Free ships make free goods.

Franklin Pierce
Second annual message, Congress
December 4, 1854

The canvas of its [America's] mariners whitens every sea.

Franklin Pierce
Fourth annual message, Congress
December 2, 1856

Europe and Africa are nearer to New York, and Asia is nearer to California, than are these two great States to each other by the sea. . . . A nation like ours cannot rest satisfied with such a separation of its mutually dependent members.

Chester A. Arthur
Message, Congress, accompanying the
    Frelinghuysen-Zavala Treaty (in support of a
    canal through Nicaragua)
December 1, 1884

Wealth and commerce are timid creatures; they must be assured that the nest will be safe before they build.

Benjamin Harrison
Speech, San Antonio, Texas
April 20, 1891

A great free-trade shadow dance.

William McKinley
Speech, congressional campaign, on the Democratic
    slogan of open world markets
1894

Good trade insures good will.

William McKinley
Speech, Commercial Club of Cincinnati
October 1897

Concessions obtained by financiers must be safeguarded by ministers of state, even if the sovereignty of unwilling nations be outraged in the process. . . . The doors of the nations which are closed must be battered down.

Woodrow Wilson
Speech, Columbia University, New York, New York
1907

I believe that if trade is not fair for all then trade is free in name only.

Ronald Reagan
Speech, business and congressional leaders,
    Washington, D.C.
September 9, 1985

As we move toward free trade, we must always remember why we're doing it: to help the working men and women of America.

Bill Clinton
Campaign address, Raleigh, North Carolina
October 4, 1992

Harry S. Truman

The people of the United States love and voted for Harry Truman, not because he gave them hell—but because he gave them hope.

Lyndon B. Johnson
Speech, signing of the Medicare Bill, Independence,
    Missouri
July 30, 1965

Whatever we say about Harry Truman, while it hurt him, a lot of people admired the old bastard for standing by people who were guilty as hell, and, damn it, I am that kind of person. I am not one who is going to say, look, while this guy is under attack, I drop him.

Richard Nixon
Comment, John Ehrlichman
April 1973

Truth

Ignorance is preferable to error; and he is less remote from the truth who believes nothing, than he who believes what is wrong.

Thomas Jefferson
"Notes on Virginia"
1781-1782

It is error alone which needs the support of government. Truth can stand by itself.

Thomas Jefferson
"Notes on Virginia"
1781-1782

At a distance from the theatre of action truth is not always related without embellishment.

George Washington
Letter, D. Stuart
July 26, 1789

Man is fed with fables through life, and leaves it in the belief he knows something of what has been passing, when in truth he has known nothing but what has passed under his own eye.

Thomas Jefferson
Letter, Thomas Cooper
1823

There is not a truth existing which I fear, or would wish unknown to the whole world.

Thomas Jefferson
Letter, Henry Lee
May 15, 1826

I love agitation and investigation and glory in defending unpopular truth against popular error.

James A. Garfield
Diary
c. 1850

We better know there is a fire whence we see much smoke rising than we could know it by one or two witnesses swearing to it. The witnesses may commit perjury, but the smoke cannot.

Abraham Lincoln
Unsent letter to J. R. Underwood and Henry Grider
October 26, 1864

The truth is accessible to you, and you will find it.

Benjamin Harrison
Speech, Indianapolis, Indiana
September 15, 1888

The bud of victory is always in the truth.

Benjamin Harrison
Speech, Indianapolis, Indiana
September 18, 1888

Intense feeling often obscures the truth.

Harry S. Truman
Address, Raleigh, North Carolina
October 19, 1948

I never did give anybody hell. I just told the truth and they thought it was hell.

Harry S. Truman
Comment, Edward R. Morrow, "See It Now," *Time*
February 10, 1958

Democracy is a constant tension between truth and half-truth and, in the arsenal of truth, there is no greater weapon than fact.

Lyndon B. Johnson
Remarks, accepting honorary membership in National Forensic League
May 12, 1964

Truth is eternal. Malice may distort it, and ignorance may ignore it, and panic deride it, but truth is always there.

Lyndon B. Johnson
Speech, dedication of the John F. Kennedy Square in Texarkana, Texas-Arkansas
September 25, 1964

I believe that truth is the glue that holds Government together, not only our Government, but civilization itself.

Gerald Ford
Inaugural address
August 9, 1974

John Tyler

Mr. Tyler . . . styles himself President of the United States, and not Vice President acting as President, which would be the correct style. It is a construction in direct violation both of the grammar and context of the constitution, which confers upon the Vice President, on the decease of the President, not the office, but the duties of the said office.

John Quincy Adams
Cited in Richard Kenin and Justin Wintle, *The Dictionary of Biographical Quotations*

A political sectarian of the slave-drawing Virginian Jefferson school, principled against all improvement, with all the interests and passions and vices rooted in his moral and political constitution.

John Quincy Adams
Cited in Richard Kenin and Justin Wintle, *The Dictionary of Biographical Quotations*

A Manifesto . . . will appear tomorrow from the Whigs in Congress reading John Tyler out of the Whig Church and delivering him over to Satan to be buffeted.

James Buchanan
Letter, Edward C. Gazzam
September 14, 1841

U

Union

The Constitution of the United States, then, forms a government, not a league.... It is a government in which all the people are represented, which operates directly on the people individually, not upon the States.

Andrew Jackson
Proclamation to the People of South Carolina
December 10, 1832

The great primary and controlling interest of the American people is union—union not only in the mere forms of government ... but union founded in an attachment of ... individuals for each other.

John Tyler
Second annual message, Congress
December 6, 1842

Ours is not a consolidated empire, but a confederated union.

James K. Polk
Fourth annual message, Congress
December 5, 1848

This, the grandest and most glorious temple which has ever been erected to political freedom on the face of the earth!

James Buchanan
Letter, union meeting
November 19, 1850

From that radiant constellation which both illumines our own way and points out to struggling nations their course, let but a single star be lost, and if [this] be not utter darkness, the luster of the whole is dimmed.

Franklin Pierce
Inaugural address
March 4, 1853

Let it be imposed upon all hearts that, beautiful as our fabric is, no earthly power or wisdom could ever reunite its brother fragments.

Franklin Pierce
Inaugural address
March 4, 1853

With the Union my best and dearest earthly hopes are entwined.

Franklin Pierce
Inaugural address
March 4, 1853

I know that the Union is stronger a thousand times than all the wild and chimerical schemes of social change.

Franklin Pierce
Third annual message, Congress
December 31, 1855

Who would wish to see Florida still a European colony? Who would rejoice to hail Texas as a lone star instead of one in the galaxy of States? Who does not appreciate the incalculable benefits of the acquisition of Louisiana? And yet narrow views and sectional purposes would inevitably have excluded them all from the Union.

Franklin Pierce
Third annual message, Congress
December 31, 1855

A house divided against itself cannot stand. I believe that government cannot endure permanently, half slave and half free.

I do not expect the Union to be dissolved—I do not expect the house to fall—but I do expect it will cease to be divided. It will become all one thing, or all the other.

Either the opponents of slavery will arrest the further spread of it, and place it where the public mind shall rest in the belief that it is in the course of ultimate extinction, or its advocates will push it forward till it shall become alike lawful in all the States, old as well as new, North as well as South.

Abraham Lincoln
Speech, Bloomington, Indiana
May 19, 1856

If we could first know where we are, and whither we are tending, we could better judge what to do, and how to do it.

Abraham Lincoln
Speech, Springfield, Illinois
June 17, 1858

We are not enemies, but friends. We must not be enemies. Though passion may have strained, it must not break our bonds of affection. The mystic chords of memory, stretching from every battle-field, and patriot grave, to every living heart and hearthstone, all over this broad land, will yet swell the chords of the Union, when again touched, as surely they will be, by the better angels of our nature.

Abraham Lincoln
First inaugural address
March 14, 1861

Is there in all republics this inherent and fatal weakness? Must a government, of necessity, be too strong for the liberties of its own people, or too weak to maintain its own existence?

Abraham Lincoln
Message, Congress, Special Session
July 4, 1861

I would save the Union. I would save it the shortest way under the Constitution. The sooner the National authority can be restored, the nearer the Union will be "the Union as it was." If there be those who would not save the Union, unless they could at the same time *save* slavery, I do not agree with them. If there be those who would not save the Union unless they could at the same time *destroy* slavery, I do not agree with them. My paramount object in this struggle is to save the Union, and is not either to save or destroy slavery. If I could save the Union without freeing *any* slave, I would do it; and if I could save it by freeing some and leaving others alone I would also do that . . . I have here stated my purpose according to my view of *official* duty; and I intend no modification of my oft-expressed *personal* wish that all men everywhere could be free.

Abraham Lincoln
Letter
August 22, 1862

Our strife pertains to ourselves—to the passing generations of men; and it can, without convulsion, be hushed forever with the passing of one generation.

Abraham Lincoln
Message, Congress
December 1, 1862

If it were my destiny to die for the cause of liberty I would die upon the tomb of the Union, and the American flag as my winding sheet . . .

Andrew Johnson
To soldiers in camp
1862

I am not for this government above all earthly possessions and if it perish I do not want to survive it. I am for it though slavery should be struck from existence—I say, in the face of Heaven, Give me my Government and let the Negro go.

Andrew Johnson
Comment, soldiers in camp
1862

And thus there will be some black men who can remember that with silent tongue, and clenched teeth, and steely eye, and well-poised bayonet, they have helped mankind on to this great consummation, while I fear there will be some white ones unable to forget that with malignant heart and deceitful speech they strove to hinder it.

Abraham Lincoln
Letter, James Conkling

The Union and the Congress must share the same fate. They must rise or fall together.

James A. Garfield
"A Century of Congress, *Atlantic*
1877

We do not want a united North, nor a united South. We want a united country.

Rutherford B. Hayes
Diary
February 25, 1877

We [South and North] have found a plane of mutual respect, and I am glad of it; and not only this, but we have found a common country.

Benjamin Harrison
Speech, Soldiers and Sailors Monument, Rochester, New York
May 30, 1892

V

Martin Van Buren

His principles are all subordinate to his ambitions.

John Quincy Adams
Memoirs of John Quincy Adams
c. 1829

I never acted with a more frank and candid man than Mr. [Martin] Van Buren. It is said that he is a great magician—I believe it, but his only wand is good common sense which he uses for the benefit of his country.

Andrew Jackson
Letter, General R. G. Dunlap
July 18, 1831

Instead of a dwarf Dutchman, a little dandy who you might lift in a bandbox, the people found him [Martin Van Buren] a plain man of middle size, plain and affable.

Andrew Jackson
Jackson Correspondence
c. 1842

Veterans

But, in a larger sense, we cannot dedicate—we cannot consecrate—we cannot hallow—this ground. The brave men, living and dead, who struggled here, have consecrated it, far above our poor power to add or detract.

Abraham Lincoln
The Gettysburg Address
November 19, 1863

They [Union soldiers and sailors] gave ungrudgingly; it was not a trade, but an offering.

Benjamin Harrison
Acceptance speech, Republican nomination,
    Indianapolis, Indiana
September 11, 1888

The Union soldiers and sailors are now veterans of time as well of war. The parallels of age have approached close to the citadels of life and the end, for each, of a brave and honorable struggle is not remote.

Benjamin Harrison
Acceptance speech, second Republican nomination,
    Washington, D.C.
September 3, 1892

Perhaps no emotion cools sooner than that of gratitude.

Benjamin Harrison
Speech, Senate and House
December 6, 1892

Veto

I consider the veto power . . . to be used only first, to protect the Constitution from violation; secondly, the people from effects of hasty legislation where their will has been probably disregarded or not well understood, and thirdly, to prevent the effects of combinations violative of the rights of minorities.

William Henry Harrison
Inaugural address
March 4, 1841

When I was a member of either House of Congress I acted under the conviction that to *doubt* as to the constitutionality of a law was sufficient to induce me to give my vote against it; but I have not been able to bring myself to believe that a *doubtful opinion* of the Chief Magistrate ought to outweigh the solemnly pronounced opinion of the representatives of the people and of the States.

John Tyler
Message, Congress
June 25, 1842

The President's power is negative merely, and not affirmative.

James K. Polk
Fourth annual message, Congress
December 5, 1848

The executive power to approve or return [bills] without approval, according to the conscience and judgment of the President, is a *trust*. It can't be given away without a violation of official oath.

Rutherford B. Hayes
Diary
April 6, 1879

The President, by the power of the veto, becomes a very large factor in determining whether a bill shall become law.

Benjamin Harrison
This Country of Ours
1897

It [the veto] is legislative in its nature, a brake rather than a steam chest.

William Howard Taft
The President and His Powers
1916

Vice President

My country has in its wisdom contrived for me the most insignificant office that ever the invention of man contrived or his imagination conceived.

John Adams
Letter written when vice president
1789

I have held the office of libelee-general long enough.

John Adams
While vice president, second term

I wish very heartily that a change of Vice-President could be made tomorrow. I have been too ill-used in the office to be fond of it.

John Adams
Letter, Benjamin Rush
April 18, 1790

Nominated.

You're not going to take it, are you?

I suppose I'll have to.

Calvin Coolidge
Comment, Mrs. Coolidge, upon receiving the nomination for vice president
November 1920

Victory

Victory and defeat are each of the same price.

Thomas Jefferson
Cited in Caroline Thomas Harnsberger, *Treasury of Presidential Quotations*

An honorable defeat is better than a dishonorable victory.

Millard Fillmore
Speech, Buffalo, New York
September 13, 1844

When the gods arrive, the half-gods depart.

Andrew Johnson
Comment, General Nathan Bedford Forrest, campaign for Senate
January 1875

I felt like anything rather than rejoicing at the downfall of a foe who had fought so long and so valiantly.

Ulysses S. Grant
On the surrender of Lee at Appomattox, Virginia, *Personal Memoirs of U.S. Grant*
1885-1886

There is no victory except through our imaginations.

Dwight D. Eisenhower
Comment, Joint Chiefs of Staff
June 19, 1954

Victory has a thousand fathers but defeat is an orphan.

John F. Kennedy
Attributed upon defeat of Bay of Pigs invasion
April 1961

Vietnam

You have the broader considerations that might follow what you would call the "falling domino" principle. You have a row of dominos set up, you knock over the first one, and what will happen to the last one is the certainty that it will go over very quickly.

Dwight D. Eisenhower
News conference
April 7, 1954

We are not about to send American boys 9,000 or 10,000 miles away from home to do what Asian boys ought to be doing for themselves.

Lyndon B. Johnson
Campaign speech
1964

This is not a jungle war, but a struggle for freedom on every front of human activity.

Lyndon B. Johnson
Speech after the second Tonkin Gulf incident
August 4, 1964

If America gives up on Vietnam, Asia will give up on America.

Richard Nixon
Speech
1965

We must realize that there is no easy way out. We either get out, surrender on the installment plan through neutralization, or we find a way to win.

Richard Nixon
Speech, Sales Executive Club of New York
January 26, 1965

There are risks, yes. But the risks of waiting are much greater. This becomes apparent when we look ahead and realize that if South Vietnam is lost, and Southeast Asia is lost, and the Pacific becomes a Red Sea, we could be confronted with a world war where the odds against us would be far greater.

Richard Noxon
Speech, Sales Executive Club of New York
January 26, 1965

There are times when Viet-Nam must seem to many a thousand contradictions, and the pursuit of freedom there an almost unrealizable dream.

Lyndon B. Johnson
Speech, presenting the Medal of Honor, posthumously, to private Milton Olive, the White House
April 21, 1966

The United States has suffered over a million casualties in four wars in this century. Whatever faults we may have as a nation, we have asked nothing for ourselves in return for those sacrifices. We have been generous toward those whom we have fought. We've helped our former foes as well as our friends in the task of reconstruction. We are proud of this record and we bring the same attitude in our search for a settlement in Vietnam.

Richard Nixon
Broadcast speech, Vietnam War negotiations
May 14, 1969

Let me be quite blunt. Our fighting men are not going to be worn down. Our mediators are not going to be talked down. And our allies are not going to be let down.

Richard Nixon
Broadcast speech, Vietnam War negotiations
May 14, 1969

If, when the chips are down, the world's most powerful nation, the United States of America, acts like a pitiful, helpless giant, the forces of totalitarianism and anarchy will threaten free nations and free institutions throughout the world.

Richard Nixon
April 30, 1970

North Vietnam cannot defeat or humiliate the United States. Only Americans can do that.

Richard Nixon
National address
November 1969

Let us put an end to self-inflicted wounds. Let us remember that our national unity is a most priceless asset. Let us deny our adversaries the satisfaction of using Vietnam to pit American against American.

Gerald Ford
Address, Congress, on Southeast Asia
April 10, 1975

We were taught that our armies were always invincible and our causes always just, only to suffer the agony of Vietnam.

Jimmy Carter
Speech, Washington, D.C.
July 15, 1979

We need compromise; we've had dissension. . . . It's been this way since Vietnam. That war cleaves us still. But friends, that war began in earnest a quarter of a century ago; and surely the statute of limitations has been reached. This is a fact: The final lesson of Vietnam is that no great nation can long afford to be sundered by a memory.

George Bush
Inaugural Address
January 20, 1989

I was opposed to the [Vietnam] war. I couldn't help that. I felt very strongly about it and I didn't want to go at the time. It's easy to say in retrospect I would have done something differently.

Bill Clinton
Presidential Debate
October 20, 1992

Vote

But I dare not say that a suffrage should never be permitted to a man who cannot read and write. What would become of the republic of France, if the lives, fortunes, character, of twenty-four million and a half men who can neither read nor write should be at the absolute disposal of five hundred thousand who can read?

John Adams
Letter, Benjamin Rush
August 28, 1811

The ballot box—that great palladium of our liberty . . .

Millard Fillmore
Letter, Isaac Newton
January 1, 1855

[Abuses] disappear before the intelligence and patriotism of the people, exerting through the ballot box their peaceful and silent irresistible power.

Franklin Pierce
Third annual message, Congress
December 31, 1855

Let us not commit ourselves to the senseless and absurd dogma that the color of the skin shall be the basis of suffrage, the talisman of liberty . . . . Let suffrage be extended to all men of proper age regardless of color.

James A. Garfield
Speech, Ravenna, Ohio
July 4, 1865

[The Fourteenth Amendment asks] nothing for vengeance but everything for liberty and safety.

James A. Garfield
Speech, House of Representatives
February 1867

I am convinced that it is my duty . . . to secure to every citizen . . . the right to cast one unintimidated ballot and to have it honestly counted.

Rutherford B. Hayes
Diary
March 27, 1879

No palliation . . . can be offered for opposing the freedom of the ballot.

James A. Garfield
Inaugural address
March 4, 1881

To violate the freedom and sanctity of suffrage is more than an evil, it is a crime, which, if persisted in, will destroy the Government itself. Suicide is not a remedy.

James A. Garfield
Inaugural address
March 4, 1881

Your every vote, as surely as your Chief Magistrate, under the same high sanction, though in a different sphere, exercises a public trust.

Grover Cleveland
Inaugural address
March 4, 1885

A trust, momentous in its influence upon our people and upon the world, is for a brief time committed to us, and we must not be faithless to its first condition—the defense of the free and equal influence of the people in the choice of public officers and in the control of public affairs.

Benjamin Harrison
Speech, Senate and House
December 9, 1891

These things will happen as long as Tom, Dick, and Harry have the right to vote.

Warren G. Harding
Comment on his defeat for governor of Ohio
1910

Votes are the professional politicians' idea of the food of gods, which is kept in pork barrels.

Herbert Hoover
Cited in Eugene Lyons, *Herbert Hoover: A Biography*

A voter without a ballot is like a soldier without a bullet.

Dwight D. Eisenhower
New York Times Book Review
October 27, 1957

I just received the following wire from my generous daddy—"Dear Jack. Don't buy a single vote more than necessary. I'll be damned if I'm going to pay for a landslide."

John F. Kennedy
Speech, Washington, D.C.
1958

Voters quickly forget what a man says.

Richard Nixon
Six Crises
1962

It is easier today to buy a destructive weapon, a gun, in a hardware store, than it is to vote.

Lyndon B. Johnson
Remarks upon accepting the report of the Commission on Registration and Voting Participation, the White House
December 20, 1963

Voting is the first duty of democracy.

Lyndon B. Johnson
Speech, ceremony marking the issuance of the "Register and Vote" stamp, the White House
August 11, 1964

The vote is the most powerful instrument ever devised by man for breaking down injustice and destroying the terrible walls which imprison men because they are different from the other men.

Lyndon B. Johnson
Speech
August 6, 1965

W

War

The animosities of sovereigns are temporary and may be allayed; but those which seize the whole body of a people, and of a people, too, who dictate their own measures, produce calamities of long duration.

Thomas Jefferson
Letter, C. W. F. Duman
1786

If America wants concessions, she must fight for them. We must purchase our power with our blood.

James Monroe
Comment, Thomas Jefferson
Early 1800s

I will hold New Orleans in spite of Urop [*sic*] and all Hell.

Ascribed to Andrew Jackson
1812

If we engage in a war, it is of the greatest importance that our people be united, and, with that view, that Spain commence it; and, above all, that the government be free from the charge of committing a breach of the Constitution.

James Monroe
Letter, General Jackson (concerning the Spanish posts taken by Jackson in Pensacola, Florida)
July 19, 1818

It is incumbent on every generation to pay its own debts as it goes—a principle which, if acted on, would save one-half the wars of the world.

Thomas Jefferson
Letter to Destutt Tracy
1820

I regret, however, to inform you that an outrage of a most aggravated character has been committed, accompanied by a hostile though temporary invasion of our territory, producing the strongest feelings of resentment on the part of our citizens in the neighborhood and on the whole border line, and that the excitement previously existing has been alarmingly increased.

Martin Van Buren
Message, Congress, on the Caroline Affair
January 8, 1838

I deem it of the most essential importance that a complete separation should take place between the sword and the purse.

John Tyler
Inaugural address
April 9, 1841

Wars will occur until man changes his nature; and duties [would be] imposed until man ceases to be selfish.

Millard Fillmore
Tariff speech
June 9, 1842

The Creator of the Universe has given man the earth for his resting place and its fruits for his subsistence. Whatever, therefore, shall make the first or any part of it a scene of desolation affects injuriously his heritage and may be regarded as a general calamity. Wars may sometimes be necessary, but all nations have a common interest in bringing them speedily to a close.

John Tyler
Second annual message, Congress
December 6, 1842

The cup of forbearance had been exhausted even before the recent information from the frontier of the Del Norte. But now, after reiterated menaces, Mexico has passed the boundary of the United States, has invaded our territory and shed American blood upon American soil. She has proclaimed that hostilities have commenced, and that the two nations are now at war.

James K. Polk
Message on war with Mexico, alleging provocation
  from Mexico
May 11, 1846

Take those guns, and by God keep them!

Zachary Taylor
Comment, Colonel William G. Belknap, war in
  Mexico
June 1846

Charge, Captain, *nolens volens*! [whether willing or not]

Zachary Taylor
Comment, Charles A. May, war in Mexico
June 1846

Colonel, lead the head of your column off to the left, keeping well out of reach of the enemy's shot, and if you think . . . you can take any of them little forts down there with the bay'net you better do it.

Zachary Taylor
Comment, Lieutenant Colonel John Garland, war
  with Mexico
September 1846

What are you using, Captain, grape or canister?

Canister, General.

Single or double?

Single.

Well, double-shot your guns and give 'em hell.

A bowdlerized version used in the 1848 presidential campaign went as follows:

A little more grape, please, Captain Bragg.

Zachary Taylor
Comment, Braxton Bragg, war with Mexico
February 1847

General, if I go into battery here I will lose my guns.

If you do not, the battle is lost.

Zachary Taylor
Comment, Braxton Bragg, war with Mexico
February 1847

There are good points about all . . . wars. People forget self. The virtues of magnanimity, courage, patriotism, etc., are called into life. People are more generous, more sympathetic, better, than when engaged in the more selfish pursuits of peace.

Rutherford B. Hayes
Letter, S. Birchard
May 8, 1861

It is now for them [the people] to demonstrate to the world that those who can fairly carry an election can also suppress a rebellion; that ballots are the rightful and peaceful successors of bullets; and that when ballots have fairly and constitutionally decided, there can be no successful appeal back to bullets; that there can be no successful appeal, except to ballots themselves, at succeeding elections. Such will be a great lesson of peace: teaching men that what they cannot take by an election, neither can they take it by war; teaching all the folly of being the beginners of war.

Abraham Lincoln
Message, Congress, Special Session
July 4, 1861

As commander-in-chief of the army and navy, in time of war I suppose I have a right to take any measure which may best subdue the enemy.

Abraham Lincoln
Reply, Church Committee
September 13, 1862

I have just read your dispatch about sour tongued and fatigued horses. Will you pardon me for asking what the horses of your army have done since the battle of Antietam that fatigues anything?

Abraham Lincoln
Letter, General Irvin McDowell
October 1862

In times like the present, men should utter nothing for which they would not willingly be responsible through time and in eternity.

Abraham Lincoln
Message, Congress
December 1, 1862

I can make a better brigadier any day, but those horses cost the government $125 a head.

Abraham Lincoln
Comment, on the loss of a small cavalry troop to the enemy
1863

There can be no army without men. Men can be had only voluntarily, or involuntarily. We have ceased to obtain them voluntarily; and to obtain them involuntarily, is the draft—the conscription. If you dispute the fact, and declare that men can still be had voluntarily in sufficient numbers prove the assertion by yourselves volunteering in such numbers, and I shall gladly give up the draft.

Abraham Lincoln
Speech
1863

I sincerely wish war was a pleasanter and easier business than it is, but it does not admit of holidays.

Abraham Lincoln
Reply, suggestion that he take a vacation
c. 1863

Fondly do we hope—fervently do we pray—that this mighty scourge of war may speedily pass away. Yet, if God wills that it continue until all the wealth piled by the bondman's two hundred and fifty years of unrequited toil shall be sunk, and until every drop of blood drawn with the lash be paid by another drawn with the sword, as was said three thousand years ago, so still it must be said, "The judgments of the Lord are true and righteous altogether."

Abraham Lincoln
Second inaugural address
March 4, 1865

Of course I deprecate war, but if it is brought to my door the bringer will find me at home.

James A. Garfield
Letter, Whitelaw Reid, on refusal to withdraw nomination of William Robertson for collector of the New York Customhouse to placate Chester A. Arthur, Roscoe Conkling, and the New York Republican machine
c. April 1881

I felt like anything rather than rejoicing at the downfall of a foe who had fought so long and so valiantly.

Ulysses S. Grant
Personal Memoirs of U.S. Grant, on the surrender of Lee at Appomattox
1885-1886

I do not think there ever was a more wicked war than that waged by the United States in Mexico. I thought so at the time, when I was a youngster, only I had not moral courage enough to resign.

Ulysses S. Grant
Personal Memoirs of U.S. Grant
1885-1886

One of the most unjust [wars] ever waged by a stronger against a weaker nation.

Ulysses S. Grant
Personal Memoirs of U.S. Grant, on war with Mexico
1885-1886

Wars produce many stories of fiction, some of which are told until they are believed to be true.

Ulysses S. Grant
Personal Memoirs of U.S. Grant
1886

When news of the [Lee's] surrender first reached our lines our men commenced firing salute of a hundred guns in honor of the victory. I at once sent word, however, to have it stopped. The Confederates were now our prisoners, and we did not want to exult over their downfall.

Ulysses S. Grant
Personal Memoirs of U.S. Grant
1885-1886

The man that would rather fight than eat has not survived the last war.

Benjamin Harrison
Speech, Indianapolis, Indiana
September 14, 1888

Half-heartedness never won a battle.

William McKinley
Speech, Canton, Ohio
May 30, 1891

War should never be entered upon until every agency of peace has failed.

William McKinley
Inaugural address
March 4, 1897

In strict confidence . . . I should welcome almost any war, for I think this country needs one.

Theodore Roosevelt
To a friend
1897

It was not civilized warfare. It was extermination.

William McKinley
First annual message, Congress, on Spanish attempts
    to repress Cuban rebels
December 6, 1897

No qualities called out by a purely peaceful life stand on a level with those stern and virile virtues which move the men of stout heart and strong hand who uphold the honor of their flag in battle.

Theodore Roosevelt
Review, Captain Alfred Mahan's *Life of Nelson, the
    Bookman*
June 1897

No triumph of peace is quite so great as the supreme triumph of war.

Theodore Roosevelt
Address, Naval War College
Spring 1897

So far as heard from, those who were so impatient at the first have not yet gone to the front.

William McKinley
Comment, Charles G. Dawes, on war with Spain
June 1899

A just war is in the long run far better for a man's soul than the most prosperous peace.

Theodore Roosevelt
Annual message, Congress
1906

When giants are engaged in a death wrestle, as they reel to and fro they are certain to trample on whoever gets in the way of either of the huge straining combatants.

Theodore Roosevelt
Prematurely arguing for neutrality in World War I,
    Outlook
August 22, 1914

I think I could do this country most good by dying in a reasonably honorable fashion, at the head of my division in the European war.

Theodore Roosevelt
Letter, William Allen White, before the United States
    entered World War I

There is no such thing as a man being too proud to fight. There is such a thing as a nation being so right that it does not need to convince others by force that it is right.

Woodrow Wilson
Speech
May 10, 1915

There may at any moment come a time when I cannot preserve both the honor and the peace of the United States. Do not exact of me an impossible and contradictory thing.

Woodrow Wilson
Speech, Milwaukee, Wisconsin
January 21, 1916

Do you remember the experience of the Spanish-American War? . . . You remember the satirical verse:

War is rude and impolite, it quite upsets a
    nation;
It's made of several weeks of fight and years of conversation.

We poured crude, ignorant, untrained boys into the ranks of those armies and they died before they got sight of the enemy. Do you want to repeat that?

Woodrow Wilson
Speech, Kansas City, Missouri
February 2, 1916

A nation is not wholly admirable unless in times of stress it will go to war for a great ideal wholly unconnected with its immediate national interest.

Theodore Roosevelt
Speech
1916

Germany is already at war with us. The only question for us to decide is whether we shall make war nobly or ignobly.

Theodore Roosevelt
Speech, Union League Club, New York, New York
March 20, 1916

Militarism does not consist in the existence of an army. . . . Militarism is a spirit. It is a point of view. It is a system. It is a purpose. The purpose of militarism is to use armies for aggression.

Woodrow Wilson
Speech, West Point
June 13, 1916

For democracy, for the right of those who submit to have a voice in their own Governments, for the rights and liberties of small nations, for a universal dominion of right by such a concert of free peoples as shall bring peace and safety to all nations and make the world itself at last free . . .

Woodrow Wilson
Asking joint session of Congress to declare war
April 2, 1917

It is a fearful thing to lead this great peaceful people into war, into the most terrible and disastrous of all wars, civilization itself seeming to be in the balance.

Woodrow Wilson
Speech, Joint Session of the two houses of Congress,
    declaration of war against Germany
April 2, 1917

We are glad . . . to fight thus . . . for the rights of nations great and small and the privilege of men everywhere to choose their way of life and of obedience

Woodrow Wilson
Speech, Joint Session of the two houses of Congress,
    Declaration of War against Germany
April 2, 1917

The world must be made safe for democracy. Its peace must be planted upon the tested foundations of political liberty. We have no selfish ends to serve. We desire no conquest, no dominion. We seek no indemnities for ourselves, no material compensation for the sacrifices we shall freely make. We are but one of the champions of the rights of mankind. We shall be satisfied when those rights have been made as secure as the faith and the freedom of nations can make them.

Woodrow Wilson
Speech, Joint Session of the two houses of Congress,
    Declaration of War against Germany
April 2, 1917

The present German submarine warfare is a warfare against mankind. . . . There is one choice we cannot make, we are incapable of making; we will not choose the path of submission.

Woodrow Wilson
Speech, calling on Congress to declare war
April 4, 1917

The idea of dethroning the Hapsburgs and the Hohenzollerns makes me weary.

Warren G. Harding
New York Times
1917

Germany has once more said that force, and force alone, shall decide whether peace and justice shall reign in the affairs of men, whether right as America conceives it, or dominion as she conceives it, shall determine the destinies of mankind. There is, therefore, but one response possible from us: force, force to the uttermost, force without stint or limit, the righteous and triumphant force which shall make right of the law of the world and cast every selfish dominion down in the dust.

Woodrow Wilson
Speech, Baltimore, Maryland
April 6, 1918

These are the ends for which the associated peoples of the world are fighting and which must be conceded by them before there can be peace.

1. The destruction of every arbitrary power anywhere that can separately, secretly, and of its single choice disturb the peace of the world . . .

2. The settlement of every question, whether of territory, of sovereignty, or economic arrangement, or of political relationship, upon the basis of the free acceptance of that settlement by the people immediately concerned . . .

3. The consent of all nations to be governed in their conduct towards each other by the same principles of honor and of respect for the common law of civilized society that govern the individual citizens of all modern states in their relations with one another . . .

4. The establishment of an organization of peace . . .

Woodrow Wilson
The Four Ends speech (of the ends of World War I)
July 4, 1918

Once lead this people into war and they'll forget there ever was such a thing as tolerance.

Woodrow Wilson
Cited in John Dos Passos, Mr. Wilson's War

And the glory of the Armies and Navies of the United States is gone like a dream in the night, and there ensues upon it, in the suitable darkness of the night, the nightmare of dread which lay upon the nations before this war came; and there will come sometime, in the vengeful Providence of God, another struggle in which, not a few hundred thousand fine men from America will have to die, but as many millions as are necessary to accomplish the final freedom of the peoples of the world.

Woodrow Wilson
Speech, St. Louis, Missouri
September 5, 1919

Why, my fellow citizens, is there any man here or any woman—let me say is there any child here—who does not know that the seed of war in the modern world is industrial and commercial rivalry?

Woodrow Wilson
Speech, St. Louis, Missouri
September 5, 1919

I can predict with absolute certainty that within another generation there will be another world war if the nations of the world do not concert the method by which to prevent it.

Woodrow Wilson
Speech, Omaha, Nebraska
September 8, 1919

It's a lie from beginning to end that we are in the war for democracy's sake.

Warren G. Harding
New York Times
January 22, 1919

We must strive for normalcy to reach stability.

Warren G. Harding
Inaugural address
March 21, 1921

Human hate demands no such toll; ambition and greed must be denied it. If misunderstanding must take the blame, then let us banish it.

Warren G. Harding
Washington Conference for the Limitation of
    Armament
November 12, 1921

The war we have just been through, though it was shot through with terror, is not to be compared with the war we would have to face the next time.

Woodrow Wilson
Cited in John Dos Passos, Mr. Wilson's War

What the end of the four years of carnage [World War I] meant those who remember it will never forget and those who do not can never be told.

Calvin Coolidge
The Autobiography of Calvin Coolidge
1929

It is well to remember that the office of Chief Executive is in part a symbol of the nation and that leaders in a nation may differ in their own house but they have instant solidarity in the presence of foreign attack.

Herbert Hoover
Speech, Gridiron Club, Washington, D.C.
April 26, 1929

The first responsibility of the President of the United States is to abate war, not to stimulate it.

Herbert Hoover
Addresses on the American Road
1933-1960

It seems to be unfortunately true that the epidemic of world lawlessness is spreading. When an epidemic of physical disease starts to spread, the community approves and joins in a quarantine of the patients in order to protect the health of the community against the spread of the disease.

Franklin D. Roosevelt
Quarantine Speech, Chicago, Illinois
October 5, 1937

Do we really have to assume that nations can find no better methods of realizing their destinies than those which were used by the Huns and Vandals fifteen hundred years ago?

Franklin D. Roosevelt
"Hands Off the Western Hemisphere," Pan-American Day Address
April 14, 1939

We are convinced that military and naval victory for the gods of force and hate would endanger the institutions of democracy in the Western World—and that equally, therefore, the whole of our sympathies lie with those nations that are giving their life blood in combat against those forces.

Franklin D. Roosevelt
Address, Charlottesville, abandoning neutrality for nonbelligerency
June 10, 1940

Never before since Jamestown and Plymouth Rock has our American civilization been in such danger as now.

Franklin D. Roosevelt
Radio speech
December 29, 1940

In all history no major war has ever been won or lost through lack of money.

Franklin D. Roosevelt
Press conference, Washington, D.C.
December 1940

Our Bunker Hill of tomorrow may be several thousand miles from Boston.

Franklin D. Roosevelt
Speech, Washington, D.C.
May 27, 1941

We have wished to avoid shooting, but the shooting has started. And history has recorded who fired the first shot. In the long run, however, all that will matter is who fired the last shot.

Franklin D. Roosevelt
Navy Day Address, Washington, D.C., on German attack on the U.S.S. *Kearny*
October 27, 1941

Yesterday, December 7, 1941—a date which will live in infamy—the United States of America was suddenly and deliberately attacked by naval and air forces of the Empire of Japan. Hostilities exist. There is no blinking the fact that our people, our territories, and our interests are in grave danger.

Message asking for war against Japan
December 8, 1941

American soil has been treacherously attacked by Japan. Our decision is forced upon us. We must fight with everything we have.

Herbert Hoover
Immediately after Pearl Harbor
December 1941

The United States can accept no result save victory.

Franklin D. Roosevelt
National broadcast, Washington, D.C.
December 9, 1941

We are going to win the war and we are going to win the peace that follows. And in the difficult hours of this day—and through dark days that may be yet to come—we will know that the vast majority of the members of the human race are with us. All of them are praying for us. For, in representing our cause, we represent theirs as well—our hope and their hope for liberty under God.

Franklin D. Roosevelt
Radio address
December 11, 1941

Delay invites great danger. Rapid and united effort by all of the peoples of the world who are determined to remain free will insure a world victory of the forces of justice and of righteousness over the forces of savagery and of barbarism.

Franklin D. Roosevelt
Declaration of War on Germany
December 11, 1941

American soil has been treacherously attacked by Japan. Our decision is forced upon us. We must fight with everything we have.

Herbert Hoover
Immediately after Pearl Harbor
December 1941

We are fighting, as our fathers have fought, to uphold the doctrine that all men are equal in the sight of God. Those on the other side are striving to destroy this deep belief and to create a world in their own image—a world of tyranny and cruelty and serfdom.

Franklin D. Roosevelt
State of the union address
January 6, 1942

The War for Survival . . .

Franklin D. Roosevelt
On World War II
Cited in Richard Hofstadter, *The Age of Reform*

People of Western Europe: A landing was made this morning on the coast of France by troops of the Allied Expeditionary Force. This landing is part of the concerted United Nations plan for the liberation of Europe, made in conjunction with our great Russian allies. . . . I call upon all who love freedom to stand with us now. Together we shall achieve victory.

General Dwight D. Eisenhower
Broadcast
June 6, 1944 (D-Day)

The mission of this Allied Force was fulfilled at 3 A.M., local time, May 7, 1945.

General Dwight D. Eisenhower
Telegram to the Combined Chiefs of Staff, at end of
    World War II, Europe

Morale is the greatest single factor in successful wars.

Dwight D. Eisenhower
New York Post
June 23, 1945

Wars are different from baseball games where, at the end of the game, the teams get dressed and leave the park.

Harry S. Truman
April 1946

I hate war as only a soldier who has lived it can, only as one who has seen its brutality, its futility, its *stupidity*.

Dwight D. Eisenhower
Cited By John Gunther, *Eisenhower*

To return to the rule of force in international affairs would have far-reaching effects. The United States will continue to uphold the rule of law.

Harry S. Truman
Statement at the start of the Korean War
June 27, 1950

Possibly my hatred of war blinds me so that I cannot comprehend the arguments that its advocates adduce. But, in my opinion, there is no such thing as a preventative war. . . . War begets the conditions that beget further war.

Dwight D. Eisenhower
Address in Pittsburgh, Pennsylvania
October 1950

It is easier to put out a fire in the beginning when it is small than after it has become a roaring blaze.

Harry S. Truman
Address to the nation, recalling General Douglas
　　MacArthur
April 11, 1951

I have always been opposed even to the thought of fighting a "preventative war." There is nothing more foolish than to think that war can be stopped by war. You don't "prevent" anything by war except peace.

Harry S. Truman
Memoirs
1952

In the final choice a soldier's pack is not so heavy a burden as a prisoner's chains.

Dwight D. Eisenhower
First inaugural address
January 20, 1953

Long faces do not win battles.

Dwight D. Eisenhower
To Cabinet
June 19, 1953

The only thing I know about war are two things: the most changeable factor in war is human nature in its day-by-day manifestation; but the only unchanging factor in war is human nature. And the next thing is that every war is going to astonish you in the way it occurred, and in the way it is carried out. So that for a man to predict what he is going to use, how he is going to do it, would I think exhibit his ignorance of war.

Dwight D. Eisenhower
Press conference, Washington, D.C.
March 23, 1954

Don't go to war in response to emotions of anger and resentment; do it prayerfully.

Dwight D. Eisenhower
News conference (after resisting five times in 1954
　　the unanimous recommendation by Joint Chiefs
　　of Staff, National Security Council and the State
　　Department to intervene in Asia, even if it meant
　　using atomic bombs)
November 1954

I always considered statesmen to be more expendable than soldiers.

Harry S. Truman
Years of Decision
1955

Unconditional war can no longer lead to unconditional victory. . . . Mankind must put an end to war or war will put an end to mankind.

John F. Kennedy
Speech, United Nations General Assembly, New
　　York, New York
September 25, 1961

The nineteen thirties taught us a clear lesson. Aggressive conduct, if allowed to go unchallenged, ultimately leads to war.

John F. Kennedy
Arms Quarantine of Cuba Speech, broadcast from the
　　White House
October 22, 1962

We no longer live in a world where only the actual firing of weapons represents a sufficient challenge to a nation's security to constitute maximum peril.

John F. Kennedy
Arms Quarantine of Cuba Speech, broadcast from the
　　White House
October 22, 1962

Our understanding of how to live—live with one another—is still far behind our knowledge of how to destroy one another.

Lyndon B. Johnson
Speech, United Nations General Assembly, New
　　York, New York
December 17, 1963

War is always the same. It is young men dying in the fullness of their promise. It is trying to kill a man that you do not even know well enough to hate. Therefore, to know war is to know that there is still madness in this world.

Lyndon B. Johnson
State of the union address
January 12, 1966

Whatever it is that we call civilization rests upon the merciless and seemingly irrational fact of history that some have died for others to live, and every one of us who enjoys freedom at this moment should be a witness to that fact.

Lyndon B. Johnson
Remarks on presenting Medal of Honor to Private Milton Olive, posthumously, the White House
April 21, 1966

When you appeal to force to carry out the policies of America abroad there is no court above you.

Dwight D. Eisenhower
To reporters
July 11, 1967

History teaches that wars begin when governments believe the price of aggression is cheap.

Ronald Reagan
Speech, Washington, D.C.
January 16, 1984

As I report to you, air attacks are under way against military targets in Iraq.... Initial reports from General Schwarzkopf are that our operations are proceeding according to plan. Our objectives are clear: Saddam Hussein's forces will leave Kuwait. The legitimate government of Kuwait will be restored to its rightful place, and Kuwait will once again be free.

George Bush
Television address
January 16, 1991

George Washington

Instead of adoring Washington, mankind should applaud the nation which educated him . . . I glory in the character of a Washington, because I know him to be only an exemplification of the American character.

John Adams
Cited in Richard Kenin and Justin Wintle, *The Dictionary of Biographical Quotations*
1785

His mind was great and powerful, without being of the very first order; his penetration strong . . . and, as far as he saw, no judgment was ever sounder. It was slow in operation, being little aided by invention or imagination, but sure in conclusion.... Perhaps the strongest feature in his character was prudence, never acting until every circumstance, every consideration was maturely weighed . . . but once decided, going through with his purpose, whatever obstacles opposed. His integrity was most pure, his justice the most inflexible I have ever known.... He was, indeed, in every sense of the words, a wise, a good and a great man.

Thomas Jefferson
Letter, Doctor Walter Jones
January 2, 1814

Washington is the mightiest name of earth—long since the mightiest in the cause of civil liberty, still mightiest in moral reformation.... To add brightness to the sun or glory to the name of Washington is alike impossible. Let none attempt it. In solemn awe pronounce the name, and in its naked deathless splendor leave it shining on.

Abraham Lincoln
Cited in Richard Kenin and Justin Wintle, *The Dictionary of Biographical Quotations*
1842

I refer you to the second term of President Washington . . . when I compare the weak, inconsequential things said about me, compared to what they said about the man who I think is the greatest human the English-speaking race has produced, then I can be quite philosophical about it.

Dwight D. Eisenhower
August 7, 1957

Washington, D.C.

Let them worry and fret and intrigue at Washington. Six weeks hence they will find themselves as wise as they were when they began.

Martin Van Buren
Letter, James A. Hamilton
Fall 1828

My God! What is there in this place that a man should ever want to get into it?

James Garfield
Remark
1881

Its official circles never accept anyone gladly. There is always a certain unexpressed sentiment that a new arrival is appropriating the power that should rightfully belong to them.

Calvin Coolidge
The Autobiography of Calvin Coolidge
1929

There are a number of things wrong with Washington. One of them is that everyone has been too long away from home.

Dwight D. Eisenhower
May 11, 1955

Washington is a city of Southern efficiency and Northern charm.

John F. Kennedy
Cited in William Manchester, *Portrait of a President*

The behind-the-scenes power structure in Washington is often called the "iron triangle": a three-sided set of relationships composed of congressional lobbyists, congressional committee and subcommittee members and their staffs.

Richard Nixon
The Memoirs of Richard Nixon
1978

Wealth

The rich are seldom remarkable for modesty, ingenuity, or humanity. Their wealth has rather a tendency to make them penurious and selfish.

John Adams
Diary
March 5, 1773

I have not observed men's honesty to increase with their riches.

Thomas Jefferson
Letter, Jeremiah Moore
1800

The prosperity of the country, independent of all agency of the Government, is so great that the people have nothing to disturb them but their own waywardness and corruption.

John Quincy Adams
Diary
October 9, 1834

Wealth can only be accumulated by the earnings of industry and the savings of frugality.

John Tyler
First annual message, Congress
December 7, 1841

Like all Americans, I like big things: big prairies, big forests and mountains, big wheatfields, railroads . . . and everything else. But no people ever yet benefited by riches if their prosperity corrupted their virtue.

Theodore Roosevelt
Speech, Dickinson, North Dakota
July 4, 1886

Wealth should be the servant, not the master of the people.

Theodore Roosevelt
"A Charter for Democracy," *Outlook*
March 2, 1912

High society is for those who have stopped working and no longer have anything important to do.

Woodrow Wilson
Speech, Washington, D.C.
February 24, 1915

Wealth comes from industry and from the hard experience of human toil.

Calvin Coolidge
The Autobiography of Calvin Coolidge
1929

Concentration of wealth and power has been built upon other people's money, other people's business, other people's labor. Under this concentration, independent business . . . has been a menace to . . . American society.

Franklin D. Roosevelt
Acceptance speech, Democratic National
  Convention
June 27, 1936

White House

I'll be glad to be going—this is the loneliest place in the world.

William Howard Taft
Comment, Woodrow Wilson, at the latter's inauguration, Washington, D.C.
March 4, 1913

The White House is a bully pulpit.

Theodore Roosevelt
Comment, George Haven Putnam, recalled by Putnam at Roosevelt eulogy, the Century Club, New York, New York
1919

There is the big white jail.

Harry S. Truman
Comment, on morning walk, reported in *New York Herald Tribune*
April 14, 1958

Woodrow Wilson

Byzantine logothete.

Theodore Roosevelt
Cited in Richard Kenin and Justin Wintle, *The Dictionary of Biographical Quotations*

Woodrow Wilson is a perfect trumpet.

Theodore Roosevelt
Written communication
1902

He advocated with skill, intelligence and good breeding the outworn doctrines which are responsible for four-fifths of the political troubles of the United States.

Theodore Roosevelt
Letter, friend
1912

[That] infernal skunk in the White House . . .

Theodore Roosevelt
c. 1914-1915

I feel certain that he would not recognize a generous impulse if he met it on the street.

William Howard Taft
Cited in Alpheus Thomas Mason, *William Howard Taft*

Women

I must not write a word to you about politics, because you are a woman.

John Adams
Letter, Abigail Adams
February 13, 1779

Too wise to wrinkle their foreheads with politics.

Thomas Jefferson
Cited in Howard Zinn, *A People's History of the United States*

The capacity of the female mind for studies of the highest order cannot be doubted, having been sufficiently illustrated by its works of genius, of erudition, and of science.

James Madison
Letter, Albert Picket
September 1821

I go for all sharing the privileges of the government who assist in bearing its burdens. Consequently I go for admitting all whites to the right of suffrage who pay taxes or bear arms (by no means excluding females).

Abraham Lincoln
Letter, *Sangamo Journal*, Springfield, Illinois
June 13, 1836

Why does it follow that women are fitted for nothing but the cares of domestic life, for bearing children and cooking the food of a family? . . . I say women exhibit the most exalted virtue when they depart from the domestic circle and enter on the concerns of their country, of humanity, and of their God!

John Quincy Adams
Speech, House of Representatives
February 1838

Female virtue is like a tender and delicate flower; let but the breath of suspicion rest upon it, and it withers and perhaps perishes forever.

Andrew Jackson
Cited in Robert Remini, *Andrew Jackson*

That which distinguishes us from other nations whose political experience and history have been full of strife and discord is the American home, where one wife sits in single uncrowned glory.

Benjamin Harrison
Speech, Salt Lake City, Utah
May 9, 1891

What men owe to the love and help of good women can never be told.

Calvin Coolidge
The Autobiography of Calvin Coolidge
1929

Where are they unequal?

Dwight D. Eisenhower
Cabinet meeting
May 17, 1954

It's hard for a mere man to believe that women don't have equal rights.

Dwight D. Eisenhower
August 7, 1957

I am unabashedly in favor of women. A writer once observed, a bit critically, that American women seek a perfection in their husbands that English women find only in their butlers. But that only proves to me that American women have a taste for style and a yearning for excellence.

Lyndon B. Johnson
Speech upon presenting the first Eleanor Roosevelt Memorial Award to Judge Anna M. Kross, Washington, D.C.
March 4, 1964

Our purpose has not been simply to end stag government.

Lyndon B. Johnson
Speech at swearing in of Mrs. Virginia Brown as Interstate Commerce Commissioner, White House
May 25, 1964

The women of America represent a reservoir of talent that is still underused. It is too often underpaid, and almost always underpromoted.

Lyndon B. Johnson
Speech, Federal Women's Award Ceremony, the White House
March 2, 1965

Work

Idleness begets ennui, ennui the hypochondriac, and that a deseased body. No laborious person was ever yet hysterical.

Thomas Jefferson
Letter, Martha Jefferson
March 28, 1787

Though I occupy a very high position, I am the hardest-working man in this country.

James K. Polk
The Diary of James K. Polk
January 28, 1847

Labor disgraces no man; unfortunately you occasionally find men who disgrace labor.

Ulysses S. Grant
Cited in Vic Fredericks, *The Wit and Wisdom of the Presidents*

It is not industry, but idleness, that is degrading.

Calvin Coolidge
The Autobiography of Calvin Coolidge
1929

I am not gifted with intuition. I need not only hard work but experience to be ready to solve problems.

Calvin Coolidge
The Autobiography of Calvin Coolidge
1929

My progress had been slow and toilsome, with little about it that was brilliant, or spectacular, the result of persistent and painstaking work, which gave it a foundation that was solid.

Calvin Coolidge
The Autobiography of Calvin Coolidge
1929

My sin is an indisposition to labor as hard as I might; a disposition to procrastinate and a disposition to enjoy the fellowhip of others more than I ought.

William Howard Taft
Cited in *Literary Digest*
March 15, 1912

The joy and moral stimulation of work must no longer be forgotten in the mad chase for evanescent profits.

Franklin D. Roosevelt
First inaugural address
March 4, 1933

Those dark days will be worth all they cost us if they teach us that our true destiny is not to be ministered unto but to minister to ourselves and to our fellow-men.

Franklin D. Roosevelt
First inaugural address
March 4, 1933

Happiness lies not in the mere possession of money; it lies in the joy of achievement, in the thrill of creative effort.

Franklin D. Roosevelt
First inaugural address
March 4, 1933

My favorite animal is the mule. He has a lot more horse sense than a horse. He knows when to stop eating. And he knows when to stop working.

Harry S. Truman
Press statement
January 1952

For me, it is often harder to be away from the job than be working at it.

Richard Nixon
Six Crises
1962

There is an old saying: "The harder you try, the luckier you get." And I kind of like that definition of luck.

Gerald Ford
"Ford Deals with New York," *New York Times*
November 27, 1975

APPENDIX

President	Birth	Death	Term of Office
George Washington	1732	1799	1789-1797
John Adams	1735	1826	1797-1801
Thomas Jefferson	1743	1826	1801-1809
James Madison	1751	1836	1809-1817
James Monroe	1758	1831	1817-1825
John Quincy Adams	1767	1848	1825-1829
Andrew Jackson	1767	1845	1829-1837
Martin Van Buren	1782	1862	1837-1841
William Henry Harrison	1773	1841	1841-1841
John Tyler	1790	1862	1841-1845
James K. Polk	1795	1849	1845-1849
Zachary Taylor	1784	1850	1849-1850
Millard Fillmore	1800	1874	1850-1853
Franklin Pierce	1804	1869	1853-1857
James Buchanan	1791	1868	1857-1861
Abraham Lincoln	1809	1865	1861-1865
Andrew Johnson	1808	1875	1865-1869
Ulysses S. Grant	1822	1885	1869-1877
Rutherford B. Hayes	1822	1893	1877-1881
James A. Garfield	1831	1881	1881-1881
Chester A. Arthur	1829	1886	1881-1885
Grover Cleveland	1837	1908	1885-1889 1893-1897
Benjamin Harrison	1833	1901	1889-1893
William McKinley	1843	1901	1897-1901
Theodore Roosevelt	1858	1919	1901-1909
William Howard Taft	1857	1930	1909-1913
Woodrow Wilson	1856	1924	1913-1921
Warren G. Harding	1865	1923	1921-1923
Calvin Coolidge	1872	1933	1923-1929
Herbert Hoover	1874	1964	1929-1933
Franklin D. Roosevelt	1882	1945	1933-1945
Harry S. Truman	1884	1972	1945-1953
Dwight D. Eisenhower	1890	1969	1953-1961
John F. Kennedy	1917	1963	1961-1963
Lyndon B. Johnson	1908	1973	1963-1969
Richard Nixon	1913		1969-1974
Gerald Ford	1913		1974-1977
Jimmy Carter	1924		1977-1981
Ronald Reagan	1911		1981-1988
George Bush	1924		1989-1993
Bill Clinton	1946		1993-

Bibliography

Abbot, W. W., ed. *The Papers of George Washington*, Dorothy Twohig, Associate ed. Charlottesville, Virginia: University Press of Virginia, 1983.

Adams, Charles Francis. *Memoirs of John Quincy Adams*. 12 vols. Philadelphia: Lippincott, 1874-77.

Adams, Henry. *History of the United States of America During the Administrations of James Madison*. New York: Library of America, Viking Press, 1986.

Adams, John Quincy. *Parties in the United States*. New York: Greenberg, 1822.

Adams, Samuel Hopkins. *Incredible Era: The Life and Times of Warren Gamaliel Harding*. New York: Capricorn Books, 1939, 1964.

Adler, Bill, ed. *The Johnson Humor*. New York: Simon and Schuster, 1965.

——. *The Kennedy Wit*. New York: Citadel Press, 1964.

——. *Presidential Wit from Washington to Johnson*. New York: Trident Press, 1966.

Alsop, Stewart. *Nixon and Rockefeller: A Double Portrait*. New York: Doubleday, 1960.

Ambrose, Stephen. *Eisenhower*. Vol. 2, *The President*. New York: Simon and Schuster, 1984.

——. *Nixon: The Education of a Politician 1913-1962*. New York: Simon and Schuster, 1987.

American Historical Association. *Autobiography of Martin Van Buren*. Annual Report. Washington, D.C., 1918.

Angle, Paul M., ed. *By These Words: Great Documents of American Liberty*. New York, Chicago, San Francisco: Rand McNally, 1954.

——. *The Lincoln Reader*. New Brunswick, N.J.: Rutgers University Press, 1947.

Badeau, Adam. *Grant in Peace: A Personal Memoir; From Appomattox to Mt. McGregor*. Hartford: Scranton, 1887.

Bailey, Thomas A. *Woodrow Wilson and the Great Betrayal*. New York: Times Books, 1972.

Bartlett, John. *Familiar Quotations*. Boston: Little, Brown, 1948.

Bauer, K. Jack. *Zachary Taylor: Soldier, Planter, Statesman of the Old Southwest*. Baton Rouge: Louisiana State University Press, 1985.

Blum, John Morton. *From the Morgenthau Diaries*, Vol I: *Years of Crisis*. Boston: Houghton-Mifflin, 1959.

Bohle, Bruce, ed., *The Home Book of American Quotations*. New York: Dodd-Mead, 1967.

Brodie, Fawn M. *Thomas Jefferson: An Intimate History*. New York: W. W. Norton, 1974.

Brown, Dee. *Bury My Heart At Wounded Knee: An Indian History of the American West*. New York: H. Holt, 1971.

Brussell, Eugene E., ed. *Dictionary of Quotable Defintions*. Englewood Cliffs, New Jersey: Prentice-Hall, 1970.

Burns, James MacGregor. *Roosevelt: The Soldier of Freedom 1940-1945*. New York: Harcourt Brace Jovanovich, 1970.

Butterfield, L.H., et al., *The Diary and Autobiography of John Adams.* 4 vols. Cambridge: Harvard University Press, 1961.

Carter, Jimmy. *Keeping Faith: Memoirs of a President.* New York: Bantam Books, 1982.

Cleveland, Grover. *Presidential Problems.* Freeport, N.Y.: Books for Libraries Press, 1904.

Cohen, J.M., and M.J. Cohen, eds. *The Penguin Dictionary of Quotations.* New York: Allen Lane/Viking Press, 1979.

Coletta, Paolo E. *The Presidency of William Howard Taft.* Lawrence, Manhattan, Wichita: University Press of Kansas, 1973.

Coolidge, Calvin. *The Autobiography of Calvin Coolidge.* New York: Cosmopolitan Book Corporation, 1929.

———. *Have Faith in Massachusetts: A Collection of Speeches and Messages of Calvin Coolidge.* Boston/New York: Houghton-Mifflin, 1919.

Cunliffe, Marcus. *American Presidents and the Presidency.* Boston: Houghton-Mifflin, 1986.

Davison, Kenneth E. *The Presidency of Rutherford B. Hayes.* Westport, Conn.: Greenwood Press, 1972.

Dickinson, John N., ed. *Andrew Johnson: 1808-1875: Chronology, Documents, Bibliographic Aids.* Dobbs Ferry, N.Y.: Oceana Publications, 1970.

Dos Passos, John. *Mr. Wilson's War.* Garden City, N.Y.: Doubleday, 1962.

Dulles, Foster Rhea. *America's Rise to World Power: 1898-1954.* New York: Harper Torchbooks/Harper and Row, 1955

Edelhart, Michael, and James Tirien. *America The Quotable.* New York: Facts On File, 1983.

Eisenhower, Dwight D. *At Ease: Stories I Tell Friends.* Garden City, N.Y.: Doubleday, Doran & Co.

Elletson, D.H. *Roosevelt and Wilson: A Comparative Study.* London: J. Murray, 1965.

Encyclopaedia Britannica. 11th ed.

Facts On File Yearbooks. New York: Facts On File Publications, 1941, 1982, 1984, 1985.

Fadiman, Clifton. *The American Treasury.* New York: Harper and Brothers, 1955.

Falkner, Leonard. *The President Who Wouldn't Retire; John Quincy Adams: Congressman from Massachusetts.* New York: Coward, McCann, 1967.

Fitzpatrick, John C., ed. *The Autobiography of Martin Van Buren (1854).* The Annual Report of the American Historical Association. Washington, D.C.: Government Printing Office, 1918.

Fredericks, Vic. *The Wit and Wisdom of the Presidents.* New York: Frederick Fell, 1966.

Furer, Howard B., ed. *Lyndon B. Johnson 1908: Chronology, Documents, Bibliographical Aids.* Dobbs Ferry, N.Y.: Oceana Publications, 1971.

———. *James Garfield 1831-1881, Chester Arthur 1830-1886.* Dobbs Ferry, N.Y.: Oceana Publications, 1970.

Goldman, Alex J., ed. *The Truman Wit.* New York: Citadel Press, 1966.

Graff, Henry F., ed. *The Presidents: A Reference History.* New York: Charles Scribner's, 1984.

Grant, Ulysses S. *Personal Memoirs of U.S. Grant.* New York: Webster, 1885-86.

Greeley, Horace. *The American Conflict.* New York: Negro University Presss, 1969.

Hamilton, S.M. *The Writings of James Monroe.* Vols. 1-7. New York: AMS Press, 1969.

Harbaugh, William Henry. *Power and Responsibility: The Life and Times of Theodore Roosevelt.* New York: Octagon Books/Farrar, Straus and Giroux, 1975.

Harnsberger, Caroline Thomas. *Treasury of Presidential Quotations.* Chicago: Follett Publishing Company, 1964.

Harrison, Benjamin. *This Country of Ours.* New York: Scribner's, 1897.

———. *Views from an Ex-President.* Indianapolis: Bowen-Merill, 1901.

———. *Public Papers and Addresses: March 4, 1889 to March 4, 1893.* Washington, D.C.: Government Printing Office, 1893. New York: Krause Reprint Company, 1969.

Hawthorne, Nathaniel. *The Life of Franklin Pierce.* New York: Garrett Press, 1970.

Hay, John. *William McKinley: Memorial Addresses.* New York: Thomas Y. Crowell and Company, 1902.

Hayes, Rutherford B. *The Diary of a President 1875-1881, Covering the Disputed Election, the End of Reconstruction, and the Beginning of Civil Service.* New York: McKay Co., 1964.

Hayes, Sarah H., ed. *The Quotable Lyndon B. Johnson.* Anderson, S.C.: Droke House, 1968.

Hedges, Charles. *Speeches of Benjamin Harrison.* New York: John W. Lovell Company, successors to United States Book Company, 1892.

Hesseltine, William B. *Ulysses S. Grant: Politician.* Dodd, Mead and Company, 1957.

Hofstadter, Richard. *The Age of Reform.* New York: Vintage Books/Random House, 1955.

——. *The American Political Tradition.* New York: Knopf, 1973.

Hoover, Herbert. *American Individualism.* Garden City, N.Y.: Doubleday, Doran, 1922.

——. *The Memoirs of Herbert Hoover: The Great Depression 1929-1941.* New York: MacMillan, 1952.

——. *The Memoirs of Herbert Hoover: Years of Adventure 1874-1920.* New York: MacMillan, 1951.

——. *Addresses Upon the American Road 1955-1960.* Caldwell, Idaho: Cayton Printers Ltd., 1968.

——. *Proclamations and Executive Orders of Herbert Hoover.* Vols. 1 and 2. Washington, D.C.: U.S. Government Printing Office, 1974.

Jefferson, Thomas. *The Life and Selected Writing of Thomas Jefferson.* New York: Modern Library, 1944.

Johnson, Lyndon B. *My Hope for America.* New York: Random House, 1964.

——. *A Time for Action: A Selection from the Speeches and Writings of Lyndon B. Johnson 1953-1964.* New York: Atheneum Publishers, 1964.

——. *The Vantage Point: Perspectives of the Presidency 1963-1969.* New York: Holt, Rinehart, and Winston, 1971.

Joslin, Theodore G. *Hoover Off the Record.* Garden City, N.Y.: Doubleday, Doran, 1934.

Kearns, Doris. *Lyndon Johnson and the American Dream.* New York: Harper and Row, 1976.

Kenin, Richard, and Justin Wintle. *The Dictionary of Biographical Quotations.* New York: Alfred A. Knopf, 1978.

Klein, Philip S. *President James Buchanan: A Biography.* University Park, Pa.: Pennsylvania State University Press, 1962.

Koch, Adrienne, and William Peder, eds. *The Selected Writings of John and John Quincy Adams.* New York: Alfred A. Knopf, 1946.

Krause, Sidney, ed. *The Great Debates: Carter vs. Ford 1976.* Bloomington, Ind.: Indiana University Press, 1979.

Lankevich, George J., ed. *Gerald R. Ford: Chronology, Documents, Bibliographical Aids.* Dobbs Ferry, N.Y.: Oceana Publications, 1971.

Leach, Margaret. *In the Days of McKinley.* New York: Harper and Row, 1959.

Lyons, Eugene. *Herbert Hoover: A Biography.* Garden City, N.Y.: Doubleday and Company, 1948.

MacDonald, William, ed. *Select Documents Illustrative of the History of the United States, 1776-1861.* New York and London: MacMillan Company, 1911.

Malone, Dumas. *Jefferson and His Time.* Vol. 6. *The Sage of Monticello.* Boston: Little, Brown, 1981.

——. *Thomas Jefferson as Political Leader.* Westport, Conn.: Greenwood Press, 1979.

Manchester, William *Portrait of a President: John F. Kennedy in Profile.* Boston: Little, Brown, 1962.

Mason, Alpheus Thomas. *William Howard Taft.* Boston: University Press of America, 1983.

McCoy, Donald R. *Calvin Coolidge: The Quiet President*. New York: MacMillan Company, 1967.

McKitrick, Eric L., ed. *Andrew Johnson: A Profile*. New York: Hill and Wang, 1969.

Mencken, H.L., ed. *A New Dictionary of Quotations on Historical Principles from Ancient and Modern Sources*. New York: Alfred A. Knopf, 1957.

Miller, Merle. *Lyndon: An Oral Biography*. New York: G. P. Putnam's, 1980.

——. *Plain Speaking: An Oral Biography of Harry S. Truman*. New York: Berkeley, 1973.

Mooney, B. *The Lyndon Johnson Story*. New York: Farrar, Strauss and Giroux, 1964.

Moran, Philip R., ed. *Ulysses S. Grant 1822-1885: Chronology, Documents, Bibliographical Aids*. Dobbs Ferry, N.Y.: Oceana Publications, 1968.

Morris, Edmund. *The Rise of Theodore Roosevelt*. New York: Coward, McCann and Geoghegen, 1979.

Nevins, Allan, ed. *Polk: Diary of a President, 1845-1849, Covering the Mexican War, the Acquisition of Oregon, and the Conquest of Florida and the Southwest*. London: Longmans, Green, 1952.

Niven, John. *Martin Van Buren: The Romantic Age of American Politics*. New York: Oxford University Press, 1983.

Nixon, Richard. *The Memoirs of Richard Nixon*. New York: Grosset and Dunlap, 1978.

——. *Six Crises*. Garden City, N.Y.: Doubleday, 1962.

Padover, Saul K., ed. *The Complete Madison: His Basic Writings*. New York: Harper and Brothers, 1953.

Pancake, John S., ed. *Thomas Jefferson: Revolutionary Philosopher; A Selection of Writings*. Woodbury, N.Y.: Barron's Educational Series, 1976.

Parker, George F., ed. *The Writings and Speeches of Grover Cleveland*. New York: Cassell Publishing Company, 1892; Krause Reprint Company, New York, 1970.

Peterson, Merrill D. *The Portable Thomas Jefferson*. New York: Viking Press, 1975.

Quaife, Milo Milton, ed. *The Diary of James K. Polk During His Presidency, 1845-1849* (4 vols.). Chicago: A.C. McClung, 1910.

Rayback, Robert J. *Millard Fillmore: Biography of a President*. Buffalo Historical Society. Vol 40. Buffalo, N.Y.: Henry Stewart, 1959.

Reader's Digest. Editors *The Reader's Digest Treasury of Modern Quotations*. New York: Reader's Digest Press, T. Y. Crowell Co., 1975.

Reed, Edward. *Readings for Democrats*. New York: Docket Series (vol. 15)/Oceana Publications, 1960.

Reeves, Richard. *A Ford, Not a Lincoln*. New York, 1975.

Reeves, Thomas C. *Gentleman Boss: The Life of Chester Alan Arthur*. New York: Alfred Knopf, 1975.

Remini, Robert. *Andrew Jackson*. New York: Harper and Row, 1969.

Rice, Arnold S., ed. *Herbert Hoover 1874-1964*. Dobbs Ferry, N.Y.: Oceana Publications, 1971.

Roosevelt, Franklin Delano. *The American Way*. New York: Philosophical Library, 1944.

Roosevelt, Theodore. *Autobiography*. New York: Scribner's, 1958.

——. *Life of Thomas Hart Benton*. Boston: Houghton-Mifflin, 1887.

——. *The New Nationalism*. New York: Outlook Co., 1911.

——. *The Works of Theodore Roosevelt*. New York: Collier, 1910.

Russell, Francis. *The Shadow of Blooming Grove: Warren G. Harding in His Times*. New York: McGraw-Hill, 1968.

Ryan, Halford Ross. *American Rhetoric from Roosevelt to Reagan: A Collection of Speeches and Critical Essays*. Prospect Heights, Ill.: Waveland Press, 1983.

Sandburg, Carl, *Abraham Lincoln: The Prairie Years* and *The War Years*. New York: Harcourt, Brace, 1936; 1936-9.

Schlesinger, Jr., Arthur M., *The Imperial Presidency*. Boston: Houghton-Mifflin, 1973.

——. *The Age of Jackson*. Boston: Little, Brown, 1946.

——. *A Thousand Days*. New York: Fawcett, 1977.

Seldes, George, ed. *The Great Quotations*. Secaucus, N.J.: Citadel Press, 1960, 1966, 1983.

Sievers, Harry J., ed. *William McKinley 1843-1901*. Dobbs Ferry, N.Y.: Oceana Publications, 1970.

Simpson, James B. *Contemporary Quotations: A Treasury of Notable Quotes since 1950*. New York: Thomas Y. Crowell Company, 1964.

Sloan, Irving J., ed. *Franklin Pierce 1804-1869: Chronology, Documents, Bibliographical Aids*. Dobbs Ferry, N.Y.: Oceana Publications, 1968.

Smith, Page. *John Adams*. Vol. 1, 2. Garden City, N.Y.: Doubleday, 1962.

Smith, Sam B. and Harriet Chappell Owsley, eds. *The Papers of Andrew Johnson*. Vol. 1, 2. Knoxville, Tenn.: University of Tennessee Press, 1980.

Sorensen, Theodore. *Decision-Making in the White House*. New York: Columbia University Press, 1963.

Steinberg, Alfred. *The First Ten: The Founding Presidents and Their Administrations*. New York: Doubleday, 1967.

Stewart, Robert. *The Penguin Dictionary of Political Quotations*. Harmmondworth, England: Penguin, 1986.

——. *The President and His Powers* (formerly titled as *Our Chief Magistrate and His Powers*, 1916). New York and London: Columbia University Press, 1967.

Taylor, John M. *Garfield of Ohio: The Available Man*. New York: W. W. Norton, 1970.

Tourtellot, Arthur Bernon. *The Presidents on the Presidency*. Garden City, N.Y.: Doubleday, 1964.

Truman, Harry S. *Memoirs: Years of Trial and Hope*. Vol. 2. Garden City, N.Y.: Doubleday, 1955-56.

Tuchman, Barbara W. *Stilwell and the American Experience in China, 1911-45*. New York: Macmillan, 1971.

Twohig, Dorothy, ed. *The Journal of the Proceedings of the President 1793-1797*. Charlottesville, Va.: University Press of Virginia, 1981.

Untermeyer, Louis, ed. *Britannica Library of Great American Writing*, Vol. 1. Chicago, Philadelphia, and New York: Britannica Press, with J.P. Lippincott Company, 1960.

U.S. Government Printing Office. *Inaugural Addresses of the Presidents of the United States from George Washington 1789 to John F. Kennedy 1961*. Washington, D.C.: U.S. Government Printing Office, 1961.

Van Buren, Martin. *Inquiry Into the Origin and Course of Political Parties in the United States*. Cambridge, 1867.

Vital Speeches of the Day. Southold, N.Y.: City News Publishing Company, 1984.

Washington Post Staff. *Commentary by the Staff of the Presidential Transcripts*. New York: Dell, 1974.

Williams, T. Harry, ed. *Hays: The Diary of a President 1875-1881*. New York: David McKay Company, 1964.

Wilstach, Paul. *Patriots off Their Pedestals*. New York: Books for Libraries Press, 1972.

Wilson, Woodrow. *The New Freedom, 1912-13 Speeches*. Englewood Cliffs, N.J.: Prentice-Hall, 1961.

Zinn, Howard. *A People's History of the United States*. New York: Harper and Row, 1980.

Author Index

Subject Index